N. EGGENHOFER

59572

E
185.63 Carroll, John
C37 Black military experience in the American West

THE BLACK MILITARY EXPERIENCE IN THE AMERICAN WEST

THE BLACK MILITARY EXPERIENCE IN THE AMERICAN WEST

EDITED BY
JOHN M. CARROLL

LIVERIGHT
New York

1. 987654321
(first edition, first printing)

International Standard Book Number: 0 - 87140 - 519 - 9
Library of Congress Catalog Card Number: 76 - 137866

Designed by Charlotte Thorp

Manufactured in the United States of America

This book is dedicated to Bennie Scott Barnes, my very young black friend who was born on September 6, 1969. It is dedicated with the wish that by the time he is able to read it, our history texts will have already been fully integrated with the historic facts of the contributions of all of America's peoples. It is my wish, too, that by then it will no longer be necessary to identify the Ninth and the Tenth Cavalry Regiments and the Twenty-fourth and the Twenty-fifth Infantry Regiments as all-black units, for that will be secondary to the real fact that they were heroic men who served their country bravely and well.

ACKNOWLEDGEMENTS

In undertaking a publication of this kind there is of necessity a great deal of letter writing involved. There are publishers, societies, authors, and directors of institutions who must be contacted for certain information and for permissions. I would like to thank all the people and institutions who came to my aid by granting permissions, giving advice, suggesting leads, granting information, and being helpful in general. In no special order, they are:

Raymond F. Locke of *Mankind Magazine,* Eleanor B. Adams of *New Mexico Historical Review,* Richard L. Polese of the Museum of New Mexico, Eugene O. Porter of *Password* in El Paso, Texas, Nicholas J. Bleser of the Fort Davis National Historic Site, Texas, Madge Grba of the West Texas Historical Association, Maxine Benson of *The Colorado Magazine,* L. Tuffly Ellis of the Texas State Historical Association, Pat Wagner of Western Publications, Inc. of Austin, Texas, Mrs. Vivian Paladin of the Montana Historical Society, John W. Cornelison of the Wyoming State Archives and Historical Department, Mr. Houston Harte of the Harte-Hanks Newspapers, Inc., of San Angelo, Texas, Robert A. Murray, the library staff of New Brunswick, New Jersey Public Library, the library staffs of Princeton and Rutgers Universities, Erwin N. Thompson, Fray Angelico Chavez, Col. William J. Buchanan, Mrs. Porter of Howard University Library, Miss Buchanan and Mr. McGraw of the Fort Leavenworth, Kansas Library Services, Col. O. W. Martin of the U. S. Armor Association, Mr. Binder of the Association of the U. S. Army, Col. Pappas and his library staff at Carlisle Barracks, Pa., Robert J. Ege, C. E. Dornbusch of Home Farm Press, Dr. Thompson of the Fort Huachuca, Arizona Museum, the staff at Arizona Pioneers' Historical Society, and to Mrs. Orville Cochran who has been so generous and patient with me since the death of her husband, my friend, Colonel Cochran of the Fort Huachuca Library and Museum.

I would like to also make recognition of all the authors of the articles in this anthology who are no longer with us and whose works have been in public domain for so very long. It only proves that they did a wonderful service in writing what they did when they did.

Special recognition is made to those authors who are represented in this anthology, but whose permissions were not sought to reprint their writings since their publishers extended the necessary permissions for them.

A great big round of applause to all my very talented friends who responded to my request for original art to illustrate this book. Their contributions are beyond a doubt the most exciting feature of this book.

Finally, to three great friends and champions of history, Colonels H. B. Wharfield, Clarence C. Clendenen, and Jerome W. Howe, I give very special thanks for their many letters of guidance, help, and their contributions of tremendous historical value. They all three knew the Tenth Cavalry as officers in it. Their contributions, after retirement, to the fields of history and education are surpassed only by their long years of loyal duty to their country.

Please forgive me if I have overlooked a responsibility. It was not intentional, I assure you.

J.M.C.

CONTENTS

III THE FORTS

IV THE CAVALRY

V ACTION ON THE FRONTIER

VI THE OFFICERS AND THE ENLISTED MEN

VII SOME HEROIC INDIVIDUALS

VIII THE MEDAL OF HONOR WINNERS

IX BLACK-WHITE RELATIONS ON THE FRONTIER

X A NEW BREED OF FRONTIER SOLDIER

ILLUSTRATIONS

ILLUSTRATIONS

The painting reproduced on the jacket – "York," by Charles Russell – appears courtesy of the Montana Historical Society.

Introduction

These writings were selected to represent the best works on the subject of the black military experience in the American West. The final choices were based upon subject, presentation, and scholarship. The choices were entirely mine, selected from my personal collection. The process of collecting and selecting the pieces indicated to me that the story of black contributions to American military history amounts to one of historical omission. I had been frustrated for years in seeking information on this subject in an effort to make my American History classes more relevant for my students. This was not always an easy task since those facts I wanted were either well hidden or totally unreported in the more popular texts and periodicals. As the years passed, however, I was successful in accumulating a wealth of information on various special subjects which, unfortunately, had no real structure and direction; I had just piled up one large repository of facts and personal profiles. Then one day I discovered a developing pattern.

For once, my total accumulation of rare and not so rare articles on the black military in the West began to fall into three broad periods: pre-1866, 1866-1900, and post-1900. Within these period classifications smaller subtopics readily fell into place, so that finally I saw that I had identified a way to share this wealth of information.

My personal historical interest had always been in the field of western Americana. The image which inevitably dominated this period of our westward expansion was the military image. Even though many blacks participated in the events of the time and were very much in evidence, they simply were not as a rule included in the textbooks—a regrettable oversight.

As my collection grew I found myself more and more interested in the military contributions of blacks during this period. Unfortunately, I could never find a good history text that did not dwell excessively upon the term "buffalo soldiers," the name given by the Indians to the black soldiers, whose hair reminded them of buffalo fur. As a result, the full story of the black trooper—his hardships and successes—was often not told. How can the dangers of Indian warfare and the ugliness of frontier life, both professionally and socially for these men, be overlooked or summed up in one or two paragraphs? How can the eighteen black winners of the Congressional Medal of Honor during this period be completely ignored? The heaviest area of concentration in textbooks dealing with black history has always been upon the periods of slavery, the Civil War, and Reconstruction. This simply is not the sum total of black American history.

Fortunately today more and more public schools and colleges are offering courses in black history and literature. I applaud this trend, for I feel from my experiences in the public schools as a teacher that these must be separate courses. This is the only way to be actually assured that the full content of these subjects will be taught. Otherwise, their special character is completely diluted and lost in the regular curricula. The trend may still be to dwell on those years of the Civil War, but there is another century beyond that which must be explored fully.

Perhaps part of the problem has been the abundance of reading and reference materials available on slavery and the paucity of materials on the black military experience on the American frontier. If this be the reason – or the excuse – then the present collection should go a long way toward correcting the problem as it exists.

Since I wanted this book to be read and appreciated for its wealth of historical information, I had to make many decisions as to which article to elect when there was more than one on a similar subject. The decisions were often made on the basis of readability – but always on the significance of the content. One very simple attribute always stood as a guideline. That attribute was the acknowledgement of human values to history; and every author's work was selected on that basis.

Much consideration was given to the span of the book. The decision was made not to end it with the close of the nineteenth century. I believe this is the right decision, and I am elated at the prospect of extending the "western image" beyond its usual limits.

Colonels Wharfield and Howe, both retired officers of the United States Army and former members of the famed Tenth Cavalry, have been extremely helpful. The assistance of Colonel Howe has been especially instrumental, since he placed into my hands many documents and letters which were of immense value and interest, such as the original of the Corporal Houston letter which is quoted in the text. These documents and letters have now been placed in the Rare Documents Collection of the library of the Military Academy at West Point for all to view and research. I would like to share part of Colonel Howe's last letter to me:

> He [Cpl. Houston] was my first striker [Orderly], at Fort Ethan Allen, Vt. where he was hardly more than a recruit himself. He was a smart looking, bright mulatto, of perhaps seventeen or eighteen. I became greatly attached to him.
>
> When the Carrizal affair came off, he was a corporal of my troop, very highly respected by all who knew him. Shortly after Carrizal, First Sergeant Page with another non-com and a squad were sent off to find some strayed horses, but they got drunk on mesqual instead. I preferred charges, and Page was deprived of his chevrons. Believing that young Houston, despite his age and short service was the best man for the job, I recommended his promotion to sergeant and then made him Top Sergeant. He never failed me.
>
> Soon afterwards I was ordered to take my troop to Guzman, nearly a hundred miles eastward of the Line of Communication, to investigate a report of a bandit attack on a train. I was not easy in my mind about this job. This jaunt sounded very like that which had taken K and C troops in the same direction to their terrible disaster [the fight at Carrizal].
>
> My troop was now completely rehabilitated, and looked very smart and military. Going toward a Carranzista garrison, I wondered what would happen this time. But now I was the only officer with these sixty black troopers. But there was competent, reliable Sergeant Houston. Well, actually, nothing happened, and I accomplished my mission.

> When soon the country became involved in war with Germany, and we were recruited to war strength, we were required to send our suitable non-coms to school to Colonel Young of our regiment, a wonderful black soldier who had been one of our squadron commanders in Mexico, to be trained to be officers of a Negro division. I sent Houston.
>
> I admired Col. Young as did all officers with whom he had served. Moreover I found him very likable. I often visited him in his quarters, and heard him play beautifully on the piano. He had a fine family, but never had them with him on a military post. He was one of three Negro officers who had graduated from West Point right after the end of the Civil War. President Roosevelt had decreed that every officer must serve with troops two years out of every six. Major Young had been serving in Liberia, Puerto Rico, and in Negro colleges. He was a fine specimen of an athletic soldier and a perfect gentleman.
>
> Houston was successful and was commissioned as was our Sergeant Queen a Captain of the Reserve, and served in France. He was never to serve with me again. Queen was a colonel in Italy in World War II and met with me when he was training a regiment at Fort Devens. Afterwards he was a high school principal in Pennsylvania. I still correspond with him.
>
> He told me that Houston, who has since died, was married and a successful electrician in San Francisco.

This is the human factor in history. This is what makes history come to life – to breathe.

An interesting aspect of my research as a teacher – and that which prompted this book – was the infuriating repetition of specific source material that was footnoted in the articles I managed to collect early in my days of searching. These sources would lead me on frustrating journeys of non-discovery, for quite often the referenced articles were not available. As my reference material began to accumulate, I realized that others might also be seeking the same information contained in these writings – hence this anthology. It is a never-ending, ever-growing interest to me as new sources are found.

It would be remiss of me not to say something about the art appearing in this book. There are over sixty presentations of black military art, the largest accumulation of this subject ever assembled. Over fifty percent of the art is original work which was commissioned specifically for the book and is now in my private collection. All the well-known artists who contributed their talents performed a remarkable task in bringing to life – pictorially – the story of the black soldier in our western history. Perhaps about twenty percent of the art is from private collections and is presented here for only the second time; some have never before been published. The balance of the pictures represents a substantial part of the output on this subject by the celebrated Western artist, Frederic Remington.

It is my great hope and expectation that the reader will find as much pleasure in reading and viewing this publication as I have experienced in accumulating its contents.

JOHN M. CARROLL

New Brunswick, New Jersey
Spring, 1971

able last [illegible] belonging to life [illegible] of [illegible] in our [illegible] twenty [illegible] private [illegible] and [illegible] have [illegible] The [illegible] represents [illegible] of the [illegible] celebrated [illegible] Frederic Remington.

It is my [illegible] that the [illegible] will [illegible] much pleasure in reading and viewing this [illegible] as I have experienced in accumulating its contents.

[illegible] CARRINGTON

New Brunswick, New Jersey,
Spring, 1971

THE BLACK MILITARY EXPERIENCE IN THE AMERICAN WEST

Seminole-Negro Indian Scout

The New World

The story of the black man in America's western history would not be complete without the first four chapters of this book. This is true because these accounts establish the presence of blacks in America beginning in 1619, more than two hundred years before 1866, the time when the four black units – the Ninth and Tenth Cavalry and the Twenty-Fourth and Twenty-Fifth Infantry – were formed.

These first accounts do not necessarily deal with men in uniform or with formal military deployments; nevertheless, they can be identified under the category of a "military experience." Nearly all the explorations in the New World had either a military or a paramilitary nature (a paramilitary experience being best defined as one that was, in some part, controlled by military figures, be they military governments of occupation or the military in the mother country, with the blessings of the court). Furthermore, uprisings or rebellions, as well as explorations, did have the structures of military operations and were usually led by militaristic forces.

Some of the events recounted in this section do not take place within the present territorial boundaries of the United States. Thus, it might be argued that it is inaccurate to include these chapters in a volume about the western United States. Their inclusion is justified, however, by stressing the fact that the western frontier in the early days was not a fixed point: It was a fluid, constantly moving line.

The first chapter concerns Estevanico de Dorantes, known as the black conquistador. He was the first black to be recorded in western American history. This exotic figure moved through the New World followed by his retinue of Indian wives, a pack of greyhounds at his heel, his body adorned with feathers and bells. He impressed the Indians with his magical powers by invoking a combination of Christian rites and Indian superstition, until, finally, he met a grisly end at the hands of the Zuñi: as he lay wounded by arrows, the skin was methodically stripped from his body.

The second chapter presents a figure whose origin in the New World is a matter of record, however sketchy. Described as being "tall, black, with very large yellow eyes," he posed as Pohé-yemo, the Pueblo sun god. He initiated the Pueblo revolt of 1680 by sending runners from pueblo to pueblo carrying thongs with knots in them indicating the number of days remaining before the Indians were to follow him against the Spanish. The revolt was quashed, but Pohé-yemo's representative was never captured.

In the late 1600s, Sebastian Rodriguez, a black from Angola, served as drummer for the Spanish soldiers in New Mexico. With his "coal-black face and toothy grin," he beat his snare drum at the head of the white troops. Although he wore the white man's uniform, however, he remained between two worlds: for example, to cure his child of an illness, he once had a mulatto "witch" place the child between her thighs and "smoke" him.

The Lewis and Clark expedition had as one of its members York, the black manservant of Captain Clark. The Indians along the way were fascinated by York, the first black man they had ever seen. At first, they would spit on his skin and rub it, thinking that he was a white man painted black. Indeed, the fact that York was black actually led the Indians to believe that he was the most heroic member of the group and, therefore, its leader: It was the custom of the plains Indians to paint their bodies black after a particular deed of bravery, and, the braver the deed, the blacker the warrior painted himself.

Although few writers have dealt with this indispensible member of the Lewis and Clark expedition, painters have not been so remiss. There follows a partial list of pictures in which York is either a central figure or is included in a panoramic Lewis and Clark scene:

York, by Charles M. Russell, Montana Historical Society.

Lewis and Clark Meet the Flathead Indians, by Charles M. Russell, State House, Helena, Montana.

Lewis and Clark on the Lower Columbia, by Charles M. Russell, Amon Carter Museum, Fort Worth, Texas.

Captain William Clark of the Lewis and Clark Expedition Meeting With the Indians in the Northwest, by Charles M. Russell, privately owned.

Five miniatures depicting various points in the journey of Lewis and Clark, by Olaf Seltzer, Gilcrease Institute, Tulsa, Oklahoma.

York, a black and white study, by Charles M. Russell, the Charles M. Russell Museum, Great Falls, Montana.

Lewis and Clark and York at Lolo Creek, by Edgar Paxson, county courthouse mural, Missoula, Montana.

Lewis and Clark on the Missouri, by J. K. Ralston, St. Louis Exposition.

Lewis and Clark and York on the Trail, by J. K. Ralston, mural at the First National Bank of Livingston, Montana.

Lewis and Clark Expedition at Celilo Falls, mural in the state capitol building, Salem, Oregon.

There are also two dioramas worthy of mention. One is at the Montana Historical Society Museum in Helena, Montana, and the other is at the Lost Trail Exhibit in the Bitterroot Mountains in Idaho.

J. CISNEROS

The Legend of the Black Conquistador

William J. Buchanan

In the rich folklore of the Zuñi Indians of New Mexico there is a legend, persisting to this day, which tells of a "black man" who intruded upon their lands in the long ago years of their ancestors: "When the roofs lay over the walls of Kyakime, when the smoke hung over the house-tops, then the black Mexicans came from their adobes in the everlasting summerland. . . ."

Dressed in the manner and finery of a god, accompanied by a retinue of servants and beautiful women from the tribes to the south, the mysterious intruder told a fantastic story of one who followed who was white, who knew the secrets of God in Heaven and had powers to bestow everlasting life. Then, so the legend goes, the stranger demanded that the Zuñis provide him with treasures, and women to replenish his harem: ". . . thus was killed by our ancients, right where the stone stands down by the arroyo of Kyakime, [the] black Mexican, a large man with chili lips . . . then the rest ran away, chased by our grandfathers, and went back toward their own country in the land of everlasting summer."

Fantasy? That the black intruder existed is historical fact. That he was indeed killed by the Zuñis, although not at the pueblo of Kyakime, was proved conclusively by the famed conquistador, Francisco Coronado. But who was this man who so indelibly stamped his image upon the

Reprinted through the courtesy of *Mankind Magazine*, ed. Raymond F. Locke, and Col. William J. Buchanan. The article first appeared in Vol. I (February, 1968), No. 5.

Zuñis that he left a legend that has been handed down for over four and one quarter centuries?

His name was Estevanico de Dorantes, Negro slave of a Spanish master. (Estevan is treated interchangeably by historians as a Negro or an Arab-Moor. Most of his contemporaries referred to him as a "black.") As chattel he did not even own his own body.

Yet, by the time of his death in 1539 he had already survived one of the most harrowing ordeals of endurance ever recorded, had won the respect of the most powerful men in the province of *Nueva España* (New Spain), and, in a final daring exploit, had opened the doorway for the Spanish exploration of what was to become the vast southwestern United States.

The story of Estevan's last journey – one of the most fascinating adventures in American history – is best told against the background of intrigue and polemics which brought it about.

In the years directly following the bloody Spanish conquest of Mexico the dominant figure in New Spain was the powerful and ambitious Captain General Hernando Cortes. With the Aztec conquest behind him, Cortes, spurred by stores of fabulous wealth awaiting discovery, carefully laid plans for an *entrada* into the vast uncharted region to the north. But the wary Charles of Spain was not amenable. Suspecting a general obsessed by dreams of empire, the emperor suddenly decreed that an *Audiencia* (governing council) be established in New Spain. Ostensibly formed to manage the affairs of the crown, the *Audiencia's* purpose was, more aptly, to hold in check the indomitable conqueror. For eight years power balanced precariously between Cortes and the *Audiencia.* Then, in 1535, with the arrival in Mexico City of Don Antonio de Mendoza as viceroy, the aging warrior's domination of events was at last greatly curtailed.

One of the most competent of the king's deputies, Mendoza was an astute administrator, more at home manipulating the affairs of state than in planning new conquests. Yet even this most level-headed official could not ignore the fevered excitement of the times, charged by persistent rumors that the long sought "Cities of Gold" of Spanish legend lay somewhere in the unexplored lands to the north.

These golden cities had their origin in the medieval legend of the Moorish capture of Mérida, Spain, in 1150. Seven bishops of the city, and their followers – the story was – fled by ship into the western ocean. Landing at last on "blessed isles" they founded seven prosperous cities. These elusive cities had been searched for by every Spanish explorer since Columbus.

Prior to Mendoza's arrival, Nuño de Guzman, then head of the *Audiencia* of New Spain, while visiting the village of Panuco near the east coast, met an Indian from the northern lands who told of seven large, rich cities just forty days' travel to the north. Guzman's report of this encounter fanned the sparks of the old legend.

In 1536, one year after Mendoza's arrival, there occurred an event which, though it perhaps did not alter the course of history, at least sped it on its way. In April of that year a Spaniard named Alvarez, leading a hunt for Indian slaves in northern Mexico just above the Rio Sinaloa, came upon a small disheveled group of wanderers.

Most were Indians. But in the group, dressed in deerskins, their weathered faces framed by long neglected hair and beards, were three white men and a large Negro. To Alvarez's astonishment they announced themselves to be Alvar Nuñez Cabeza de Vaca, Castilla Maldonado, Andres Dorantes, and Estevan – a slave belonging to Dorantes.

Escorted to Mexico City these men told an incredible story of deprivation, agony, and endurance. Sole survivors of the ill-fated Narvaez expedition of 300 men which vanished in Florida in 1528, they had wandered across the vast country in the north (now Texas and Northern Mexico) for eight years, searching for the settlements of New Spain. Often slaves of the Indians, later worshiped as healers, they were with one tribe or another for almost the entire time. One incident they told about fired the imagination of their listeners. While with the Opatas of the upper Sonora valley they had heard of a region to the north populated by several large wealthy cities – and Estevan had been shown the trail leading to them!

Here was heady news for the restless adventurers of New Spain. These were not itinerant Indians, but men of their own culture who had traveled widely in the beckoning north country. Though they had not actually seen the golden cities they had wandered so near that one of them now had knowledge of the route leading to them. The possessor of this knowledge, however, was not truly a Spaniard, but a Negro – and a slave.

From all accounts of the de Vaca ordeal this Negro's extraordinary character emerges with striking clarity. It was Estevan who most readily adapted to the hostile environment in which the four struggled for survival. He quickly absorbed the ways of the Indians, learned their speech, and in fact did most of the negotiating for the party. Passing from tribe to tribe, Estevan acquired a strange and mysterious influence over the admiring natives.

Cabeza de Vaca later wrote, "The Negro was in constant conversation. He informed himself about the ways we wished to take, of the towns there, and the matters we desired to know." At the end of their ordeal, Estevan, who could neither read nor write, spoke at least six of the varied Indian languages of the upper region and knew all the important sign languages.

Such attributes were not lost on the wily viceroy. While Mendoza had soberly dismissed the old legend, he fully realized the impact de Vaca's report would have at the Court of Spain. The Opatas' story would certainly be investigated, and fortune awaited him who proved it true. Thus, recognizing Estevan's special gift for dealing with Indians, Mendoza shrewdly purchased the slave from Dorantes. Then to further enhance his scheme, he retained in his service the Indians found with Estevan above the Rio Sinaloa.

As Mendoza anticipated, wild speculation as to what lay above the Opatas' lands erupted anew. In Old Spain excitement was stirred by de Vaca himself who returned there soon after rescue. Cortes, still a threat, hastily readied an expeditionary fleet to push to the head of the Gulf of California. Simultaneously from Madrid came reports that another experienced New World explorer, Hernando de Soto, had obtained royal approval for an expedition penetrating the continent westward from the Florida coast. De Soto's attempt to enlist Cabeza de Vaca as a lieutenant revealed one of his goals.

Seeing Cortes and de Soto as ominous threats to his plans, Mendoza finally decided to act. Typically, the viceroy's efforts were subtle. Since King Charles had not yet authorized a northward *entrada* a large expeditionary force could not be risked. But a small reconnoitering party could. Mendoza chose his men with special care. Scholars have long speculated as to why Mendoza chose Marcos. Though he was apparently esteemed by his church superiors there is enough of a shadow on his integrity to prompt the question. Some believe he was chosen because Mendoza knew that no matter what the friar saw he could be trusted to return a report supporting a full expedition.

Estevan, of course, would be the guide. Then, to imply ecclesiastical approval and lend a missionary tone to the undertaking, Mendoza chose as leader one Fray Marcos de Niza, a Franciscan monk of some repute as an explorer. The Indians previously retained would go along as servants, interpreters, and couriers for important news back to Mendoza. Another friar, Anoratus, chosen by Marcos as a companion, took ill and had to be left at Petatlan.

In the fall of 1538 the little party was escorted from Mexico City to the northernmost Spanish outpost of San Miguel de Culiacan by one of Mendoza's prize protégés, twenty-eight-year-old Captain Francisco Vasquez de Coronado. En route, at Tonala (now Guadalajara), Coronado delivered the viceroy's written instructions to Fray Marcos.

Probably intended for eyewash at the Court of Spain rather than for any serious attempt at fulfillment, Mendoza's instructions were a large order for the small force. Among other things they were to admonish the Spaniards of San Miguel to forgo slavery and treat the Indians well; report on Coronado's manner in his new post as Governor of New Galicia; observe and report on geography, topography, climate, flora, fauna, minerals, and the various Indian tribes encountered; leave markings to establish their route for others to follow; search out large settlements suitable for the establishment of monasteries; claim lands for the emperor. Notwithstanding these orders there is little doubt that Estevan and Marcos clearly understood that their true mission was to seek out the golden cities and report their location to Mendoza with all possible haste.

One of Mendoza's instructions stands out. The viceroy took pains to caution Marcos that Estevan was to obey him ". . . in all and by all that you command him, as he would himself; and if he does not do so he shall incur jeopardy and the penalties which befall those who do not obey the persons who have authority from His Majesty to command them." Very clearly, Mendoza recognized an emerging independence in the slave. It was a prophetic observation. In March, 1539, after final preparations and instructions from Coronado, Estevan and Marcos at last departed San Miguel in search of the wondrous cities that had teased men's imaginations for four hundred years.

From the start Estevan's bearing was regal. Two sleek greyhounds trotted at his side. In his packs, carried by Indian servants, was his personal dinner service of various colored dishes. As a talisman to impress the natives he carried an ornamented calabash – a gourd rattle decorated with colored feathers, strings of beads, and rows of snake rattles – given to him as a symbol of power and authority by admiring Indians during his odyssey with de Vaca. It would have been better had he left it in San Miguel.

Somewhat less impressive, Fray Marcos, sandal shod and dressed in a habit of grey zaragoza cloth, carried only his cross and staff. But in his packs, along with his vestments of office, were pearls, gold, and precious stones, samples to determine from the Indians along the way what treasures they knew.

The first part of the trail northward from San Miguel was the same Estevan had followed southward three years earlier. Skirting the coast it led through the small village of Petatlan to a more populous one called Vacapa, probably near the northern border of the present state of Sinaloa. Here after eleven days' travel Marcos abruptly altered the makeup of the expedition.

In his account of the journey, written later for Mendoza, Marcos says that when they reached Vacapa, "I sent Estevan Dorantes the Negro another way, whom I commanded to go directly northward for fifty of threescore leagues, to see if by that way he might learn any news of any notable thing which we sought." Since Estevan could neither read nor write he was to report his finding to Marcos by Indian couriers bearing signs: ". . . that if it were but a mean thing, he would send me a white cross of one handful long; and if it were any great matter, one of two handfuls long; and if it were a country greater and better than the Nueva España, he should send me a great cross."

Why was he really sent ahead? Though Marcos implies it was purely an exploratory expediency, Castaneda (soldier-chronicler and member of the Estevan-Marcos journey), who knew them both, gives us a more interesting explanation: "It seemed that after the Friars I have mentioned and the Negro had started, the Negro did not get on well with the Friars because he took the women that were given him and collected turquoises and got together a stock of everything. Besides, the Indians in those places through which they went got along better with the Negro because they had seen him before. This was the reason he was sent ahead."

On Easter Sunday, with his Indian servants and bevy of women, Estevan took leave of Fray Marcos – his last earthly master. Four days later a courier reported back to Marcos bearing a cross as large as a man!

Had the slave truly found a country "greater and better than New Spain?" Though no Spaniard ever again saw the black man, his subsequent activities and fate were investigated and recorded by his contemporaries – chiefly Marcos, Castaneda, and Coronado himself. What follows is constructed mostly from their accounts.

From the moment he left Marcos, Estevan inquired constantly about the golden cities. Then only two *jornadas* from Vacapa he came upon a tribe who told him of "a very mighty province." These Indians told Estevan that only thirty *jornadas* to the north was a land of seven rich cities all under the rule of one lord. In the first of these cities, named Cibola by Marcos, well-dressed people lived in large, multi-storied stone houses with high porches and walls inlaid with ornamented turquoise.

At once Estevan dispatched the courier bearing the man-sized cross. He also sent along one of the Indians who had seen Cibola to describe its greatness to the friar. Then, ignoring Marcos' order to proceed no further but to wait for him if anything of great value was learned, Estevan set out immediately for Cibola. Castaneda says of Estevan at this point: ". . . he thought he could get all the reputation and honor himself, and that if he should discover those settlements with such famous high houses, alone, he would be considered bold and courageous. So he proceeded with the people who followed him." Whether Estevan's thinking was that farsighted, or whether he was more interested in protecting a newfound status, he had no intention of allowing Marcos to catch up with him.

While the agitated friar tried desperately to overtake him, Estevan hastened toward Cibola. And as the distance between them increased, the slave, master at last, rapidly reverted to a role he relished once before. Imitating the powerful shamans he had seen in Texas, he adorned his ankles, legs, and arms with brightly colored plumes and tinkling bells. With native cunning he combined the rich ceremonies of his Catholic masters with the weird rituals of a medicine man and performed mystical rites before awestruck natives.

Indians along the way, convinced that he possessed divine powers, joined his procession. Each village brought its sick and lame to him for cure. Over these infirm he flourished the sacred calabash and performed the healing liturgies he had learned with de Vaca. In return for these ministrations, he extorted gifts of tribute from each tribe and selected their comely women to replenish his harem.

As the ardor of his growing band of followers approached reverence his rule became absolute. Indeed, there is evidence that he exercised a despot's ultimate power and summarily condemned to death those who displeased him – including women. The slave had assumed the role of God.

Up the Sonora valley past the sites of present-day Bacoachi and Cananea, Estevan led his colorful assemblage. Not entirely disloyal to Marcos, at each evening camp he had his servants prepare two shelters, one for himself and one to be waiting for the following friar. As stories of Cibola grew ever more wonderful he sent reports back imploring Marcos to come with all possible haste. Then, perversely, to protect his growing lead, he would strike out again.

Marching over twenty miles a day he soon reached the San Pedro River and followed it northward across the present international boundary to a point somewhere between modern Benson and Cascabel, Arizona. Here he swung northeasterly across the Arivaipa valley, passed between the Santa Teresa and Pinaleno mountains, then turned northward again to the Gila River. Before him lay the last great wilderness before Cibola. In high spirits he sent a report back to Marcos that he had entered upon the last great *despoblado* (wilderness) leading to Cibola and that he was very happy because he was now more certain than ever that he would find the grandeur they sought. It was the last message he would ever send.

He proceeded northward until, at last, his Indian guides told him that Cibola lay one day ahead. (At this point Estevan was somewhere near the present town of St. Johns, Arizona.) Here, as was his custom, Estevan dispatched messengers to announce his coming. Entrusting them with his calabash he ordered them to carry this symbol of authority to the Cibolans and tell them that he came in peace to speak of a great lord and to cure the sick. Then he prepared his final camp to wait for the certain news that his arrival was eagerly awaited.

The next day the messengers returned visibly shaken and filled with fear. They told Estevan that they had done as he commanded and had delivered the calabash to the Cibolans. The Lord of Cibola had taken the mace and studied it carefully for a moment, then, in a great fury, dashed it to the ground. Turning his rage upon the messengers he told them that he recognized the cascabels on the gourd as belonging to a people hostile to the Cibolans. He had then commanded the messengers to return to Estevan and tell him to turn back at once, and, if not, not one man among them would remain alive.

With typical disdain Estevan dismissed the warning. Boasting that they would be grandly received he calmed his followers and started his final procession towards Cibola. It was near the first day of May, 1539. In haughty splendor, Estevan with his retinue now numbering nearly a hundred arrived at Cibola just before sundown. Before him stood not a "City of Gold," but a clustered group of mud and stone huts, together no larger than a modest apartment house in New Spain.

The Cibolans stopped the procession before it reached the gates of the village. At that moment Estevan learned that this was not going to be another triumphant entry. Curious about his color and trappings, but deeply suspicious of his mission, the Cibolans unceremoniously placed him under guard in a large stone hut outside the village walls. Immediately a council of elders and leaders began to interrogate him. From them Estevan may have learned that he was now at the pueblo of Hawikuh, one of six (not seven) pueblos of the people later to be known as Zuñis.

In reply to their questions Estevan told the council about Fray Marcos and the mission they had undertaken by order of a great white lord. To the Cibolans his story was utter nonsense. Castaneda says: "For three days they made inquiries about him and held a council. The account which the Negro gave them of two white men who followed him, sent by a great lord, who knew about the things in the sky, and how these were coming to instruct them in divine matters, made them think that he must be a spy or a guide from some nations who wished to come to conquer them, because it seemed to them unreasonable to say that the people were white in the country from which he came and that he was sent by them, he being black."

Even at this juncture Estevan might have appeased the Cibolans had he not foolishly considered them on the same level as the lesser tribes he had awed with his posturings. But insight failed him. Perhaps by now believing himself that he was a god, he made his usual demand for tribute and women. The insult sealed his fate.

The early morning sun had just broken above the horizon when Estevan, led by some of the headmen of Cibola, stepped outside his hut. Suddenly, as if on cue a great horde of Cibolans came rushing from out of the pueblo toward them. Their intent was unmistakable. At the sight of them Estevan started to run. The attempt to escape was futile. Slowed by arrows the fleeing Negro was soon overtaken. The Cibolans fell upon him and methodically stripped the flesh from his body.

Gathering his fleetest runners the Lord of Cibola gave each one a piece of the black man's flesh to carry to the chiefs of surrounding tribes as grisly proof that the "black god" was mortal and existed no longer. To the tribes of the south he sent a warning that if other Christians should come their way, as Estevan had said, they should kill them at once for there was nothing special about them. And if any tribe was afraid they were to send for the Cibolans at once so that they might do what others feared to do.

From the Indians who came with Estevan the Cibolans selected a few young men to be adopted into the tribe. The rest were sent on their way back home. For his own pleasure the Lord of Cibola took Estevan's greyhounds, colored dinner dishes, and treasures the Negro had collected and cherished. A year later they would all be found when a vengeful Coronado would succeed in conquering Hawikuh.

Some weeks later a badly frightened Fray Marcos reported back to Coronado in Culiacan with a story of mixed horror and splendor. Marcos avowed that in spite of Estevan's fate, which he heard in detail from the fleeing Indians, he would continue on toward Cibola; and finally he viewed the pueblo from a nearby hilltop. Whether he stayed, or whether he turned at once and fled back to Mexico, has been hotly debated for centuries.

There is no doubt, however, about the story he told of Cibola's grandeur: "It has the appearance of a very beautiful town, the best I have seen in these parts. The houses are . . . all of stone, with their stories and terraces, as it appeared to me from a hill where I was able to view it. The city is bigger than the City of Mexico."

As a result of this fantastic report Viceroy Mendoza, apparently without the crown's approval, authorized the historic Coronado expedition. Coronado's search for the "golden cities of Cibola" led, of course, to the mud and stone hovels of New Mexico. Disillusioned, Coronado returned from the expedition in disgrace. But his fruitless journey discredited for all time the legend of the "Cities of Gold." Viceroy Mendoza seems to have escaped the stigma of the failure of his plans. By the end of his rule in 1550, he was considered one of the king's most successful deputies.

The Zuñis long ago abandoned their six remote villages and banded together in the pueblo they inhabit to this day. Hawikuh today is a bleak ruin, a small dim outline in the arid desert floor in western New Mexico, nearer in size to half a city block than "bigger than the City of Mexico." Left to the elements and the erosive sands it serves only as a forlorn monument to a wayward slave who, seeking glory, once led a resplendent march across the American southwest. Somewhere at the base of its crumbling walls rests all that remains on earth of Estevanico de Dorantes – the black conquistador.

J. CISNEROS

Pohé-yemo's Representative and the Pueblo Revolt of 1680

Fray Angelico Chavez

The point of highest drama in New Mexico's long history is the Indian Pueblo Revolt of 1680, when the Pueblos managed to unite briefly for one concerted effort which put an end to the Spanish colony and the Franciscan missions for a time. Twenty-one friars and several Spanish families were massacred in one day, August 10, and the Spaniards were soon forced to retreat to the distant and southernmost mission center of Guadalupe del Paso, now Ciudad Juárez in Mexico. The causes for the rebellion were several, but ancient Pueblo belief was the one adduced by the main leaders as the rallying cry. It was the "ancient ones" of the Pueblos versus the God and the saints of the Spaniards. For eighty years the Franciscans had clamored for the complete elimination of the estufas (now called kivas), which in their estimation were hotbeds of idolatry; also, that of the masked dances and related native practices which they considered not only idolatrous, but grossly immoral from the Christian point of view. These they lumped together under the term *cachinas.* Simply to provoke the missionaries, or else bribed by the Indian ritual leaders, certain Spaniards in the succession of governors and their henchmen refused to cooperate, so that the abolition of kivas and cachinas was occasional and sporadic; those eliminated were promptly restored in most pueblos.[1]

Reprinted through the courtesy of the *New Mexico Historical Review,* ed. Eleanor B. Adams, and Fray Angelico Chavez. The article first appeared in Vol. XLII (April, 1967), No. 2.

Such internal Church-State dissensions, to be sure, did nothing to improve the Indian ritual leaders' regard for the Spaniards. Moreover, and this is something never considered before by historians, some of the principal and most intelligent ones among the leaders were not pure-bred Pueblo Indians. Some were the offspring of an unscrupulous Spanish colonist and a Pueblo woman; others were descended from Negroid-Amerindian servants, brought from New Spain by the first colonists, who married into the Pueblos; and so during those first eighty years certain mestizos gravitated into Pueblo life. A complicated inner resentment against the prevailing caste system had made them identify themselves further with the Pueblo Indian and his beliefs, while their native and acquired capabilities were superior to those of the inbred Pueblos who knew little outside their individual restricted cosmos. Otherwise, the ordinary run of Pueblo Indians had been happy with the many material benefits brought them by the padres. Their limited grasp of Spanish Catholic doctrine and external worship dovetailed nicely with a native mythology which was their very life. They appreciated the protection which Spanish arms afforded against their perennial enemies, the Apache and other marauding tribes. In a way, for these common people, who in their simplicity had quietly combined interior ancestral belief with the external Catholic forms of worship, any demands made by the friars were less onerous than those made by their own ritual leaders, from whose complete influence they were being wooed. Native Pueblo ritual and government required total surrender of the person.

It was the ritual leaders in each pueblo, the "representatives" of superior beings in a native mythology, which we will have to consider briefly, who resented European domination, no matter what the material benefits. The most resentful, and also potentially dangerous, were those hybrid leaders just mentioned. Nor can we eliminate a certain amount of laudable nativistic feeling on the part of the people in general, although it was far from the modern notion of "patriotism" anachronistically attributed to them by current American writers. Power and revenge, in the guise of native belief, were the prime motivators. We might compare the situation with that of the fifteenth-century monarchy of Spain, with its closely interlaced feudal nobility and church hierarchy, which set up the Inquisition under the banner of the Faith to consolidate and preserve its position against the divisive forces that it saw in the Moors, the Jews, and the Protestant

Reformation. Except that these poor Indian leaders in the past had been altogether incapable of conjuring up any such Inquisition, or even a swift and definite revolution. The Pueblo people in general, besides being satisfied with things as they were, were slow to respond to a war cry. Their agelong sedentary life of primitive agriculture and continuous ceremony had made them a "peaceful people," seldom able to defend themselves against the warlike Apache hunters who from time immemorial had invaded the pueblos at harvest time. To stand up to Spanish firearms and European martial skills was suicidal, as some few found out on different occasions during that eighty-year period. Moreover, different pueblo groups were divided from each other by language and ancient animosities. And there was that internal struggle of long standing among the ritual leaders themselves in each pueblo, a fact noted by modern anthropologists as well as the pioneer missionaries.[2]

But the fact is that the many pueblos did manage to unite most effectively in that year of 1680, to the great surprise of the Spaniards, and to the wonder of serious historians ever since. In all subsequent histories the tactical genius has been thought to be El Popé of San Juan, from many scattered testimonies recorded in the Otermín journals of 1681. Yet, from the very start, Governor Otermín and his captains sensed that El Popé could not have done it all alone, and therefore tried to discover the chief culprit, or culprits, by interrogating their first prisoners. On August 9, 1680, two young men from Tesuque were caught bearing a message of rebellion and a hide thong with two knots signifying the number of days left. All that the frightened youths could reveal under pressure was a "common report among all the Indians that there had come to them from very far away toward the *north* a *letter* from an *Indian lieutenant [teniente] of Po he yemu* to the effect that all of them in general should rebel, and that any pueblo that would not agree to it they would destroy, killing all the people. It was reported that this *Indian lieutenant of Po he yemu was very tall, black, and had very large yellow eyes,* and that everyone feared him greatly."[3] The Spanish officials simply took this for a fable, concluding that the Indian leaders had deluded these youths and the people in general with this reference to one of their heathen "gods" or "spirits." It is evident that the young pair had divulged all they knew, and that Otermín and his men failed to detect a real human instigator behind their statement. For it certainly looked like the description of some grotesquely masked mythological creature which the Spaniards regarded as the "devil."

Again, a similar interrogation took place on August 20, after the governor's forces broke a painful siege of Santa Fe by putting more than fifteen hundred warriors to rout, killing three hundred, and taking forty-seven prisoners. On being questioned, these unfortunate captives confessed that they "had a mandate of an *Indian* who lives a very long way from this kingdom, toward the *north,* from which region *Montezuma came,* and who is the *lieutenant of Po he yemu;* and that this *person* ordered all the Indians to take part in the treason and rebellion. . . . *For fear* of this they all joined together, killing the priests and the Spaniards. . . ."[4] Once again it is evident that this was all the poor prisoners knew, else at least one of the forty-seven would have revealed the identity of that "person." And again Otermín took this as an affront to his intelligence; in his anger he had them all shot for mocking him with a mere Indian fable. To him and his men the person of the *teniente* and *Pohé-yemo* himself were one and the same pagan demon.[5] But we shall soon see that he was a very human person – I shall translate *teniente* as "representative" from now on. It expresses more fully the double function of someone "taking the place of" and "assuming the person" of Pohé-yemo. The French-derived "lieutenant" has too many European military and political connotations.

What first led me to suspect a real human person in the representative of Pohé-yemo, a man who was unusually tall and black in comparison with the average small and not too tawny Pueblo Indian, and one with big yellow eyes, which promptly suggests a mulatto, was the records of a controversy in Santa Fe in 1766. It involves five generations of the Naranjo family of the Santa Cruz-Santa Clara valley whose antecedents were Negroid and who, most significantly, were accused of having fomented Indian insurrections in the past.[6] Then, there is an amply documented legend, originating with the ordinary Spanish colonists of those revolt times, which told of the devil appearing as a black giant during the 1680 siege of Santa Fe.[7] All this provided me with enough incentive and material for a thorough investigation of the problem, concerned mainly with a big Negro or black-complexioned mulatto named Naranjo, who at some period before the revolt of 1680 insinuated himself among the ritual leaders of the Pueblos, several of them hybrid individuals like himself. Either to enjoy personal power, or to avenge himself on the Europeans who for so long, and sometimes most cruelly, had lorded it over the primitive colored races, or for both reasons, he most cleverly employed the myth of Pohé-yemo to unite the ever-dissident Pueblo Indians for a successful blow. It is not the first time that an African spoiled the best-laid plans of the Spaniard in American colonial times, but it was the most dramatic. More active and restless by nature than the more passive and stolid Indian, he was more apt to muddle up some serious Hispanic enterprise.[8]

In order to grasp the truth and flavor of the whole episode, we need to have some knowledge and sympathetic understanding of Pueblo Indian mythology and its workings on Indian behavior – in this case particularly concerning a mythical being called Pohé-yemo. This is something the captains and friars neglected to procure, to their sorrow. As they kept repeating in their official acts and letters, it was Satan himself and none other who had inspired the "apostasy and rebellion" against the twin Majesties of God and Catholic King.

I. PUEBLO MYTHOLOGY AND POHÉ-YEMO

The daily life of the Pueblo Indians was closely and intricately bound with year-round rites and ceremonials intended to tap, as it were, the mysterious Power permeating their little world of earth and sky.[9] The Power was impersonal, nothing more than the invisible energy that made nature tick. Each pueblo's cosmos was limited to the visible horizon around it. Upon the earth the Power made trees and plants grow and the wild animals to reproduce themselves; and from the sky above the Power supplied sunlight and rain, all to insure a food supply for the people in their planting and hunting. Also, through herbs and animals the Power furnished means for curing the people when sick. Naturally, the Power also made human babies grow from their parents to insure the continuity of the community. And, as with other primitives, there was a division of the Power's activities into male and female: sky phenomena were masculine as compared with the passive feminine reproduction in the earth. Hence fertility rites acquired certain open sexual manifestations, pointed out by ethnologists, and by some of the old padres who naturally labeled them obscene.

Because the Power was so erratic in its activities, mainly as regards rainfall and fertility in an arid land, what was needed to insure good crops, good hunting, a healthy people, and healthy newborn, was the right effective knowledge, or "know-how," that could make the Power work in their behalf. All that one needed was "to know." This "know-how" rested in their ritual leaders, the representative chieftains and medicinemen, to whom it had been passed down through countless generations from the "ancient ones" since the Pueblo people came out of the earth. The ritual leaders, according to each one's office, prepared themselves by purificatory bathing, fasting, and considerable vomiting, in order to better "represent" the "ancient ones" in putting the "know-how" to work. The better the preparation, the closer a leader came to "becoming" an "ancient one" for that particular function. And the greater the results.

Now, the Pueblos had no creation myth. Their ancestors came out of a hole, or vertical cave, in the already existing earth. It lay somewhere beyond the northern horizon of each Pueblo's little world. These first people were as ignorant and helpless as babies emerging from the womb. But just as helpless infants have parents and adult clan relatives to assist them through childhood, so the first people encountered other people, and also animals, who were ready to help and teach them. These were the "ancient ones." These primordial counterparts of the ordinary human and animal world were real corporeal beings. They differed from ordinary folk and animals in this one important respect – they had a perfect "know-how" for using the Power. Through this perfect knowledge they made themselves immortal, and they could perform all sorts of marvelous feats, like making themselves invisible and changing from one place to another in the twinkling of an eye. This instant travel was sometimes done with the aid of primordial birds and animals having the same "know-how." Each one of them specialized in the phenomena of one distinct phase of nature.

These benign "ancient ones" stayed with those first people and taught them how to plant and hunt and fend for themselves. Those who were animals taught them the art of curing with herbs and chants. But there were skeptics even in those days, folks who said the "ancient ones" were nothing but ordinary people disguised in masks and paint and feathers. This unbelief hurt those benefactors, so they decided to go away from the ordinary people forever. But, before departing, they taught the true believers how to use their masks and perform dances with them, and how to employ other paraphernalia such as feather bunches, feathered sticks, and tiny stone fetishes, and how to sing the right songs, to make sure that the people would always have a means of tapping the Power for corn and meat and health, even if in a much more limited degree.

Chief among these kindly beings were the Earth-Mother *(Yaya)* who dwelt by the Hole of Emergence *(Shipapu),* and the Twin-Warriors and Hunters *(Másewi* and *Oyóyewi),* who stayed with her but frequently roamed all over. Most popular were the *Shiwanna* or Rain-Makers who dwelt beyond the western horizon, or some other direction, depending on a particular pueblo's location with regard to prevailing rain clouds. Among these many single individuals controlling some phase of nature was *Pohé-yemo,* who made the sun shine upon the people when they first came out upon the dark and dreary earth's surface. He and the other beings varied in name, concept, and particular functions among the different Pueblos, and even in those of the same linguistic group.[10]

Pohé-yemo is called *Pose-yemo* among the Tewa (Santa Clara where Naranjo lived). It means "he who strews morning dew." Another name is *Pose-ueve* (dew from sky), but he is also referred to as *Pose-yemo T'ansendo* (our sun father *Pose-yemo).* The Keres of Santo Domingo know these Tewa terms but also have their own: *Payatyamo* (youth) who is the being in charge of the sun. In Cochiti *Payatyama* (sun-father) is used in contradistinction to *Sanatyaya* (moon-mother), but in action he is identified with *Oshatsh,* the sun. Both in Santo Domingo and San Felipe, *Payatyamo* appears among the fetishes used in preparing for the cachina dances. There are two masks among those of the minor side-dancers which are called *Payatyamo,* resembling the mask of the sun, *Oshatsh.* Dances originally performed for *Payatyamo* now are directed to the Rain-Makers, both at Santo Domingo and Cochiti. From this and other instances, it is clear that the person of the sun-youth was considerably less "performed" than those of the bringers of rain, and this is very natural. In the arid Southwest the sun shines perennially, and therefore needs much less invoking than those beings who control the much needed rain clouds, or those who cause the corn to grow and the wild game to multiply abundantly. Santo Domingo also uses the term *Poshaiyanyi* (our father from east coming with sun), but this is plainly a derivation from the Zuñi *Poshaiyankia.* He is the being who taught the Zuñi, the Taos, and other peoples, the arts of planting and ceremonial curing. Among the Jemez, *Pestya-sode* figures in a legend similar to one among the Zuñi, the prefix *pe* meaning "sun" in their language. But they also use *Peyatyambo* (their version of Keres "youth") for the ritual leader of the Pecos sun clan. The mask of *Pehehmiyoe* (sun on head) has features of the Keres sun-mask, *Oshatsh.*

In short, the original concept of this youth and father having the "know-how" of the sun has not only gotten mixed up in linguistic form but also in the "know-how" pertaining to other mythical persons. He also figures in later tales of the Zuñi, Jemez, Tewa, and Keres, as relayed by investigators like Bandelier and Cushing, but these are more properly current folktales than old ancestral mythology. What we have been arriving at is the fact that, in that fateful year of 1680, all the pueblos knew of Pohé-yemo under one linguistic form or another, when word came from a kiva in Taos that a Chieftain or Medicineman therein had a most extraordinary "know-how" of Pohé-yemo and was *representing* him. In performing the preparatory rites he must have fasted and vomited so effectively that he now represented Pohé-yemo to perfection – he *was* Pohé-yemo at this time. El Popé and the few select leaders let the people know that he was a black giant with big yellow eyes for greater effect. This created more than the usual fear and awe. His human identity was of no consequence, for at the time he fully represented Pohé-yemo.

Why Naranjo chose to represent Pohé-yemo instead of the mighty Twin-Warriors, *Másewi* and *Oyóyewi,* we do not know. But we can guess. It could be the connotation of "sun" with "fire." For Naranjo himself knew of the Aztec god of fire and war, as we shall see later on. Reared among the Spaniards and cognizant of the real Indian idolatry of New Spain, he imbued his self-assumed mysterious personality with a cruel inner strength unknown to the placid and less sophisticated Pueblos. He could communicate with some of the principal leaders in their own tongue, but also in Spanish with those outstanding ones who were mestizos and *coyotes;* and to some of these he could send written letters. His grasp of Spanish psychology showed him how to catch the enemy off guard, and how to hide his identity from them in case the plot should fail, as it almost did. Because the captains as well as the padres looked upon the "ancient ones" of the pueblos as the evil spirits given in the Bible, Pohé-yemo would be regarded as the Devil himself. And so he was.

The blow fell on August 10, 1680, and the success was almost perfect, marred only by the bloody resistance of the Spaniards in Santa Fe. Governor Otermín and his people held on to the villa for a spell, but considered it wise to abandon it and the whole kingdom for the time being. In his questioning of Indian captives, for future reprisals, Otermín got nothing from them, even when they unwittingly described Naranjo physically. For he had made his personal identity known only to a few main leaders, perhaps instructing them not to reveal it to the Pueblo people in general. But as soon as the Spaniards left, the Pueblos fell away from each other, forgetting all about Pohé-yemo's representative. For the deed was done. And no ritual leader, after all, could "represent" an "ancient one" indefinitely. At the same time the other ritual leaders of separate pueblos assumed their own little stances of importance, especially El Popé, who went about boasting that he alone had at last defeated the invincible Spaniard and restored the influence of thc "ancient ones." Many among the common people did not like this new surge of tyranny, which now had more of a sharp European flavor than the halcyon former rule of the "ancient ones." If Naranjo himself had harbored any ambition of making himself the supreme lord of all the Pueblos, it was a rude awakening.

Otermín's return with his forces in the following year was largely one of reconnaissance. Individual Indians of every type were captured from among the southern Rio Grande Pueblos, then questioned minutely as to the leaders and causes of the revolt. The governor's findings were mostly a confirmation of what he had heard the previous year, and these were written down by his clerks in Spanish Christian terms and concepts. One old Indian of Alameda said that Indian resentment had built up from the very beginning of the colony and missions, because the friars and Spaniards took away their *idols* and forbade *sorceries and idolatries.*[11] Another accused El Popé of San Juan, whom all feared because he *talked with the Devil;* he killed his own son-in-law, who was the (Spanish-imposed) governor of San Juan, because he was too friendly with the Spaniards and might reveal the plot to them. He went about with El Saca of Taos boasting that he alone had carried out the uprising, and proclaiming that the *Devil was very strong and much better than God.*[12] Another told a captain that El Popé had made all the Indians crazy and was like the whirlwind. He had given them to understand that the *father of all the Indians, their great chieftain, who had been such since the Deluge,* had ordered El Popé to make all the Pueblos rebel, or else be laid waste.[13] Still others declared that the rebellion had been motivated by the Taos and El Popé, whom all regarded as a *great sorcerer,* and who presented himself as a great chieftain. He went about destroying Christian vestiges and enforcing the ancient customs.[14] Friars and captains wrote that it all was the result of *diabolical* cunning and conspiracy, discord which *the Devil had sown,* apostasy caused by *blind fiends of the devil.* After eighty years of baptism, the *most intelligent and favored* among them, with complete secrecy, acted as the moving spirits and guides.[15] They pointed out some of these intelligent leaders: besides El Popé there were Alonso Catiti, *coyote* of Santo Domingo, Luis and Lorenzo Tupatu of Picuris, Nicolás Jonva, and Francisco El Ollita, *coyote* of San Ildefonso. But nobody mentioned a certain Naranjo, the *negro* or *mulato* of Santa Clara operating from a kiva in Taos. His identity had been kept too well hidden except for that dangerously close description of the previous year: a black giant with big yellow eyes. However, certain Naranjo individuals did enter the picture at this time, and these will now be treated more at length as we work out the Naranjo family relationship.

II. THE NARANJO FAMILY

In the year 1766, the colonial militia officials of Santa Fe and Santa Cruz were up in arms because a certain José Antonio Naranjo claimed to be, by a title conferred by the Viceroy, the overall field commander of colonial troops in New Mexico. At the moment Governor Vélez Cachupín had acknowledged the claim on the basis of documents which Naranjo had presented purporting to prove that not only he, but his father, grandfather, and great-grandfather before him, had received the title from successive Viceroys in Mexico City. Futhermore, his great-grandfather had been a first conquistador of the kingdom. The Spanish officers countered by saying that the military title in question was that of *Capitán Mayor de Guerra* for auxiliary Indian troops only, not for Spaniards, that Naranjo's remote ancestors were not Spanish conquistadores but a Negro slave and an Indian female servant, and that his subsequent black ancestors in the line had been the instigators of Indian uprisings in the past. Governor Cachupín then reviewed the case by interrogating witnesses, and by examining the archives in Santa Fe and the papers in Naranjo's possession. From all this we have a good picture of five generations of the Naranjo family, which are first stated briefly for greater clarity, then considered singly in full detail.

1) The original ancestor, when the New Mexico colony was founded (1598-1600), was a very black Negro slave or servant, married to a female Indian servant. 2) They had a son, Domingo Naranjo, who was born after the Conquest and was involved in Indian uprisings. 3) Domingo's son, José (López) Naranjo, attached himself to the Reconquistador Vargas (1692) and became a Major War-Captain of Indian auxiliary troops. 4) His son, José Antonio Naranjo, also held the same position and title. 5) His son, José Antonio Naranjo (II), the man making these outlandish claims in 1766, enjoyed the same title, but for Indian troops only, and was a consummate rascal and livestock rustler besides.[16] Now we can proceed to identify each generation according to the minute evidence offered in this case, as also from many other sources, in our endeavor to pin down the Naranjo who was the representative of Pohéyemo in 1680.

First Generation:

The anonymous Negro and his anonymous Indian wife: All that we know from this investigation of 1766 is that he was very black-complexioned Negro *(negro atezado),* a slave or servant who married an Indian *criada* of Juana de los Reyes, the wife of an original New Mexico settler of the Martines family.[17] There is only one male Negroid servant mentioned in the Oñate papers, 1597-1600. It is a most interesting single document concerning a recently freed mulatto who did come in the expedition of 1600 as a squire to a minor officer, Juan Bautista Ruano. He is described as a *mulato* by the name of *Mateo,* twenty years of age, "a tall man branded on the face as a slave and with other letters not well outlined," who presented an affidavit from his former master. It gave him his freedom on the sole condition that he serve his Majesty by joining the expedition going to New

Mexico in 1600. His generous master had been Mateo Montero, resident of Puebla de los Angeles, who had purchased him from Alonso de la Torre, resident of the mines of Pachuca. The instrument was officially executed in the city of Los Angeles on January 26, 1600.[18] The soldier, Juan Bautista Ruano, did not stay in New Mexico, but Mateo was obliged to remain under the stipulations of his freedom papers. Hence he must have entered the service of another soldier who settled in the new land.

There was a soldier in this same expedition by the name of *Alonso Martines,* or *Martín,* a native of Higuera de Vargas in Estremadura, the son of Benito Díaz, with complete armor for himself and steed. In all he had ten horses, twenty-four cows, and many household chattels,[19] more than many an unattached officer or soldier had. He is also referred to as Alonso Martín *Naranjo.*[20] No wife is mentioned, as with other settlers, but his many household possessions suggest that he did have one, by the name of Juana de los Reyes, who could have been overlooked when the muster rolls were drawn up. Or else he acquired one not long thereafter, perhaps a Spanish colonist's daughter. Or, from the name "Juana de los Reyes," we might suppose that he married along the way a Mexican Indian servant, of which there was a supply. (Juan Bautista Ruano had also brought along two Indian women, one of them called "Juana," who had left her man in New Spain.) At any rate, it does seem that Mateo became Naranjo's *peón*, for when Governor Oñate's activities were being investigated down in Mexico City in 1601, his chief auditor testified that Oñate's livestock at a pueblo called Santa Clara was in the care of "a certain Naranjo."[21] Since the auditor could not recall the man's first name, and since the independent character of those colonial soldiers would not let them stoop to be Oñate's herders (nor could they be spared for such menial tasks), it seems as though our mulatto Mateo is being referred to here. All this is mere reasoned supposition, yet it fits well with subsequent facts, such as the eventual settlement of the black Naranjos in the environs of Santa Clara.

A similar hypothesis may be advanced regarding Mateo's wife. In addition to Ruano's two Mexican Indian women, there is another one by the name of María, who was brought by the soldier Juan López. She is mentioned again in a list of female servants as presented by their respective masters, and most of these women seem to be of low caste.

But there are three Tlascaltec sisters who stand out above the rest for being the daughters of a Don Joseph of Tepeaca. They were brought along by Juan López. One was *María,* unmarried, with a little daughter Mariana; the other was Catalina, unmarried, with a child called María; the third was Agustina, married to the Indian Francisco, also a servant of Juan López.[22] Whether or not this Juan López stayed in New Mexico, we do not know. But in either case María, if not Catalina, could have joined the household of Alonso Martín Naranjo and thus came to marry Mateo, who was in the same employ. What is more, Mateo had lived in Puebla, and she was from Tepeaca nearby. They could have become well acquainted during the long trek north, if they had not known each other before. This supposition rests not only on the fact that a notorious grandson sometimes used the double surname of *López* Naranjo, but on the superior vitality, sagacity, and intelligence displayed by some of their descendants down several generations. The girls were the daughters of *Don* Joseph, which means that he was a major Tlascaltec chieftain or governor who had been found worthy to use such a title by the officialdom of New Spain; perhaps the girls had been left orphans and destitute, and so were persuaded by Juan López to find a new life in New Mexico. The marriage of one to tall Mateo, whose personality and intelligence must have prompted his kind master to grant him his freedom, insured a very superior progeny. It also serves to explain why the representative of Pohé-yemo was so conversant with Mexican Indian lore in all his crafty dealings.

Second Generation:

Domingo Naranjo, son of the *negro atezado* (Mateo Naranjo) and of (María or Catalina López), Indian house-girl *(criada)* of Juana de los Reyes of the Martines (Naranjo) family. In 1766 Domingo's great-grandson claimed that he had been one of the Spanish conquistadores of the kingdom, that he had received the title of *Capitán Mayor de la Guerra,* and that his son Joseph (López) Naranjo had succeeded him in office.[23] Not so, said the Spanish officers of the colonial militia. Domingo, the *tronco* of these rebellious Naranjos of Santa Clara, could not have been a conquistador since he was the son of *un negro atezado y una india criada* of a Martines housewife. These Naranjo ancestors came as slaves or servants of the first conquerors and settlers. The greatest honor that Domingo Naranjo ever enjoyed—and this is most unlikely—was to be the Chief War-Captain of Indians, not of Spaniards. There were no Naranjos with any titles to be found in Otermín's lists of colonists at the time of the Revolt of 1680, declared Governor Cachupín after consulting the archives.[24] This is all we know about Domingo Naranjo as such. He appears by name in no other documents that might identify him as the tall black representative of Pohé-yemo with the big yellow eyes. But the times and topography point directly to him as the black Tewa of Santa Clara who, sometime before 1680, hid himself in a kiva of Taos to plot and carry out the terrible rebellion of that year.

We do, however, meet with a contemporary bearing the name *Pedro* Naranjo. When Governor Otermín reached the pueblo of Isleta in his reconnaissance expedition of 1681, his men arrested a very old Indian who gave this as his name; he was found to be a great sorcerer who had come down from the upper pueblos to teach his superstitions. In order to gather more evidence against him, Otermín dispatched troops to reconnoiter the upper pueblos.[25] Old Naranjo claimed that he was a Keres of San Felipe, yet he spoke not only Keres and Tewa (of Santa Clara!), but made himself very well understood in Castilian. He understood the nature of an oath and formally took it when questioned on December 18; and his knowledge of Spanish-Indian relations in the past decades is most revealing.[26] He said that since the days of Governor Ugarte y de la Concha (1650), the pueblos had planned rebellions on various occasions through the conspiracy of Indian sorcerers.[27] The message was accepted in some pueblos, but not in others, so they failed. Seven or eight Indians were hanged as a result, and the unrest subsided. Sometime thereafter, "they" sent from Taos to all the pueblos two deerskins with pictures painted on them calling for a new rebellion.[28] The deerskins went as far as the Hopi pueblos, which refused to accept them, and the rebellion failed once more. But the idea "was kept in their hearts." Finally it materialized under El Popé, who was said to have *communication with the Devil.* "It happened that in an estufa of the pueblo of Los Taos there appeared to the said Popé *three figures of Indians* who never came out of the estufa. They gave the said Popé to understand that they were going underground to the *lake of Copala.* He saw these figures *emit fire* from the extremities of their body, and that one of them was called *Caudi,* another *Tilini,* and the other *Tleume,* and those three beings spoke to the said Popé, who was in hiding from the secretary Francisco Xavier,[29] who wished to punish him as a sorcerer. They told him to make a *cord of maguey fiber* and tie some knots in it,[30] which would signify the number of days that they must wait for the rebellion." After relating how the knotted cord had gone from pueblo to pueblo, Naranjo told how a proclamation went forth for all the pueblos to obey the command of their *"father whom they did not know,*[31] which would be given either through *El Caydi* or El Popé." Alonso Catiti brought the message from Santo Domingo to San Felipe, with orders that those who disobeyed would be *beheaded.*[32] The reason for rebelling, Naranjo went on, was "because they had always desired to live as they had when they came out of the lake of *Copala."* After the Spaniards departed, El Popé went about telling the Pueblos to break all images, bells, and crosses, to wash off the water and holy oils of baptism by bathing in the river with yucca-root soap, and to *put away their wives and take on new ones.*[33] This mandate came from *El Caydi* and the other two spirits in the Taos kiva who emitted fire, and the Indians "thereby returned to the state of antiquity, as when they came from the *lake of Copala."* Those Christian Indians who refused were killed by orders of El Popé. To further terrorize the others, El Popé and the *three demons* announced that any Indian harboring any affection for the priests and the Spaniards would be promptly executed. *The demons in the Taos kiva* also said that if the Spaniards ever returned, all the Pueblos would fight to the death. The demons would issue a warning as soon as the Spaniards started out for the north. Pedro Naranjo finished his testimony by saying that he had come to the Southern Pueblos out of fear (!) to teach them idolatrous dances, "in which he greatly fears in his heart that he may have offended God, and that now *having been absolved and returned to the fold* of the church, he has spoken the truth." He gave his age as eighty, and *signed his name* to the declaration.[34]

Pedro Naranjo's testimony is purposely given here in detail, and with several words and phrases in italics, to show that here was no mere Pueblo Indian speaking in Pueblo terms and concepts, but a man well versed by birth and upbringing in matters wholly foreign to Pueblo mentality. He seems to have been lying when he said he was a native Keres of San Felipe, and one cannot help but suspect that he also altered his name a bit, that he actually was Domingo Naranjo of Santa

Clara. And yet we would think that Domingo's unusual size, his Negroid color and features, and his yellow eyes, should have made the Spaniards suspect that he was not a San Felipe Keres. Hence it could well be that Pedro Naranjo was Domingo's brother, smaller in stature and more Indian in appearance, and was his agent in the southern pueblos. How he slyly tried to steer the Spaniards away from the representative of Pohé-yemo (himself or his brother) is evident from the three spirits he now invented. To say, as the prisoners questioned at the time of the revolt did, that the coordinator of it was a black giant with big yellow eyes would be coming too close for comfort. Therefore, it was *El Caudi, Tilini,* and *Tleume* emitting fire from their extremities – names that have the sound and look of Nahuatl rather than of any of the Pueblo tongues. They also suggest, more specifically, the Aztec god of Fire and War.[35] Then there is Pedro Naranjo's reference more than once to the lake of Copala, which he confuses with the Pueblo Indians' *Shipapu* or Hole-in-the-earth whence their ancestors emerged, thus also making it an underground lake. (Allied to this concept is that reference the year before about a far place to the north whence *Montezuma* came.) In all the revolt annals Pedro Naranjo is the only one who mentions the three spirits and the lake of Copala. Nor does the word "Copala" figure in connection with New Mexico Pueblo myth. Here we have a Hispanic-Indian concoction from New Spain being grafted onto Pueblo mythology. It had to come from the Mexican Indians in general; specifically, from Naranjo's own parents and the New World Spanish milieu in which he and his parents grew up.[36]

Finally, we have Pedro Naranjo's age of eighty, his ability to sign his name, his thorough grasp of the nature of an oath, his ability to make a well ordered (if fraudulent) sacramental confession to Father Ayeta. His age places his birth at San Gabriel (or Santa Clara) in the beginning of the century, perhaps the first-born of the mulatto-Tlascaltec couple. His literacy and easy familiarity with Spanish civil and religious practices set him apart from the illiterate Pueblo natives who at best had but a vague comprehension of Spanish Catholic practices. For the only "Pueblo Indians" conversant with writing and such practices at this period were some of the Mexican Indians among them, like the faithful Bartolomé de Ojeda at Zia, for example, whose full Spanish names and surnames identify them as non-Pueblo Indian in origin, and some of the resentful rebel *mestizos, coyotes,* and *lobos* who carried out the revolt for Naranjo in their respective pueblos. But still the actual representative of Pohé-yemo, the Naranjo individual from Santa Clara who went to Taos and from there engineered the rebellion under this clever mystic guise, remains to be fully identified. Apparently his name was Domingo Naranjo. But were Domingo and Pedro the same man?

Third Generation:

Joseph (López) Naranjo, son of Domingo Naranjo: As young men, he and his brother Lucas (whom he killed years later) might have had some active part in the revolt of 1680. Their own children could not, of course. But these succeeding generations have to be considered here for the light which their testimonies and lives throw on Pohé-yemo's representative. Joseph Naranjo, his grandson claimed in 1766, had succeeded his father Domingo as Major War-Captain (not true). He received his title from the Viceroy Duque de Linares and also performed outstanding deeds for the kingdom of New Mexico (true).[37] But, protested the Spanish officers, he was war-captain for Indian auxiliaries only, because he was not even Spanish. One witness who remembered knowing Joseph said that his complexion was decidedly black and that he was nicknamed *"el Mulato."* Another also remembered his color as black, and that some called him *"el Negro,"* others *"el Mulato."*[38] In bewilderment Governor Chachupín consulted the archives, then declared that the only Naranjos he could find therein were an Indian Naranjo (Pedro) whom Otermín found at Isleta, and among the Keres two mulatto brothers also called Naranjo.[39] If Cachupín had perused these Otermín *autos* of 1681 more studiously, he might have detected among them a certain bright young Spanish-speaking Indian by the name of *Josephe.*

After sly old Pedro Naranjo was arrested at Isleta on December 8, 1681, Otermín sent some men up to San Felipe in order to find more evidence against him. On December 18 Juan Domínguez brought in five prisoners to the governor, who was then encamped in the Alameda-Sandía area. These captives were Juan of Tesuque; *Josephe,* a Spanish-speaking youth who did not reveal his tribe; *Lucas,* who claimed to be a Piro from Socorro; and *two mulatto lads* called Juan Lorenzo and Francisco Lorenzo, who lived with their mother near San Felipe, and whose elder brother, Bartolomé Naranjo, had been killed by the San Felipe Indians during the Revolt.[40] It is very significant that the depositions of Josephe, Lucas, and Pedro Naranjo were taken in this order on December 19, and then those of the two Lorenzo brothers on the following day, all in succession.

Josephe, without offering a surname or his pueblo, or even hinting that he knew his captured companions, stated in good Spanish that he had been an employed servant of the Sargento Mayor Sebastián de Herrera when the revolt broke out.[41] He said that he had joined the Spanish refugees going down to Guadalupe del Paso, but many months later he ran away from La Toma (Real de San Lorenzo) with another young Indian called Domingo. When they got back to the northern pueblos, the rebels executed Domingo because they had seen him fighting on the Spanish side during the siege of Santa Fe. Now, said Josephe, he had voluntarily rejoined the Spaniards to warn them of Indian treachery after they had made peace offers. As the instigators of the revolt he named El Popé and other pueblo leaders of San Juan, Taos, and San Ildefonso. He did not mention any leader from Santa Clara. To the interrogator he seemed to be about twenty years old, but could well have been younger. He did not know how to sign his name.

His declaration was followed by that of Lucas, who looked to be more than twenty years old, and who claimed to be a Piro of Socorro captured by the rebels. He knew only the Piro language, he said. He swore through an interpreter that he did not know who had plotted the Revolt; the Tiwa of Isleta had picked up him and his companions by orders of a chief – "he does not know who he is." He had but recently joined the Keres, yet he understood the details of their current plotting without knowing their language. He had surrendered voluntarily because a brother of his was with the Otermín forces and had sent word ahead for Lucas to join him. This shifty character is pointed out here for being circumstantially allied with Josephe and with Pedro Naranjo, although acting as a stranger to both[42] – and because Joseph Naranjo had a brother Lucas whom he slew during a subsequent rebellion.

Old Pedro Naranjo was interviewed next, and it was a long process as we have seen, which left the two mulatto brothers for questioning the following day.[43] These are also important to know, since they have some bearing on the Naranjo relationship, a branch of which was not on the side of the rebels. Their names were Juan Lorenzo and Francisco Lorenzo, and they spoke good Spanish. When the revolt broke out they were living with their mother at a little rancho near San Felipe, not in the pueblo itself. They had gone to the pueblo on that fateful day of August 10, 1680, to hear Mass in honor of St. Lawrence, when their elder brother Bartolomé Naranjo arrived from somewhere and began upbraiding the San Felipes for rebelling. For this they pounced upon him and killed him with their war clubs. This faithful Christian Naranjo was in all probability the young man working in Santa Fe whom Governor Otermín had sent down to San Felipe to inquire about the state of affairs in the southern pueblos.[44] The two boys did not implicate any Naranjos, only El Popé, most likely because they did not know anything else. If they did know old Pedro Naranjo, they could have kept silent out of fear. In this connection there was another Naranjo by the name of Pascual, who had lived with his family in the Analco ward of Santa Fe. He could well have been an uncle of the slain Bartolomé, by being the brother of the woman living just outside of San Felipe with her two Lorenzo youngsters by a different man or husband. For all were referred to as mulattoes, and a mulatto of the previous generation had resided at a rancho called Tungue near San Felipe.[45] The inference is that only the immediate family of Domingo and/or Pedro Naranjo was connected with the revolt, while the other kin remained faithful to the Spaniards and the Faith. Because of their length these complicated matters, like other arguments previously offered, are relegated to the notes.

To get back to Joseph Naranjo, or Josephe, we meet him a full decade later under similar circumstances. On January 8, 1682, Josephe and Juan of Tesuque had escaped from Otermín's party on its way back to Guadalupe del Paso, and had fled once more to the northern pueblos.[46] Possibly fearing retaliation from the Keres and the Tewas, Josephe went to live in Taos – where his father Domingo Naranjo had directed the revolt and perhaps was still there. For here the army of Governor Vargas encountered him on October 7, 1692. The pueblo of Taos was found abandoned, but after a while two Indians came down from the mountains to parley with Vargas.[47] One was the governor of the Taos, Francisco Pacheco.[48] The other was a young Indian *ladino* (meaning very glib in Spanish) who called himself *Josephillo* (little Joe) and was referred to by the Taos as "el Español" because of his proficiency in the language. (And very possibly because Taos Tiwas knew that he was not a Pueblo Indian, but descended from alien people who had come with the Spanish colonists.) For some reason, Governor Vargas took an immediate liking to him, showing him many kindnesses at their first meeting, and from this moment on Josephe or Josephillo cast his lot for good with the Spaniards.[49] After a decade of vacillating between loyalty to the native pueblos and to the Spaniards, he saw a brighter personal future with the latter.

His "peaceful Entrada" of 1692 accomplished, Vargas returned to Guadalupe del Paso with his army, and we presume that Josephillo went along,[50] to return with the army and the colonists in the second Vargas Entrada of 1693. In this final entry into New Mexico, Vargas soon discovered that his easy "pacification" of the previous year was only a delusion. Serious signs of resistance appeared everywhere, but especially in the northern pueblos. He learned that the leaders were the brothers Luis and Lorenzo Tupatú of Picuris, Antonio Bolsas of the Tano Indians occupying Santa Fe, and "el mulato Naranjo del pueblo de Santa Clara."[51] This turned out to be Lucas Naranjo, brother of Joseph, who was to engineer the new revolt of the Tewas in 1696 and the martyrdom of five more Franciscans, and then meet his end at the hands of his brother. Although Joseph is not mentioned in these 1693 annals, he must have witnessed the battle for Santa Fe and the defeat of the Tano and their Tewa and Tiwa allies. Most likely he accompanied Vargas and his forces in the various sorties that followed up until the next major outbreak in 1696. In this year he was living in the brand-new villa of Santa Cruz. On June 5 the five missionaries were slain, as also were several of the colonists; the Indians of most of the Rio Grande pueblos then fled up to their nearby mountain fastnesses. On June 13, when Joseph Naranjo and other men of Santa Cruz were gathering wood near the swollen Rio Grande, an Indian came down and confided to him that the combined Hopi, Zuñi, and Acoma were returning to help the local Pueblos to destroy the Spaniards as soon as the river current subsided. Naranjo then notified the Alcalde of Santa Cruz, Roque de Madrid, to whom he had attached himself, and a general alarm was given.[52] Joseph must have known that his brother Lucas at Santa Clara was at the head of the new rebellion, or else he learned of it for sure from various testimonies taken from prisoners when the alarm was spread.[53]

This presented him with a wonderful opportunity to further ingratiate himself with Governor Vargas and with his mentor, Roque de

Madrid. Somehow he managed to find his brother and killed him; then he cut off his head and presented it to Vargas. This act likewise put an end to this rebellion. As Joseph's grandson boasted in 1766, it was a heroic act which was officially certified by the Cabildo of Santa Fe, when "he killed his brother Lucas in the sorry uprising of the Tewa whom he headed, cutting the head off him and presenting it to the Governor; with the deed the rebels subsided." But a Spanish officer of 1766 countered by saying that the action was not so heroic, since Joseph Naranjo thus erased the infamy of his past life, and likewise got himself pardoned for having lived as an apostate among the gentile Apache of El Cuartelejo for many years, and cohabiting with an Apache squaw; there is where he learned other Indian languages.[54] But from then on Joseph Naranjo's rise among the Spaniards was swift and effective.

By 1700 he was Alcalde Mayor of Zuñi, when he went with the padre to the Hopi pueblos to confer with the mestizo Espeleta, leader of the Hopi.[55] The following year he formulated a petition which is extraordinarily revealing. It betrays long-harbored ambitions, born perhaps on the day when Vargas took him under his wing. Just as he had the bloody execution of his brother certified by the Santa Fe Cabildo, now in 1701 he approached the Franciscan Custos, Fray Antonio Guerra, asking him to write up his past accomplishments. His purpose, as it turned out, was to get the title of Chief War-Captain over all Indian troops from the Viceroy himself. He began by stating that he was "a native of the kingdom," and had already served his Majesty as Alcalde Mayor and War-Captain of Acoma and Zuñi. When he first got these titles from the Governor, the Acoma and Laguna were entrenched on the great rock of Acoma, and the Zuñi on their own fortress mountain, and he all alone persuaded the Laguna and the Zuñi to come down and return to their pueblos. No Spaniard helped him – only his own Christian zeal! (Joseph, unlike his grandson, was not trying to pass himself off as a Spaniard.) Then the Governor in Santa Fe ordered him to enter the ferocious Hopi nation, which he did with the Custos, Father Zavaleta, and with Father Garaycoechea of Zuñi and Father Miranda of Acoma. The party was sorely threatened by the Hopi, but he effectively defended the fathers at the risk of his life. When the Santa Clara Tewa on the rock of Walpi showed signs of surrender, he went up there against the prudent advice of the padres, and brought these people back to Santa Fe. Again, he returned to Walpi with Father Garaycoechea to bring back the Tano Indians living there. The good father tried to dissuade him from risking his life but he, after making his confession, bravely went up and argued with the Tano all night in their kiva; he could not persuade them to return to their pueblos, yet he got them to make peace with the Spaniards. Of the families he himself brought back from the Hopi pueblos, eight were Santa Claras now living in San Juan, six were San Ildefonsos, nine were Cochiti, four were Santo Domingos, six were Galisteos, and also the entire Jemez population now living in their pueblo. All this was done at his own expense without royal aid, as the friars who went with him could testify. This declaration he asked Father Guerra to certify formally, and with the signature and rubic of Joseph Naranjo.[56]

This is followed by an order from the Custos for Fathers Miranda and Garaycoechea to confirm it, and they do in glowing terms, affixing their signatures. Next is a previous certification by Governor Pedro Rodríguez Cubero, who states that Joseph Naranjo, vecino of this kingdom, requested of him the titles of Alcalde Mayor and Capitán de Guerra of Taos when for a year no one had dared go near the pueblo; upon receiving the titles, Naranjo went there and the natives were instructed in the Faith; he not only persuaded the Taos to receive Father Alvarez as their missionary, but got them to help him build the church before the padre got there. Therefore he is found worthy of any honor and grants which the King might choose to bestow on him. This statement is purportedly signed and sealed with his arms in Santa Fe, December 18, 1798 (1698).[57]

This declaration and the several certifications were obviously intended to obtain a more ambitious title as Chief War-Captain of all Pueblo auxiliary troops, and he evidently did get it from the Duke of Linares. For this is not contradicted in a statement made by Naranjo before interim Governor Valverde y Cosío, August 13, 1719, that he was *Cabeza Mayor de la Guerra con título y nombramiento que hizo el Exmo. Virrey que fue, duque de Linares; nor in another, June 2, 1720, Capitán .... que lo es Mayor de la Guerra de los naturales de este Reino, con título del Superior Gobierno.*[58] This last quotation also shows that the title of War-Captain was meant to be for Indian warriors only, and that Joseph did not claim command over Spanish soldiers and militiamen. Nevertheless, it was indeed a high and noteworthy position, for no individual "Indian" had ever exercised a general command over all Pueblo auxiliary troops.

Nor do subsequent documents imply that his petition of 1701 contained empty boasts. In February 1702 he was still Alcalde Mayor of Zuñi, and very hopeful of reducing the Hopi to Christianity.[59] In March of the same year he and his Pueblo troops were on a campaign under Captain Juan de Ulibarrí, when he declared having heard from the Acoma and Laguna Indians that the Zuñi and Hopi were passing around a "knotted thong" *(correa)*. At this time he gave his age as thirty-five (probably off by several years), and he did not sign his name for not knowing how.[60] On March 4, 1703, the Zuñi killed three Spanish vecinos in their pueblo. At the time the solders and Naranjo were away, and on March 7 Father Garaycoechea wrote to Governor Cubero that the rebels were lying in wait night and day for Naranjo to return in order to kill him also. On March 12 Father Miranda wrote from Acoma to Governor Cubero that fifty Acoma warriors were ready and eager to leave for Zuñi and rescue Father Garaycoechea, but he was holding them back because the good padre had written that he would not leave his post without the permission of the major superior. Father Miranda also stated that Naranjo was especially anxious to go himself, but in his letter the priest of Zuñi had written that the Zuñi had laid ambushes for him along the way, and so he held him back also.[61] With Governor Vargas' return to Santa Fe for a second term, Naranjo must have been summoned to his side, for we find him as captain of Indian spies or scouts at Bernalillo in 1704, during the fateful Apache campaign when Vargas took sick and died.[62] During Ulibarrí's famed journey to El Cuartelejo in 1706, Naranjo headed a hundred Indians from every pueblo and did yeoman service as a guide and in contacts with the Apache chieftains. He discovered a needed water-spring which thereafter bore his name, Ojo de Naranjo, and he managed to have the Apache release the Picuris and let them return to their pueblo.[63]

In 1707 he was residing at Santa Cruz, where his good friend Roque de Madrid was still Alcalde Mayor of the villa. His name is the sixteenth on the list of the villagers, married to Catalina, with a family of seven persons.[64] This Catalina was the bastard daughter of a certain Matías Luján of Santa Cruz. Naranjo also owned lands across the Rio Grande at La Vega (present Española), south of those belonging to an Antonio Salazar. These most likely were the ancestral lands which he inherited *in toto* after the death of his rebel brother Lucas. Of his several children, we know the name of his eldest son and heir, José Antonio Naranjo.[65]

In February 1709, after the Navajo stole some livestock from the Santa Clara side of the river, Naranjo and a captain went alone and followed their trail, and Governor Chacón sent out a troop to help the brave men.[66] In October 1713 the Navajo raided the livestock of San Ildefonso, and Governor Mogollón dispatched a troop of seventy Spaniards and one hundred fifty Pueblo auxiliaries, Naranjo in full command of the latter.[67] Again, in 1715 Naranjo led the auxiliaries in another Navajo campaign.[68] As a permanent seal or symbol for all these activities, his name is found carved on Inscription Rock.[69]

Joseph subsequently appears, and still most active, in the two military documents of 1719 and 1720, already referred to in connection with the titles obtained from the Viceroy.[70] In the first, Governor Valverde conferred with his Spanish captains, and Naranjo also on the advisability of waging a compaign against the Ute. Naranjo, still a resident of Santa Cruz, gave his reasons for attacking them. In the second, the same Governor asked his officers' opinions on the Viceroy's idea of establishing a garrison of twenty-five men and their families at El Cuartelejo, with friars to evangelize the gentile Indians. Here Naranjo gave the first "parecer," demonstrating the impracticality of such a plan, and all the Spanish officers seconded his opinion. This is the last we hear of him. But he must have lived on for many years, long enough to be remembered by some witnesses in 1766 as a black-complexioned individual with the soubriquets of "el Negro" and "el Mulato."

Fourth Generation:

José Antonio Naranjo I: One witness of 1766 stated that he was somewhat lighter in complexion than his father Joseph, but did not know for sure if father and son were mulattoes or Indians; they had lived next to the pueblo of Santa Clara. Another flatly stated that José Antonio was an Indian from Santa Clara. Governor Cachupín then declared that, following the death of his father Joseph, José Antonio had moved to Santa Fe and received his title of War-Captain from Viceroy Revilla Gigedo.[71] This means that José Antonio, as the eldest son, had left the household in Santa Cruz to take care of the ancestral lands north of Santa Clara. Then, after his father's death, he went to

Santa Fe in order to engage in the politics necessary to have his father's title conferred upon himself. José Antonio had married Juana Márquez de Ayala, of the colonists brought from Zacatecas by Vargas. Their eldest son was likewise named José Antonio (II), and they had a daughter Catalina, the wife of Salvador de Torres. Another son of theirs was most likely a Gerónimo Naranjo who married María Trujillo in 1743, and for whom Salvador de Torres and Catalina Naranjo stood as witnesses. Possibly another son, or perhaps a brother, was a Matías Naranjo, living in the same Santa Clara district with his wife María Varela. In 1731 José Antonio Naranjo had murdered a man and fled the kingdom.[72]

Fifth Generation:

José Antonio Naranjo II, the man who in 1766 caused such a furor by wanting to be the field commander of Spanish troops as well as Indian: In 1747 he had gone all the way to Mexico City, and without permission. There he wangled an interview with the Viceroy himself to present the documents that compose this case. Apparently the Viceroy believed his story about his being descended from an original Spanish conquistador of New Mexico, and about his direct ancestors all the way back having held the title of general commander of all colonial troops in the field. For in January 1748 the Marqués de las Amarillas conferred on him the title of "Capitán Mayor de la Gente de Guerra, en la villa de Santa Fe," in the place of his father José Antonio Naranjo (I). Later, Governor Marín del Valle (1754-1760) had angrily suspended the title because of gross disobedience and other charges. But after Vélez Cachupín came as Governor (1762-1767), Naranjo began working for his reinstatement. He got a glowing writ of commendation from Fray Juan José de Toledo, and his henchman Cristóbal Vigil gathered an impressive batch of signatures in his favor. First, Cachupín assigned him to the valley and pueblo of Taos with the "honorific title of Capitán y Justicia Mayor," Later, he apprised the militia of his intention of reinstating Naranjo according to the tenor of the documents which he presented.[73] This is what started the alarm among the Spanish officers and men and prompted Cachupín to look into the governmental archives in Santa Fe. As was mentioned before in connection with his father and grandfather, some thought he was a pure Tewa from Santa Clara while others declared that his forebears were a mixture of Negro and Indian. His title, if legitimate, was as war-captain for Indians only. Besides not being an "español," he was utterly incapable of exercising any military command for many serious reasons. For one thing, he was a notorious horse thief and cattle rustler. His no-good son, José, had recently murdered the son of Roque Jaramillo of Santa Cruz with bow and arrows. The details of his rascality run into many pages, but are here passed over since they contribute nothing to the Naranjo family relationships and their connection with the Representative of Pohé-yemo.

Governor Cachupín's judgment was final. "All this proves that the title conferred on the present José Antonio Naranjo must be understood as *Capitán Mayor,* not of Spaniards, but of Indians (which was the one that his father and grandfather held). . . . Concerning the other Naranjos, whom Vargas found in the year ninety-three, and one of them was the already mentioned first Captain (Joseph Narango), their (racial) quality is not specified in the documents of that archive. The witnesses say, almost all, that they know the grandfather of José Antonio Naranjo. And he, according to their testimonies, turns out to be a *Lobo, ó Mulato, ó Indio.* And what is certain is that, after the defect of his *calidad* had been set forth by the militia officials, he did not dare deny it. . . ."[74] In short, the results of the investigation were sent to Mexico City, and the Viceroy stripped Naranjo of his titles, ordering the local authorities to punish him and his companions in crime according to their deserts.[75]

It is of interest to note that in one of these papers Naranjo employs his mother's family name, Márquez de Ayala. His wife was Manuela Armenta, whom he had married in Santa Fe in 1749. She, like his mother, belonged to the colonists from Zacatecas. Other activities recorded about him, in addition to the case we have been treating, were a land transfer in 1752, a trial in 1756 for mistreating his Armenta wife, and other charges for assault in 1758.[76] These, and the entire epidsode of 1766, sadly demonstrate how much the main line of the vigorous and gifted black Naranjo family had fallen from the bizarre genius displayed by the great-grandfather in the Revolt of 1680, and from the enviable heights of achievement reached by the grandfather, Joseph López Naranjo, at the turn of the century.

III. CONCLUSION

That the famous Pueblo Revolt of 1680 was successfully planned and carried out, not alone by individual ritual leaders of each pueblo, but by a very real representative of Pohé-yemo – a tall black man with big yellow eyes by the name of Naranjo – is amply demonstrated, I believe, by all the foregoing evidence. Whether or not Domingo Naranjo and Pedro Naranjo were one and the same man remains a moot question, although I incline toward the belief that they were brothers: Domingo the Representative of Pohé-yemo in Taos, and Pedro carrying out his orders at San Felipe. If Governor Otermín so officiously failed to recognize the chief culprit under his clever disguise, the basic truth did survive, even if in a confused way, in the long memory of the common Hispanic folk, as shown in the testimonies of 1766. It also had been preserved, although in a more legendary manner, in the tradition of Nuestra Señora de la Macana, in which the Devil himself is said to have appeared in the form of a black giant during the 1680 siege of Santa Fe.[77]

We can close this study most appropriately with a Pueblo folktale about the Pohé-yemo which was still being told in Santo Domingo not too long ago. Because the story concerns an "ancient one" who in latter times is but a minor being among the *kopershtaya* or fetishes of the Indians, it must go back to those faraway times when the person of Pohé-yemo had been greatly magnified and emphasized for the moment. And because the tale's form and flavor is not characteristic of the Indian genre of storytelling, but rather of the Spanish picaresque story, it could well have been composed just before the Revolt of 1680 by Naranjo himself and disseminated among the pueblos. The use of the form *Poshaiyanyi* for Pohé-yemo suggests that it came back to Santo Domingo by way of Zuñi:

> God and Poshaiyanyi were going to have a contest to see which one had the most power. They were going to shoot at a tree. God shot at it with a gun and cut a gash in the bark. Poshaiyanyi struck it with a bolt of lightning and split the trunk in half. Next they were going to see which one had the best things to eat. God had a table with lots of good things on it. Poshaiyanyi ate on the ground; he had some fat deer meat and some tortillas. God watched Poshaiyanyi eat for a while, then he got down on the ground and ate with him.

Then they were going to see who could get some water from Shipap first. God wrote a letter. Poshaiyanyi made a wabani (feather bunch). He got water while someone was reading God's letter.

The next was to see who could make the best music. God had a horn and blew on it. Poshaiyanyi used a drum and sang. After a while God got tired and gave up. God went home on a cloud; Poshaiyanyi left on the back of a duck.

The next day they met again. They were going to shoot again. They shot at a rock this time. They decided to bet on the outcome. God bet some horses, cows, sheep, and one daughter. Poshaiyanyi bet corn and watermelons. God shot first; he just made a little nick in the rock. Poshaiyanyi struck it with a bolt of lightning and shattered it into bits. So Poshaiyanyi won again. He took the girl and started to go home. God got mad and sent some soldiers after him. But Poshaiyanyi got on a duck's back and went away to Wenima.[78]

Before he left he told the Indians that there wouldn't be any more war between the Indians and anyone. If there were he would come back. He would gather all the Indians in one place and separate the good people from the witches. Then the earth will crack. Then everything will be new again—"when a mule has a baby."[79]

J. CISNEROS

DeVargas' Negro Drummer

Fray Angelico Chavez

Oftentimes the little people in regional history, forgotten because the writers of history are entirely preoccupied with the deeds of the mighty, prove more interesting than the great from a human point of view. Precisely because of their secondary status, material concerning them is scant; yet bits of information here and there sometimes provide enough facts for the portrayal of such an individual, especially if he took part in the great events often written about. Such a character is Sebastián Rodríguez, who feverishly beat his snare-drum to encourage the Spanish soldiery at every martial encounter or parade during the First and Second *Entradas* of Governor de Vargas, as well as in subsequent campaigns. That he was a pure bred Negro from Africa makes him all the more fascinating.

The earliest mention of him is in 1689 (May 29), when he gave his name as Sebastián Rodríguez Brito, *"de nación angola,"* in his petition to contract a marriage at Guadalupe del Paso, where the exiled New Mexicans were awaiting the reconquest of their homeland. The only page left of this petition consists of an objection made by his master, Don Pedro Reneros de Posada, then in his last year as Governor. Posada stated that Rodríguez who had been in his service for three years, was already married.[1] This shows that Rodríguez was a newcomer with a past unknown to the inhabitants there; it cannot be ascertained

Reprinted through the courtesy of *El Palacio*, ed. Richard L. Polese, and Fray Angelico Chavez. The article first appeared in May, 1949.

whether Posada's objection was justified, or whether Rodríguez gave proof that his former spouse was already deceased. A different matrimonial investigation three years later, however, partially supplements this incomplete record. Rodríguez was called as a witness to prove the freedom to marry of a certain Antonia Naranjo, daughter of a *mulato,* Pascual Naranjo, who was to marry a certain Pacheco Pérez. Here Rodríguez deposed that he was fifty years old, a native of San Pablo de Luanda, and a resident of El Paso for seven years as official drummer of the garrison; he also testified that he had once been engaged to Antonia Naranjo, but that she had refused to marry him because of the rumor that he was already married.[2]

Some two or three years later, he did succeed in marrying a certain Isabel, or Ana, Olguín, the widow of a certain Madrid.[3] It is from his next marriage, in 1697, that fuller details of his origin are made known. Sebastián Rodríguez is his name, and he is the widower of Isabel Olguín, and holds the position of drummer of the Santa Fe garrison. He is a native of Rio Llanero, the son of Manuel Rodríguez and María Fernández, both *"negros bosales,"* and natives of San Pablo de Luanda; therefore, Sebastián is a true black, since both of his parents were "jungle" Negroes. The woman he now married was a *coyota,* Juana de la Cruz, of unknown parentage, native of the Salinas district of New Mexico.[4] Called to testify on another occasion, he stated further that San Pablo de Luanda was in Guinea.[5]

From all this, as well as from his family names, we conclude that he was born in Portuguese Guinea on the bulging west coast of Africa north of the equator in about the year 1642. Rio Llanero does, indeed, sound like the Portuguese colony of Rio de Janeiro, and it could be that he might have come to New Spain by way of Brazil; his birthplace, however, was most likely a small river or the name of a district in Luanda, Africa. From New Spain he came north in the service of Governor Posada (as drummer, no doubt), in 1686. Undoubtedly, he had married at least once before in his fiftieth year, but whether he had a wife or wives living in New Spain or in the West Indies, at the time he contracted subsequent marriages in New Mexico, is something to conjure with.

With the arrival in 1691 of a new Governor, Don Diego de Vargas, the New Mexican colony at Guadalupe del Paso bestirred itself for the epic return home after twelve years of exile. Drills and maneuvers and reviews were the order of the day and in these operations, the drummer played an indispensable part. One can see his ivory-toothed grin as he frantically beat his drum, while armored horses and men drew in the reverberations of the martial spirit. Rodríguez was, besides, the governor's herald or town-crier, who went through the civilian and military camps proclaiming his orders or the decrees received from the Viceroy. On August 9, 1692, for example, de Vargas' decision to lead his first expedition into New Mexico "was publicly announced to the sound of the war drum and bugle and with the customary solemnity in the most public places, loudly and intelligibly by voice of Sebastián Rodríguez. . . ."[6] Throughout the campaign journals of that memorable expedition, the name of Sebastián Rodríguez is not mentioned, but his personality sounds forth mightily every time de Vargas calls for the drum and bugle for a skirmish with the Indians or for a solemn parade, such as the one which took place in the famous first entry into Santa Fe.

After receiving the peaceful submission of the Pueblos, the Governor and his forces returned to El Paso in order to gather the old exiled families and newly arrived colonists for a final grand colonizing expedition. Again the same drummer is heard, by the sound of his *caja de guerra* if not by name; and we must revise our mental picture of the Spanish soldiery in shining armor during the battle of Santa Fe, and the triumphant ceremony of possession in that December of 1693, by including the coal-black face and toothy grin of Sebastián Rodríguez, strutting high, manipulating his drumsticks as only a Negro can.

It was after this event that he married Isabel Olguín, for her Madrid husband was then buried in the Santa Fe cemetery. Rodríguez settled in Santa Fe as official drummer of the garrison. He was affluent enough some years later to purchase property between the lands of Captain Medina on the west and of Ana Luján on the east, and south of the property of Antonio Lucero.[7] This was in the year 1697, when his Olguín wife died and he married Juana de la Cruz. Other Indian campaigns followed during the last years of the century in which he and his drum took part. It seems that he was a quiet man and well-respected, for he himself was not mixed up in any fights or scandals of the period. One interesting note is struck by his self-identification in 1698, when he said that he was a native of San Pablo de Luanda and the drummer of the Santa Fe garrison and — "*de Nacion*

Moreno."[8] It was as if he had said "colored" instead of the blunt Spanish word for black.

Rodríguez continued as drummer under de Vargas' successor, Governor Cubero (1696-1703). He is mentioned as such in an incident when an Indian came into his house at midnight to warn him and the Spanish of a Zuñi and Apache plot.[9] De Vargas returned for a second term, and Rodríguez was with him again as drummer in the 1704 Sandía Mountain Campaign, when the great Captain-General sickened and died.[10] The last date in which his name appears is 1706; he sold some land "on the other side of the Santa Fe River" to Micaela de Velasco.[11] In that same year he also appeared in an affair concerning his family, described below. Perhaps he died in Santa Fe sometime after, or maybe he moved away – the earliest Santa Fe burial book extant dates from 1726, and therefore there is no way of checking.

The last woman Rodríguez had married, Juana de la Cruz (also called Maese or Apodaca) was sometimes embroiled in hexing or similar superstitious affairs which came up for trial, and this is how her husband's name sometimes was drawn in. One of these trials took place in 1704. A Spanish woman claimed that she had been bewitched by some Tesuque Indians; the hysterical plaintiff asserted that Juana de Apodaca and her daughter had taken part in this hexing.[12] A similar trial in 1706 concerned several *mulato* and Indian women of the lowest stratum in Santa Fe, who were allegedly casting all sorts of spells on each other and on their respective consorts; again Juana de Apodaca and her daughter were named. Rodríguez himself appeared voluntarily in court to disclaim any part in the matter; he said that certain people considered him, his wife, and his step-daughter as witches, but that it was false. "*Primero es Dios que quanto ay,*" he said. Then he proceeded to show how the accusers themselves had tried to inveigle his wife and step-daughter into taking part in certain superstitious practices. In doing so, he showed how he himself firmly believed (as did all and sundry, for that matter) in the "evil eye." He accused a *mulato* hag, called "La Lozana," of having played the evil eye upon his little son Melchor. To cure his boy, he himself sneaked behind her on the street one day, secretly cut off some hair from one of her braids, and brought it home to cure the child. He burned the hair and was in the act of "smoking" the child with it in the form of a cross, when La Lozana came in and told him that the weather was too cold for the remedy to take effect. So she put the child under her skirts between her thighs and "smoked" him there. In her own testimony, the child's mother declared that her little Melchor did not get well until she took him to church and the Fathers prayed over him.[13]

Whether little Melchor grew up to be a healthy man and had children is something not yet discovered. Nor do we know if Sebastián Rodríguez had other progeny. The garrison drummer in 1716 was a man by the name of Esteban Rodríguez, who was still alive in 1757, when Governor del Valle ordered him back to duty to train a successor for this "most necessary function which arouses the soldiers and terrifies the enemy." We do not know if he was related to Sebastián, or if he, too, was colored – unless he is the same Esteban Rodríguez, Negro, who was involved in a marital scandal in Santa Cruz.[14]

L. Bjorklund.

YORK

John M. Carroll

Perhaps the least known, yet one of the most important, members of the famous Lewis and Clark expedition was a black manservant to Captain Clark named York. There was no other distinguishing name recorded for him other than that single sobriquet. It was neither first nor last name; it was sufficient identification for him then, and it is a standout to the researchers of today.

It is doubtful that York had much to say about whether he would go on the expedition or not. He had been recently inherited by Captain Clark from his father who had died shortly before the expedition was to begin. Had he been given any opportunity to choose, it would have been likely that he would have elected to go, for the pattern of his behavior throughout the entire trip indicated a man who had strong preferences for the outdoors, for adventure, and for excitement.

The story of York can only be told through the brief mentions he is awarded in the journals kept by the leaders of the expedition. What is more improbable, but true, however, is his presence and obvious importance to the expedition as recorded by many of America's greatest painters of the western American scene.

York's value as a manservant, and then as a full-fledged important member of the expedition, slowly evolves as one reads the journals. It is made very obvious by the types of entries that appear. They begin as:

This selection is being published for the first time in this volume.

> June 5th Tuesday 1804 . . . which we named Sand C., here my Servant York Swam to the Sand bar to geather Greens for our Dinner, and returned with a Sufficient quantity wild *Creases [Cresses]* or Tung grass.[1]

and then progressed to:

> . . . About the only members of the party who could be counted on to do as told were Clark's servant York and Lewis's big dog, Scannon.[2]

It was not until the Indians began to demonstrate a more than casual interest in York that Lewis and Clark began fully to appreciate his true value, not only to themselves but to the success of the expedition. Evidence of this began to appear early as described here:

> . . .Of the other members of the exploring party, York, Captain Clark's Negro servant, attracted the most attention from both the Hidatsa and Mandan Indian. They had never before seen a Negro and did not know quite what to make of him. York himself, a dark, corpulent man, tried to make the Indians believe he had been wild like a bear and tamed. One Eye, the principal Hidatsa chief, examined York closely, spit on his hand and rubbed the Negro's skin, believing that he might be a painted white man. Possibly this Indian reaction to York survives in the name for Negro in the languages of some of the Upper Missouri tribes, which may be translated as "black white man."[3]

and:

> . . .But they [Lewis and Clark] must wait while the airgun was shot or one of the men went into a jig or someone struck up a tune on the violin to keep the Indians in a negotiating mood. When they ran out of diversions, a display of York's black skin and wiry curls made a good show. "We have learnt by experience," Lewis explained, "that to keep the savages in good humor their attention should not be wearied by too much business. . .matters should be enlivened with what is new and entertaining."[4]

As the expedition made its way across this vast uncharted continent, so too did word of the black man who was with them. Tribe after tribe knew, mysteriously, about York long before the expedition reached their villages.

> . . . River Maropa 9th of October 1804. Tuesday. . .Sorry [several] Canoos of Skins passed down from the 2 Villages a Short distance above, and many Came to view us all day, much astonished at my black Servant, who did not lose the opportunity of [displaying] his powers Strength &c. &c. this nation never Saw a black man before.[5]

. . .15th of October Monday 1804. . .Those people [recares] are much pleased with my black Servent. Their womin verry fond of carressing our men &c.[6]

. . .Sunday 28th of October 1804. . .we made up the presents and entertained Several of the Curious Chiefs whome, wished to see the Boat which was verry curious to them viewing it as great medison, as they also Viewed my black Servent.[7]

It must have been somewhere, sometime, during this phase of their arduous journey that it became more evident to Lewis and Clark that York was really their ambassador – their ticket – their passport from tribe to tribe. It was as much York as anyone who made the trek an easier one for all concerned. It explained, too, in part, why there were fewer hostile tribes than they originally expected to find.

Indeed, Lewis and Clark may very well have had reason to feel slighted at times, for York took preference to anything else when meeting a new tribe.

. . . Friday August 15th, 1805. . .I [Lewis] had mentioned to the chief several times that we had with us a woman of his nation who had been taken prisoner by the Minnetaries, and that by means of her I hoped to explain myself more fully than I could do signs. some of the party had also told the Indians that we had a man with us who was black and had short curling hair. this had excited their curiossity very much, and they seemed quite as anxious to see this monster as they wer[e] the merchandize which we had to barter for their horses.[8]

It is unnecessary at this point to indicate that York enjoyed his new-found fame. That goes without saying. How could anyone not? He surely viewed it with pleasure as the following will attest:

. . . He brought back to camp two Frenchmen, named Gravelines and Tabeau, who were trading with the Indians. Both understood the Indian language well. The captains asked them to arrange the usual conference with the chiefs of the nation.

. . . The Indians came and were amazed by Clark's giant servant, York. He was the first black man they had ever seen. The natives "all flocked around & examined him from top to toe," Clark said. York enjoyed the situation immensely. "He carried on the joke himself and made himself more turribal than we wished him to doe." He told the Indians he was a wild animal Clark had captured and tamed. A horde of little boys followed him at a safe distance wherever he went. York loved it. He would turn and bare his teeth or growl and the small fry would scatter screaming, only to gather again immediately when he turned his back.

> ...The Arickara men were generous and their wives amorous and pretty. Most of the men withstood the temptation well, but York took full advantage of his popularity. One warrior, considerate of his wife's every desire, invited York to his tepee and stood guard at the entrance. He even refused Clark the privilege of contacting his servant until a reasonable time had elapsed.[9]

One of the most interesting observations – and really a testimonial to York's true importance to the expedition – is recorded below:

> ...The two captains advanced and shook hands with the chief, who commanded his people to refrain from any evil-doing toward them. The white men removed their pack-saddles from their horses and sat down on the ground. The chief said: "They have no robes to sit on. Some Indians have stolen them. Bring them robes." Buffalo-skins were brought, but instead of sitting on them, the white men threw them about their shoulders. One of them had a black face, and the Indians said among themselves, "See, his face is painted black! They are going to have a scalp-dance.[10]

On the surface, and without a proper explanation, this episode would appear to be meaningless, except to students of ethnology. It was the practice of some of the plains Indians, when returning from battle or a raid or a coup, to stop outside the village area and paint portions of their bodies with charcoal. This black indicated bravery to all who would see him ride slowly and triumphantly into the village later. The more of the body that was painted black, the braver the deed. Consequently, when these Indians first viewed York it was difficult – if not impossible – for them to accept Lewis and Clark as the leaders of the expedition when truly the bravest one of all, a man colored black from head to toe, side to side, front to back, sat with them in council. And everyone knew that the bravest was the leader.

Without a retelling of the whole journey, it is a recorded fact, of course, that the members of the expedition were successful in reaching the Pacific. What is not known, however, is that Captain Clark, in gratitude for the services York rendered him as his manservant, and in recognition of his part in the success of the journey – accidental or not – granted full and total emancipation to his servant and friend upon their return.

York lived in Tennessee until his natural death some years later. Since there is no record of his death nor any details of his burial, it is impossible to identify exactly when, where, and how the end came.

However, from personal memoirs of other settlers in that area, it has been learned that York became a rather successful businessman and never wanted for that which he could not buy.

In attempting to arrive at an epitaph for this remarkable man, I was reminded of a Langston Hughes poem which ended: "I, Too, Am America." So that all the world may know and appreciate York and his contribution to our history, I paraphrase with: "He, too, was America."

The Four Black Regiments

The following four excerpts give a brief outline of the organizational history of the major all-black units, the Ninth and Tenth US Cavalry Regiments and the Twenty-fourth and Twenty-fifth US Infantry Regiments. Many of the episodes touched on here – for example, General Grierson's Victorio campaign, Captain Nolan's lost expedition, the Wham paymaster robbery – will be treated in greater detail elsewhere in the book.

The selections are from a common source, *"The Army of the United States,"* by Theodore F. Rodenbough and William J. Haskin, which was published in 1896. The authors were military men who took their material from actual regimental records; and the information contained therein is reliable and accurate through the year 1896.

The excerpt pertaining to the Ninth, brief as it is, is the only history of that regiment. Unlike the other three, the Ninth never had an active regimental historian, which, in part, explains why the Tenth has probably always been the "glamor" unit of the two. This is not to say that the Tenth does not deserve all the written credits it has received; it is rather to assert that the Ninth was also very much in the frontier picture.

This account shows the humble beginnings of the Ninth in New Orleans: When the soldiers were originally mustered to form the unit, empty cotton presses were used as barracks, and mess was cooked over open fires. Since formal education had been virtually denied the black man in these years, only one soldier was found in the regiment who could read well enough to perform the duties of Sergeant-Major. The duties of the Ninth were to protect the stagecoach lines, to establish law and order along the Mexican border, and to keep the Indians on reservations. It is clear from this brief history that garrison life in Texas was far from glamorous: there were no such amenities as bathtubs, for example, and the entire water supply was limited to a huge tank on wheels that rolled around the post "with eight mules and a surly driver."

The Tenth Cavalry is more well known than the Ninth for its frequent encounters with hostile Indians. At its inception, the commander, Colonel Grierson, was determined to fill the ranks only with men of the highest quality. Orders went out to recruit none but "superior men . . . who would do credit to the regiment." The descriptions throughout the book of the Tenth bear witness to the fact that Grierson achieved his goal. One example of their ability to respond to a call for action concerns Lt. Colonel Forsyth's battle with the Indians. The relief troops of the Tenth were the first to come to the rescue of Forsyth and his men, who were cornered on an island in the Republican River. The black troopers found the men out of rations and living on horseflesh "without salt or pepper." All the horses were dead, and their rotting carcasses "impregnated the air with a terrible stench."

The two infantry regiments, the Twenty-fourth and the Twenty-fifth, are also not as heavily chronicled as the Tenth Cavalry. They did, however, perform valuable service on the frontier, their duties being described as the following: engaging in expeditions against the Indians, guarding strategic points, building roads, hunting horse thieves, building and repairing military posts, erecting telegraph lines, and performing escort and guard duties.

The service performed by all four units was instrumental in ending Indian hostilities on the western frontier and opening the country to settlers.

Paul A. Rossi

The Ninth Regiment of Cavalry

Lieutenant Grote Hutcheson (Adjutant Ninth U.S. Cavalry)

The subject of this sketch first came into existence by virtue of an act of Congress entitled "An Act to increase and fix the military peace establishment of the United States," approved July 28, 1866. To the six regular cavalry regiments then in service, this Act added four additional ones, "two of which shall be composed of colored men, having the same organization as is now provided by law for cavalry regiments." The organization of the colored regiments was modified in a few particulars, notably, by including a regimental chaplain, whose duties were enlarged to include the instruction of the enlisted men. Up to this time all chaplains had been appointed in the army, designated to posts, and known as post chaplains.

The original vacancies in the grades of first and second lieutenant were to be filled by selection from among the officers and soldiers of volunteer cavalry; two-thirds of the original vacancies in the higher grades by selection from among the officers of volunteer cavalry; and one-third from among officers of the regular army. It was further provided that to be eligible for selection, an active service of two years in the field during the War of the Rebellion was necessary; also that applicants should have been distinguished for capacity and good conduct.

This selection was first published in Theodore F. Rodenbough and William J. Haskin, *The Army of the United States* (New York, 1896).

Another enactment considerably affecting the composition of the regiment, and which, because its requirements have been so enlarged by recent legislation as to embrace nearly the entire commissioned force of the regular army, may be deemed of particular interest, is that referring to the examination of officers prior to appointment. It directed that no person should be commissioned in any of the regiments authorized by the Act, until he had passed a satisfactory examination before a board to be composed of officers of the arm of the service in which the applicant was to serve. This board was to be convened by the Secretary of War, and was to inquire into the service rendered during the war by the applicant, as well as into his capacity and qualifications for a commission in the regular forces. Appointments were to be made without reference to previous rank but solely by a consideration of present qualifications and past meritorious services.

On August 3, 1866, Major General Philip H. Sheridan, then commanding the Military Divison of the Gulf, at New Orleans, Louisiana, was authorized to raise, among others, one regiment of colored cavalry to be designated the Ninth Regiment of US Cavalry, which was to be enlisted within the limits of his own command. Men serving in volunteer colored regiments who desired to enlist in regular regiments were authorized to be discharged from the volunteer organizations. This class of men was desired and many took advantage of the opportunity to join the regular service, and later proved of some value as noncommissioned officers.

The mustering officer at New Orleans was directed to take temporary charge of the recruiting, and shortly afterwards it was transferred to Major Francis Moore, Sixty-fifth US Colored Infantry. The men obtained by Major Moore formed the nucleus of the enlisted strength, and were principally obtained from New Orleans and its vicinity. A little later in the autumn recruiting was established in Kentucky, and all the men for the new regiment were obtained from that State and Louisiana. The horses were obtained at St. Louis, and proved to be an excellent mount.

About the middle of September all recruits were assembled in New Orleans, and preparations made for organization. Empty cotton presses were used as barracks and the ration was cooked over open fires. In the latter part of September an epidemic of cholera caused the camp to be moved to Greenville, and later, for other reasons, it was moved to

Carrollton, both of which places are suburbs of New Orleans.

During the winter of 1866-67, every effort was made to bring about an efficient state of drill, discipline and organization. The orders regarding stables and the performance of that duty were especially strict. Few officers had as yet joined, and the number on duty with the regiment was so small, that a scheme of squadron organization was resorted to so that at least one officer might be present with each squadron for every drill or other duty. The entire enlisted strength was woefully ignorant, entirely helpless, and though willing enough to learn, was difficult to teach. By assiduous labor and constant drilling much headway was made, however, and by the end of March, 1867, a change of station was determined upon. The middle of this month found the regiment with nearly its full strength, the return at that time showing a total of 885 enlisted men, or an average of over 70 to a troop.

The regiment, now practically organized yet still far from being in anything approaching a perfected state, was ordered to proceed to San Antonio, where it arrived early in April and formed a camp of instruction. Troops L and M, however, proceeded direct to take station at Brownsville, Texas, near the mouth of the Rio Grande, where they remained several years. This command was under First Lieutenant J.M. Hamilton (now a major of the First Cavalry), then an officer in the Ninth US Colored Infantry, he being one of a number of volunteer officers who had been temporarily continued in their volunteer commissions for the purpose of assisting in the organization of the new regiments until the arrival of the regularly appointed officers. Upon these officers much heavy work fell during the winter of 1866-67, as the regular officers arrived slowly until after the camp at San Antonio was established, when they began to report rapidly.

The camp near San Antonio was continued for some three months, and the time spent there was profitably employed in completing and perfecting the organization and drill, already well under way from the efforts of the preceding winter. The officers of the regiment were now nearly all appointed, and during the summer of 1867 they were as follows:

Colonel Edward Hatch.
Lieutenant-Colonel Wesley Merritt.
Majors James F. Wade, George A. Forsyth, and Albert P. Morrow.
Chaplain John C. Jacobi.

Captains J.S. Brisbin, W. Bayard, G.A. Purington, J.M. Bacon, G.H. Gamble, Henry Carroll, A.E. Hooker, W.T. Frohock, J.C. DeGress, T.A. Boice, F.S. Dodge, and E.M. Heyl.

First Lieutenants Michael Cooney, I.F. Moffatt, J.G. Birney, Charles Parker, J.L. Humfreville, Francis Moore, F.W. Smith, L.H. Rucker, Byron Dawson, J.S. Loud, Patrick Cusack, F.S. Davidson, D.H. Cortelyou, G.B. Bosworth, and W.B. Brunton.

Second Lieutenants I.W. Trask, F.R. Vincent, I.M. Starr, F.P. Gross, E.D. Dimmick, W.W. Tyler, G.W. Budd, T.C. Barden, and J.C. Edgar.

It is difficult nowadays fully to appreciate all the work and labor devolving upon the officers in those early days. The men knew nothing, and the noncommissioned officers but little more. From the very circumstances of their preceding life it could not be otherwise. They had no independence, no self-reliance, not a thought except for the present, and were filled with superstition. To make soldiers of such material was, at that time, considered more of an experiment than as a fixed principle. The government depended upon the officers of those early days to solve the problem of the colored soldier.

The colonel of the regiment was Edward Hatch, a young man full of energy and enthusiasm. He went right manfully to work, determined to succeed, and in this he was ably seconded by his officers. They were all equally enthusiastic in proving the wisdom of the experiment of colored soldiers, and in forcing the issue to a successful solution were compelled, not only to attend to the duties that naturally attach to the office of a troop commander and his lieutenants, but, in the endeavor to make finished individual soldiers of the Negro and to feel that the troop, taken as a unit, was an independent fighting force, well drilled, well clothed, well fed, suitably armed and equipped, and thoroughly able to take care of itself in garrison or campaign, they were forced to enter into the minutest details of military administration, and personally to assume nearly all the duties of the non-commissioned officer. For some years the latter, from lack of education, were such only in name, and the process of molding them into a responsible and self-reliant class was a slow one. Troop officers were in fact squad commanders, and it took both time and patience to teach the men how to care for themselves.

The amount of writing devolving upon officers during the earlier years of the regiment is not to be passed over lightly. Fully to appreciate this, it must be borne in mind that the enlisted men were totally uneducated; few indeed could read and scarcely any were able to write even their own names. It is related that but one man in the entire regiment was found able to write sufficiently well to act as sergeant-major. It was not an uncommon thing for a captain to assist his first sergeant in calling the roll, and every record, from the morning report to the monthly return, was prepared by an officer. In time the simpler reports were mastered, but it is only in later years that troop clerks are found, and even now considerable difficulty is experienced at times in finding reliable men of sufficient education to conduct properly the routine clerical work pertaining to a troop.

Early in June the regiment was ordered into western and southwestern Texas to assist in opening up once more that vast territory, extending from Fort Clark to El Paso, and from the Rio Grande to the Concho. By this time the regiment was deemed sufficiently well organized, equipped, and disciplined, to be sent to the extreme frontier, and capable of undergoing the long and trying march into the wild and unsettled country that lay before it.

The regiment was distributed as follows: Headquarters and Troops A, B, E, and K, General Hatch commanding, at Fort Stockton; Troops C, D, F, G, H, and I, Lieutenant Colonel Merritt commanding, at Fort Davis. Troops L and M had previously been sent to Brownsville.

The principal duty of the command in western Texas was to open up and protect the mail and stage route from San Antonio to El Paso; to establish law and order in the country contiguous to the Rio Grande frontier, which had been sadly interfered with by Mexicans as well as Indians during the Civil War; to prevent marauding by Indians and to capture and confine to their reservations all roving bands; in fact, to help pave the way for the western advance of civilization, and to add their part in the great work of opening to settlement the vast resources of the great West.

Having landed the regiment in this far away part of the country, a word or two of every-day garrison life during those early days, when the nearest railroad was six hundred miles distant, may be of interest. In many respects the every-day life of the men in garrison was similar to that of the present time. There was the same drill, stables, and parade; the amount and kind of fatigue bore a strong resemblance to that of today; there were logging teams for the sawmill and special details for the garden; men mixing mud for adobes and burnishing brasses for orderly; but guard duty, though no more tedious than now, was spiced with an element of danger which added zest to the duty. Strict orders prohibited all persons from leaving the immediate limits of a garrison, except in small parties, and they were enjoined always to carry their carbines. Heavy herd guards were detailed, and lookouts were posted on high ground during grazing hours.

The appliances for the personal comfort of the soldiers were few, and should the improvements now surrounding them be suddenly exchanged for what they had then, there would be such a scurrying off of recruits that I doubt if the whole state of Kentucky could furnish satisfactory material to fill the depleted ranks. Ashen slats on bunk irons and a bedsack filled with straw made a very good bed for its fortunate possessor, while the less favored ones were often at their wits' end to improvise a comfortable resting place out of two blankets. Sheets, pillows, white shirts, linen collars, and barrack shoes were not dreamed of, and bathtubs were unknown, for the water system was limited to a huge tank on wheels, with eight mules and a surly driver.

The stomachs of the men, even more than their bodies, were subject to a Spartan simplicity, and the numerous delicacies now supplied them could not then be found on officers' tables. The commissary kept only the component parts of the regular ration, and the pound of fresh vegetables was not a part of it.

The banishment from the gentler influences of settled communities and separation from the varied society of large cities was keenly felt by officers, and the exiles' life they were forced to lead caused a few to give up in disgust and resign; but the majority continued in service, fighting bravely against the hardships surrounding them. Of luxuries they had none, of comforts, few; but the canvas homes and outdoor life furnished good digestions and hearty appetites for the limited bills of fare presented at the mess. Nearly all were bachelors, with the careless habits this class of army officers are noted for, though the presence of an occasional lady served to check in part the familiarity engendered by lack of privacy and constant association – serious objections to any long continued camp.

Horseback riding on pleasant days was almost the only outdoor amusement, but the danger from Indians so contracted the safety limits, that all ground was soon visited, and only the hope of a shot at a stray wolf or coyote, or the rare advent of some visitor to be entertained, kept up interest in this kind of outing. A great event was the distribution of the mail, and whether weekly, semi-weekly, or daily, the hour of its arrival was looked forward to by all, and, as the cloud of dust in the distance heralded its approach, the entire garrison, from the commanding officer to the latest recruit, hastened to the post office where they formed an eager crowd, anxious for the latest news from the States, or in happy anticipation of the expected letter from sweetheart, wife, or mother.

The regiment remained in Texas for eight years, spending the greater portion of the time in the field, patrolling the vast stretches of prairie in innumerable scouts after depredating Indians, and gradually freeing the country from this scourge of settlers. There is not space to describe minutely even the more important of these expeditions, and I shall only summarize the following:

1867

October 1, near Howard's Wells, Texas, two men killed while escorting the mail; December 5, Eagle Springs, Texas, one man killed; December 26, Camp Lancaster, Texas, Troop K persistently attacked for two days by a large force of Indians who were finally driven off, three men killed.

1868

January, Fort Quitman, Troop F attacked sixteen times by a large band; August, Fort Quitman, Troop H attacked, Indians driven off without loss; September 12, Horsehead Hills, Texas, Lieutenant Cusack with 60 men surprised a large party of Indians, killing 25 and capturing all their horses, ponies, and supplies. But one man was wounded in this affair, which was reported as a very brilliant and successful coup against the wandering bands.

1869

June 5, Johnson's River, Texas, Troop L, no loss; June 7, on Pecos River, Texas, 32 men of Troop G under Captain Bacon; September 15, on the Brazos River, Troops F and M under Captain Carroll, had a skirmish, and again on the 20th and 21st, the same command being augmented by detachments from Troops B and M, engaged the same band of Indians; October 28 and 29, Troops B, E, F, G, L, and M had a running fight of 40 miles at the head waters of the Brazos River, killing a number of Indians. This is the affair to which the late General Sherman so often referred with his quizzical inquiry as to which way Bacon ran; November 29, head of Llanos River, Texas, Troops L and M under Captain E.M. Heyl had a desperate fight and this officer was seriously wounded; December 25, five men of Troop E defeated a band of 20 Indians which attempted to surprise the mail coach.

1870

January 6, Guadaloupe Mountains, Texas, Troop H; January 11, Lower Pecos River, Troop L; January 16, Troop G and detachment of L, under Captain Bacon, surprised an entire village, capturing 83 head of stock and all supplies; January 21, a command of Troops C, D, I, and K, under Captain Dodge engaged in a skirmish in the Guadaloupe Mountains; April 3, 15 men of Troop H, under a noncommissioned officer, ran into some Indians near San Martin's Springs, killing one; April 25, Crow Springs, Texas, 50 men from Troops C and K, under Major Morrow, captured 30 horses and the supplies of a village; May 19 and 20, at Kickapoo Springs, Texas, Sergeant Emanuel Stance with five men of Troop F surprised and attacked a small village, wounding four Indians and capturing two white boy prisoners and 15 horses; May 29, Bosaler Canyon, Texas, Troop I.

1872

April 20, Howard's Wells, Troops A and H. Lieutenant Vincent killed.

I have only mentioned the affairs in which an actual engagement took place. The many scouts, long marches, the weeks and months spent in campaign are omitted, but during the eight years of duty in Texas, as well as afterwards and until the regiment was sent to the Department of the Platte, more time was spent in campaign than in garrison, and the troops covered thousands of square miles of territory.

In the latter part of 1875 the regiment was transferred into New Mexico, with headquarters at Santa Fe, and the troops scattered all over that territory and even beyond. The general duty was about the same as in Texas, and during the time the regiment remained there, various troops and detachments were employed in capturing and returning to their reservations innumerable roving bands of the wily and treacherous Apache tribes, the more important of which were those headed by Nana and Victoria. During the five years spent in this section the more important affairs were as follows:

1876

April 15, in the Florida Mountains, Troop F, one Indian killed and 11 horses captured; September 2, in the Cuchillo Negro Mountains, detachment of Troops C and E, under Lieutenant Wright, small camp captured and number of lodges destroyed.

1877

January 23, Florida Mountains, nine men under Lieutenant Wright killed 5 Indians and captured 6 horses; January 28, Sierra Boca Grande Mountains, Mexico, detachments of Troops C and A captured a small camp.

1878

August 6, Dog Canyon, New Mexico, Troop H was engaged.

1879

January 15, Troop A under Lieutenant Day, was engaged and captured a number of horses and mules; March 8, Ojo Caliente, Troop I; May 28, in the Black Range, Troops C and I under Captain Beyer captured a camp and 16 horses, losing one man killed and 2 wounded; September 4, Ojo Caliente, four men were killed; September 8, West Las Animas River, 24 men of Troop G under Lieutenant Hugo were engaged losing one man; September 18, Las Animas River, Troops A, B and C, one man killed and 2 wounded; September 29 and 30, on the Cuchillo Negro River, parts of Troops B, C, E and L, under Major Morrow, 1 man killed; October 2 and 3, at Milk River, Colorado, Troop D went to the relief of Thornburgh's command and succeeded in reaching it losing all its horses; October 27, in the Guzman Mountains, Mexico, Troops B, C, G, and H, under Major Morrow were engaged, losing one man and one scout.

1880

January 12, on the Rio Percho, Troops B, C, D, F, H, and M, under Major Morrow, were again engaged, losing one man; January 17, in the San Mateo Mountains, Troops B, C, F, H, and M, under Major Morrow, were again engaged, losing one officer (Lieutenant French) killed, and one man wounded; January 30, in Caballo Mountains, detachment of Troops B and M, under Captain Rucker, loss of 3 men wounded; February 3, in the San Andreas Mountains, Troops B, C, F, H, and M, under Major Morrow, were engaged, losing 4 men wounded; February 28, and again April 5, in the San Andreas Mountains, Lieutenant Conline with Troop A was engaged, losing one man and one citizen wounded; April 6, in the same mountains, Troops A, D, F, and G, under Captain Carroll, were engaged, Captain Carroll and 6 men being severely wounded; April 7, Major Morrow with Troops H and L continued this affair; May 14, near old Fort Tulerosa, Sergeant Jordan with 25 men repulsed a force of more than a hundred Indians under Victoria; June 5, Cook's Canyon, Troop L, loss of 2 men; May, in the San Francisco Mountains, Troop C and detachment scouts, 2 men killed and one wounded; June 11 and 12, near Fort Cummings, Troop B; September 1, in the Sacramento Mountains, 11 men of Troop G, 2 men wounded.

1881

In February and again in April, a detachment under Lieutenant Maney, Fifteenth Infantry, was engaged in southern New Mexico, one man wounded; July 25 at White Sands, July 26 in the San Andreas, and August 3 at Santa Monica, 20 men of Troop L were engaged.

In August there were a number of engagements: – In Carrizo Canyon, 19 men of Troop K, under Captain Parker, 2 men killed; in the San Mateo Mountains, detachments of Troops B and H, under Lieutenant Taylor; in Cuchillo Negro Mountains, Troop I, Lieutenant Valois, 2 men wounded; in Cavilare Pass, detachment of Troops B and H, Lieutenant Smith, 3 men and one citizen killed, 3 men wounded.

October 4, in the Dragoon Mountains, Troops F and H, 3 men wounded.

1887

November 5, Crow Agency, Montana, Troops D and H.

1890

December 30, Troop D, under Captain Loud, was attacked while escorting a wagon train near Pine Ridge Agency, South Dakota, losing one man killed. Later in the same day Troops D, F, I, and K, under Major Henry, were engaged near the Drexel Mission, South Dakota, no casualties.

In June, 1881, the regiment was moved from New Mexico to Kansas and Indian Territory, where it remained until 1885. Most of these years were spent in garrison, though the intruders upon the Oklahoma Territory, which at that time was not open for settlement, kept a number of troops busy moving over that country and patrolling the northern portion of Indian Territory and southern Kansas.

In the summer of 1885, the regiment was moved to the Department of the Platte, where it has since remained enjoying a well-earned rest after the many scouts and campaigns of the preceding eighteen years. The only campaign worthy of mention is that of 1890-91, during the uprising of the Sioux, when the regiment was the first in the field in November, and the last to leave late in the following March, after spending the winter, the latter part of which was terrible in its severity, under canvas.

At present (February, 1895) the regiment is commanded by Colonel James Biddle, and eight troops garrison the post of Fort Robinson, Nebraska. Troops B and F, under Major Randlett, are at Fort Duchesne, Utah; while Troops L and M are continued with a skeleton organization.

Every effort is made to keep the regiment in a high state of efficiency, and with nearly all its officers present for duty – with the ranks filled to the authorized strength and with an excellent and ample mount – the Ninth Cavalry stands ready today for any service it may be called upon to perform, filled with a just pride in its past achievements and anxious again to seek "the bubble reputation even in the cannon's mouth."

Paul A. Rossi

The Tenth Regiment of Cavalry

Lieutenant John Bigelow, Jr.
(U.S.A., R.Q.M., Tenth Cavalry)

Section 3 of an "Act to increase and fix the military peace establishment of the United States," approved on the 28th day of July, 1866, provides "That to the six regiments of cavalry now in service, there shall be added four regiments, two of which shall be composed of colored men. . . . " The six regiments referred to as already in service were composed of white men.

The colored regiments were to be organized on the general plan of the white regiments, modified in a few particulars. They were each to have a regimental chaplain whose duty should include the instruction of enlisted men in the common English branches. Up to that time all chaplains had been appointed not in regiments but in the Army. The colored regiments were also given two veterinary surgeons each, whereas the white regiments had but one.

Another enactment which more or less affected the composition of these additional cavalry regiments, both white and colored, and which is deemed of peculiar interest, was the following:

> That no person shall be commissioned in any of the regiments authorized by this act until he shall have passed a satisfactory examination before a board to be composed of officers of that arm of the service in which the applicant is to serve, to be convened under the

This selection was originally published in Theodore F. Rodenbough and William J. Haskin, *The Army of the United States* (New York, 1896).

> direction of the Secretary of War, which shall inquire into the services rendered during the War, capacity and qualifications of the applicant; and every such appointment when made, shall be without regard to previous rank, but with sole regard to qualifications and meritorious services.

Congress having created the Tenth Cavalry in law, the first step towards its creation in fact was taken, it seems, by Lieutenant-General Sherman, commanding the Military Division of the Mississippi, in an order from his headquarters dated St. Louis, Missouri, August 9, 1866, which read as follows:

> *G.O. No. 6*
>
> I. Commanders of military departments within this division in which colored troops are serving, will proceed at once to enlist men for two regiments of colored regulars, under the Act of Congress approved July 28, 1866, entitled "An Act to increase and fix the military peace establishment of the United States"; one of cavalry, to be entitled the Tenth Regiment United States Cavalry, and one of infantry to be entitled the Thirty-eighth Regiment United States Infantry.
>
> II. Fort Leavenworth, Kansas, is hereby named as the headquarters and rendezvous of the Tenth Cavalry, and Jefferson Barracks, Missouri, the headquarters and rendezvous of the Thirty-eighth Infantry.
>
> III. Commanding generals of the Departments of the Missouri, Arkansas, and Platte, will detail one or more officers of the Regular Army, who will proceed to canvass the regiments of colored troops now serving in their respective departments and enlist men for the new regiments above named, the cavalry for five years and the infantry for three years. The men so enlisted will be discharged from their present obligation and grouped into companies under officers to be selected by the colonels or regimental commanders hereafter to be appointed, but will be retained for the present at or near their present station. The number of privates allowed to a company is sixty-four. The men of existing colored regiments not willing to enlist in the new organization will, for the present, be consolidated into companies under the direction of their immediate commanders, and held to service until the new army is sufficiently organized to replace them.
>
> IV. The field officers of these regiments will, on arrival at these headquarters, proceed to the posts herein named and organize their new regiments according to law and regulations, but will not withdraw the new companies from their present stations without consent of department commanders, or orders from these headquarters . . . .

The first regimental return was rendered on the 30th of September, 1866. It showed the aggregate strength of the regiment, present and absent, to consist of two officers – Colonel Benjamin H. Grierson, and Lieutenant-Colonel Charles C. Walcutt – and gave the number of recruits required as 1092. Colonel Grierson was reported present with the regiment, and Colonel Walcutt absent on regimental recruiting service.

The first commander of the Tenth Cavalry is doubtless known personally as well as by reputation to most of the readers of this sketch. His raid through Mississippi in 1863 is the historic operation on which his reputation chiefly rests. It has placed him among the foremost cavalry leaders of the War, and seems destined, as it becomes better known and more justly appreciated, to add honor and distinction to his name. Lieutenant-Colonel Walcutt never joined the regiment, and resigned shortly after his appointment. The recruiting for the regiment was in the main regimental, that is, by officers of the regiment detailed to recruit for it. At the end of the year 1866, the Tenth Cavalry consisted of two field officers, one company officer, and 64 unassigned recruits. It was still without a staff or a single organized company. For seven months of the new year the headquarters of the regiment went on but continued to make slow progress. This was due in the main to two causes, the want of clerical assistance at recruiting stations and the high standard fixed for the recruits by the regimental commander. Recruiting officers were not allowed to hire clerks and had extreme difficulty in securing any among their recruits or the members of their recruiting parties. With a view to securing an intelligent set of men for the ranks, the colonel had Captain Louis H. Carpenter, who was recruiting at Louisville, Kentucky, ordered to Philadelphia, Pa., to open a recruiting station there. Writing to Captain Carpenter, the colonel says, after referring to the captain's knowledge of Philadelphia: "I requested you to be sent there to recruit colored men sufficiently educated to fill the positions of noncommissioned officers, clerks, and mechanics in the regiment. You will use the greatest care in your selections of recruits. Although sent to recruit men for the positions specified above, you will also enlist all superior men you can who will do credit to the regiment."

During its last month at Fort Leavenworth the regiment lost heavily from disease, caused in the main by a cholera epidemic. From a death rate which did not average one a month for the preceding ten months, the loss by death during the month of July, 1867, rose to 23. On the 6th of August, 1867, the headquarters of the regiment left Fort Leavenworth for Fort Riley, Kansas, where they were established on the 7th.

Let us take a general look at the regiment as it existed just prior to this change. We find the field and staff still incomplete, being composed as follows:

colonel, B.H. Grierson
lieutenant-colonel, J.W. Davidson
majors, J.W. Forsyth and M.H. Kidd
chaplain, W.M. Grimes
adjutant, H.E. Alvord

The regiment now comprises eight troops. Their designation, date of organization, original composition and color of horses are as below:

Troop A.—color, bay; organized February 18, 1867; captain, Nicholas Nolan; lieutenants, G.W. Graham and G.F. Raulston.

Troop B.—color, bay; organized April 1, 1867; captain, J.B. Vande Wiele; lieutenants, J.D. Myrick and J.W. Myers.

Troop C.—color, bay; organized May 15, 1867; captain, Edward Byrne; lieutenants, T.C. Lebo and T.J. Spencer.

Troop D.—color, bay; organized June 1, 1867; captain, J.W. Walsh; lieutenants, Robert Gray and R.H. Pratt.

Troop E.—color, gray; organized June 15, 1867; captain, G.T. Robinson; lieutenant, J.T. Morrison.

Troop F.—color, gray; organized June 21, 1867; captain, G.A. Armes; lieutenants, P.L. Lee and J.A. Bodamer.

Troop G.—color, bay; organized July 5, 1867; captain H.T. Davis; lieutenants, W.B. Kennedy and M.J. Amick.

Troop H.—color, black; organized July 21, 1867; captain, L.H. Carpenter; lieutenants, T.J. Spencer and L.H. Orleman.

These troops were posted at Fort Hays, Fort Harker, and other points along the Smokey River, Kansas, on the line of the Kansas Pacific Railroad, then in the course of construction. They had been put in the field for the protection of the railroad as fast as they were organized. The strength of the regiment, present and absent, amounts to 25 officers and 702 enlisted men.

The first engagement in which any part of the regiment participated occurred a few days before the regimental headquarters left Fort Leavenworth. Troop I, under Captain Armes, numbering 34 men and two officers, fought a party of 300 Indians near Saline River, 40 miles northeast of Fort Hays. The engagement lasted six hours and resulted in the troops being forced to retreat with the loss of Sergeant W. Christy, killed, and Captain Armes, wounded. On the twenty-first of the same month Captain Armes had another fight, the second on record in the regiment. Forty men of his troop, together with 90 men of the Eighteenth Kansas Volunteers, engaged about 500 Indians northeast of Fort Hays. The losses in this fight were one soldier killed and scalped, and 13 wounded; fifteen men of the volunteers and two guides wounded, twelve horses killed, and three wounded.

Troops I, K, L and M, were organized from the new headquarters at Fort Riley as here indicated:

Troop I.–color, bay; organized August 15, 1867; captain, G.W. Graham; lieutenant, Silas Pepoon.

Troop K.–color, bay; organized September 1, 1867; captain, C.G. Cox; lieutenants, R.G. Smither and B.F. Bell.

Troop L.–color, sorrel; organized, September 21, 1867; captain, R. Gray; lieutenant, C.E. Nordstrom.

Troop M.–color, mixed ; organized October 15, 1867; captain, H.E. Alvord; lieutenants, P.L. Lee and W.R. Harmon.

In September, 1867, the field officers were increased in number to their full complement by the appointment of Major J.E. Yard. In the same month the position of regimental quartermaster was taken by Lieutenant W.H. Beck. Thus were filled the last of the original vacancies in the field and staff.

The headquarters remained at Fort Riley until April 17, 1868. The troops were about evenly distributed between Kansas and Indian Territory and were employed in the perfection of their drill and discipline, and in the protection of the Union Pacific Railroad and exposed settlements. The only engagement of this period took place about 45 miles west of Fort Hays. Sergeant Davis and nine men of Troop G were attacked by fifty or sixty Cheyennes. They drove the Indians off in confusion, losing one private wounded.

From Fort Riley the Headquarters of the regiment went to Fort Gibson, Indian Territory. At this time General Sheridan was in the field directing military operations. The Indians had brought on a war by their characteristic restlessness and deviltry. They were attached to agencies to which they came in from time to time for supplies, but they were not confined to any reservations. General Sheridan determined to put them and keep them on reservations, or, if that could not be done, to show them that winter weather would not give them either rest or impunity. The consequence was the winter campaign of 1867-68, which resulted in the destruction of Black Kettle's band of Cheyennes, the worst lot of Indians in the territory. The Tenth Cavalry was in the field and came in for a good share of hard marching and fighting.

On the 15th of September, 1868, Troop I, Captain Graham, was attacked by about 100 Indians. It fought until dark, losing ten horses killed and captured, and killing seven Indians.

On the 27th of this month Lieutenant-Colonel G.A. Forsyth, A.D.C. to General Sheridan, with a party of white scouts, was attacked and "corralled" by a force of about 700 Indians on an island in the Republican River. Two of Forsyth's scouts stole through the Indian lines and brought word of the perilous situation of the command to Fort Wallace. Parties were soon on the way to its relief. First and last the following troops were started towards it from different points. Captain Bankhead with about 100 men of the Fifth Infantry, Captain Carpenter with Troop H and Captain Baldwin with Troop I, of the Tenth Cavalry, and two troops of the Second Cavalry under Major Brisbin.

Captain Carpenter's troop was the first of these commands to arrive upon the scene. It found Forsyth's command out of rations, living on horseflesh without salt or pepper. All its officers had been killed or wounded. Every horse and mule, too, had been killed. Forsyth, who had been twice wounded, was lying in a square hole scooped out in the sand, within a few feet of a line of dead horses which half encircled the hole and impregnated the air with a terrible stench. Captain Carpenter immediately pitched a number of tents in a suitable place nearby, had the wounded men carried to them, and the rest removed to a more salubrious air. Twenty-six hours later Captain Bankhead arrived bringing with him the two troops of the Second Cavalry.

On the 24th of the following month, two weeks after he had returned to Fort Wallace with the wounded of Forsyth's command, Captain Carpenter was ordered to take his own troop and I Troop of the Tenth Cavalry and escort Major Carr, of the Fifth Cavalry, to his command, supposed to be on Beaver Creek. On the march he was attacked by a force of about 500 Indians. After proceeding, regardless of the enemy's firing and yelling, far enough to gain a suitable position, he halted his command, had the wagons corralled close together, and rushed his men inside at a gallop. He had them dismount, tie their horses to the wagons, and form on the outside around the corral. Then followed a volley of Spencers which drove the Indians back as though they were thrown from a cannon. A number of warriors, showing more bravery than the others, undertook to stand their ground. Nearly all of these, together with their ponies, were killed. Three dead warriors lay within fifty yards of the wagons. The Indians were so demoralized by these results that they did not renew the attack, and the troops accomplished their march without further molestation. They were back at Fort Wallace on the 21st, having travelled 230 miles in about seven days. For their gallantry in the fight, which took place on Beaver Creek, the officers and men were thanked by General Sheridan in a general field order, and Captain Carpenter was breveted Colonel.

Regimental headquarters remained at Fort Gibson until March 31, 1869, when they were moved to Camp Wichita, Indian Territory, where they arrived on the 12th of April. Camp Wichita, an old Indian village, was selected by General Sheridan as a site for a military post and the Tenth Cavalry was ordered there to establish and build it. Some time in the following month of August the post was given the name of Fort Sill, by which name it will be designated in these pages.

The military duty of the regiment was now that of an army of occupation, to hold the country from which the Indians had been expelled and to keep the Indians within the bounds assigned them. It gave rise to frequent scouting for trespassers and marauders and occasional reconnaissance and demonstration in considerable force. More than once the garrison of Fort Sill had to apprehend an attack upon the post.

On the 11th of June Camp Supply was alarmed by a party of Comanches charging through it, shooting and yelling, with the object of stampeding the horses on the picket line, and they succeeded in stampeding a few. These were pursued by Troops A, F, H, I, and K, Tenth Cavalry, and Companies B, E, and F, Third Infantry, commanded by Lieutenant-Colonel Nelson, Third Infantry. The Indians turned on their pursuers and attacked them, wounding three soldiers and killing two horses. Six Indians were killed and ten wounded.

During the 22nd and 23rd of August the Wichita Agency was subjected to a fierce attack by the Kiowa and Naconee Indians. The Agency was defended by Troops C, E, H, and L, Tenth Cavalry, commanded by Lieutenant-Colonel Davidson. The main object of the attack, as expressed in the vigorous language of the hostiles, was to "wipe out" the buildings and settlement. Attempts were made to do so by setting fire to the prairie at different points, but the tireless and well-directed efforts of the defenders succeeded in extinguishing the flames and saving the buildings. Repeated assaults were made by the Indians in numbers ranging from 50 to 500, at different points of the line, all of which were repulsed with the infliction of heavy losses and great disorder upon the assailants. The decisive feature of the engagement was a charge made by Captain Carpenter's troop. His men routed a body of over 150 warriors, who were about to take up a commanding position in the rear of the troops. The loss of the troops was only four men wounded. That of the Indians was quite large, but owing to their well-known custom of carrying off their dead and wounded could not be definitely ascertained.

From Fort Sill the regimental headquarters moved back to Fort Gibson. They left Fort Sill on the 5th of June, 1872. During the three years and two months of their stay at that station a majority of the regiment – for a time there were eleven troops – was constantly at headquarters. The monthly rate of desertion fell from 7 to 3; the rate of discharge by courtmartial from 2.5 to 1.5. In fact, the deportment of the regiment attested the advantage to discipline of large commands and varied and interesting occupation for the troops.

Among the stations other than Fort Sill held by troops of the Tenth Cavalry were Forts Dodge, Gibson, and Arbuckle, Camp Supply, and Cheyenne Agency. Having remained at Fort Gibson until April 23, 1873, the regimental headquarters then returned to Fort Sill. In the meantime there had been a few skirmishes unattended by any casualties.

A movement of troops was now underway looking to a transfer of the regiment to the Department of Texas, and the end of April found Troops E, I, and L at Fort Richardson, Texas; and Troops C, D, and F en route, the two former for Fort Griffin, the latter for Fort Concho,

Texas. The headquarters were reestablished at Fort Sill on the 4th of May, 1873, and remained there until the 27th of March, 1875. During this time the regiment continued serving partly in Texas and partly in the Indian Territory. The troops that were serving in the Indian Territory took part in the campaign of 1874-75 against the Kiowas and Comanches. This campaign was but a continuation of the campaign of 1867-68, and, like the latter, was directed by General Sheridan. There were four columns in the field operating separately under the following commanders:

Lieutenant-Colonel Neill, Sixth Cavalry; Colonel N.A. Miles, Fifth Infantry; Lieutenant-Colonel Davidson, Tenth Cavalry; Colonel R.S. Mackenzie, Fourth Cavalry.

The first capture of the campaign was made by a portion of Davidson's column. On the 25th of October, 1874, Troops B and M, Tenth Cavalry, and one company of the Eleventh Infantry, under the command of Major Schofield, while in pursuit of Indians near Elk Creek, pressed them so hard that the whole band surrendered. They numbered 68 warriors, 276 squaws and children, and about 1500 ponies. These prisoners, and others taken subsequently, were put in camp at Fort Sill, the more dangerous bucks being closely confined. At the close of the campaign the ringleaders were sent to Fort Marion, Florida, under charge of Captain Pratt. This officer never returned to the regiment. He is now justly distinguished for his work as an educator of Indians, especially in the superintendence of the Carlisle Indian School.

On the 6th of April, 1875, Black Horse, one of the Cheyenne ringleaders who was billeted for Fort Marion, broke from his guard at the Cheyenne Agency and ran towards the camp of his people nearby. He was pursued by Captain Bennett, Fifth Infantry, with the guard, who fired upon Black Horse and killed him. Several shots passed beyond him and wounded some people in the camp. After firing a volley of bullets and arrows at the guard, about one-half of the Cheyenne tribe abandoned their camp and fled to a group of sand hills on the south side of the Canadian River opposite the Cheyenne Agency. They were followed by a company of the Fifth Infantry, a troop of the Sixth Cavalry, and Troops D and M of the Tenth Cavalry, all under the command of Lieutenant-Colonel Neill, Sixth Cavalry. Being well-armed and well-posted, the Indians held their ground until nightfall and then stole away. The troops took up the trail and followed it about ten days, at the end of which time it was covered up by rains. Troops from other posts were ordered to assist in the pursuit, and eventually most of the fugitives gave themselves up. In the fight at the Agency the Indians lost eight killed. The Tenth Cavalry lost 12 men wounded, one mortally.

When moved for the second time from Fort Sill the regimental headquarters were transferred to Fort Concho, Texas, where they were established on the 17th of April, 1875. The First of May found the troops of the regiment located in Texas and Indian Territory as follows:

Troops A, F, G, I, and L, at Fort Concho; B and E at Fort Griffin, C and K at Fort McKavett; H at Fort Davis, D and M in the field at Buffalo Springs, Indian Territory. During the month of May, troops D and M moved from the Indian Territory, the former to Fort Concho, the latter to Fort Stockton.

In the course of the next two years the disposition of the troops was modified so as to scatter the regiment over the length and breadth of Western Texas. Its headquarters, however, were destined to remain at Fort Concho for more than seven years. During this period the regiment continued with some variation its past experience in Indian fighting. Its campaigning consisted mainly in pursuing small bands of marauding Apaches. This carried the troops – now across the border into the unknown territory of the "Gringo" - hating Mexicans, now over the scorching wastes of the Staked Plains, now up and down the rocky fastnesses of the Guadaloupe Mountains and the badlands bordering the upper Rio Grande.

The following are a few instances of this kind of service:

In July, 1876, Troops B, E, and K crossed into Mexico as part of a column commanded by Lieutenant-Colonel Shafter, Twenty-Fourth Infantry. A detachment of this command, made up of twenty picked men of Troop B under Lieutenant Bullis, Twenty-Fourth Infantry, made a march of 110 miles in 25 hours and thereby succeeded in surprising a camp of 23 lodges of hostile Lipans and Kickapoos near Saragossa, Mexico. They killed ten Indians and captured four, and also captured about 100 horses. They then made a bonfire of the camp material and with their prisoners and captured stock rejoined the main column as fast as their jaded horses would carry them.

On the 10th of July, 1877, Troop A left Fort Concho under command of Captain Nolan for a scout on the Staked Plains. The command got lost, and, as a consequence, Captain Nolan, Lieutenant Cooper, Sergeant Jackson, and about ten privates were 96 hours without water. Four of the men died. Other parties were from 24 to 38 hours without water. The command was found and brought back to Fort Concho by a party sent out from there to search for it.

In 1880 the regiment was engaged in what is known as the Victoria campaign, a series of operations directed against the Mescalero Apache chief Victoria, who, with his whole band, had escaped from the military authorities in New Mexico. On the 30th of July Colonel Grierson, with a party of only six men, was attacked by this band between Quitman and Eagle Springs. Lieutenant Finley with fifteen men of Troop G came up, engaged the Indians, and held them in check until the arrival of Captains Viele and Nolan with Troops C and A. In an engagement, which lasted four hours, seven Indians were killed and a number wounded. On the side of the troops one soldier was killed and Lieutenant Colladay wounded. The hostiles were driven off and pursued to the Rio Grande. In the course of the pursuit a running fight of at least fifteen miles was maintained near the Alamo by a detachment under Corporal Asa Weaver of Troop H. Private Tockes, Troop C, was killed. His horse went to bucking and then ran directly into the Indians. When last seen alive this devoted trooper had dropped his reins, drawn his carbine, and was firing to right and left. His skeleton was found months afterwards. For his gallant conduct in this affair Corporal Weaver was promoted to a sergeant on the ground. The same day Captain Lebo, with Troop K, followed an Indian trail to the top of the Sierra Diabola, captured Victoria's supply camp of twenty-five head of cattle, and a large quantity of beef and other provisions on pack animals.

The decisive blow of the campaign was struck a few days later by Colonel Grierson. Being on the trail of Victoria, heading northward through the Carrizo Mountains, Grierson switched off to his right, and, by a forced march of sixty-five miles, swung around the flank of the unsuspecting Apaches and struck them in front, forcing them southward across the frontier. Victoria never went raiding again on American soil. He was subsequently killed by the Mexican troops near Lake Guzman, Mexico.

In July, 1882, regimental headquarters was moved from Fort Concho to Fort Davis, where it remained until March 30, 1885.

During this time the regiment saw little active field service.

In the spring of 1885 the regiment moved from the Department of Texas to the Department of Arizona, marching along the Southern Pacific Railroad. When the column took up its march from Fort Davis it comprised eleven troops and the band. At Camp Rice it was joined by Troop I, and from this point to Bowie Station, Arizona, the twelve troops continued together. They had never been together before and never have been since. At Bowie the troops separated to go to their several stations. The headquarters went to Fort Apache, where they arrived on the 20th of May.

The Geronimo campaign had just commenced, and on the 19th of May a battalion formed of Troops D, E, H, and K, under Major Van Vliet, was sent out from Fort Grant in search of hostiles. They marched to Fort Bayard, New Mexico, and through the Mogollon Mountains, but saw nothing of them. The greater part of the regiment was in the field during the whole campaign. Several of the officers, anxious to be where there was most to be done, had themselves detached from their troops to do duty with Indian scouts at the front. Thus, Lieutenant Shipp was with Captain Crawford in Mexico when that officer was killed. Lieutenant Finley accompanied Captain Lawton in his long, hard chase of Geronimo, which led to his surrender. Lieutenant Clarke patrolled the Mexican border. The latter especially distinguished himself in an engagement which Troop K, under command of Captain Lebo, had with Geronimo's band in the Pineto Mountains in Mexico. His conduct on this occasion has recently won for him a Medal of Honor.

After Geronimo had surrendered to Captain Lawton, a remnant of his band under Chief Mangus, who was still defying the Government of the United States, was run down in handsome style by Troop H, under the command of Captain Cooper.

Such instances of distinguished service are the more creditable as the opportunities therefore were extremely rare. To the greater part of the regiment the Geronimo campaign was a dismal succession of inglorious days devoted to the guarding of waterholes, mountain passes, and so forth.

In 1887, part of the regiment was in the field in search of "the Kid," a former follower of Geronimo, who had never been caught, and has not been yet. Lieutenant Carter P. Johnson especially distinguished himself by the skill, energy, and perseverance with which he pursued this Indian.

On the 15th of April, 1890, the regiment lost the colonel who had commanded it from its organization by his promotion to a brigadier-general. The vacancy was filled by the promotion of Lieutenant-Colonel J.K. Mizner, Eighth Cavalry, who is the present chief of the regiment. Regimental headquarters was moved by Colonel Mizner to Fort Grant, where it now (1891 is.

Infantry firing with the Texas grip. *Frederic Remington*

The Twenty-fourth Regiment of Infantry

Lieutenant H. W. Hovey (Twenty-fourth U.S. Infantry)

The present Twenty-fourth Infantry is an example of the injustice done to regiments of a standing army by the statutes of a republic not forced by its surroundings to maintain a large military organization. The laws governing the consolidation of regiments at the conclusion of our wars, during which the number of organizations has been increased, have resulted in stamping out regimental traditions in many organizations and have left this one without any, although its number has been borne twice by regiments in the regular establishment, which after honorable service have been consolidated with others, thereby losing all identity, and forfeiting records which would have given honor to them in history.

The existing Twenty-fourth can, therefore, under the conditions of its organization claim for itself none of the honors of war won by its predecessors; and, except for the war records of officers who have served or are now serving in it, and by the honorable service of the few enlisted men who served in the late war, it can present but a short history of duties performed, often under adverse circumstances but always cheerfully and uncomplainingly.

Under the Act of July 28, 1866, the Thirty-eighth and Forty-first Regiments of Infantry were organized both to consist of colored men. All of the officers in both regiments except the chaplains had seen

This selection was originally published in Theodore F. Rodenbough and William J. Haskin, *The Army of the United States* (New York, 1896).

service during the War of the Rebellion either with the regular or volunteer forces, and all but one had been breveted for services performed under perilous or other entitling conditions. Of the Thirty-eighth Infantry, Brevet Major General William B. Hazen was colonel, Brevet Major General Cuvier Grover, lieutenant colonel, and Brevet Colonel Henry C. Merriam, major. Of the ten captains who were assigned to the regiment at or near the time of its organization there are now in active service but three, and but five of the eighteen lieutenants.

The Forty-first Infantry was commanded by Brevet Major General Ronald S. Mackenzie, with Brevet Brigadier General William R. Shafter, lieutenant colonel, and Brevet Brigadier General George W. Schofield, major. Of the ten captains assigned to it at or near its organization but two are now in active service, and but four of the eighteen lieutenants.

The Thirty-eighth was distributed along the transcontinental railroads then building, and in New Mexico, and the Forty-first was in Louisiana and Texas during the same period. The work performed by these regiments is a part of the history of the departments in which they served.

Under the Act of March 3, 1869, the Thirty-eighth and Forty-first Regiments were consolidated and became the Twenty-fourth Infantry, and as thus reestablished has since continued in service. Under this reorganization Ronald S. Mackenzie became colonel, William R. Shafter, lieutenant colonel, and Henry C. Merriam, major. Of the captains assigned to the new regiment there are in active service at this writing six, but two only serving in it; and of the twenty lieutenants there are also six, but four only remaining in it. A few of the enlisted men who served in the War of the Rebellion or in the Thirty-eighth or Forty-first Regiments may still be seen in its ranks.

The regiment was in Texas from 1869 to 1880, and at some time during that period the several companies were stationed at all or nearly all of the many posts and permanent camps in that great state.

The duties falling to it were many, consisting of expeditions against Indians over the Staked Plains and other sections, guarding strategic points, building roads, hunting horse thieves, and in other ways performing arduous service which brought no fame, but required of its officers and men constant vigilance, discretion, and care in the performance of the service; and it thus aided in clearing western Texas of Indians, opening the country to settlers. On December 15, 1870,

General Mackenzie was assigned to the Fourth Cavalry and Brevet-Major-General Abner Doubleday succeeded him as colonel, remaining in that position until December, 1873, when, upon his retirement, Brevet-Brigadier-General Joseph H. Potter became the colonel.

In the autumn of 1880 the regiment changed to Indian Territory and the several companies were stationed at Forts Supply, Reno, Sill, Cantonment on the north fork of the Canadian River, and again a part of it in Texas at Fort Elliot. During this time no campaign service fell to its lot.

In April, 1886, Colonel Potter having been appointed a brigadier general, Colonel Zenas R. Bliss succeeded him and is still in command of the regiment.

In June, 1888, the regiment moved to the Department of Arizona with headquarters and three companies at Fort Bayard, N.M., the remainder of the companies being distributed in Arizona at San Carlos and Forts Grant and Thomas, and for nearly four years they performed all the infantry duty at these posts. The duty at San Carlos was particularly trying under circumstances of danger and discomfort, but no serious trouble with the Indians occurred to require unusual work, and the only incident of note was the fight of Paymaster Wham's escort, composed of men of the Twenty-fourth Infantry and Tenth Cavalry, who when attacked by a gang of robbers made a brave stand, for which Medals of Honor or certificates of merit were given according to rank.

The companies of the regiment which have been distributed at the before-mentioned posts were in 1892 sent to Fort Huachuca, and as two companies had in the meantime been skeletonized, the regiment now became equally divided, with headquarters, D, E, F, and G, at Fort Bayard, New Mexico, and Companies A, B, C, and H at Huachuca, where at this writing they still remain.

The "Dough-boys" on the March

The Twenty-fifth Regiment of Infantry

Lieutenant George Andrews (Twenty-fifth U.S. Infantry)

The Act of July 28, 1866, added to the nineteen regiments of infantry then in service, "Eight new regiments of ten companies each, four regiments of which shall be composed of colored men." Accordingly the Thirty-eighth, Thirty-nineth, Fortieth, and Forty-first were so composed, while the Forty-second, Forty-third, Forty-fourth, and Forty-fifth were designated Veteran Reserves. The eighteen regiments between the Nineteenth and Thirty-eighth were provided by erecting the second and third battalions of each of the three-battalion regiments (Eleventh and Nineteenth, inclusive) into separate regiments. The same Act contained the following provision, which has not since been modified: "The President may, by and with the advice and consent of the Senate, appoint a chaplain for each regiment of colored troops."

The Act of March 3, 1869, provided for the consolidation of the forty-five regiments into twenty-five, and also that "The enlisted men of two regiments of infantry shall be composed of colored men." General Orders issued from Army Headquarters in May, 1869, directed the "Twenty-fifth Infantry (colored), to be composed of the Thirty-ninth and Fortieth Regiments," and ordered that "The Thirty-nineth, now in North Carolina, will be relieved as soon as possible and will proceed to New Orleans, there to be consolidated with the Fortieth, now in the Department of Louisiana. The field officers

This selection was originally published in Theodore F. Rodenbough and William J. Haskin, *The Army of the United States* (New York, 1896).

will be: Joseph A. Mower, colonel; Edward W. Hinks, lieutenant-colonel; Zenas R. Bliss, major."[1]

The Twenty-fifth Infantry of 1866 conveyed its personnel to the Eighteenth; probably its records and colors were returned to the War Department. Although from a legal standpoint the Twenty-fifth Infantry has had a continuous existence since 1866, it is evident that for all purposes of tradition, the present regiment sprang into existence in 1869, and has no connection with any regiment that has previously borne the number. The regiment is, therefore, the lineal descendant of the Thirty-ninth and Fortieth Regiments.

By the end of April, 1869, the organization of the regiment had been completed, and the special return shows a full complement of officers and 1045 men. Colonel (and Brevet Major-General) Mower was commanding the 1045 men; Colonel (and Brevet Major-General) Mower was commanding the Department of Louisiana with headquarters at New Orleans; Lieutenant-Colonel (and Brevet Brigadier-General) Hinks commanded the regiment with headquarters, Companies D, G, and K, at Jackson Barracks, Louisiana; Major (and Brevet Lieutenant-Colonel) Bliss with Companies E, F, and I garrisoned Ship Island, Mississippi; Company A was at Fort Pike, Louisiana; Companies B and H at Fort Jackson, Louisiana; Company C at Fort St. Philip, Louisiana. By the end of the year, 532 men had been discharged by expiration of service alone, and, as little recruiting was done, the effectives had fallen to about 500 men, from which it has not since varied materially.

General Mower died at New Orleans January 6, 1870, and was succeeded by Colonel (and Brevet Major-General) J.J. Reynolds who was placed in command of the Department of Texas the following April, without having joined the regiment. In May, 1870, the regiment was on its way to that department, going by steamer to Indianola, Texas, thence marching to San Antonio. Colonel Bliss with Companies B, C, and G arrived at the latter place on June 3 and encamped at San Pedro Springs where they were joined by the rest of the regiment, under General Hinks, on the 9th. The march to stations began June 22nd. The main body took the Fort Clark road, while Companies C and H diverged on the road to Fort McKavett. At Rio Frio, Companies E and I marched for Fort Duncan, under Colonel Bliss. July found headquarters, Companies D and F established at Fort Clark; Company K at Fort Stockton; Companies A and G at Fort Davis; Company B did not reach its distant station, Fort Quitman, until August.

In December, 1870, General Reynolds transferred to the Third Cavalry and General Hinks retired from active service; they were succeeded by Colonel John D. Stevenson and Lieutenant-Colonel George L. Andrews, the latter becoming colonel of the regiment January 1, 1871, when Stevenson resigned. Colonel Andrews joined the regiment at Fort Clark June 18, 1871. In May, 1872, the regiment marched to western Texas and established its headquarters at Fort Davis. Company I, Captain Lawson commanding, participated in the engagement with Indians at the Wichita Indian Agency, Indian Territory, August 22 and 23, 1873, having one man wounded. Company B, Captain Bentzoni commanding, was with General Mackenzie's expedition into Mexico in June, 1878.

The history of the ten years' service in Texas is the record of a continuous series of building and repairing of military posts, roads, and telegraph lines; of escort and guard duty of all descriptions; of marchings and counter-marchings from post to post, and of scouting for Indians which resulted in a few unimportant skirmishes.

In April, 1880, the regiment was ordered to the Department of Dakota, exchanging with the First Infantry. Headquarters and four companies took station at Fort Randall, South Dakota, in June and remained there until the arrival of the Fifteenth Infantry in November, 1882, when they were transferred to Fort Snelling, Minnesota, relieving the Seventh Infantry. During this period four companies were stationed at Fort Meade, South Dakota, and two at Fort Hale, South Dakota. The latter post was abandoned in May, 1884, and the garrison transferred to Fort Sisseton, North Dakota.

In May, 1888, the regiment was transferred to Montana, exchanging stations with the Third Infantry. Headquarters and four companies were located at Fort Missoula, while four companies went to Fort Shaw and two to Fort Custer.

In September, 1890, companies I and K were skeletonized pursuant to orders from the War Department. Lieutenant-Colonel Van Horn, with companies C, E, F, and H, arrived at Fort Keogh the last of November, 1890, and remained there in camp until February 5, 1891, when they returned to their stations, nothing further having been required of them during that short but eventful campaign against the hostile Sioux.

Of the original officers of the regiment there are now but six on the rolls, *viz.:* Captains John W. French, Charles Bentzoni (Brevet Lieutenant-Colonel), and Gains Lawson (Brevet Lieutenant-Colonel), and Second Lieutenants (now captains) David B. Wilson, Owen J. Sweet and Henry P. Ritzius. It may also be interesting to note that Colonel Andrews, who has been colonel of the regiment for over twenty years, is the only colonel who ever commanded it; that during its twenty-two years of existence, the whole regiment has been together but fourteen days, and that but one captain (Van Valzah) has attained his majority by regular promotions.

THE FORTS

At the outset, one of the "strikes" against the black regiments was the fact that they had, in the early garrisons, the worst imaginable living conditions. They were, nevertheless, expected to be constantly prepared for action. (There were twelve Apache attacks in the first month that the Ninth Cavalry was at Fort Quitman.) One visitor remembers Fort Quitman as follows: ". . .a few houses and some rude stick tents, deep sand and broad sunshine as hot as I ever felt. . . . The river was rising and threatened to overflow the place." By 1890 a letter from Major Morrow to the Department Inspector General depicts graphically that living conditions had become well nigh intolerable:

> The buildings on the post are no longer tenable. . .during heavy rain yesterday, the guardhouse fell in and guard and prisoners narrowly escaped injury. . . .As the offices are all dripping and filled with mud, I have no place to write this letter in and trust its appearance will be excused as it is being written under the shelter of a piece of canvas held over my head.

The land around the fort was hostile territory, and with the danger of Indian attack ever present. An incident occurred on August 9th, 1880. At that time, General J.J. Byrnes was killed when the stagecoach in which he was riding was ambushed in Quitman Canyon: "The stage driver. . .escaped death by quickly turning his team and outracing the savages to Quitman five miles away with Byrnes' body hanging half way out of the coach. . . ."

As time passed, however, the situation in the West and Southwest assumed such importance that newer and more permanent bases of operations for the troops were needed. A brief history of one such post, Fort Davis, is included. The men at Fort Davis did not suffer as many hardships, personal and geographical, as men at other posts at that time. Although perhaps not typical in this regard, the function of Fort Davis within the histories of all four black units is real enough. It represented "home" to all the units at one time or another. At Fort Davis, there seemed to be more regard than at benighted Fort Quitman for a proper military appearance: for example, some of the officers' wives kept chickens, but Major Bliss thought that they made the post look "unmilitary." So he decreed that "On and after February 1, 1874, no fowls will be kept within the limits of this garrison."

For diversion, the post had a band, library, chapel, and a school. The women organized balls, dinner parties, and weddings. Recreation of a different sort could be found in the nearest town of Chihuahua; this town, filled with gamblers and prostitutes, was totally dependent on the Army for its livelihood and was the scene of frequent violent shootings and knifings.

And yet, life at Fort Davis was not without its degree of hardship. In 1878, there was an epidemic of dysentary, traceable, it was discovered, to the fact that the post pigs were bathing in the spring that was the fort's water supply.

9
H
US
US
J. CISNEROS

Quitman: The Worst Post at Which I Ever Served

George Ruhlen

So wrote Lieutenant Zenas R. Bliss, Eighth US Infantry of Fort Quitman, Texas when he served there in 1861.[1] There was much about this typical frontier outpost to warrant the lieutenant's opinion, although there were some who described the fort as being pleasantly situated on the bank of the Rio Grande with its adobe buildings "resembling marble in their several coats of whitewash."[2]

If it were not a pleasant post at least it was an essential one, for a fort on the Rio Grande near where the El Paso-San Antonio road left the river had been recommended for several years prior to its establishment. Colonel J.K. Mansfield had so recommended in his 1853 report.[3] In 1854 the Department of New Mexico Commander, Brigadier General Garland, reported that due to Indian attacks near Eagle Springs[4] he had detached one of the companies at Fort Bliss to take post near there, even though outside his Department, until other arrangements could be made to assure safe transportation of mail and protection for California bound emigrants.[5]

General David Twiggs, commanding the Department of Texas, citing a recent attack on San Antonio drovers en route to El Paso, stated that most Indian depredations were committed between Fort

Reprinted (in excerpted form) through the courtesy of *Password*, Quarterly of the El Paso (Texas) County Historical Society, ed. Eugene O. Porter. The article first appeared in Vol. XI (Fall, 1966), No. 3.

Davis and El Paso, and that with the current amount of daily travel there were not enough forces or forts in the Department to provide proper protection. He considered the post about to be established on the Rio Grande where the road struck the river to be of great importance to the security of travelers and to the mails. Garrisoning the post with two companies of infantry, Twiggs planned to abandon the defensive and carry the war to the Indians.[6]

In early September, 1858, companies C and H, Eighth Infantry at Fort Davis were ordered to be prepared to establish a post on the Rio Grande pending completion of a reconnaissance and recommended location by Captain A.T. Lee, Eighth Infantry.[7] On 22 September, these two companies comprising 2 officers, 1 Assistant Surgeon and 144 men left Fort Davis and arrived six days later at the selected site 85 miles downriver from El Paso.[8] Three weeks before its establishment it had been named Fort Quitman in honor of the distinguished former Governor, Congressman, and soldier from Mississippi, John Anthony Quitman, recently deceased, whose gallantry and conduct as a major general in the Mexican War had been recognized by a joint resolution of Congress which also tendered him a testimonial sword.[9]

Twenty-four soldiers on extra duty commenced construction of buildings immediately. Lumber was obtained from Tularosa, 300 miles away, and Mexicans were employed to teach the soldiers how to make adobes and build flat roofs.[10] These prosaic occupations were not without hazard; for in early 1859 the Mescalero Indians repeatedly harrassed the El Paso road and in their third foray in a two week period attacked settlers making lime as well as a government wagon train only a mile and a half from the post.[11] Nevertheless, by June, Captain Bomford, commanding Company H and the post, was able to report that during the last nine months construction had been completed on two sets of company quarters with messes and kitchen, a commissary and storehouse and four sets of officers quarters; nearing completion were a blacksmith shop and guardhouse. Barracks were 26 feet by 74 feet, messes and kitchens 18 by 50, officers quarters 18 by 36, all about 9 feet high. The condition of the quarters was reported good, all adobe walls coated with gypsum wash and windows glazed. Planned construction included a commanding officer's set, 6 small houses for married men, a bakery, a wall for the corral and two storerooms, and a hospital 26 by 72 feet.[12] The latter would be needed if the garrison were to remain at two companies; but since the recent departure of Company C it had consisted of only 2 officers and 66 men.

Despite this heartening description there must have been certain undesirable features about life at Quitman; for it was designated a double ration post in May, 1859, and one traveler, Bishop Pierce, left his impression of the post as

> a few houses and some rude stick tents, deep sand and broad sunshine as hot as I ever felt. . . . When we stopped to deliver the mail a gentleman came up to inquire of a train behind. He seemed to long for its arrival, that he might hasten his escape from what he called "this God-forsaken country." The river was rising and threatened to overflow the place. The people were full of fear, for their adobe houses were certain to cave in if the water reached them.[13]

The Bishop was traveling on stages of the San Antonio-San Diego mail route. In August the mail under contract by the Butterfield line which heretofore had traveled up the Pecos River and then along Delaware Creek, through Guadalupe Pass to El Paso, was changed to run via forts Stockton, Davis, and Quitman to El Paso. This was done to provide semi-weekly mails to these Army posts as well as to use a route only slightly longer but with assured sources of water, including, of course, the 85-mile stretch along the river from Quitman to El Paso. Fort Quitman was not a station of the Butterfield Overland Mail; coaches made only brief stops there for mail and passengers. The actual stage station was located five and a half miles down river from the post where Quitman Canyon (formerly called *Cañón de los Lamentos,* probably because of the innumerable tragedies from the Indian attacks on this dangerous trail) joined the Rio Grande valley. This area, where the El Paso trail first reached the river, had been a camping and rest area for mail riders, stages, and travelers as long as it had been traveled.[14]

The absence of troops on the frontier during the war years had emboldened the Indians to such an extent that travel on the El Paso road became increasingly hazardous. Early in December, 1867, the mail escort was attacked near Eagle Springs and in the same month some nine hundred Indians attacked Company K, Ninth Cavalry near Fort Lancaster.[15] Conditions were reminiscent of those in '58, so again troops were ordered to Quitman. Company F, Ninth Cavalry with two officers and eighty-one men departed from Fort Davis and arrived at Quitman on January 1, 1868.

Indian reaction was immediate. The new garrison's first month was enlivened by twelve different Apache attacks – each successfully driven off.[16] The post was officially reestablished by Department orders of 25 February which also increased the garrison. It is interesting to note that whereas the initial post returns of 1858 stated that communications should be addressed through San Antonio, upon reestablishment the best means of communication was given as through Santa Fe. The garrison was augmented in May by the arrival of Company H, Forty-first Infantry, and companies H and I, Ninth Cavalry, although the latter soon left for station at Eagle Springs.[17] Usual garrison duties, including crude temporary repairs to buildings and regular escorts for the mails, occupied the troops' time, with little else to relieve the monotony. The Negro troops must have been reasonably content however; for the desertion rates for 1868 of the Ninth Cavalry and Forty-first Infantry regiments – forty-eight and thirty-one respectively – were among the lowest in the Army and were about one-tenth those of the famed Second, Seventh or Eighth Cavalry regiments.

In the late summer good grass and water near the post brought an increase in Indian raids and retaliatory forays by the Ninth Cavalry. In late August a 250 mile chase succeeded in recovering stock stolen near the post, and October was marked by minor Indian troubles. There is little record of events during the next few years other than changes in garrison units and commands. Company F departed for Fort Davis in August, 1868, and Major A.P. Morrow, Ninth Cavalry, assumed command in December. During that time various losses occurred due to desertion, discharge, and death from disease or bullet wounds, including one poor soul reported as "died of disease in post hospital."

Early in 1869, a month after Judge Hubbell of El Paso and the driver of his stage were murdered by Indians near Fort Quitman, Lydia Lane, Army wife and veteran of a dozen years on the frontier, passed through the post and later wrote:

> When we sighted the Rio Grande, five miles below Fort Quitman, a sense of relief took the place of my recent uneasiness and fear; and when we drove into the forlorn and tumble down adobe built fort, I wanted to greet everybody as a friend and brother. The troops stationed there were colored, and as we passed the guardhouse I noticed a sergeant in full dress jumping rope! I felt rather shocked to see a soldier in uniform so disporting himself, but concluded if any one at

> Quitman could feel cheerful enough to enjoy so innocent a pastime he was to be congratulated. . . . From Quitman to Fort Bliss the journey was comparatively a safe one. . . .[18]

In November, 1869, Company H, Forty-first Infantry, was redesignated Company H, Twenty-fourth Infantry, but remained at Quitman. During this time the post garrison reached its all time high in strength, 7 officers and 230 men. The major events of the year 1870 were scouting expeditions against the Indians of greater strength and longer duration than previous ones – 30 to 70 men in the field from four to six weeks on each scout – but their exhausting efforts brought only meager results. Mail guards and escorts continued. In August, Company B, Twenty-fifth Infantry under Captain Bentzoni arrived to become part of the garrison.[19]

While Quitman troops were occupied in the monotonous routine of a frontier garrison, its commanders were engrossed in other problems, possibly monotonous but not routine. These were the post war years when war claims against the Government were legion. One claimant filed for $5,000 for transportation of baggage and supplies from forts Quitman, Bliss, and Davis in 1861 when Twiggs ordered those posts to be evacuated. Two Mexicans submitted claims for injuries inflicted and robberies committed by soldiers from Fort Quitman in 1859. Three citizens of San Lorenzo, across the river from Quitman, demanded $100,000 for grass and wood taken from the village by U.S. troops in 1861. At least one officer characterized these claims as attempts to swindle the government.

Of more concern to the post commander was the deplorable condition of the buildings. During the war they had been stripped of everything that could be carried away. Now, in the summer of 1870, the only buildings having doors were the officers' quarters; all windows were covered with cloth only and, due to crowded conditions, many of the officers lived in tents.[20] Major Morrow's letter to the Department Inspector General presented a dismal picture of conditions at the post as these excerpts depict so vividly:

> The buildings on the post are no longer tenable . . . during heavy rain yesterday, the guardhouse fell in and guard and prisoners narrowly escaped injury . . . barracks fell in on Company H, 25th Infantry . . . houses are not fit to stable cattle in . . . if the rain continues, all must move into tents. . . . Many buildings are beyond repair. . . . As the

> offices are all dripping and filled with mud, I have no place to write this letter in and trust its appearance will be excused as it is being written under the shelter of a piece of canvas held over my head. . . . Quarters have a wagon load of silt on rugs, furniture, etc. . . . Complete plans and a hundred or more reports have been made on conditions at Quitman and action to be taken to improve buildings and build new ones . . . [but] as yet no action has been taken. . . . The post is a disgrace to the government and a gross injustice to troops to station them there. . . .[21]

Morrow's letter brought results as well as divergent views on ways to improve post accommodations. The Department Quartermaster General stated that eight months previously a survey showed the quarters were not worth repairing. He proposed new construction on an austere basis by contract rather than troop labor. The Department Commander, General Reynolds, agreed but considered that the construction criteria should be the same as approved for other posts, for "not one post in Texas has adequate shelter for troops, animals or stores." As planned, Fort Quitman was to have 13 new sets of officer's quarters, 4 company barracks, 3 stables, storehouses, offices, commissary, and a hospital. The total cost was estimated at $249,500. Alas for the hopes that had been raised! In view of the cost involved, approval was withdrawn in favor of making economical repairs to existing buildings – a policy still popular almost a century later.

Troop accommodations at the fort were indeed not only substandard, but inadequate and unhealthy, as four companies (H and I, Ninth Cavalry; H of Twenty-fourth Infantry, and B of the Twenty-fifth Infantry) now occupied a post which could not shelter two properly. The sick reports for 1870-71 reflect the result of these conditions. The number of dysentery cases was more than one-third the mean strength of the command with intermittent fever and bronchitis running close seconds. In fact the hospital record presents a pretty dismal picture of life at Quitman; with a mean strength of 7 officers and 184 men, 234 cases of disease are recorded, 46 cases of accidents and injuries and 4 deaths, two of them from gunshot wounds. Early in 1871, Assistant Surgeon Guinn, soon to die at Fort Quitman, protested the inadequacy of hospital facilities such as inadquate space, no convalescent ward, no attendants' quarters and inadequate privies, among others.

From February 7 to March 29 Major Morrow conducted one of the longest and most prolonged scouts against the Indians combing the

Sacramento Mountains with four companies of the Ninth Cavalry, including the two from Quitman, but with insignificant results. The infantry companies continued to escort the mail and perform garrison duties, which consisted at this time mainly of repairing buildings. Twenty-man scouts of two weeks duration through the Carrizo Mountains, Alamo Springs and Eagle Springs area in June and July returned without sighting any hostiles. In the meantime troop changes in May and June had reduced the Quitman garrison to Company K, Ninth Cavalry and Company B, Twenty-fourth Infantry.[22]

February of 1872 saw the garrison depleted to sixty-three men, which caused the commanding officer to write that conditions were "about as bad as can be . . . . The garrison," he continued, "is too few to be of any service . . . at least another company of cavalry is needed . . . more posts are recommended to be established on Delaware Creek and to the west to keep the White Mountain Apaches under control."[23] A month later the garrison had dwindled to forty men upon the departure of the infantry company for fort Stockton.

During the latter half of 1872, Company D, Twenty-fifth Infantry arrived from Fort Clark, Company K, Ninth Cavalry departed for that post, and Company B, Twenty-fifth Infantry arrived from Fort Bliss. Guard detachments at the Eagle Springs and Van Horn Wells mail stations were continued throughout the year and with good reason, for in August thirty horses belonging to Mexicans were stolen by Indians less than thirty miles from the post. In November Company D, Twenty-fifth Infantry was transferred to Fort Davis leaving only Company B, Twenty-fifth Infantry under Captain Bentzoni to garrison Fort Quitman – a disposition which was to remain unchanged until the next abandonment of the post.

An insight into the effect of the government's procrastinating business practices is gained from a report of post inspection submitted by Bentzoni in December, 1872. He stated that the high costs of maintaining Fort Quitman were due primarily to:

> a constant want of funds. . . . There are not more than six to ten men in this part of the country whose capital will admit of taking contracts if they must wait an indefinite period for payment after delivery. Competition having as its object not to bid under certain figures is the inevitable result. Under prompt payment hay should not be more than $12 per ton, yet the present contract price is $22. The contract price at

Bliss in 1871 was only $13 per ton and the contractor turned it over to a poor man who filled it for $11 a ton.[24]

A report of the Surgeon General gives a fairly good description of the post at that time. The buildings, constructed of adobes with earth roofs, had been made comfortable during the past three years, particularly the officers' quarters, by repairs made by their individual occupants. Married soldiers and laundresses occupied an old set of officer's quarters. Although the hospital boasted of two bath tubs, its arrangement was inconvenient and with neither floor nor ceiling nor lavatory was most inadequate. All attempts to cultivate a post garden had failed and although milk and sometimes butter, eggs, and chickens could be procured locally, fresh vegetables and fruits had to be hauled over dusty roads from the El Paso area, 50 to 75 miles away. Food prices reflected this inconvenience of supply. Many supplies, particularly military, were brought by wagon train from San Antonio, 595 miles away. It was truly a remote post which well tested the hardihood and character of those who lived there, particularly members of that gallant and unsung band – the Army wives.[25]

Garrison duties for the next few years followed much the same pattern as before, enlivened somewhat by an earthquake on February 7, 1873, a visit by the Inspector General of the Army, and an inspection by the Department Commander. Periodic scouts of some 200 miles to ascertain Indian movements were made through the Eagle Mountains, Carrizo Mountains, Hot Springs, and down the Rio Grande, with negative results except for one incident in May, 1874. Undertaking these patrols concurrently with essential mail escort duty and usual garrison chores became increasingly difficult as the strength of the garrison decreased. As early as August, 1874 Captain Bentzoni had estimated that by the following June he would lose 33 men of his 46 man command due to expiration of their terms of service, of whom 8 might possibly reenlist. He was not far wrong, for in June, 1875 Quitman's garrison consisted of only 2 officers and 18 men present for duty.

One of Bentzoni's letters reveals the kind of commander he must have been. The Department Quartermaster stated that "All posts between Concho and El Paso are garrisoned by colored troops and details from them would not as a rule be reliable." Bentzoni was quick to reply that in justice to the troops he commanded he:

> must point out that the letter of September 22nd last directing troops to carry mail was received at 5:00 P.M. on October 11 and the first mail left at 11:00 P.M. that night. . . . It has been carried seven times both ways and once on a double route for a total of some 2,140 miles . . . and has arrived and departed punctually and been delivered in good order. No civilians have been employed for this task . . . [as] soldiers are competent to perform this and similar duties.[26]

During the following two years regimental changes of station brought a welcome influx of visitors and transients to Quitman with the unanticipated surprise and pleasure, so typical of Army life, of again seeing old friends and acquaintances. Troops of the Eighth Cavalry en route from Fort Selden, New Mexico to Fort Clark, Texas and those of the Ninth Cavalry going in the opposite direction, paused at Quitman sporadically from July, 1875, through March, 1876; Companies C and H, Twenty-fifth Infantry, exchanging station between forts Bliss and Davis stopped for a day or two in September and October as did other troops engaged in the interminable "scouts for hostiles." At least one scout of 300 miles in February, 1876, was partially successful, resulting in a minor skirmish and destruction of considerable Indian supplies.

In December, 1876, the Division of the Missouri approved previous recommendations of the Department of Texas and authorized the discontinuance of the posts of Quitman and Bliss and movement of their garrisons to Forts Clark and Concho respectively. Major Zenas R. Bliss, once again Quitman's commander after fifteen years, was ordered from Fort Davis to command Clark.[27] On January 5, 1877, he abandoned Fort Quitman for the second time.[28]

The Salt War incident near El Paso soon showed that withdrawal of these frontier garrisons was premature and ill advised. A report by First Lieutenant L.H. Rucker, Ninth Cavalry, who was instrumental in saving Judge Howard's life the first time he was threatened by an irate mob of "Spanish-Americans" and Mexicans, emphasized that the presence of troops was necessary to protect life and property. The endorsement of General Sheridan, Missouri Division Commander, was irate and terse. He had "never recommended abandonment of Bliss . . . done while he was away . . . recommended by Department Commander and approved by the Secretary of War . . . request authority of the Secretary of War to reoccupy Quitman."[29] Sheridan prompty received the authority he requested and on 26 November

1877 directed the Department of Texas Commander to reoccupy the fort whenever he considered the public service required it.[30] Such was not done but instead various company strength camps were established throughout the newly formed District of the Pecos, among them one at Eagle Springs in another attempt to make the mail route and settlements safe by forcing the Indians from its vicinity.

This scheme was not too successful due to some extent to the improper selection of the military district limits. For example, the Commander of the District of New Mexico had responsibility as far south as San Elizario but no farther, although the entire lower valley is a geographical entity.[31]

In 1879 a stage station was established on the site of the abandoned post. Less than a year later Apache raids made travel in the Quitman-Eagle Springs area as hazardous as it had ever been. The Tenth Cavalry was constantly in the field attempting to exert a measure of control over the elusive Apaches. In February, 1880, Captain L. H. Carpenter was ordered to visit Fort Quitman and report on the feasibility of reestablishing the post.[32] Buildings and facilities were in such poor condition that this was not done. However, during the campaign against Victorio in 1880 – last of the Indian campaigns in Texas – General Grierson did use the old post as a camp and tactical base in the successful execution of his plan which prevented Victorio's Apaches from reaching the Guadaloupe Mountains and turned them into Mexico to their eventual annihilation. One company of cavalry was usually encamped at or near the old fort during the summer of 1880. Such a disposition probably saved General Grierson's life, for in July, 1880, Apaches surrounded his small party at Eighteen Mile Water Hole and were driven off only when Company A, Tenth Cavalry arrived at a gallop from Fort Quitman. In a few days most of the regiment had assembled at Eagle Springs to intercept Victorio and his band.[33] These precautions limited but did not stop Apache depredations. On August 9th, General J.J. Byrnes was murdered when the stage in which he was travelling was ambushed in Quitman Canyon. The stage driver, Ed Walde, escaped death by quickly turning his team and outracing the savages to Quitman five miles away with Byrnes' body hanging half way out of the coach.[34]

When Brigadier General C.C. Augur assumed command of the Department of Texas in January, 1881, he abolished the military district organization but made commanders responsible for the security of their area to half the distance to adjacent posts. He also established a series of subposts satellited on the permanent forts; thus Pena Colorado, Camp Presidio, and Fort Quitman became subposts of Fort Davis.[35] The detachment of Company A, Tenth Cavalry stationed at Quitman since the previous summer was relieved on January 12, 1881, by Company E, Sixteenth Infantry commanded by First Lieutenant S.R. Whitall. To protect the mail route between forts Davis and Quitman, other detachments from the company were stationed at Eagle Springs, Van Horn Wells; Ojo del Muerto, and Barilla Springs.[36] The duty continued until the infantrymen at Quitman were replaced in April by Company K, Tenth Cavalry.[37]

To the duties so familiar to the Tenth of patrolling for Indians, escorting the mails, and repairing the telegraph lines, was soon added a new one – protecting the engineers and workmen who were steadily pushing the tracks of the Texas and Pacific Railroad to their eventual junction with the Southern Pacific at Sierra Blanca. In October, Company A, Tenth Cavalry, relieved from duty protecting the railroad crews, was ordered to replace K Company as Quitman's garrison – its last as it turned out.[38]

The end of the Apache menace to West Texas marked a definite change in the character and purpose of the military posts in that area. The railroad had replaced the stage route as the main artery of travel. Security of the border south of Fort Bliss from intrusions of marauders and smugglers from Mexico became the primary military mission. Even as the troops at Quitman were fruitlessly scouting for Indians south of Eagle Springs, in April, 1882, plans were being developed in accordance with General Sherman's views to establish a post west of Sierra Blanca where the Southern Pacific Railroad reached the Rio Grande. Lieutenant Nordstrom, commanding troops at Quitman, was directed to examine the country near Camp Rice, initially a railroad construction camp some thirty-seven miles northwest of Sierra Blanca and to select a site in that vicinity suitable for a camp of one company of cavalry.[39]

Nordstrom reported a favorable location existed about two miles north of Camp Rice and that abandonment of Fort Quitman would present no problem as the troops there were housed only in tents. Fort Davis' commander recommended establishment of the new camp and abandonment of Quitman. The Department of Texas commander, concurring in these views, so directed by telegram on July 5, 1882. Five days later Company A, Tenth Cavalry marched from Quitman to its new station at Camp Rice, fifteen miles distant, and Fort Quitman – defender of the frontier for almost twenty-five years – was abandoned forever.[40] It was a typical prototype of the frontier posts as they actually were – far different from those portrayed in paperback novels, motion pictures, or television.[41]

About thirty years ago, a few of the old adobe walls of the post buildings could still be faintly identified. Since then irrigation projects and levee construction have completed nature's erasures of man's temporary works. Today no trace of old Fort Quitman remains. About 65 miles south of El Paso State Road 34 joins Interstate Highway 10. If one drives south on State 34 about six miles, an old cemetery will be found a few dozen yards to the west of the road. Approximately 150 yards west of the cemetery is the site of the old fort – unmarked, little known, and practically forgotten. About five miles farther south the road turns east away from the river into gloomy, once dreaded Quitman Canyon – *Cañón de los Lamentos* – which even today requires no great imagination to people it with the ghosts of Apache warriors, stage drivers and blue clad troopers. From the top of the canyon, no more than thirty minutes drive due east over a range road lies Sierra Blanca.

Full-dress parade *Paul Rossi*

Fort Davis

Robert M. Utley

Nestled at the eastern base of the scenic Davis Mountains in West Texas, Fort Davis guarded the Trans-Pecos segment of the southern route to California. From 1854 to 1891, except for the Civil War years, units of the United States Army garrisoned this remote post beyond the frontiers of Texas. They patrolled the San Antonio-El Paso road, escorted stagecoaches and guarded mail relay stations, policed the Mexican border, and skirmished with Comanche and Apache warriors whose raiding trails to Mexico sliced across the deserts of West Texas. Troops stationed here played a major role in the campaigns against the able Apache Chieftain Victorio, whose death in 1880 terminated Indian warfare in Texas. Today the remains of Fort Davis commemorate a significant phase of the advance of the frontier across the American continent.

On October 23, 1854, General Persifor F. Smith issued orders establishing Fort Davis, which was named for Secretary of War Jefferson Davis. The general himself chose the spot where the post was to rise. It was in a canyon about a quarter of a mile south of the Painted Camp. On three sides palisaded rock walls rose abruptly from the canyon floor, terminating at the top in grassy hills. Considering the tactical situation, this was not the wisest choice, for an enemy could, and later did, approach very near without discovery. Seawell wished

Reprinted (in excerpted form) from *The Fort Davis Historical Handbook*, U.S. Department of the Interior, No. 38 (Washington, 1965).

instead to establish the fort near a bubbling spring on the prairie opposite the mouth of the canyon. where it was in fact rebuilt after the Civil War. Whether he voiced this opinion to General Smith is not known, but throughout his service at Fort Davis he clung to the hope of one day building a fine new post of stone outside the canyon. Meanwhile, he contented himself with erecting temporary structures of pine slabs and canvas on the site inside the canyon designated by General Smith.

A NEW FORT

For nearly 2 years after the Confederate surrender at Appomattox, the Texas frontier and the road to El Paso lay exposed to Comanche and Apache raiders. The Reconstruction policies that followed the war kept Federal troops in Texas too occupied to devote much attention to the Indian menace. Attacks on frontier settlements and the El Paso road, however, finally brought about the reactivation of the frontier defense system. The Ninth U.S. Cavalry, one of two newly organized mounted regiments composed of Negros with white officers, was assigned to Fort Davis. On June 29, 1867, four troops of the regiment under Lieutenant Colonel Wesley Merritt, distinguished Civil War General, marched into the wrecked post on Limpia Creek.

On the prairie at the mouth of the canyon, Colonel Merritt began building a stone post such as Colonel Seawell had planned in the years before the war. A row of nineteen sets of officers' quarters with separate kitchen buildings would face, across a five hundred foot parade ground, a row of six barracks, with offices and other utility buildings fronting the parade ground at each end. Although only a few structures were finally built of stone and some originally planned never emerged from the drawing board, the post that took shape proved commodious and vastly more comfortable than its predecessor.

About two hundred civilian carpenters, masons, and laborers went to work on Fort Davis. By March, 1869, nearly two years later, they had finished about half the buildings and begun work on the rest. On March 20, however, the department quartermaster inspected the post and, probably for reasons of economy, ordered all work halted. Thereafter, the fort expanded sporadically as limited construction funds became available. Not until the middle 1880s did it assume its final form. During the period of active field operations, therefore, the garrison occupied ten sets of officer's quarters and two barracks and discharged the routine duties of the post in limited office and utility space. Most of the structures were built of adobe bricks, in the manufacture of which the Mexican laborers who lived in the neighborhood were experts.

During the decade of the 1880s, even though the Indian menace had been eliminated, the garrison was increased beyond any previous number, and new buildings were therefore necessary.

Band barracks, infantry barracks, and two new cavalry barracks were built in this period, together with additional quarters for officers. A new twelve-bed hospital had been erected in 1874-75 to replace the temporary structure in use since 1868, and in the eighties this was enlarged by the addition of a second ward. The installation of an iceplant, gas street lamps, and a water system added a touch of civilization to the remote frontier. By 1890, the number of buildings at Fort Davis had risen to more than sixty.

GARRISON OF FORT DAVIS, 1867-81

The fifteen years from 1867 to 1881 spanned the period of active operations against hostile Indians in West Texas. The history of Fort Davis during these years is the history of four regiments, all Negro with white officers – the Ninth and Tenth Cavalry and the Twenty-Fourth and Twenty-Fifth Infantry. Gradually the garrison grew from four companies of both infantry and cavalry to twelve – from eight officers and two hundred enlisted men to thirty officers and six hundred men. The Ninth Regiment supplied the cavalry until 1875, when the Tenth took over and served until 1885. The infantry were drawn from the Twenty-fourth until 1870, from both the Twenty-fourth and Twenty-fifth until 1872, and from the Twenty-fifth from 1872 until 1880.

Organized shortly after the Civil War, these regiments were composed largely of former slaves, and many in the Army and out watched them closely to see how the experiment would work. Like all other regiments, they had their share of bad soldiers. Led by some capable officers, however, the Negro units soon won a secure place in the frontier Army and for nearly three decades participated creditably in Indian campaigns all over the West. The troops stationed at Fort Davis compiled an impressive record in the late 1860s and the 1870s and played a significant role in destroying the Indian barrier of West Texas.

Like the enlisted complement, the officer corps of Fort Davis usually contained a few men poorly equipped for the difficult task of presiding over the destinies of the troops they were supposed to lead. But most were capable professionals. Except for second lieutenants recently graduated from West Point, the officers were veterans of the Civil War. Some had commanded regiments, brigades, or even divisions in ranks much higher than the shrunken peacetime Army could now offer. Many held brevet ranks awarded for gallantry in action during the war, and it was not unusual for a first lieutenant or captain at Fort Davis to be addressed as major or colonel in recognition of his brevet grade.

LIFE AT FORT DAVIS

Life at Fort Davis differed little from life at other frontier posts of the time. Scouts, patrols, escort duty, and campaigns were part of the life throughout the period of Indian hostility. For most, these were welcome diversions, for the routine of garrison existence accounted for the greater share of one's service. Day after day, official activities followed the same monotonous pattern: mounted and dismounted drill, target practice, care of weapons and stock, fatigue labors, guard duty, inspections, parades, and a variety of other tasks.

Under the post commander, each officer and man had his part to play. The post adjutant and the sergeant major were the administrative voices of the commanding officer, with whom they shared offices at post headquarters on the north edge of the parade ground. Most of the commander's orders were transmitted through these men. The post quartermaster officer and sergeant were responsible for clothing, housing, and supplying the garrison, the post commissary officer and sergeant for feeding it. They occupied offices and warehouses south of the corrals during the 1870s, then moved to new buildings north of the corrals in the 1880s. The post surgeon, aided by the noncommissioned hospital steward, presided over the hospital behind officers' row and also looked after the sanitary condition of the fort. Each company was supposed to have a captain and two lieutenants, but this was an ideal rarely achieved. Company officers could be found supervising their units in the field or occupied with paper work in the company orderly room in the barracks. Sergeants and corporals of the line usually stayed with the troops. Numerous enlisted specialists – blacksmith, farrier, saddler, wagoner, wheelwright – worked in shops that formed part of the quartermaster and cavalry corrals. At specified times of the day, an infantry bugler or cavalry trumpeter blew the appropriate calls that regulated the routine of the military community.

The troops ate their meals in buildings housing kitchen and messroom adjoining each set of barracks. Staple fare had changed little since the 1850s. In 1877 the meat ration consisted of three-tenths bacon and seven-tenths fresh beef. Beans and flour were purchased locally, and bread came daily from the post bakery. Scurvy swept the garrison in the spring of 1868, and the surgeon, Dr. Daniel Weisel, stressed the necessity of including plenty of fresh vegetables in the diet. In 1869 he persuaded Colonel Merritt to start a post garden. Two were planted, one of four acres on Limpia Creek for the post and one of three acres at the spring southeast of the corrals for the hospital. These gardens flourished year after year until abandonment of the fort in 1891. Some of the officers' wives kept chickens, but Major Bliss thought that they made the post look unmilitary, and he decreed that "On and after Feb. 1, 1874, no fowls will be kept within the limits of this garrison." Dr. Weisel thought it worth noting that, unlike white troops, Negro soldiers customarily ate their entire ration.

Water for all purposes was hauled from the Limpia in water wagons. The troops suffered from chronic dysentery, and everyone blamed the water. Dr. Weisel, however, insisted that it was pure and that "the water is made a shield of carelessness and neglect in enforcing necessary hygienic and sanitary measures." Nevertheless, in 1875 the spring was substituted for the Limpia as the source of water. By 1878 the drainage ditch leading to the spring had become "the resort of pigs" (chickens were probably back, too, now that Major Bliss had been transferred), and the water took on impurities. Finally, in 1883, construction began on a new water system, with a well and a steam pump on the Limpia and pipes leading into the post.

The state of sanitation was a constant worry to the post surgeon. Dr. Weisel complained that the squad rooms in the barracks were "very untidy, dirty and disorderly," that the kitchens and messrooms were equally dirty, that the sinks were "in a very bad condition," and that "offal and slops" were not hauled away as often as necessary. The doctor also tried to get orders issued requiring every soldier to bathe in Limpia Creek at least twice a week during the summer, but he appears not to have been successful. "The difficulties of a medical officer . . . at a frontier post," he wrote, "can only be fully estimated by actual and trying experience." And, he added, "much more might be said."

For diversion, the troops had a band, a library, a chapel, and a school, the last usually presided over by the chaplain. But the chief off-duty pastimes were gambling, drinking, and sampling the pleasures of the village of Chihuahua, just off the reservation. Boasting a population of about 150 Mexicans and 25 Americans, all dependent on the Army or the stage line for a living, Chihuahua was the scene of frequent violence. In October 1870, for example, someone shot Private Anderson Merriweather with an army pistol. The bullet tore up his stomach, and Dr. Weisel could not save him. Several months later Private John Williams got into a scrap with a comrade and was killed instantly with a butcher knife. Similar incidents occurred regularly. Diversions took their toll on officers, too.

Many of the officers had their wives and families at the fort, and the women took an active lead in organizing social diversions. Balls, charades, dinner parties, and weddings were frequent and well-attended events. The arrival of official visitors from other posts or from department headquarters in San Antonio always prompted parties of one kind or another; and such occasions as the inspection of Fort Davis in 1882 by General of the Army William T. Sherman and staff were highlights of the continual war on monotony.

The Cavalry

The five chapters that follow deal with the Tenth Regiment of Cavalry. In some sections, events are presented in a strictly chronological form, with great attention to historical detail. At other points, the exploits of the Tenth are explored in a more impressionistic fashion, in descriptive prose that is powerfully evocative of the American West as it was experienced by the black soldier.

In the first chapter, "Early Field Service," the official historian of the Tenth describes chronologically some of the details of military life and some of the specific engagements that were fought against the "enemy," the Indian. There is an account here of the dramatic incident that occurred when Generals Sherman and Grierson were challenged by two Kiowas with rifles:

> . . . Lone Wolf, a vicious and desperate Kiowa chief, rode up, dismounted, and came on the porch, smiling and ejaculating the familiar Indian greeting, "How, How," threw aside his blanket, and disclosed two loaded carbines, one of which he passed to another Indian. With an almost superhuman effort, General Grierson sprang upon the two Indians, seized the muzzles of the carbines, and sat both Indians squat upon the porch floor.

Grierson's men, it is clear from this account, were a worthy complement to his strength and leadership. "In the years 1882-85," wrote the company historian, "they were close to being a perfect cavalry fighting machine; they were lean and hard and grizzled and loved a fight."

In "The Buffalo Soldiers in Arizona," the same writer gives a full picture of the Apache Campaign, as it came to be called in textbooks. This campaign involved, for one thing, the famous chase of Geronimo through the territory. But it also involved the ignominious tasks of confining and disciplining the red man. Even when performing this regrettable activity, however, the troopers acquitted themselves creditably. When, in the summer of 1897, the Tenth was called out to arrest several "bad Injuns" among the Cheyennes, there was no resistance from the rest of the assembled tribe, due "not a little to the respect of the Cheyennes for their old friends the buffalo soldiers."

The two articles, "A Scout with the Buffalo Soldiers" and "Vagabonding with the Tenth Horse," are probably the most famous eyewitness accounts of life in the Tenth by one of America's most distinguished reporter-artists, Frederic Remington. From the beginning, it is apparent that Remington had respect for the abilities of the black troopers. His respect, alas, often emerged with a tinge of condescension as, to his apparent surprise, he discovered that black men were as good at soldiering as were white men. He also falls into the dangerous trap of trying to report in writing exactly what he heard – in this case, dialect, in its most embarrassing presentation. Although today we bristle at so narrow a view of the black man, it is important to keep in mind the fact that Remington was writing in the 1880s and 1890s and that his writing reflected the prejudices of those years, not too long after the Civil War. If only for that reason, as a mirror of the times, the articles remain authentic and worthwhile documents of history. The articles are included here primarily for the vivid accounts of day-to-day life that Remington recorded on the march with the Tenth. What also makes Remington's writing valuable are the drawings seen throughout this volume portraying the black military man under the best and the worst of conditions, at leisure, in combat, and on the trail. This marks the first time that art of this nature ever appeared in such quantity and quality depicting the black man in America in such a heroic and positive manner.

In the fifth article, "The Tenth Cavalry in the Early Days," Colonel William Wharfield, a painstaking chronicler of his regiment, presents the most readable and informative early history of the Tenth. This chapter provides valuable information without which no account of the Tenth would be complete: His footnotes are precise and meticulous, giving almost as much information as does the article; and the history is a complete one up to the turn of the century.

A halt to tighten the packs

EARLY FIELD SERVICE

Edward Glass

[After the Tenth Cavalry had been assembled] little time was lost in placing the regiment in the field. The First and Second Squadrons were detailed on the list of the Kansas Pacific Railroad, guarding it and protecting the working parties. Fort Hays, Fort Harker, and other posts along the Smoky Hill River, Kansas, were the outposts of civilization. Beyond lay the hunting grounds of the Indians, and they looked with dread and anger at the advancement of civilization westward.

The colors of the regiment first came under fire on August 2, 1867, about forty miles northeast of Fort Hays, near the Saline River. Company F, patrolling the railroad, was attacked by a band of three hundred Indians. The troop comprised two officers and thirty-four men. The fight lasted six hours. The troop, badly outnumbered, was in the end forced to retire, after inflicting heavy losses on the hostiles. Captain Armes was wounded, and Sergeant William Christy killed.

On the 21st of the same month the second baptism of fire was had. Captain Armes with forty of his men, together with ninety men of the Eighteenth Kansas Volunteers, engaged some thousand hostiles in about the same locality as the first fight. They were hampered by a large wagon train loaded with supplies. The engagement lasted all the afternoon, with severe losses on both sides. One private of F Company was killed and nineteen wounded. The volunteers lost fifteen wounded.

Reprinted (in excerpted form) from Edward Glass, *History of the Tenth Cavalry* (Tuscon, 1921).

Fifteen horses were killed and many wounded. A first-hand account of this engagement would be most valuable; unfortunately, it is doubtful if there survives today any participant.

On September 15, 1868, a detachment of Company G, Sergeant Davis and nine men, was attacked by sixty Cheyennes. The Indians were badly beaten, with the loss of one private wounded and two laborers killed.

The headquarters of the regiment remained at Fort Riley until April 17, 1868. The regiment was scattered throughout Kansas and Indian Territory (Oklahoma); the troops were very much occupied learning their drill, patrolling the Union Pacific Railroad and protecting the far-flung settlements.

The winter of 1867-68 found the regiment engaged in General Sheridan's winter campaign against Black Kettle's band of Cheyennes. This tribe bore one of the worst reputations of any of the plains Indians. They were not confined to reservations, but came in to designated agencies to draw rations, blankets, and other supplies. Black Kettle was a wily chief, and much hard riding and scouting was required before his band was broken up and their capacity to commit depredations ruined. This winter campaign taught them that the troopers could and would follow them to any length, and the Tenth Cavalry did an equal share in wiping out their menace. In one march the regiment was caught in a terrible blizzard and lost over a hundred horses through starvation and freezing.

In the fall of 1868 actual service was seen again. Company I fought a drawn battle with one hundred Cheyennes at Big Sandy Creek on September 15th, losing ten horses, but killing seven hostiles.

In the same month Companies H and I formed part of the relief party to the rescue of Lieutenant Colonel George A. Forsyth, who, with a party of scouts, was attacked and "corralled" by a force of about 700 Indians on an island in the Republican River. Two of Forsyth's scouts stole through the Indian lines and brought word of the perilous situation of the command to Fort Wallace. Parties were soon on the way to its relief. First and last the following troops were started toward it from different points: Captain Bankhead with about one hundred men of the Fifth Infantry, Captain Carpenter with Company H, Captain Graham with Company I of the Tenth Cavalry, and two companies of the Second Cavalry under Major Brisbin.

In April, 1869, headquarters and troops moved to Camp Wichita in Indian Territory.

Camp Wichita was established on the flat directly northeast of the site selected for the post, on the bank of the Medicine Bluff Creek near its junction with Cache Creek.

The only shelter they had was the tentage which they brought with them, much of which had been condemned. An old saw mill was moved up from Fort Arbuckle, fatigue parties were detailed to cut logs in the Wichita Mountains west of the camp, rock quarries were opened in the vicinity, and the erection of temporary shelter for men and animals commenced. These were "jackal" buildings with mud roofs and floors.

Very few of the recruits assigned to the regiment could read or write, many of them being plantation hands from the South. Seldom could one be found capable of clerical duty, so that the officers were obliged to do most of their paper work. Quite a number of the recruits had served in the colored regiments during the Civil War, and these furnished the noncommissioned officers. On the whole the men were obedient, amenable to discipline, and anxious to learn, besides being proud of their uniform.

Even the band was organized, not from musicians, but by selecting men who could read and write and teaching them music. General Grierson, who was himself an accomplished musician, gave them his personal attention and soon succeeded in having a competent leader enlisted and assigned to the regiment.

With this handicap in the way of skilled men, the erection of the permanent post was commenced, principally with the labor of the troops. The government was very penurious in the matter of furnishing skilled labor and material. Very few skilled mechanics were allowed and these only for superintendents and overseers. The soldiers ran the saw mill, quarried rock, burned lime, and dressed and laid the stone in the walls. In this way a post for ten troops of cavalry, officers' quarters, barracks, stables, and storehouses were built.

In the summer of 1872, General Sherman, then in command of the Army, made a tour of inspection of the posts in the Department of Texas. When between Forts Griffin and Richardson they met a contractor's mule train hauling supplies to Fort Griffin. Soon after General Sherman and his party arrived at Fort Richardson a teamster from this train arrived at the post with information that the train had been captured by a party of Indians, the teamsters, except this one, who had escaped, were killed, the wagons burned and the mules driven off. The general and his party continued their journey to Fort Sill. The day after their arrival, being ration day, the Kiowas and Comanches in large numbers, probably seven or eight thousand, men, women, and children, came into the agency, which was on the military reservation about half a mile from the post. "Satanta," a chief of the Kiowas, openly boasted that he was the leader of the band which had captured the train. The Indian agent sent a note to the post commander requesting that he be arrested, also "Satank," another influential chief, and a young Indian named "Big Tree." In the meantime, Satanta and Satank came into the post to see the "Big Chief," who, they learned, was at the commanding officer's house.

The troops had orders to "saddle up" and remain in the stables where they could not be seen. While the conversation between General Sherman and the two chiefs was being conducted on the commanding officer's portico, "Big Tree" rode by on his way to the trader's store. The adjutant was directed to take a detachment and arrest him. He was found in the rear of the store, and upon seeing the guard pulled his blanket about his head and jumped through a window, carrying sash and glass with him, vaulted over a high stockade fence and ran like a deer through the troop gardens toward a thicket. The guard fired several shots at him, and the adjutant (Lieutenant Woodward) mounted, pursued, and caught him just as he was about to enter the thicket, bound him with a lariat and took him to the commanding officer's quarters. In anticipation of the final decision to confine Satanta and Satank, a dismounted detachment had been secretly sent, one by one, to enter the commanding officer's house by the rear and was concealed in a front room ready for an emergency. When the general indicated that he wished them arrested, the guard filed out and surrounded the porch. At this juncture, Lone Wolf, a vicious and desperate Kiowa chief, rode up, dismounted, and came on the porch, smiling and ejaculating the familiar Indian greeting, "How, How," threw aside his blanket and disclosed two loaded carbines, one of which he passed to another Indian. With an almost superhuman effort, General Grierson sprang upon the two Indians, seized the muzzles of the carbines, and sat both Indians squat upon the porch floor. The guard levelled their carbines, but General Grierson's action prevented what, for a moment, threatened a serious tragedy.

Indians were passing through the post and exhibited much excitement. As a precaution, a small detachment of mounted troops was placed at each of the four corners of the parade. Some Indians riding into the post from the southeast, perceiving the commotion on the porch, fired upon one detachment, wounding a horse, and fled. This detachment pursued and fired upon them and killed one, his companion closing in on him and carrying him off mounted. The firing was heard by the Indians at the agency and a wild stampede occurred.

Satanta, Satank, and Big Tree were confined in the guard house and a short time afterwards were turned over to General MacKenzie, colonel of the Fourth Cavalry who came through the post with a detachment of his regiment, with orders to turn them over to the civil authorities of Texas to be tried for murder. As the three Indians were brought from the guard house to be put in a wagon, Satank started a weird chant, which we afterwards learned was his "death song." No one understood him except the other two Indians, who, fearing the consequencies of an outbreak by him, caught him and put him forcibly into a wagon, taking the precaution to get in another wagon themselves. In the wagon with Satank was a soldier of the Fourth Cavalry who was unable to ride his horse. A short distance from the post, Satank, who had concealed a knife about his person, attacked and stabbed the soldier and seized his carbine, which was loaded. The soldier rolled out of the wagon, and the Indian attempted to fire on the guard which surrounded the wagon, but a shot broke his wrist and others soon ended his earthly career.

During the seven years the regiment was at Fort Sill, besides watching and controlling the Indians, it was largely engaged in suppressing horse and cattle thieves and whiskey peddlers.

After establishing and building a post there, this camp was named Fort Sill. Life at Sill was not a picnic. More than once the garrison stood to arms in apprehension of an attack. Scouting parties were continually in the field running down marauders, desperadoes, outlaws, hostiles on the war path, and many times only a demonstration in force succeeded in keeping the Red Men within their bounds.

An example of the manifold duties falling to the troops during this period, is the entry in the regimental return: "Company D – February

25th. Left Fort Arbuckle for Cottonwood Grove to assist Indian agent in reclaiming white children held captives by Indians."

On the 11th of June, 1871, Camp Supply was charged by a horde of Comanches, who endeavored to pursue their favorite tactics of stampeding the horses and stock. The Indians were promptly driven off and pursued by Companies A, F, H, I, K, and three companies of the Third Infantry. In the fight that ensued three soldiers were wounded and several horses killed. The Indians lost six killed and ten wounded.

It was about this time that the colored troopers became known among the Indians as the "Buffalo Soldiers." Years later, when a design for the regimental coat of arms was being prepared, the buffalo was adopted as a crest. The Indians of that day learned a wholesome respect for the tireless troopers who, once on the trail, could not be shaken off.

Among the stations garrisoned by the regiment in this period were Forts Dodge, Gibson, and Arbuckle; Camp Supply and the Cheyenne agency, in the Indian Territory.

A pitched battle was staged in August, 1874, between the hostiles and the defenders of the Wichita agency. The Kiowas and Naconees strongly resented the establishment of the post, and had planned a coup to wipe out the settlers, soldiers, and every building. The hostiles numbered some five hundred. Companies C, E, H, and L of the Tenth Cavalry comprised the garrison.

The attack was launched from all sides by the determined red men. The surrounding prairie was fired at many points, with the purpose of burning the defenders out, stampeding horses, and burning the buildings. The soldiers had their hands full fighting the fires and repulsing the repeated attacks by the encircling Indians, which were delivered with great courage. Affairs were about to become serious, when Captain Carpenter mounted his company (H) and charged through their center. This charge broke the spirit of the attackers, who fell back in confusion, leaving on the field a large amount of booty.

In April, 1873, a part of the regiment made the acquaintance of Texas. Companies E, I, and L were stationed at Fort Richardson; C at Fort Griffin; F at Fort Concho. Headquarters remained at Fort Sill until March, 1875. The troops remaining in Indian Territory took part in the campaign of 1874-75 against the Kiowas and Comanches. In this campaign, Companies D and M, with one Company of the Eleventh Infantry, commanded by Major Schofield, captured a band of more than three-hundred hostiles and fifteen-hundred ponies at Elk Creek, Indian Territory, October 25, 1874.

On the 6th of April, 1875, occurred the chase after Black Horse's band. He was at the Cheyenne agency awaiting transportation to Fort Marion. Knocking down his guard, he escaped and ran for the camp of his tribe nearby. He was killed as he ran by Captain Bennett, Fifth Infantry. This was the signal for an exodus. Practically the whole tribe abandoned camp that night and took to the hills, but not before engaging in a brisk skirmish with Companies D and M, in which one soldier was killed and twelve were wounded. The Indians lost eight killed. Tenth Cavalry marksmanship was improving with practice. After a ten day chase most of the Indians returned to the agency.

Those were the days that tried men's souls, and welded the organizations into bands of true and tried veterans. Captain Bourke, of the Third Cavalry, has written of those days:

> To march into battle with banners flying, drums beating, and the pulse throbbing high with the promptings of honorable ambition and enthusiasm, in unison with the roar of artillery, does not call for half the nerve and determination that must be daily exercised to pursue, mile after mile, in such terrible weather, over rugged mountains and through unknown canyons, a foe whose habits of warfare are repugnant to every principle of humanity, and whose presence can be determined solely by the flash of the rifle which lays some poor sentry low, or the whoop and yell which stampeded our stock from the grazing grounds. The life of a soldier, in time of war, has scarcely a compensating feature; but he ordinarily expects palatable food whenever obtainable, and good, warm quarters during the winter season. In campaigning against the Indians, if anxious to gain success, he must lay aside every idea of good food and comfortable lodgings and make up his mind to undergo with cheerfulness privations from which other soldiers would shrink back dismayed. His sole object should be to strike the enemy and to strike him hard, and this accomplished should be full compensation for all privations undergone. With all its disadvantages this system of Indian warfare is a grand school for the cavalrymen of the future, teaching them fortitude, vigilance, self-reliance, and dexterity, besides that instruction in handling, marching, feeding, and fighting troops which no school can impart in textbooks."

The frontier was an imaginary line when pursuing marauders. A picked detachment of Company B, under Lieutenant Evans, and two Seminole scouts, surprised a camp of the Lipans and Kickapoos near

Saragossa, Mexico, on July 30, 1876, after a forced march of 110 miles in twenty-five hours. Ten Indians were killed, 93 captured, with the loss of one horse. Twenty-three lodges were destroyed. Captain Lebo also led Companies B, E, and K into the Pinto Mountains of Mexico and destroyed a village on August 12, 1876.

The Victoria compaign of 1880 resulted in the breaking up of that wily chieftain's band, teaching it such a lesson that he never again came north of the Rio Grande.

In July of that year, Victoria and all his band broke out from the Mescalero reservation in New Mexico and started through Texas on a reign of terror, murder and pillage.

Colonel Grierson, on a scout with only six men, was attacked by this band near Eagle Springs, and was barely rescued by a reinforcement from Company C, of Lieutenant Finley with fifteen men. Later, Companies A and C came up, driving the Apaches off after a four-hour fight. The pursuit was carried to the Rio Grande.

Under the "Record of Events," the following are typical:

Co. K–Sculptured Tanks, Guadalupe Mountains, April, 1880.
Left Salada Water Holes, Texas, April 1st, arrived at Black River Falls, N.M. Marched thence northward through the Guadalupe Mountains by way of Guadalupe Creek to the Rio Panasco in the Sacramento Mountains, thence to the agency and took part in the disarming and dismounting the Mescalero Indians. April 9th struck the camp of a small party of Mescaleros at Shakehand Springs, New Mexico. Killed one buck, captured four squaws and one child, released from captivity a small Mexican boy (Cayetana Segura) aged 11. Captured 21 head of horses and mules, and destroyed their camp. Distance marched, 417½ miles.

Company A–Near old Fort Quitman, Texas, August, 1880.
Left Eagle Springs, Texas, August 2nd and marched to Van Horn's Wells. August 3rd, marched to Devil's Race Course. August 4th, marched to Rattlesnake Springs; 6th 7th, and 8th, engaged in scouting and picketing the passes of the Sierra Diablo. August 10th, marched to Ash Springs. August 11th, discovered and followed trail of Victoria's band of Apaches from 8:00 P.M. until 11:45 A.M. of the 12th, when, after marching and reaching the Rio Grande, the pursuit ended by reason of the enemy crossing the river into Mexico. Distance marched by company and detachments, 748 miles.

Company G–Sulphur Water Hole, Texas, August, 1880.
Left Eagle Springs, Texas, August 3rd, arriving at Van Horn, Texas, the

> same night; August 4th, 5th, marched to Rattlesnake Springs, Texas. August 6th, engaged with hostile Indians near Rattlesnake Springs. No casualties. August 7th, marched to Sulphur Water Hole, Texas. August 3rd, Private Julius London, one of the party of scouts, was engaged and wounded in action with hostile Apaches near Eagle Springs, Texas. Distance marched 1256 miles.
>
> *Company H—Near Hot Springs, Texas, August, 1880.*
> August 1st, engaged in furnishing pickets and scouts from Eagle Springs, Texas. August 3rd, Corporal A. Weaver, with Private Brent of H Company, and a small detail from other companies, while on picket at Alamo Springs, discovered Victoria's band of Indians after they had crossed the Rio Grande and had an engagement and running fight for fifteen miles. August 3rd, left Eagle Springs in pursuit of Victoria's band. Marched to Van Horn and thence to Devil's Race Course, thence across to the Rattlesnake Springs. August 6th, participated in an engagement with Victoria's band with Companies B, C, and G, under command of Captain L.H. Carpenter, the Indians being repulsed and fleeing to the mountains. Private Wesley Hardy missing in action. Distance marched by company and detachments, 1250 miles.

On January 1, 1881, the designation was changed from "Company" to "Troop."

Regimental headquarters moved to Fort Davis in July, 1882, and remained until March, 1885. In these three years the troops performed the same old dismal frontier service, with few comforts, and no luxuries. But they were close to being a perfect cavalry fighting machine; they were lean and hard and grizzled, and loved a fight. This entry appears in Troop M's records:

> Jan., '84, Piña-Colorado, Texas. Saddler Ross mentally wounded. Sergeant Winfield Scott and Private Augustus Dover slightly wounded, while arresting a desperado on the military reservation. The desperado, W.A. Alexander, was killed while resisting arrest.

The Buffalo Soldiers in Arizona

Edward Glass

In the Spring of 1885, the regiment moved westward into the Department of Arizona, where the Apaches held sway. Geronimo, the Kid, Mangus, Cochise, Alchise, Aklenni, Natsin, Eskiltie, and other chieftains had dotted the plains and canyons of Arizona with the graves of thousands of emigrants, settlers, and prospectors. The department was commanded by that famous Indian fighter and administrator, General Crook.

Marching along the Southern Pacific Railroad, the column was joined at Camp Rice by Troop I. For the first time in its history the regiment was gathered together. The twelve troops, headquarters, and band, continued together to Bowie Station, Arizona, in the Chiricahua Mountains. Here the troops again separated to go to their posts, as follows:

Headquarters and Troop B, Whipple Barracks; A. Fort Apache; C, F, and G, Fort Thomas; D, E, H, K, and L. Fort Grant; I and M, Fort Verde. Lieutenant Colonel Wade took station at Apache; Major Mills at Thomas; Major McClellan at Verde; and Major Van Vliet at Grant. The chaplain held out at Apache.

The Geronimo campaign was under way, and immediately a squadron composed of Troops D, E, H, and K was put in the field under Major Van Vliet. They ransacked every trail in the Mongollon

Reprinted (in excerpted form) from Edward Glass, *History of the Tenth Cavalry* (Tuscon, 1921).

Mountains, even as far as Fort Bayard, New Mexico, but were evidently on the wrong trail. All the troops of the regiment were in the field in this campaign.

Several officers used pull and had themselves detailed with Indian scouts, hoping in that way to get to the front of the front. Lieutenant Shipp was thus with Captain Crawford in his tragic expedition way down in Mexico. Lieutenant Finley accompanied Captain Lawton, Fourth Cavalry, when he forced the surrender of Geronimo and his band.

The second Medal of Honor in the regiment was won by Lieutenant Powhatan H. Clarke, who had accompanied Captain Lebo's troop (K) from Calabasas into Mexico. On May 3rd, 1886, the troop, after a remarkable march of over two hundred miles, came up with Geronimo's band in the Pinito Mountains. The fighting was of a most desperate character; the Indians were in their own chosen positions, in gorges and on inaccessible cliffs. Corporal Scott was wounded seriously, and lying exposed to the enemy's fire. Lieutenant Clarke ran, without hesitation, to his aid, picked him up and carried him to safety through a hail of missiles.

In October, Chief Mangus and his band were run down by Troop H in the White Mountains, east of Fort Apache, after a running fight of forty-five miles over almost impassable country. Captain Cooper then had H Troop.

For most of the troops there was little glory in this campaign. Theirs was the harder duty, to prevent outbreaks, rather than chase the renegades back onto their reservations. Theirs was the dismal duty to guard mountain passes, waterholes, and trails that did not lead to glorious fighting.

In 1887, about half the regiment pursued the "Kid," one of Geronimo's disciples. It was a hard campaign, but unsuccessful. He was never caught; he may still be running. Lieutenant Carter P. Johnson gained commendation by the skill, energy, and endurance with which his outfit pursued this outlaw.

Headquarters move to Fort Grant in July, 1886, thence to Santa Fe, New Mexico, in November of the same year.

The following order was published to the troops in Arizona:

Headquarters Department of Arizona
Willcox, A.T., October 7, 1886.

General Field Orders No. 12:

It is gratifying to the Commanding General to announce to the troops serving in this Department the close of the Indian campaign and the establishment of permanent peace and security against future depredations of the hostile Apaches, as the result of the fortitude and endurance of the troops in the field.

You have effected the subjugation of the hostiles under Geronimo and Natchez, and with the exception of one small thieving party now in Chihuahua, Mexico, all have been removed to a place of safe custody. At the same time the entire tribe of Chiricahua and Warm Springs Indians, whose presence has been a menace to the settlements and whose camps have for years been the rendezvous, the source of supplies, and the safe refuge of the hostile element, have been entirely removed from these territories.

For centuries the warlike Apaches have been a terror to this country. Neither Indian nor Spaniard have been able to successfully cope with them in their peculiar methods of savage warfare, and for years they have retarded the progress of civilization and industry. It was against such an enemy as this, and in a wild, arid country, traversed by a series of rugged and almost impassable mountain ranges, with great scarcity of water, that the troops, already worn and tired, reentered the field.

In the early days of April last, the hostiles, then in Sonora, Mexico, began their depredations, and on the 27th of that month invaded the territory of Arizona. They at once met active opposition; Captain T. C. Lebo, Tenth Cavalry, true to his reputation as a gallant and successful cavalry leader, moving first against them. He followed the hostiles rapidly for over two hundred miles, and finally, on May 3rd, forced them to an encounter. During this spirited engagement the officers and men evinced great bravery, contending against an enemy on ground of their own choosing, among rugged cliffs almost inaccessible. During the engagement, Corporal Scott, a brave soldier, lay disabled with a serious wound, exposed to the enemy's fire, and Lieutenant P. H. Clarke, Tenth Cavalry, rushed to his assistance, carrying him to a place of safety. Such acts of heroism are worthy of great praise. After the engagement the hostiles continued their flight, and for nearly a fortnight the troops, under Lieutenant Benson, Captains Lebo and Lawton, continued the pursuit without cessation . . . .

. . . .Subsequently the trail of the hostiles was taken up by several other detachments acting in concert, each commanded by energetic and capable officers, until Captain J. T. Morrison, Tenth Cavalry, near Fort Apache, captured all their horses, and they took flight on foot south and were driven across the Mexican boundary. The other band, meanwhile, had been pursued by other commands through the Santa Rita, Whetstone, Santa Catalina, and Rincon Mountains, and on the evening of June 5th, when in the Patagonia Mountains, were surrounded and much of their stock and equipment captured by Lieutenant R.D. Wash, Fourth Cavalry.

. . . .The march of Lebo's troop, 20 miles in two hours; Benson's ride of 90 miles in 19 hours, and Dr. Wood's skill and remarkable marches with a detachment of infantry, are worthy of mention.

. . . .Now that all has been accomplished, the troops in this Department will duly appreciate the feeling of relief as expressed by the people of Sonora, Mexico, through their governor, Louis E. Torres, the resolution of thanks for your heroic services offered by all parties in every section of Arizona and New Mexico; the approval of General Sheridan and Secretary Endicott, all of which are most gratifying, but you will regard higher than all praise, the deep and lasting gratitude which comes from the thousands of homes scattered over this vast area to which you have given security and happiness.

By command of Brigadier General Miles:

Wm. A. Thompson,
Captain Fourth Cavalry, A.A.A.G.

Official;
G.B. Russell, Acting Assistant Adjutant General

The regiment was now to lose its colonel, who relieved General Nelson A. Miles in command of the Department of Arizona. His last official act was a farewell to the regiment:

Headquarters Tenth Cavalry
Santa Fe, New Mexico, December 1st, 1888.

Orders No. 51:

In pursuance of General Orders No. 97, current series, Headquarters of the Army, announcing his assignment to the command of the Department of Arizona, the undersigned relinquishes command of the Tenth U. S. Cavalry.

In doing so he desires to express his deep regret at being thus separated from the regiment he organized and has so long commanded, but he is gratified to be able, at this time, to refer, even briefly, to its splendid record of nearly twenty-two years service to the Government, while under his command; rendered, as it has been, in the field and at the most isolated posts on the frontier; always in the vanguard of civilization and in contact with the most warlike and savage Indians of the plains.

The officers and enlisted men have cheerfully endured many

hardships and privations, and in the midst of great dangers steadfastly maintained a most gallant and zealous devotion to duty, and they may well be proud of the record made, and rest assured that the hard work undergone in the accomplishment of such important and valuable service to their country, is well understood and appreciated, and that it cannot fail, sooner or later, to meet with due recognition and reward.

That the high standard of excellence gained by the regiment for discipline and efficiency in the past will be fully sustained in the future; that the most signal success will ever attend the officers and soldiers of the Tenth Cavalry in all their noble efforts and undertakings, official or otherwise, is the heartfelt wish of their old commander.

(Signed) Benjamin H. Grierson,
Colonel Tenth U. S. Cavalry, Brevet Major-General.

Colonel Grierson was promoted to Brigadier in April, 1890, and retired July 8, in the same year, dearly beloved by every man in the regiment.

Colonel J. K. Mizner was next assigned to command, and joined in August, 1890, at Fort Apache. Lieutenant Colonel George C. Hunt was commanding in the meanwhile. The field and staff then comprised in addition: Majors C. B. McClellan, Van Vliet, and Norveil; 1st Lieutenant T. W. Jones, Adjutant; 1st Lieutenant L. Finley, Quartermaster; F. H. Weaver, Chaplain.

The Indians were by now fairly well settled down to farming on their reservations, and except for sporadic outbreaks by a few of the worst, there was little field service. Lieutenant Clarke, with a detachment of picked men and scouts, had a roving commission to run down the few hostiles still "out," and did excellent work.

In 1891 there were two expeditions sent into the Moki country. General Corbin accompanied the latter expedition of Troops B and E.

Colonel Mizner wrote to the Adjutant General in August, 1891, drawing attention to the fact that for twenty consecutive years the Tenth Cavalry had served south of the thirty-sixth latitude, in the most undesirable stations known to any branch of the service, and with fewer accommodations as to quarters or barracks, and requested a gradual change to a northern climate, preferably not further than Kansas. With characteristic kindness, orders came to move at once to Montana, detraining there in midwinter, in a blizzard. The regiment left Arizona in the southern spring.

Relieving the First Cavalry, the Tenth Cavalry took over their horses, troop for troop. Troop A of the First was in Virginia, so to mount our own A troop, Montana horses were secured, brand new to military service. The regiment took stations in the Department of Dakota as follows:

Headquarters and Band, Fort Custer, Montana.
Troop A, Fort Custer, Montana.
Troop B, Fort Custer, Montana.
Troop C, Fort Assinniboine, Montana.
Troop D, Fort Keogh, Montana.
Troop E, Fort Custer, Montana.
Troop F, Fort Assinniboine, Montana.
Troop G, Fort Custer, Montana.
Troop H, Fort Buford, North Dakota.
Troop I, Fort Leavenworth, Kansa.
Troop K, Fort Custer, Montana.
Troop L and M, which were skeletonized, were considered at headquarters.

Life in Montana and North Dakota was a great relaxation for our veterans after their strenuous work in Arizona. They enjoyed the hunting and change of scenery and became acquainted with the country, making long practice marches, sometimes in the dead of winter, through blizzards. Forts Keogh and Buford earned the reputation of being the coldest stations in the country.

The regiment lost Lieutenant Clarke, who was drowned in the Little Big Horn River on July 21, 1893. His death was keenly felt by his comrades. In February, 1894, Lieutenant Finley was injured at drill when his horse fell and crushed his leg. He failed to recover from the amputation; thus in less than a year two well loved officers came to an untimely end.

Troops, B, E, G, and K had some relaxation when they were called out in April, 1894, to suppress a part of "Coxey's Commonwealers." These had held up a Northern Pacific train and were generally obnoxious. Parts of the regiment were called out this summer on strike duty to protect the railroad from strikers.

Headquarters moved to Fort Assinniboine November 20, 1894.

Troop I mourned the loss of First Sergeant James Brown, who was frozen to death in a blizzard February 5, 1895. One of the best types of old soldier, his death was grieved throughout the regiment.

In the summer of 1896 the whole regiment was in the field

rounding up Cree Indians, who were still off their reservations in Canada, and had been stealing and committing minor depredations since 1877. Great bands of Indians were gathered in and turned over to the Canadians at the border. Lieutenant Pershing, commanding Troop D, was out all summer, marching over 600 miles.

Colonel Mizner was promoted to be Brigadier General in June, 1897. His farewell to the regiment is expressed in the following:

Headquarters Tenth U.S. Cavalry,
Fort Assinniboine, Montana, June 7th, 1897.

General Orders No. 1:

The President having been pleased to advance the undersigned to the grade of Brigadier General, he hereby relinquishes command of the Tenth Cavalry and of the post of Fort Assinniboine, Montana.

In severing his connection with the Tenth U. S. Cavalry, of which he has been Colonel for more than seven years, it affords him unbounded pleasure to commend both officers and men for their loyalty to their country and for their devotion to every duty, however trying and arduous.

For efficiency and discipline and valuable service the regiment has a history of which it may justly be proud.

With a sense of deep obligation to the officers for their zealous support and generous courtesies and high appreciation of the excellent soldierly conduct and good behavior of the men, he wishes for each a prosperous and happy future and bids them all farewell.

(Signed) J.K. Mizner.
Brigadier General U. S. Army.

Lieutenant Colonel Baldwin commanded until the arrival of Colonel Guy V. Henry on October 29, 1897.

During this summer. Troops A, E, and K were called out under Major Norvell to arrest several "bad Injuns" near the Tongue River Agency. Trouble was anticipated in arresting the bucks, "Whirlwind," "Shoulder Blade," "Yellow Hair," and "Sam Crow," on account of the attitude of the rest of the Cheyenne tribe. However, owing to the skill and diplomacy of Major Norvell and Captain Read, and not a little to the respect of the Cheyennes for their old friends the "Buffalo Soldiers," the arrests were made without untoward incident, and the troops were recalled.

The War Department saw fit to order the abandonment of Fort Custer this winter (1897) and the garrison moved to other posts. The change was made in December, with the thermometer flirting around the 40° mark below zero.

January 1st, 1898, found the regiment assembled at Fort Assinniboine, less Troops A, B, and E, at Fort Keogh, Montana.

Marching on the mountains (Frederic Remington is fourth in line)

A Scout with the Buffalo Soldiers

Frederic Remington

I sat smoking in the quarters of an army friend at Fort Grant, and through a green lattice-work was watching the dusty parade and congratulating myself on the possession of this spot of comfort in such a disagreeably hot climate as Arizona Territory offers in the summer, when in strode my friend the lieutenant, who threw his cap on the table and began to roll a cigarette.

"Well," he said, "the K. O. has ordered me out for a two-weeks' scouting up the San Carlos way, and I'm off in the morning. Would you like to go with me?" He lighted the cigarette and paused for my reply.

I was very comfortable at that moment, and knew from some past experiences that marching under the summer sun of Arizona was real suffering and not to be considered by one on pleasure bent; and I was also aware that my friend the lieutenant had a reputation as a hard rider, and would in this case select a few picked and seasoned cavalrymen and rush over the worst possible country in the least possible time. I had no reputation as a hard rider to sustain, and, moreover, had not backed a horse for the year past. I knew too that Uncle Sam's beans, black coffee, and the bacon which every old soldier will tell you about would fall to the lot of any one who scouted with the Tenth Dragoons. Still, I very much desired to travel through the country to the north and in a rash moment said, "I'll go."

Reprinted from *The Century Magazine* (April, 1889).

"You quite understand that you are amenable to discipline," continued the lieutenant with mock seriousness, as he regarded me with that soldier's contempt for a citizen which is not openly expressed but is tacitly felt.

"I do," I answered meekly.

"Put you afoot, citizen; put you afoot, sir, at the slightest provocation, understand," pursued the officer in his sharp manner of giving commands.

I suggested that after I had chafed a Government saddle for a day or two I should undoubtedly beg to be put afoot, and, far from being a punishment, it might be a real mercy.

At the adobe corral the faded coats of the horses were being groomed by black troopers in white frocks; for the Tenth United States Cavalry is composed of colored men. The fine alkaline dust of that country is continually sifting over all exposed objects, so that grooming becomes almost as hopeless a task as sweeping back the sea with a housebroom. A fine old veteran cavalry horse, detailed for a sergeant of the troop, was selected to bear me on the trip. He was a large horse of a pony build, both strong and sound except that he bore a healed-up saddle-gall, gotten, probably, during some old march upon an endless Apache trail. His temper had been ruined, and a grinning soldier said, as he stood at a respectful distance, "Leouk out, sah. Dat ole hoss shore kick youh head off, sah."

The lieutenant assured me that if I could ride that animal through and not start the old gall I should be covered with glory; and as to the rest, "What you don't know about cross-country riding in these parts that horse does. It's lucky there isn't a hole in the ground where his hoofs trod, for he's pounded up and down across this territory for the last five years."

Well satisfied with my mount, I departed. That evening numbers of rubber-muscled cavalry officers called and drew all sorts of horrible pictures for my fancy, which greatly amused them and duly filled me with dismal forebodings. "A man from New York comes out here to trifle with the dragoon," said one facetious chap, addressing my lieutenant; "so now, old boy, you don't want to let him get away with the impression that the cavalry don't ride." I caught the suggestion that it was the purpose of those fellows to see that I was "ridden down" on that trip. and though I got my resolution to the sticking-point, I knew that "a pillory can outpreach a parson," and that my resolutions might not avail against the hard saddle.

On the following morning I was awakened by the lieutenant's dog-rubber and got up to array myself in my field costume. My old troop-horse was at the door, and he eyed his citizen rider with malevolent gaze. Even the dumb beasts of the army share that quiet contempt for the citizen which is one manifestation of the military spirit, born of strength, and as old as when the first man went forth with purpose to conquer his neighbor man.

Down in front of the post-trader's was gathered the scouting party. A tall sergeant, grown old in the service, scarred on battlefields, hardened by long marches – in short, a product of the camp – stood by his horse's head. Four enlisted men, picturesquely clad in the cavalry soldier's field costume, and two packers, mounted on diminutive bronco mules, were in charge of four pack-mules loaded with *apperajos* and packs. This was our party. Presently the lieutenant issued from the headquarters' office and joined us. An orderly led up his horse. "Mount," said the lieutenant; and swinging himself into his saddle he started off up the road. Out past the groups of adobe houses which constitute a frontier military village or post we rode, stopping to water our horses at the little creek, now nearly dry – the last water for many miles on our trail – and presently emerged upon the great desert. Together at the head of the little Cavalcade rode the lieutenant and I, while behind, in single file, came the five troopers, sitting loosely in their saddles with the long stirrup of the United States cavalry seat, forage-hats set well over the eyes, and carbines, slickers, canteens, saddle-pockets, and lariats rattling at their sides. Strung out behind were the four pack-mules, now trotting demurely along, now stopping to feed, and occasionally making a solemn and evidently well-considered attempt to get out of line and regain the post which we were leaving behind. The packers brought up the rear, swinging their "blinds" and shouting at the lagging mules in a manner which evinced a close acquaintance with the character and peculiarities of each beast.

The sun was getting higher in the heavens and began to assert its full strength. The yellow dust rose about our horses' hoofs and settled again over the dry grass and mesquite bush. Stretching away on our right was the purple line of the Sierra Bonitas, growing bluer and bluer until lost in the hot scintillating atmosphere of the desert horizon.

Overhead stretched the deep blue of the cloudless sky. Presently we halted and dismounted to tighten the packs, which work loose after the first hour. One by one the packers caught the little mules, threw a blind over their eyes, and "Now, Whitey! Ready! eve-e-e-e – gimme that loop," came from the men as they heaved and tossed the circling ropes in the mystic movements of the diamond hitch. "All fast, lieutenant," cries a packer, and mounting we move on up the long slope of the mesa toward the Sierras. We enter a break in the foothills, and the grade becomes steeper and steeper, until at last it rises at an astonishing angle.

The lieutenant shouts the command to dismount, and we obey. The bridle-reins are tossed over the horses' heads, the carbines thrown butt upwards over the backs of the troopers, a long drink is taken from the canteens, and I observe that each man pulls a plug of tobacco about a foot long from one of the capacious legs of his troop-boots and wrenches off a chew. This greatly amused me, and as I laughed I pondered over the fertility of the soldier mind; and while I do not think that the original official military board which evolved the United States troop-boot had this idea in mind, the adaptation of means to an end reflects great credit of the intelligence of someone.

Up the ascent of the mountain we toiled, now winding among trees and brush, scrambling up precipitous slopes, picking a way across a field of shattered rock, or steadying our horses over the smooth surface of some boulder, till it seemed to my uninitiated mind that cavalry was not equal to the emergencies of such a country. In the light of subsequent experiences, however, I feel confident that any cavalry officer who has ever chased Apaches would not hesitate a moment to lead a command up the Bunker Hill Monument. The slopes of the Sierra Bonitas are very steep, and as the air became more rarified as we toiled upward I found that I was panting for breath. My horse – a veteran mountaineer – grunted in his efforts and drew his breath in a long and labored blowing; consequently I felt as though I was not doing anything unusual in puffing and blowing myself. The resolutions of the previous night needed considerable nursing, and though they were kept alive, at times I reviled myself for being such a fool as to do this sort of thing under the delusion that it was an enjoyable experience. On the trail ahead I saw the lieutenant throw himself on the ground. I followed his example, for I was nearly "done for." I never had felt a rock that was as soft as the one I sat on. It was literally down. The old troop-horse heaved a great sigh, and dropping his head went fast asleep, as every good soldier should do when he finds the opportunity. The lieutenant and I discussed the climb, and my voice was rather loud in pronouncing it "beastly." My companion gave me no comfort, for he was a "soldier, and unapt to weep," though I thought he might have used his official prerogative to grumble. The Negro troopers sat about, their black skins shining with perspiration, and took no interest in the matter in hand. They occupied such time in joking and in merriment as seemed fitted for growling. They may be tired and they may be hungry, but they do not see fit to augment their misery by finding fault with everybody and everything. In this particular they are charming men with whom to serve. Officers have often confessed to me that when they are on long and monotonous field service and are troubled with a depression of spirits, they have only to go about the campfires of the Negro soldier in order to be amused and cheered by the clever absurdities of the men. Personal relations can be much closer between white officers and colored soldiers than in the white regiments without breaking the barriers which are necessary to army discipline. The men look up to a good officer, rely on him in trouble, and even seek him for advise in their small personal affairs. In barracks no soldier is allowed by his fellows to "cuss out" a just and respected superior. As to their bravery, I am often asked, "Will they fight?" That is easily answered. They have fought many, many times. The old sergeant sitting near me, as calm of feature as a bronze statue, once deliberately walked over a Cheyenne rifle-pit and killed his man. One little fellow near him once took charge of a lot of stampeded cavalry-horses when Apache bullets were flying loose and no one knew from what point to expect them next. These little episodes prove the sometimes doubted self-reliance of the Negro.

After a most frugal lunch we resumed our journey towards the clouds. Climbing many weary hours, we at last stood on the sharp, ridge of the Sierra. Behind us we could see the great yellow plain of the Sulphur Spring Valley and in front, stretching away, was that of the Gila, looking like the bed of a sea with the water gone. Here the lieutenant took observations and busied himself in making an itinerary of the trail. In obedience to an order of the department commander, General Miles, scouting parties like ours are constantly being sent out from the chain of forts which surround the great San Carlos reservation.

The purpose is to make provision against Apache outbreaks, which are momentarily expected, by familiarizing officers and soldiers with the vast solitude of mountain and desert. New trails for the movement of cavalry columns across the mountains are threaded out, waterholes of which the soldiers have no previous knowledge are discovered, and an Apache band is at all times liable to meet a cavalry command in out-of-the-way places. A salutary effect on the savage mind is then produced.

Here we had a needed rest, and then began the descent on the other side. This was a new experience. The prospect of being suddenly overwhelmed by an avalanche of horseflesh as the result of some unlucky stumble makes the recruit constantly apprehensive. But the trained horses are sure of foot, understand the business and seldom stumble except when treacherous ground gives way. On the crest the prospect was very pleasant, as the pines there obscured the hot sun; but we suddenly left them for the scrub mesquite which bars your passage and reaches forth for you with its thorns when you attempt to go around.

We wound downward among the masses of rock for sometime, when we suddenly found ourselves on a shelf of rock. We sought to avoid it by going up and around, but after a tiresome march we were still confronted by a drop of about a hundred feet. I gave up in despair; but the lieutenant, after gazing at the unknown depths which were masked at the bottom by a thick growth of brush, said, "This is a good place to go down." I agreed that it was if you once got started; but personally I did not care to take the tumble.

Taking his horse by the bits, the young officer began the descent. The slope was at an angle of at least sixty degrees, and was covered with loose dirt and boulders, with the mask of brush at the bottom concealing awful possibilities of what might be beneath. The horse hesitated a moment, then cautiously put his head down and his leg forward and started. The loose earth crumbled, a great stone was precipitated to the bottom with a crash, the horse slid and floundered along. Had the situation not been so serious it would have been funny, because the angle of the incline was so great that the horse actually sat on his haunches like a dog. "Come on!" shouted the redoubtable man of war; and as I was next on the ledge and could not go back or let anyone pass me, I remembered my resolutions. They prevailed against my better judgment, and I started. My old horse took it unconcernedly, and we came down all right, bringing our share of dirt and stones and plunging through the wall of brush at the bottom to find our friend safe on the lower side. The men came along without so much as a look of interest in the proceeding, and then I watched the mules. I had confidence in the reasoning powers of a packmule, and thought that he might show some trepidation when he calculated the chances, but not so. Down came the mules, without turning an ear, and then followed the packers who, to my astonishment, rode down. I watched them do it, and know not whether I was more lost in admiration or eager in the hope that they would meet with enough difficulty to verify my predictions.

We then continued our journey down the mountains through a box canyon. Suffice it to say that, as it is a cavalry axiom that a horse can go wherever a man can if the man will not use his hands, we made a safe transit.

Our camp was pitched by a little mountain stream near a grassy hillside. The saddle, packs and *apperajos* were laid on the ground and the horses and mules herded on the side of the hill by a trooper, who sat perched on a rock above them, carbine in hand. I was thoroughly tired and hungry, and did my share in creating the famine which it was clearly seen would reign in that camp ere long. We sat about the fire and talked. The genial glow seems to possess an occult quality: it warms the self-confidence of a man; it lulls his moral nature; and the stories which circulate about a campfire are always more interesting than authentic. One old packer possessed a wild imagination, backed by a fund of experiences gathered in a life spent in knocking about everywhere between the Yukon River and the City of Mexico, and he rehearsed tales which would have staggered the Baron. The men got out a pack of Mexican cards and gambled at a game called "Coon-can" for a few nickles and dimes and that other soldier currency – tobacco. Quaint expressions came from the card party. "Now I'se a-goin' to scare de life outen you when I show down dis han'," said one man after a deal. The player addressed looked at his hand carefully and quietly rejoined, "You might scare *me* pard, but you can't scare de fixin's I'se got yere." The utmost good-nature seemed to prevail. They discussed the little things which make their lives. One man suggested that "De big jack mule, he behavin' hisself pretty well dis trip. he hain't done kick nobody yet." Pipes were filled, smoked, and returned to that cavalryman's grip-sack, the boot-leg, and the game progressed until the fire no longer gave sufficient light. Soldiers have no tents in that country, and we rolled ourselves in our blankets and, gazing up, saw the weird figure of the sentinel against the last red gleam of the sunset, and beyond that the great dome of the sky, set with stars. Then we fell asleep.

When I awoke the next morning the hill across the canyon wall was flooded with a golden light, while the gray tints of our camp were steadily warming up. The soldiers had the two black camp pails over the fire and were grooming the horses. Every one was good-natured, as befits the beginning of the day. The tall sergeant was meditatively combing his hair with a currycomb; such delightful little unconventialities are constantly observed about the camp. The coffee steamed up in our nostrils, and after a rub in the brook I pulled myself together and declared to my comrade that I felt as good as new. This was a palpable falsehood, as my labored movements revealed to the hard-sided cavalryman the sad evidence of the effeminacy of the studio. But our respite was brief, for almost before I knew it I was again on my horse, following down the canyon after the black charger bestrided by the junior lieutenant of K troop. Over piles of rocks fit only for the touch and go of a goat, through the thick mesquite which threatened to wipe our hats off or to swish us from the saddle, with the air warming up and growing denser, we rode along. A great stretch of sandy desert could be seen, and I foresaw hot work.

In about an hour we were clear of the descent and could ride along together, so that conversation made the way more interesting. We dismounted to go down a steep drop from the high mesa into the valley of the Gila, and then began a day warmer even than imagination had anticipated. The awful glare of the sun on the desert, the clouds of white alkaline dust which drifted up until lost above, seemingly too fine to settle again, and the great heat cooking the ambition out of us, made the conversation lag and finally drop altogether. The water in my canteen was hot and tasteless, and the barrel of my carbine, which I touched with my ungloved hand, was so heated that I quickly withdrew it. Across the hot-air waves which made the horizon rise and fall like the bosom of the ocean we could see a whirlwind or sand-storm winding up in a tall spiral until it was lost in the deep blue of the sky above. Lizards started here and there; a snake hissed a moment beside the trail, then sought the cover of a dry bush; the horses moved along with downcast heads and drooping ears. The men wore a solemn look as they rode along, and now and then one would nod as though giving over to sleep. The pack-mules no longer sought fresh feed along the way, but attended strictly to business. A short halt was made, and I alighted. Upon remounting I threw myself violently from the saddle, and upon examination found that I had brushed up against a cactus and gotten my corduroys filled with thorns. The soldiers were overcome with great glee at this episode, but they volunteered to help me pick them from my dress. Thus we marched all day, and with canteens empty we "pulled into" Fort Thomas that afternoon. I will add that forageless cavalry commands with pack-animals do not halt until a full day's march is completed, as the mules cannot be kept too long under their burdens.

At the fort we enjoyed that hospitality which is a kind of freemasonry among army officers. The colonel made a delicious concoction of I know not what, and provided a hammock in a cool place while we drank it. Lieutenant F—— got cigars that were past praise, and another officer had provided a bath. Captain B—— turned himself out of doors to give us quarters, which graciousness we accepted while our consciences pricked. But for all that Fort Thomas is an awful spot, hotter than any other place on the crust of the earth. The siroccos continually chase each other over the desert, the convalescent wait upon the sick, and the thermometer persistently reposes at the figures 125° F. Soldiers are kept in the Gila Valley posts for only six months at a time before they are relieved, and they count the days.

On the following morning at an early hour we waved adieus to our kind friends and took our way down the valley. I feel enough interested in the discomforts of that march to tell about it, but I find that there are not resources in any vocabulary. If the impression is abroad that a cavalry soldier's life in the Southwest has any of the lawn-party element in it, I think the impression could be effaced by doing a march like that. The great clouds of dust choke you and settle over horse, soldier, and accouterments until all local color is lost and black man and white man wear a common hue. The "chug, chug, chug" of your tired horse as he marches along becomes infinitely tiresome, and cavalry soldiers never ease themselves in the saddle. That is an army axiom. I do not know what would happen to a man who "hitched" in his saddle, but it is carefully instilled into their minds that they must "ride the horse" at all times and not lounge on his back. No pains are spared to prolong the usefulness of any army horse, and every old soldier knows that his good care will tell when the long forced march comes some day, and when to be put afoot by a poor mount means great danger in Indian warfare. The soldier will steal for his horse, will share his camp bread, and will moisten the horse's nostrils and lips with the precious water in the canteen. In garrison the troop horses lead a life of ease and plenty; but it is varied at times by a pursuit of hostiles, when they are forced over the hot sands and up over the perilous mountains all day long, only to see the sun go down with the rider still spurring them on amid the quiet of the long night.

Through a little opening in the trees we see a camp and stop in front of it. A few mesquite trees, two tents, and some sheds made of boughs beside an *acequia* make up the background. By the cooking fire lounge two or three rough frontiersmen, veritable pirates in appearance, with rough flannel shirts, slouch hats, brown canvas overalls, and an unkempt air; but suddenly, to my intense astonishment, they rise, stand in their tracks as immovable as graven images, and salute the lieutenant in the most approved manner of Upton. Shades of that sacred book the *Army Regulations,* then these men were soldiers! It was a camp of instruction for Indians and a post of observation. They were nice fellows, and did everything in their power to entertain the cavalry. We were given a tent, and one man cooked the army rations in such strange shapes and mysterious ways that we marveled as we ate. After dinner we lay on our blankets watching the groups of San Carlos Apaches who came to look at us. Some of them knew the lieutenant, with whom they had served and whom they now addressed as "Young Chief." They would point him out to others with great zest and babble in their own language. Great excitement prevailed when it was discovered that I was using a sketchbook, and I was forced to disclose the half-finished visage of one villainous face to their gaze. It was straightway torn up, and I was requested, with many scowls and grunts, to discontinue that pastime, for Apaches more than any other Indians dislike to have portraits made. That night the "hi-ya-ya-hi-ya-hi-yo-o-o-o-o" and the beating of the tom-toms came from all parts of the hills, and we sank to sleep with this gruesome lullaby.

The following day, as we rode, we were never out of sight of the brush huts of the Indians. We observed the simple domestic processes of their lives. One naked savage got up suddenly from behind a mesquite bush, which so startled the horses that quicker than thought every animal made a violent plunge to one side. No one of the trained riders seemed to mind this unlooked-for movement in the least beyond displaying a gleam of grinning ivories. I am inclined to think that it would have let daylight upon some of the "English hunting-seats" one sees in Central Park.

All along the Gila Valley can be seen the courses of stone which were the foundations of the houses of a dense population long since passed away. The lines of old irrigating ditches were easily traced, and one is forced to wonder at the changes in Nature, for at the present time there is not water sufficient to irrigate land necessary for the support of as large a population as probably existed at some remote period. We "raised" some foothills, and could see in the far distance the great flat plain, the buildings of the San Carlos agency, and the white canvas of the cantonment. At the ford of the Gila we saw a company of "doughboys" wade through the stream as our own troop horses splashed across. Nearer and nearer shone the white lines of tents until we drew rein in the square where officers crowded around to greet us. The jolly post commander, the senior captain of the Tenth, insisted upon my accepting the hospitalities of his "large hotel," as he called his field tent, on the ground that I too was a New Yorker. Right glad have I been ever since that I accepted his courtesy, for he entertained me in the true frontier style.

Being now out of the range of country known to our command, a lieutenant in the same regiment was detailed to accompany us beyond. This gentleman was a character. The best part of his life had been spent in this rough country, and he had so long associated with Apache scouts that his habits while on a trail were exactly those of an Indian. He had acquired their methods and also that instinct of locality so peculiar to red men. I jocosely insisted that Lieutenant Jim only needed breech-clout and long hair in order to draw rations at the agency. In the morning, as we started under his guidance, he was a spectacle. He wore shoes and a white shirt, and carried absolutely nothing in the shape of canteens and other "plunder" which usually constitute a cavalryman's kit. He was mounted on a little runt of a pony so thin and woe-begone as to be remarkable among his kind. It was insufferably hot as we followed our queer guide up a dry canyon, which cut off the breeze from all sides and was a veritable human frying-pan. I marched next behind our leader and all day long the patter, patter of that Indian pony, bearing his tireless rider, made an aggravating display of insensibility to fatigue, heat, dust, and climbing. On we marched over the rolling hills, dry, parched, desolate, covered with cactus and loose stones. It was Nature in one of her cruel moods, and the great silence over all the land displayed her mastery over man. When we reached water and camp that night our ascetic leader had his first drink. It was a long one and a strong one, but at last he arose from the pool and with a smile remarked that his "canteens were full." Officers in the regiment say that no one will give Lieutenant Jim a drink from his canteen, but this does not change his habit of not carrying one, nevertheless, by the exercise of self-denial, which is at times heroic, he manages to pull through. They say that he sometimes fills an old meat tin with water in anticipation of a long march, and stories which try credulity are told of the amount of water he has drunk at times.

Yuma Apaches, miserable wretches, come into camp, shake hands gravely with every one, and then in their Indian way begin the inevitable inquiries as to how the coffee and flour are holding out. The campfire darts and crackles, the soldiers gather around it, eat, joke, and bring out the greasy pack of cards. The officers gossip of army affairs, while I lie on my blankets, smoking and trying to establish relations with a very small and very dirty little Yuma Apache, who sits near me and gazes with sparkling eyes at the strange object which I undoubtedly seem to him. That "patroness of rogues," the full moon, rises slowly over the great hill while I look into her honest face and lose myself in reflections. It seems but an instant before a glare of sun strikes my eyes and I am awake for another day. I am mentally quarreling with that insane desire to march which I know possesses Lieutenant Jim; but it is useless to expostulate, and before many hours the little pony constantly moving along ahead of me becomes a part of my life. There he goes. I can see him now – always moving briskly along, pattering over the level, trotting up the dry bed of a stream, disappearing into the dense chapparal thicket that covers a steep hillside, jumping rocks, and doing everything but "halt."

We are now in the high hills, and the air is cooler. The chapparal is thicker, the ground is broken into a succession of ridges, and the volcanic boulders pile up in formidable shapes. My girth loosens and I dismount to fix it, remembering that old saddle gall. The command moves on and is lost to sight in a deep ravine. Presently I resume my journey, and in the meshwork of ravines I find that I no longer see the trail of the column. I retrace and climb and slide down hill, forcing my way through chapparal, and after a long time I see the pack-mules go out of sight far away on a mountain slope. The blue peaks of the Pinals tower away on my left, and I begin to indulge in mean thoughts concerning the indomitable spirit of Lieutenant Jim, for I know he will take us clear over the top of that pale blue line of far-distant mountains. I presume I have it in my power to place myself in a more heroic light, but this kind of candor is good for the soul.

In the course of time I came up with the command, which had stopped at a ledge so steep that it had daunted even these mountaineers. It was only a hundred-foot drop, and they presently found a place to go down, where, as one soldier suggested, "there isn't footing for a lizard." On, on we go, when suddenly with a great crash some sandy ground gives way, and a collection of hoofs, troop-boots, ropes, canteens, and flying stirrups goes rolling over in a cloud of dust and finds a lodgment in the bottom of a dry watercourse. The dust settles and discloses a soldier and his horse. They rise to their feet and appear astonished, but as the soldier mounts and follows on we know he is unhurt. Now a coyote, surprised by our cavalcade and unable to get up the ledge, runs along the opposite side of the canyon wall. "Pop, pop, pop, pop" go the six-shooters, and then follow explanations of each marksman of the particular thing which made him miss.

That night we were forced to make a "dry camp"; that is, one where no water is to be found. There is such an amount of misery locked up in the thought of a dry camp that I refuse to dwell upon it. We were glad enough to get upon the trail in the morning, and in time found a nice running mountain-brook. The command wallowed in it. We drank as much as we could hold and then sat down. We arose and drank some more, and yet we drank again, and still once more, until we were literally water-logged. Lieutenant Jim became uneasy, so we took up our march. We were always resuming the march when all nature called aloud for rest. We climbed straight up impossible places. The air grew chill, and in a gorge a cold wind blew briskly down to supply the hot air rising from sands of the mesa far below. That night we made a camp, and the only place where I could make my bed was on a great flat rock. We were now among the pines, which towered above us. The horses were constantly losing one another in the timber in their search for grass, in consequence of which they whinnied, while the mules brayed, and made the mountain hideous with sound.

By another long climb we reached the extreme peaks of the Pinal range, and there before us was spread a view which was grand enough to compensate us for the labor. Beginning in "gray reds," range after range of mountains, overlapping each other, grow purple and finally lose themselves in pale blues. We sat on a ledge and gazed. The soldiers were interested, though their remarks about the scenery somehow did not seem to express an appreciation of the grandeur of the view which impressed itself strongly upon us. Finally one fellow, less aesthetic than his mates, broke the spell by a request for chewing tobacco, so we left off dreaming and started on.

That day Lieutenant Jim lost his bearings, and called upon that instinct which he had acquired in his life among the Indians. He "cut the signs" of old Indian trails and felt the course to be in a certain direction – which was undoubtedly correct, but it took us over the highest points of the Mescal range. My shoes were beginning to give out, and the troop-boots of several soldiers threatened to disintegrate. One soldier, more ingenious than the rest, took out some horse-shoe nails and cleverly mended his boot-gear. At times we wound around great slopes where a loose stone or the giving way of bad ground would have precipitated horse and rider a thousand feet below. Only the courage of the horses brings one safely through. The mules suffered badly, and our weary horses punched very hard with their foreparts as they went down hill. We made the descent of the Mescals through a long canyon where the sun gets one in chancery, as it were. At last we reached the Gila, and early downed a pack-mule and two troopers in a quicksand. We began to pass Indian huts, and saw them gathering wheat in river bottoms, while they paused to gaze at us and doubtless wondered for what purpose the buffalo soldiers were abroad in the land. The cantonment appeared, and I was duly gratified when we reached it. I hobbled up to the "Grand Hotel" of my host the captain, who laughed heartily at my floundering movements and observed my nose and cheeks, from which the sun had peeled the skin, with evident relish at the thought of how I had been used by his lieutenant. At his suggestion

I was made an honorary member of the cavalry, and duly admonished "not to trifle again with the Tenth Nubian Horse if I expected any mercy."

In due time the march continued without particular incident, and at last the scout "pulled in" to the home post, and I again sat in my easychair behind the lattice-work, firm in the conviction that soldiers, like other men, find more hard work than glory in their calling.

Marching in the desert (Frederic Remington is second in line)

VAGABONDING WITH THE TENTH HORSE

Frederic Remington

When once an order is published in the military way it closes debate, consequently, on the day set by order for the troops to take up their outward march from Fort Assiniboine it was raining; but that did not matter. The horses in front of the officers' club stood humped up in their middles, their tails were hauled down tight, and the water ran off their sides in tiny rivulets. If horses could talk they would have said, D–– the order, or at least I think they felt like their riders, and that is what they said.

It is not necessary to tell what we did in the club at that early hour of the day; but Major Wint slapped his boot leg with his quirt and proceeded toward the door, we following. Major Kelly, who was to stay behind to guard the women and children, made some disparaging remarks about my English "riding things" – called them "the queen's breeches" – but he is not a serious man, and moreover he is Irish.

Down at the corrals the trumpets were going and the major mounted his horse. Three troops and the band of the Tenth marched out of the post and lined up on the prairie. Down the front trotted the major to inspect, while the rain pattered and drained on the oilskin "slickers" of the cavalrymen. I rode slowly up behind the command, enjoying myself – it being such a delight for me when I see good horses and hardy men, divested of military fuss. The stately march of the

Reprinted from *Cosmopolitan Magazine*, XXII (February, 1897), No. 4.

Seventh New York, or Squadron A, when it is doing its prettiest, fills my eye; but it does not inflate my soul. Too deadly prosaic, or possibly I discount it; anyhow, the Tenth Cavalry never had a "soft detail" since it was organized, and it is full of old soldiers who know what it is all about, this soldiering. They presently went slipping and sliding into the column, and with the wagons following the march begins.

"Did you forget the wash-basin, Carter?" asks one of our mess.

"Yes. D—— modern invention! If this rain keeps up we won't need it," replies my host as he muffles up in his slicker; and, turning, says, "Sergeant, make that recruit sit up in his saddle – catch him lounging again make him pull mud."

"Man, sit up thar; yu ride laik yu wus in a box-car; be hittin de flat fust, yu reckon," reiterates the noncom.

And it rains, rains, rains, as mile after mile the little column goes bobity-bobity-bob up and down over the hills. But I like it. I am unable to say why, except that after I left school I did considerable of this bobity-bob over the great strange stretches of the high plains, and I have never found anything else so fascinating. The soldiers like it too, for while it is set, in its way, it is vagabonding nevertheless. I have often thought how fortunate it is that I am not secretary of war, because I should certainly burn or sell every barrack in the country and keep the soldiers under canvas and on the move.

The cavalrymen wear great oilskin coats which cover them from hat rim to boot sole, in the buying of which they imitate the cowboys, a thing which is always good for cavalry to do. There are some Montana horses in the command, fierce, vicious brutes, which do a little circus as we pass along, making every one grin smoothly except the man on the circus horse. His sentences come out in chucks: "Dog-gone, yu black son," and the horse strikes on his forefeet; "I'll break yu haid wid –" up goes the horse in front, the carbine comes out at the socket " – a rock." His hat goes off and his cup, canteen, bags, and rope play a rataplan. In plugs the spur, up mounts the pony like the sweep of an angel's wing. Oh, it is good to look upon.

In the afternoon, far on ahead, we see the infantry tents with the cook-fires going. They had started the day before and were now comfortable. As the cavalry passed the "dough-boys" stood grinning cheerfully by their fires.

"Say, honey; is yu feet muddy?" sings out an ironical cavalryman to the infantry group; but the reply comes quickly, "Oh, Mr. Jones, can I come up and see yu groom yu horse this evenin'?" A great guffaw goes up, while the mounted one shrugs up in his slicker and spurs along.

The picket lines go down, the wagons are unpacked, and the herds of horse go trotting off over the hill to browse and roll. Every man about camp has something to do. Here is where the first sergeant looms up, for he who can get the most jumps out of his men has the quickest and neatest camp. It takes more ability to be a good first sergeant than it does to run a staff corps. Each troop has its complement of recruits who have never been in camp before, and to them the old noncom addresses himself as he strides about, overlooking things.

"You sergeants stand around her laik a lot of come-latelies; get these men to doin' somethin'. Throw dat cigarette away. Take hold of this pin. Done yu talk back. I'll tak hold of yu in a minute, and if I do I'll spoil yu."

In the colored regiments these first sergeants are all old soldiers – thirty years and upward in the frontier service. What will be done to replace them when they expire is a question; or rather nothing will be done. Their like will never come again, because the arduous conditions which produced them can never reoccur, unless you let me be secretary of war and burn the barracks.

The tents being up we managed a very bad supper. We had suspected, but we did not know until now, that the officer who was appointed to run our mess was in love. "All the world loves a lover," but he was an exception. That night I did not sleep a wink, having drunk a quart cup of coffee – that kola-nut of the American soldier and the secret of the long marches he has made in his campaigns. I had made out to drowse a little toward morning, when a tender young Missouri mule began a shrill "haugh-ha, haugh-ha," at the approach of the hour for half rations of grain, while presently the bugles split the dawn. Shortly an orderly came in and wanted to know if he could do up my bedding. Before having fairly gotten my boots on, the tent was pulled down over my head, and there I sat in an ocean of frosty grass bounded on one side by mountains covered with snow. Across the horizon was a streak of light, before which stood my tentmates humped in their "slickers" and stamping from one foot to another as they talked.

"How are you this fine morning, you old citizen?" asks my host.

"If I wasn't a d—— fool I'd be miserable, thank you."

The horses are released from the picket lines and go thundering off over the hills, kicking and neighing, glad to get the frost out of their muscles. A herder tries to mount his excited horse bareback; it plunges, rears, and falls backward, spilling the man, and before he recovers the horse has got away.

"Huh!" says a soldier pulling tentpegs near me; "dats de old Caesar horse; I knows him. 'Pears laik he knows a recruit when he sees one."

"What have you got for breakfast?" I ask of the lover.

"Crackers and canned tomatoes – our mess kit is not yet in order. I'll give you your breakfast bacon for dinner," he answers: but he forgets that I am solid with the infantry mess, where I betook myself.

After breakfast the march begins. A bicycle corps pulls out ahead. It is heavy wheeling and pretty bumpy on the grass, where they are compelled to ride, but they managed far better than one would anticipate. Then came the infantry in an open column of fours, heavy-marching order. The physique of the black soldiers must be admired – great chested, broad shouldered, upstanding fellows, with bull necks, as with their rifles thrown across their packs they straddle along.

United States regular infantry in full kit and campaign rig impresses one as very useful and businesslike. There is nothing to relieve the uniform or make it gay. Their whole clothing and equipment grew up in the field, and the field doesn't grow tin pots for head gear or white cross belts for the enemy to draw dead-centers on. Every means are used to keep men from falling out of ranks, for almost any reason they may allege as an excuse. Often to fall out only means that when camp is reached the unfortunate one must continue to march backward and forward before the company line, while his comrades are making themselves comfortable, until – well, until he is decided that he won't fall out again.

"I know why so many of dem battles is victorious," said one trudging darkey to another.

"Why?" he is asked.

"Dey march de men so hard to get thar, dat dey is too tired to run away."

Very naturally when with infantry and transportation, the cavalry have time to improve their mind. Later in the day the sun came out, and Major Wint made them do "some of the things which the fools write in the books," as I heard it put. We were on a perfectly flat plain where you could see for ten miles – an ideal place for paper work. The major threw an advance and flankers, and every one had a hack at the command. I forget how many troops of cavalry I represented, but I did not have enough, and notwithstanding the brilliancy of my attack I got properly "licked." At any rate, after it was all over we knew more than the fellows who write the books, and besides, it was great fun. Handling cavalry troops is an art, not a science, and it is given to few men to think and act quickly enough. As for mistakes, it is a question how many an officer ought to be allowed to make before he has to hunt up another business where he will not have to decide between right and wrong or good and bad in the fraction of a second. It is quite startling how quickly good cavalry "rides home" over eight hundred yards of ground, and when one has to do something to meet it, he has no time to whittle a stick over the matter. Moreover, I never expect to meet any really great cavalrymen who weigh over one hundred and sixty pounds.

Some of the old sergeants have been taught their battle tactics in a school where the fellows who were not quick at learning are dead. I have forgotten a great many miles of road as I talked to old Sergeant Shropshire. His experiences were grave and gay and infinitely varied.

"We used to have a fight every day down on the Washita, Mr. Remington," said he, "and them Indians used to attack accordin' to your ideas. A feller on the flanks nevah knew what minute he was goin' to have a horserace back to the command, with anywhar from ten to five hundred Indians a close second.

"Ah, Mr. Remington, we used to have soldiers in them days. Now you take them young fellers ahead thar – lots of 'em 'll nevah make soldiers in God's world. Now you see that black feller just turnin' his head; well, he's a 'cruit, and he thinks I been abusin' him for a long time. Other day he comes to me and says he don't want no more trouble; says I can get along with him from now on. Says I to that 'cruit, 'Blame yer eyes, I don't have to get along wid you; you have to get along wid me. Understand?' " The column halted.

"What is the trouble, Shropshire?"

"Mule got disgusted, I reckon, sah," said he; and I rode ahead to find a "government six" stuck in the bed of a creek. I sat on the top of the bank as the dismounted men and mules and whips and sand flew, while to my ears came the lashing, the stamping, yelling, and profanity. The thing was gotten out when the long lines of cavalry horses stood under the cut bank and drank at the brook, greenish-yellow with the reflection of the bank above, while the Negro cavalrymen carried on conversations with their horses. Strange people, but yet not half as strange as Indians in this respect, for between these natural people and horses there is something in common which educated white men don't know anything whatever about. It is perfectly apparent that the horses understand them when they talk. This is not true of all the men, but of the best ones. That is one reason why it ought to be legally possible, when a recruit jerks his horse's head or is otherwise impatient with him, to hit the recruit over the head with a six-shooter, whereas all an officer can now do is to take him to one side and promise faithfully to murder him if he ever repeats the error.

In due time the major made a permanent camp on a flat under the Bear Paw range and everything was gotten "shipshape" and "Bristol fashion," all of which nicety is to indicate to the recruit that when he rolls over in his sleep, the operation must be attended to with geometrical reference to the center-pole of the major's tepee. All about was an inspiring sweep, high rolling plains, with rough mountains, intersecting coulées and a well-brushed creek bottom, in all, enough land to maneuver forty thousand men under cover, yet within sight of the camp, and for cavalry all one could wish. Officer's patrols were sent out to meet each other through the hills. I accompanied the major, and we sat like two buzzards on a pinnacle of rock, using our field glasses so cleverly that no one could tell what we saw by studying our movements through their own, yet we had the contestants under sight all the time.

There was an attack on the camp led by Mr. Carter Johnson, one of the most skillful and persistent cavalrymen of the young men in the army, General Miles has said. His command was the mounted band which was to represent three troops, and with these he marched off into the hills. The camp itself was commanded on one side by a high hill on top of which the infantry rifle pitted and lay down. From here we could see everywhere, and I had previously told Mr. Johnson that I thought the camp perfectly safe, covered as it was by the intrenched infantry. It is a fact that officers have such enthusiasm each for his own arm that infantry take calvalry as they do "summer girls," whereas cavalrymen are all dying to get among "foot" and hack them up. Neither is right but both spirits are commendable.

A few cavalry orderlies stood near me while the infantry were intrenching.

"How much dirt does a dough-boy need for to protect him?" asked the saber.

"There ought to be enough on 'em to protect 'em," laughs his comrade.

But Mr. Johnson had told me that he was going to charge the infantry just for the lark, and for this I waited. I cannot tell all that happened on that field of battle, but Mr. Johnson snapped his "wind jammers" over those hills in a most reckless manner. He met the subtle approaches of his enemy at every point, cut off a flank of the defending party, and advanced in a covered way to the final attack. He drew the fire of the infantry while replying, dismounted at long range, disappeared and reappeared, coming like mad down a cut right on top of a troop of defenders. From here on I shall not admit it was "war, but it was magnificent." On he came, with yells and straining horses, right through the camp, individual men wrestling each other off their horses, upsetting each other over the tent ropes, and then in column he took off down a cut bank at least six feet high, ploughed through the creek with the water flying, and disappeared under our hill. In an instant he came bounding up, his squad in line, the horses snorting and the darkies' eyes sticking out like saucers. It was a piece of daring riding and well delivered as a charge, but the festive dough-boys lighted cigarettes and said, "Carter, your d—— band ought to be ready for burial long before now." Heroism does not count in maneuvers and miracles are barred.

This is, in my opinion, the sort of thing our militia should undertake, and they ought to eliminate any "cut-and-dried" affairs. It should be done in September, when the weather is cool, because men not accustomed to outdoor life cannot stand immediately either extreme heat or cold and do what should be expected of them.

Permanent camps like Peekskill are but one step in advance of an armory. They were good in their day but their day is passed in our militia – we have progressed beyond it. Men will be found to like "life on the road," and officers will find that where the conditions of country are ever changing, a week's "advance and outpost" work will eclipse all the books they have ever indulged in. One of the most intelligent of military authorities, Colonel Francis Green, says that our troops will never be called on to fight rural communities, but will operate in cities. This is probably true, but practice marches could be made through populous sections, with these villages, railroad tracks, fences, stone walls, and other top-hamper to simulate conditions to be expected. Such a command should be constantly menaced by small detachments, under the most active and intelligent officers belonging to it, when it will be found that affairs usually made perfunctory begin to mean something to the men.

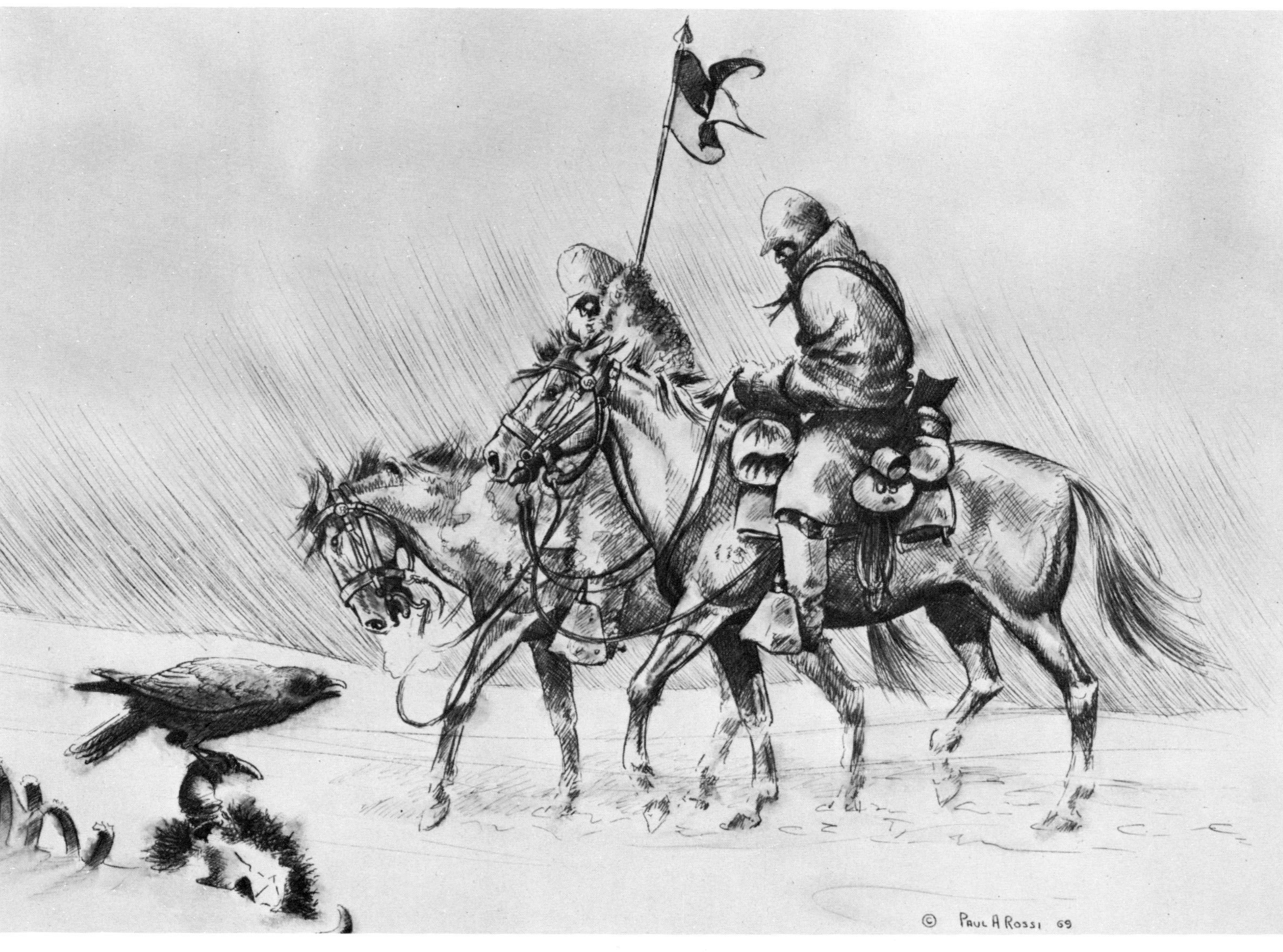

Winter Campaign

The Tenth Cavalry in the Early Days

Colonel H. B. Wharfield

After the Civil War the regular army cavalry was increased by the addition of four regiments, one of which was the Negro enlisted Tenth U.S. Cavalry. The initial strength-return report of the regiment from Fort Leavenworth, Kansas, on September 30, 1866 listed Brevet Major General Benjamin H. Grierson as colonel commanding, Lieutenant-Colonel Charles C. Walcutt absent on recruiting, and the full strength of 1092 Negroes as zero. However some progress in strength was reported on December 31, 1866, with one company officer and sixty-four unassigned recruits increase. During 1867 the recruiting results proved successful and many former slaves from Arkansas and neighboring states were enlisted including Negro soldier veterans with Civil War experience.

It was not long before the Tenth Cavalry started its career as an Indian fighting regiment, which extended throughout the years to Geronimo's time and even beyond to the last Indian fight in the West of 1918 against a band of Yaqui.

The Headquarters was moved to Fort Riley, Kansas, troops[1] were organized, and the units were detailed to guarding working parties of the Kansas Pacific Railroad against the plains Indians. During August and September 1867 Troop F had the initial fighting experience against Cheyenne while patroling the railroad northeast of Fort Hayes, Kansas.

Reprinted (in excerpted form) through the courtesy of Colonel H. B. Wharfield from *Tenth Cavalry and Border Fights* (El Cajon, California, 1964).

Later in the fall Troops G, H, and I had fights with Cheyenne and Comanche.

During General Phil Sheridan's winter campaign 1867-68 against the Cheyenne of Black Kettle's band, the regiment was a part of the forces. Later in 1868 Troop I fought at Big Sandy Creek in Kansas. Then in September Troops H and I and two troops of the Second Cavalry (later designated Fifth Cavalry) rescued Lieutenant Colonel George A. Forsyth's[2] scouts and soldiers at the Beecher Island siege. On this island in the Republican River in Nebraska the small force of beleaguered men had fought off the wild savages for almost four days.

In October two troops, while escorting Major Eugene A. Carr[3] Fifth Cavalry, repulsed some five hundred Comanche at Beaver Creek, Kansas. Captain L.H. Carpenter, commanding Troop H, was decorated with the Congressional Medal of Honor and breveted a colonel for his heroic conduct. General Sheridan in a general field order cited the officers and men for gallantry.

Fort Arbuckle near the present day Davis, Oklahoma, was reoccupied in 1867 by Troup D under Captain J. W. Walsh and Troop L with Captain R. Gray and two companies of the Sixth Infantry. The mixing of cavalry and infantry at the small post resulted in frequent personal clashes. At a time when an infantry captain was in command the hostilities broke out. An official letter was written by a cavalry officer that his troop was getting a raw deal in post fatigue and special duty. That was followed with one complaining that the post surgeon was keeping the cavalry patients for lengthy periods as kitchen police and orderlies.[4] Then the commander had the morale problem of Civil War captains complaining about taking orders from the younger officers who outranked them.

Outside troubles started by the Comanche bothering the Indian agency at Fort Cobb, some distance away, relieved the pressures of post life. At Fort Cobb an advocate of peaceful treatment as the solution for the Indian problems was putting his theories into practice. He was J. H. Leavenworth, a son of General Henry Leavenworth for whom Fort Leavenworth had been named. This offspring's views that peaceful methods could change the savages into farmers were short-lived. After a number of scares and frantic requests for army protection, upon the approach of a Comanche war party in May 1868 he decamped and fled the country.

Thereafter the Department headquarters ordered Colonel Benjamin H. Grierson, Tenth Cavalry, to make a reconnaissance of the Fort Cobb area and southward in the Wichita Mountains for the purpose of selecting a site for a new post. It was desired to have the fort within the Indian reservation where the tribes could be observed. Near Cache Creek and Medicine Bluff he picked out an area which was to become Fort Sill. The expedition went as far west as the ruins of Camp Radziminski, where the gorge of Otter Creek comes out of the hills between two granite peaks.[5]

It was not until the next year, 1869, that General Sheridan decided to build a fort near the Medicine Bluff-Cache Creek area. The task was assigned to the Tenth Cavalry, which moved to the location, and established Camp Wichita. There they built temporary accommodations of condemned tentage with wooden frames and log huts for the officers. The Seventh Cavalry wanted the permanent camp named Fort Elliot in honor of a young officer killed in an Indian fight. The Nineteenth Kansas Volunteers called it Camp Starvation, and the Comanche and Kiowa used Indian names meaning "where the soldiers live at Medicine Bluff." But General Phil Sheridan decided on the name of Fort Sill in honor of one of his officers, Brigadier General Joshua W. Sill, killed at the battle of Stone River, Tennessee, in 1862. The Department of Missouri issued a general order, dated July 2, 1869, establishing the name of Fort Sill.[6]

The next year the permanent buildings got underway. Oak and cottonwood logs were made into lumber by a sawmill moved from Fort Arbuckle, and a limestone hill supplied the rock and material for lime. Many of the original rock buildings still stand (1965). One of the interesting structures is the stone corral, now bearing a historical sign that it was built by the Tenth Cavalry.

The Tenth was stationed at Fort Sill for seven years, but separate troops were detailed at various places such as Fort Gibson, Fort Arbuckle, Camp Supply, the Cheyenne agency, and in Texas at Fort Concho, Fort Richardson, and Fort Griffin during the period.

Not all the duties were construction, drill, and garrison. Chasing renegade savages during the raiding seasons from spring to the fall months further enhanced the reputation of the troopers as Indian fighters. It was during this period that the native tribes called them Buffalo Soldiers because their kinky hair resembled that of "God's cattle." This was a name given in respect, and accepted by the Tenth. Subsequently the buffalo was adopted as the main character in the regiment's coat of arms.

The Kiowa under Santana, Big Tree, and Satank caused much trouble in 1871. During the summer the Comanche attempted to run off the animals at Camp Supply, but were thoroughly whipped during pursuit by Troops A, F, H, I, K, and three units of the Third Infantry.

In 1872 the Comanche and Kiowa were on thieving and "revenge" expeditions in Texas. One night that summer a few Comanche braves successfully raided the stone corral at Fort Sill and ran off the entire horse and mule herd. Major George W. Schofield[7] Tenth Cavalry, then in temporary command of the post, was greatly embarrassed (and what junior field grade officer wouldn't be?) and he made a scanty report to the Department on the matter. One of the raiders, who in later times lived near the post, recounted the story of his youthful adventure with much glee to Captain Wilbur S. Nye. Captain Nye is the author of the story of old Fort Sill, "Carbine and Lance."

1873 was quiet insofar as the movement of large hostile bands was concerned, but small raiding parties continually harrassed the Texas frontier.

The next year the Kiowa and Comanche became restless because of the inroad of whites and the killing off of the buffalo. Many went on the warpath to save their hunting grounds. The peace policy of the Department of Interior, in charge of agents belonging to the Quaker church, could not cope with the problem of taming the Indians. The military was ordered to take over.

General Sheridan's plan of campaign was based on encirclement by all of his forces, and continued pursuit to starve the tribes into surrender. Colonel Ranald S. Mackenzie with the Fourth Cavalry was to move northward from Fort Concho, Texas; Colonel Nelson A. Miles and his column of the Fifth Infantry including Captain Adna R. Chaffee with Sixth Cavalry units southward from Camp Supply; Lieutenant Colonel "Black Jack" Davidson with the Tenth Cavalry to the west from Fort Sill, and Major Will Price with the Eighth Cavalry and Navajo scouts east from Fort Union, New Mexico. Also Lieutenant Colonel Buell's column with Indian scouts were to plug the gap between Mackenzie and Davidson.

This 1874 campaign resulted in forcing the wild hordes of

Comanche and Kiowa to accept restriction to the Indian reservation. From then on the Indian troubles were limited to raiding parties of the young bucks and a few restless renegades.

TEXAS

Texas became the next station of the Tenth Cavalry for a period of seven years. On April 17, 1875, headquarters was established at Fort Concho and troops detailed to Fort Stockton, Fort Griffin, Fort McKavett, Fort Davis, and Fort Elliott. However during 1877 to 1879 two troops under Lieutenant Colonel Davidson returned to Fort Sill for duty. One of the officers there in Captain Nicholas Nolan's troop A was Second Lieutenant Henry O. Flipper, who was the first Negro graduate of the United States Military Academy at West Point.[8]

It was the fate of the army in the West that a regiment seldom had its units at the same post. The Tenth Cavalry, according to my information, did not have all of its troops at one station until the mobilization at Chickamagua Park, Georgia in 1898 for the Spanish-American War.

The duties in Texas were concerned chiefly with chasing small bands of hostile Indians, patrolling the frontier, and endless marching over the deserts or the Staked Plains, the mountains, through the Big Bend country and on occasions crossing the Rio Grande River into Mexico in hot pursuit of Indians.

Two expeditions entered Mexico in 1876 and successfully attacked renegade Indians. The most extensive compaign was the Tenth Cavalry participation in the final 1880 struggle against Victorio and his Warm Springs Apache, who had some months before decamped from the San Carlos reservation where they had been moved.

Prior to the Civil War those Warm Springs Indians had been located by the government on a reservation west of Fort Craig, New Mexico Territory. After the disputatious John P. Clum became the Apache agent at San Carlos, the Indian Commissioner's policy of concentrating all Apache bands at that area was vigorously carried out. However raiding by small groups sorely distressed the frontiers.

When Geronimo, Ponce, Gorde, and other Chiricahua sought refuge with Victorio's Indians in 1877, Clum was ordered to take his

Indian police, asking for military aid if necessary, and apprehend the renegades on the Hot Springs Reservation. This assignment developed into a feud between Clum and General August V. Kautz of the Department of Arizona.

At the agency on April 12, 1877, during a conference with Geronimo and six other renegades, some eighty San Carlos police suddenly charged out of a building and grabbed the seven Chiricahua. This was the "capture" of Geronimo which Clum flaunted before the military as the only time that the renegade had been seized. The Chiricahua and Victorio's band were all moved to San Carlos. For a year or more the various groups remained on the reservation; some peaceful and others out on sporadic raids. Then in 1878 large numbers of Chiricahua broke out for Mexico. Thereafter Victorio and many of his tribesmen also left, and returned to the mountains of their old reservation, hiding out and thieving and killing in New Mexico and Texas.

Troops from various stations took part in the 1880 campaign against Victorio and Loco bands. Among the regiments involved was the Ninth Cavalry (Negro). Since its organization the Ninth had been stationed in the Indian country, mainly at posts in Texas and New Mexico.

An incident during one fight showed the character of seasoned troopers. A patrol of the Tenth under a corporal attacked a band. During the engagement an arrow hit the horse ridden by a brave soldier named Private Tockes, and ran wild into the horde of savages. Nothing done would stop the animal. When last seen the gallant trooper had dropped the reins and was shooting his carbine at the surrounding Indians. Months afterwards his skeleton was found in the area.

In the late summer Victorio and his renegades were driven across the Rio Grande into Mexico. During October 1880 they were ambushed by Mexican soldiers, and Victorio along with many of his followers were annihilated. The Mexican commander was Major Mauricio Corredor, who had been a notorious bounty hunter after Apache scalps. He was subsequently killed during the melee between his nacionales Tarahumari Indian soldiers and Captain Emmet Crawford's forces in the Sierra Madre Mountains. On that fateful day of January 11, 1886, Captain Crawford was fatally wounded while trying to stop the shooting.

In July 1882 the headquarters was transferred to Fort Davis, twenty miles north of Marfa, Texas; remaining there until 1885.

ARIZONA

In the spring of 1885 the regiment was transferred to Arizona for the purpose of increasing General Crook's strength in the planned campaign into Mexico against Geronimo and other marauding Chiricahua. The troops were stationed at Whipple Barracks (Prescott), which Colonel Grierson used for headquarters, at Fort Apache under Lieutenant Colonel Wade, Fort Thomas with troops under Major Anson Mills, units at Fort Verde, and five troops at Fort Grant under Major Frederick Van Vliet.

During the 1885-86 campaigns into Mexico, the Tenth Cavalry was used for duty on the reservation and along the southeastern Arizona border. The soldiers called it the "water hole campaign." A good diary record of the border service out from Fort Huachuca has been edited by Arthur Woodward, "On the Bloody Trail of Geronimo." The recitals give an intimate story of border duty, somewhat similar in general nature to that experienced by the Tenth during later years in that region.

From the strenuous years of field duty the troops now settled down to garrison life at posts on or along the southern perimeter of the Apache reservation.

It is of interest that frontier posts had never been established in the regions between the Apache and Navajo for the purpose of controlling inter-movement between the Indians, such as on the plains.

The relationships between the two groups were minor in nature, due in part to the different cultures. The nomadic Apache had but scant goods to trade with the Navajo, who were a herding people. Furthermore the vigorous Navajo tribesmen were sufficient reason for the Apache to turn southward against the weaker Mexican ranches and settlements for plunder.

It was to some extent a standoff and a case of mutual fear; each avoiding the other. However by chance or otherwise there were some few interchanges between the two peoples. Barnes in his "Apaches & Longhorns" tells about Navajo visiting Fort Apache in 1880 to trade blankets, and of Zuñi from New Mexico with large burro trains of fresh fruit. Perhaps the trading was limited and of recent origin because the Apache made only buckskin garments and woven baskets; and basket making was a common art among all Indians. Trade with all peoples is dependent on a desire for the articles and available routes.

Barnes tells an interesting incident about some visiting Navajo women salvaging condemned army blue uniforms at the post dump. The woolen threads were unraveled and the blue yarn woven into Navajo blankets. My friend, Dr. Cornelius C. Smith, Jr., has a blue Navajo blanket which was secured by his father, Colonel C. C. Smith, commander Tenth Cavalry during 1918-19.

During my assignment at Fort Apache in 1918, a small group of Navajo visited with First Sergeant Chicken's family. They were relatives of the scout's wife, according to a statement of Scout Jesse Palmer. I went over to the wickiup to buy a saddle blanket. However the initial price of fifteen dollars, then "maybe ten do-lar", was twice the price at a Whiteriver agency trading store; so there was no sale.

The mutiny of Apache Kid and his four scout companions at San Carlos on June 1, 1887, was the beginning of numerous scouting expeditions throughout central and southwestern Arizona. This alliance, growing out of a tulapai drinking party, was precipitated by some of the Kid's reservation Apache friends shooting Al Sieber, chief of scouts, in the foot. Thereupon the five scouts and their friends fled and hid out in the mountains. However the Kid was never apprehended. Troop K and Apache scouts with Lieutenant J. W. Watson and Lieutenant Powhatan H. Clarke took an active part in the field. Details of the Apache Kid Incident are set forth in the historical booklet "Apache Indian Scouts" and "Apache Kid and the Record."

In 1891 the Tenth Cavalry sent a troop from Fort Apache to the Oraibi pueblo village on the Hopi (Moki, Moqui) Indian Reservation. Indian trouble had started the previous winter by the government school superintendent enforcement of the compulsory attendance policy of the Department of Interior. It is likely that the soldiers were less than enthusiastic seizing Hopi children and taking them to the agency school. Throughout the spring and summer of 1891 the unrest reached a serious stage. During July military forces under command of Lieutenant Colonel Henry C. Corbin from Fort Wingate together with Troop B and E, Tenth Cavalry, were sent to the reservation. A conference with the hostile Hopi settled the difficulties, and the arrested trouble-makers were taken to Fort Wingate.

Action on the Frontier

There probably has never been a period in American history that has so captured the imagination of millions of people like the time when the Indian Wars were fought. These battles raged all over the West from the Plains to the southwest, from the snow-covered mountains to the prairies and deserts. Playwrights, scenarists, historians, novelists, painters, and poets have all captured, in one way or another, some exciting aspect of this overly romanticized era. Unfortunately, not too many of them have told the full story.

For the most part, western art failed to make clear that this was a period of national disgrace, when the government used the Indians as pieces in a human chess game. Thousands of human beings were fighting for their rights as provided by the treaties which they had signed in good faith but which the government had broken whenever convenient. They were fighting for the preservation of their homelands, their way of life, and their religion. These were familiar rallying cries in American history, but, somehow, were never applied to the "savage" Indian.

Into the forefront of this struggle were pushed the newly organized black units. Their assignment was a price that they paid for having won their victory on the battlefield during the Civil War. They had won their freedom, and now they came to erase the same for another suppressed people.

The four all-black military units built roads where nothing but Indian trails had existed before, while suffering from heat or extreme cold, bad water, unhealthy living conditions, inadequate food, and the possibility of death by hidden sniper at any moment. They soon learned to live under such conditions and to take them as a matter of course. When they were not building roads or serving escort duty they were fighting skirmishes against the Indians. Such, however, was the exception and not the general rule for every cavalry unit in the West. Most engagements in the Indian Wars were ambushes, chases, and roundups for the reservations.

In between these exploits of strength and bravery were short periods of rest and relaxation – usually hundreds of miles away from the nearest center of civilization and from civilian companionship. It may have been these very elements of denial and hardship that made the beginning of the "golden years" for these troops become a reality. After all, before and during the Civil War, denial was a way of life for most of them. The only difference now was the lay of the land and the nature of the "enemy." They were disciplined men; they were anxious men. Their strong desire to succeed existed not only for themselves as soldiers and citizens but also for all the blacks in America. Public opinion – albeit a minority one – would make their presence a difficult one at times. At times it would defeat them; but from defeat grew stronger men.

One of the first major engagements for some of these soldiers came early in 1867, just a year after legislation creating them as a unit, and less than a year after training. The recounting of this episode was discovered within the pages of a book by Elizabeth Custer who had chronicled her experiences along with those of her famous husband while in Texas shortly after the close of the Civil War. As in many other cases the black soldiers' participation in certain combats is reported as secondary to the original intent of the writer. (Also, as has been observed on the part of other writers in the volume, Mrs. Custer falls prey to reproducing the speech of the black soldiers in stereotyped dialect.) In this case, Mrs. Custer was reporting the first fight of the white Seventh Cavalry; but also involved in this fight were black soldiers from another post who were at Fort Wallace.

In 1868, just two years after the organization of the Tenth Cavalry, these troopers were engaged in a rescue mission that was more organized than the rescue role they played as reported by Elizabeth Custer. The second chapter of this section describes this engagement, known as the Battle of Beecher Island, so named after a young officer who lost his life there. Roman Nose was the antagonist – or protagonist, depending upon how one might view the Indian policy existing at the time – in this drama. The episode is made even more dramatic since it was written by a trooper of the Tenth who was there and participated in the rescue.

Before the Victorio and Nana Campaigns got underway, the soldiers had to become familiar with the country through such explorations as those undertaken by Shafter in Texas. They had to know all the conditions that existed in the area, the water-hole locations, where the best river crossings existed, and the topography of the countryside in general. It was necessary to know about the various Indian tribes that lived in the area, their strengths and weaknesses.

In the accounts of the Apache Wars that follow, not only is the thoroughness of the army recounted but also the complete boredom and frustrating routine of this type of military duty. It has been stated that this kind of boredom prompted a great many of the desertions of that time.

In the 1870s there was a long and difficult campaign against the Apache chief Victorio. (His name is variously spelled Victoria and Victorio.) Chief Victorio made all the Trans-Pecos country, which includes parts of Texas, New Mexico, and Mexico, rumble and tremble with rifles and thundering hooves. This campaign against him was made more difficult because of the Mexican border – a line which the troops observed but Victorio did not. The following chapters give a very good insight into the various aspects of this campaign. The strategic aspects of warfare were often as responsible for the defeat of the military as were the human factors. During this time, supplies for troopers as well as horses could not be flown to their rescue whenever they were in need. Indeed, feed and supplies often had to be carried along. When a unit was outfitted for four days' maneuvers, four days it was. Any time beyond the planned period worked against them and aided their enemy. In order to win this campaign, the troopers had to stop thinking in terms of traditional tactics and to start using those of the Indians. It is fortunate that competent men such as Colonel Grierson were able to so expertly use their knowledge of the Indian to aid their campaigns.

The pursuit of Geronimo had been in progress for a few years under the leadership of General Crook. If this heroic leader, well-known for his brilliance of command during the Civil War, had a fault, it was his humanitarianism: He knew, understood, and appreciated the Indian as a human being. In 1876 he had suffered a reverse at the hands of the Sioux just eight days before these same Sioux defeated Custer at the Little Big Horn. His cautiousness and awareness of the limitations of the endurance of men under strain caused him to change his part in the campaign and to retreat, regroup, and resupply. He could have just as eaily plunged pell-mell into battle against the Indians with tired troops and mounts and little ammunition – and might even have won – but he insisted that the men be cared for and his command restored to fighting strength before pushing on.

For far too long, the Geronimo Campaign had been a constant worry to the government and they wanted it ended. Those tactics that had won General Crook plaudits and praise previously were now earning him the disfavor of the government. Another factor which the government did not like – or understand for that matter – was the enlightened attitude which General Crook expressed about the Indians, his "enemies." The General had long since become disillusioned over the government's Indian policy. How it must have plagued this man when he had to make a decision between his sworn duty and his conscience! Letters were exchanged, tempers flared, and General George Crook was replaced in the field by General Nelson Miles. Not long afterward, General Crook resigned his commission and devoted many productive years to working for the Indian rather than fighting against him.

General Miles, fresh from his "victory" over Chief Joseph and the Nez Percé Indians, arrived upon the scene with everything already working in his favor. A new method of communication, heliography, made it possible to send messages swiftly, thereby cutting to a minimum all the advantages of terrain and maneuverability then held by the Indians. New international agreements were also made which allowed our troops to cross into Mexico in pursuit of the Indians, so that the border was no longer an assurance of safety for Indians being pursued. General Miles made short work of the Geronimo Campaign and won the praise of government and citizens alike. In so doing, he also shaved off all the last vestiges of human dignity then possessed by the Apaches.

The century literally ended for the black military in the West in the early 1890s. Of course there were other isolated minor incidents and duties, but the Sioux Campaign of 1890-91 in South Dakota marks the end of their major activities against the Indians in that century. They were to serve in various posts, and were later to be engaged in the Spanish-American War in Cuba. The Twenty-fifth Infantry played a minor, but important role in the Pine Ridge incident. The Ninth Cavalry played a major, but unheralded role in that Sioux campaign. It was yet another incident in which the black troopers' presence would save the day for others.

With Custer in Texas

Elizabeth B. Custer

The first fight of the Seventh Cavalry was at Fort Wallace. In June, 1867, a band of three hundred Cheyennes, under Roman Nose, attacked the stage-station near that fort, and ran off the stock. Elated with this success, they proceeded to Fort Wallace, that poor little group of log huts and mud cabins having apparently no power of resistance. Only the simplest devices could be resorted to for defense. The commissary stores and ammunition were partly protected by a low wall of gunnysacks filled with sand. There were no logs near enough, and no time, if there had been, to build a stockade. But our splendid cavalry charged out as boldly as if they were leaving behind them reserve troops and a battery of artillery. They were met by a counter charge, the Indians, with lances poised and arrows on the string, coming on swiftly in overwhelming numbers. It was a hand-to-hand fight. Roman Nose was about to throw his javelin at one of our men, when the cavalryman, with his left hand, gave a saber thrust equal to the best that many good fencers can execute with their sword arm. With his Spencer rifle he wounded the chief and saw him fall forward on his horse.

The post had been so short of men that a dozen Negro soldiers, who had come with their wagon from an outpost for supplies, were placed near the garrison on picket duty. While the fight was going on, the two officers in command found themselves near each other on the

Reprinted from Elizabeth Custer, *Tenting on the Plains* (New York, 1887).

skirmish line and observed a wagon with four mules tearing out to the line of battle. It was filled with Negroes, standing up, all firing in the direction of the Indians. The driver lashed the mules with his blacksnake and roared at them as they ran. When the skirmish line was reached, the colored men leaped out and began firing again. No one had ordered them to leave their picket station, but they were determined that no soldiering should be carried on in which their valor was not proved. The officers saw with surprise that one of the number ran off by himself into the most dangerous place, and one of them remarked, "There's a gone nigger, for a certainty!" They saw him fall, throw up his hands, kick his feet in the air, and then collapse – dead to all appearances. After the fight was over, and the Indians had withdrawn to the bluffs, the soldiers were called together and ordered back to the post. At that moment a Negro, gun in hand, walked up from where the one supposed to be slain had last been seen. It was the dead restored to life. When asked by the officer, "What in thunder do you mean, running off at such a distance into the face of danger, and throwing up your feet and hands as if shot?" he replied, "Oh, Lord, Massa, I just did dat to fool 'em. I fot deyed try to get my scalp, thinkin' I war dead, and den I'd jest got one of 'em."

The following official report, sent in from some colored men stationed at Wilson's Creek, who were attacked, and successfully drove off the Indians, will give further proof of their good service, while at the same time it reveals a little of other sides of the Negro, when he first began to serve Uncle Sam:

"All the boys done bully, but Corporal Johnson – he flinked. The way he flinked was, to wait till the boys had drove the Injuns two miles, and then he hollered, 'Gin it to 'em!' and the boys don't think that a man would flink that way out to have corporal's straps."

In order to give this effort at military composition its full effect, it would be necessary to add the official report of a cut-and-dried soldier. No matter how trifling the duty, the stilted language, bristling with technical pomposity, in which every military move is reported, makes me, a noncombatant, question if the white man is not about as absurd in his way as the darkey was in his.

Paul A. Rossi

History of a Slave Written by Himself at the Age of Eighty-nine Years

Reuben Waller

I was born January 5th, 1840, and the first sensation of my life was the falling stars in 1849. All the slaves and their masters got together and began a mighty fixing for the Judgement Day. Of course our masters had a greater cause for fixing up things, than we poor slaves did, but we followed their advice.

Well, the next was the '56 Border Ruffian War, and the comet in 1860 just before the Civil War. Well, we all got scared at the comet as its tail reached from West to East. It did look frightful. As we think of it now we believed it was a token of the great Civil War and the completing of our freedom, four million of us.

Well, I come now to the War of the Rebellion. My master was a general in the rebel army, and he took me along as his body servant and I was with him all through the war, was with him in twenty-nine battles.

On one occasion my master's regiment was whipped by General Bank's black soldiers and they captured several hundred of our soldiers and they slaughtered most all of them, crying "Remember Fort Pillow."

We were with General Forest at the shameful massacre at Fort Pillow of six hundred colored troops. And in several battles after that I saw our rebel soldiers reap what they had sown at Fort Pillow.

Reprinted from the *Beecher Island Annual* on the Ninety-third Anniversary of the Battle of Beecher Island, September 17, 18, 1868.

I told my master that the black men done our men like we did them at Fort Pillow, and I asked him why it was that way, as they had slaughtered his son and several boys who were raised with me, and his son that was raised at my mother's breast with me, all was slaughtered as the result of the Fort Pillow massacre. Being a slave and ignorant, I could not understand it and master did not enlighten me on the subject, and I never really understood it till I saw Master Robert E. Lee hand his sword to General Grant at Appomattox Court House.

Well, while being with Stonewall Jackson's cavalry, I engendered a great liking for the cavalry soldiers, and on July 16, 1867, I went to Fort Leavenworth, Kansas, and Colonel L. H. Carpenter was raising the Tenth U. S. Cavalry, and I enlisted on the sixteenth day of July, 1867, for the Indian war that was then raging in Kansas and Colorado. Well, we plunged right into the fights – Beaver Creek, Sand Creek, Cheyenne Wells, and many others. One great sensation was the rescue at Beecher Island, on the Arickare Creek, in Colorado, September, 1868. The Indians had surrounded General Forsyth and fifty brave men, and had killed and wounded twenty men, and had compelled the rest to live on dead horse flesh for nine days on a small island. Colonel L. H. Carpenter, with his Company H, Tenth U. S. Cavalry, was at Cheyenne Wells, Colorado, one hundred miles from Beecher Island. Jack Stillwell brought us word of the fix that Beecher was in and we entered the race for the island, and in twenty-six hours, Colonel Carpenter and myself, as his hostler, rode into the rifle pits. And what a sight we saw – thirty wounded and dead men right in the midst of fifty dead horses, that had lain in the hot sun for ten days.

And these men had eaten the putrid flesh of those dead horses for eight days. The men were in a dying condition when Carpenter and myself dismounted and began to rescue them.

By this time all the soldiers were all in the pits and we began to feed the men from our haversacks. If the doctor had not arrived in time we would have killed them all by feeding them to death. The men were eating all we gave them, and it was a plenty. Sure, we never gave a thought that it would hurt them. You can imagine a man in starvation, and plenty suddenly set before him. He can't think of the results until too late. That is the condition that Company H, Tenth Cavalry, fixed for the Beecher Island men. We were not aiming to hurt the boys. It was all done through eagerness and excitement.

God bless the Beecher Island men. They were a noble set of men.

Now, I shall explain this fight as told to me by the men at the time I rescued them. There were two thousand Indians under the great Chief Roman Nose. They were preparing to raid Kansas and Colorado, and there were no soldiers within two hundred miles and all Roman Nose had to oppose him and his two thousand braves was Major Forsyth and fifty scouts, all dead shots and armed with the famous Spencer seven-shot carbines, a very deadly weapon. The Indians surrounded Beecher, Forsyth and fifty men on this island, which was not protected by anything but a sandbar.

The men dug rifle pits in the sand with their spoons and pocket knives. Well, the Indians shot their fifty horses in about forty-five minutes. Every horse was dead, and the men made breastworks of the dead horses till they could dig rifle pits in the sand, but before this was done, five men were killed and several wounded, and by this time they had dug deep pits in the sand, and had good rifle pits with high banks of sand. You know a bullet can't have good luck going through ten inches of sand. After Roman Nose had killed all the horses, he was sure he had the fifty men at his mercy and so he fixed up a grand charge that he thought would be fatal to the white men, but he had better not have made the charge. It was the greatest mistake that Roman Nose ever made.

He had several rounds with him and he was always careful about mistakes when he met regular soldiers, he was too smart for us. We most always had "heap too many" (buffalo soldiers) and I suppose he thought fifty whites "heap little," but also his fatal mistake.

Well, now to the fight as explained to me by the rescued men. After the horses were all killed and five men killed, the rest of us by this time were well concealed in the sand pits. The grand charge formed. Here they come, one hundred yards away, two hundred in number, three hundred in ambush, open forty-five Spencer brand new carbines. Roman Nose and his grand charge is wiped off the face of the earth. Only thirty-five brave scouts did this job so you see by the brave stand made by the Forsyth and Beecher scouts, hundreds of lives of settlers of Kansas and Colorado were saved from massacre and destruction, by the brave stand of fifty brave men.

Let me say here that I had many fights with the Indians for ten years after the Beecher fight, and I never saw anything to equal it. I say it was the greatest fight that ever was fought by any soldiers of the regular army at any time, not excepting the Custer fight or the massacre at Fort Phil Kearney, and I say further that in all the fights we had with the Indians, I mean the regular army, we never killed as many Indians. I saw Lone Wolf, who was in the Beecher fight, and he told us that they lost four hundred killed and fatally wounded in the Beecher fight. Well, after the fight and rescue we stayed at the island three days. We buried the five men who were killed. Lieutenant Beecher, Dr. Mooers, Louis Farley, and others, with military honors. We used the funeral flag of Company H to bury the dead, which flag I now have in my possession.

At present I have in my possession a scalping knife and a horseshoeing knife that I picked up on the battlefield.

We arrived at Fort Wallace and the scouts were disbanded, and were reorganized under the leadership of Lieutenant Pappoon and rendered military service under the leadership of Lieutenant Pappoon.

Well, after we had been at Fort Wallace about two weeks and the scouts had gotten rested a lot of us soldiers took French leave one night and went to Pond Creek, three miles west of Wallace. Well, when we got there we met the Beecher scouts, as they had been paid off. They sure treated us black soldiers right for what we had done for them.

Of course we lost all respect for prohibition, and of course all got on a very wet drunk. The scouts would have us drink, and we did not resent their courtesy, and everyone in town was on a drunk, and we had everything going our way. But, listen! BANG! BANG! BANG! rang out the shots from a sod house saloon. We rushed in to see what the trouble was and found Sharp Grover lying on the floor with one shot through the brain and one through the heart. Killed by one of the boys who was in the Beecher fight with him. I know the man's name who fired the shots, but I will leave a blank. He (Sharp Grover) came to his death from a pistol shot, in the hands of one named ———.

It will be remembered that in April or May, 1868, five miles southwest of Fort Wallace that one William Comstock had a ranch and was one of the greatest scouts on the plains. He had charge over all the scouts. In the U.S. service, whenever the army wanted a scout we just called on Comstock and he would furnish the man we wanted.

He had under him at his ranch twelve good scouts. He had sent them all out but Sharp Grover, and Sharp one morning came galloping into the fort with the tale that the Indians had attacked him and

Comstock and had killed Comstock. I myself was in the party that charged out to the Comstock ranch to find him shot through the back and through the head. Sharp went back with us. We examined the battlefield. It was a sandy field and it had been tracked, it looked like, by many ponies, in the way the Indians attack. But when we got through we compared the pony tracks to the pony Sharp had ridden to the fort with the report. All the tracks absolutely corresponded with the tracks made by Sharp's pony.

You see, it was this way. Mr. Comstock was brutally murdered, and Sharp marked the battlefield by riding over it to show that the Indians had attacked him. Well, one of the soldiers said, "Sharp, this looks most damn suspicious, and you had better come across."

We arrested him and took him back to the fort. But he convinced Colonel Bankhead and got out of it. But the man who killed Sharp knew all about how Comstock was killed. Comstock is buried in the old cemetery at Fort Wallace. Sharp is also buried there.

I was at the old cemetery in September, 1928, and saw the grave of Comstock, but I could not find just where Sharp was buried, but I know he was buried there for I helped bury him.

Well, we wintered at Fort Wallace, and in the spring of 1869 we took our last farewell of Fort Wallace and we never returned there any more.

We went on a long Indian campaign, almost two years in the cavalry saddle. In the winter of 1870 we go to Camp Supply and build winter quarters for men and horses. Here we had six thousand Indians on our hands to feed. We had to herd cattle for their beef. Well, we had some exciting times getting acquainted with the Indians. They were on a treaty, you know, and just as we were getting acquainted, every devil of them broke and went on the warpath. We lost several men.

There was a stage station about thirty miles from the fort, taken care of by eight white soldiers. They knew the Indians were at peace at the fort and the Indians were at the station every day to trade with the soldiers. But the soldiers didn't know that they had "broken for the warpath," and the Indians slaughtered them at one stroke.

Now came some hard times for us worn out soldiers. We had a hard campaign all winter, but in the spring of 1870 we rounded them up at Fort Sill, Indian Territory. We had the same gang that we had at Fort Supply. We got them all good and fat and they broke again and raided a family by the name of John Friend, scalped Mrs. Friend, brutally outraged several young girls, and killed several others.

Well, we were on their trail. We followed them down through Mexico and back through Colorado and Kansas and rounded them up at Fort Sill. Old Chief Santank and Santa, Lone Wolf and Big Tree, were the chiefs that were at the head of all this.

Well, you see they had out-generaled the soldiers and got to Fort Sill five days ahead of us. When we arrived they were all in camp playing "good Indians." We had two prisoners and some ponies we got from them and they could not deny their guilt. General Sherman had come through Texas and saw and knew all they had done, and was waiting at Fort Sill until we brought them in, so the next day we reported and produced the prisoners and ponies. General Sherman had boots and saddles sounded, mounted seven companies of cavalry, and surrounded the Indian camp. He demanded that they bring out Santank, Lone Wolf, and Big Tree. And they refused to comply, and Sherman gave the command, "Ready, Aim." He gave them five minutes before the word "Fire." Well, they came across very quick. Well, it sure saved an awful slaughter for there were two thousand Indians in the camp. Every man, woman and child in the camp was ready to fight, and if they had not complied with Sherman's request that would have been one of the greatest massacres in the history of Indian wars. Well, we arrested the chiefs, to send to Texas, and the Second white cavalry came after them, and when they started back to Texas with them the Indians broke, but the troops were all in the saddle when they broke.

Well, two mighty dark hours. I hate to talk of it. The Second cavalry had to kill Santank before they left the fort. He concealed a knife under his blanket and attacked his guard and died "game."

Well, I was discharged from the army honorably after ten years, and came to Eldorado, Kansas, and have made my home here since.

Well, after a period of sixty years, there is printed at St. Joseph, Missouri, a small paper called Winners of the West, printed in the interest of the Indian War Veterans, and after sixty years, and in this little paper, I wrote a letter describing the Beecher Island fight of September, 1868, not knowing that there was a survivor of that yet alive. After a few days there was a big automobile rolled up to my door, and who should it be but J. J. Peate, of Beverly, Kansas, one of the survivors who was there with me at the rescue. And all honor to J. J.

Peate. Peate and myself want to be at the monument this September, 1929, if we can. As far as we know there are only three living who were at the rescue, J. J. Peate, Thomas Murphy, and Ruben Waller, who were with Colonel Carpenter at the rescue. One word more about Sharp Grover. He was Beecher's chief scout and should have been the one to go for relief, but he failed to volunteer to do anything to help.

Major Forsyth, in his write up of that fight, named one man his scout who proved to be a coward, in the person of a man named Lane. He must have made a mistake in the name. I don't know why it was not "Grover." It is all over now, only the rising generation ought to have the truth in history.

I visited in June, 1929, I think, as far as I know, the only survivor of the Beecher fight, Thomas Murphy, at Corbin, Kansas. He was in the fight. Well, as my memory fails me in remembering so many things of the past I conclude by saying I have told the facts as near as I could remember them.

I remain,
Yours truly,

Reuben Waller

(Eldorado, Kansas, July 23, 1929 late Co. H., 10th U.S. Cavalry)

Sergeant—Major, Retired, Medal-of-Honor winner

Pursuit of Chief Victoria

William A. DuPuy

In September, 1879, the notorious Chief Victoria with his murdering and thieving band of Indians held New Mexico in a state of terror by his raids and outrages on the settlers. Coming out of Old Mexico these maurauders practically swept over the whole territory of New Mexico, and so rapid were their movements that the military had great difficulty in following them up.

The first attack made by the hostiles was upon the herd guard of Troop E, Ninth Cavalry, near Ojo Caliente and the attack was so well conducted by them that no less than eight men were killed in the short struggle. Victoria's band which had been reenforced by Mescaleros and some Chiricahuas prior to this attack, then made for the hills, and although pursued by the troops they succeeded in carrying off with them about fifty horses. With this attack began a series of fierce and murderous raids, which struck terror to the hearts of the people throughout the territory for it was evident that the few troops alone could not check these maurauding Indians. Citizens at once organized themselves into quasi-military companies and volunteered to aid in checking and subduing these savages.

Near Hillsboro a party of these citizens encountered about one-hundred of Victoria's followers, and in the ensuing engagement they displayed great courage but were unable to inflict much damage

Reprinted from William A. DuPuy and John W. Jenkins, *World War and Historic Deeds of Valor* (Chicago: 1919).

on the redskins whose spirits were buoyed up by reason of their successful escape from the troops and the fact that they were fighting with armed citizens and not trained soldiers. The Indians therefore brought into play their worst traits of savagery with the result that the whites were driven back with a loss of ten killed, a number wounded and scalped, and all their stock captured. This occurred on the seventeenth of September, and on the eighteenth another fierce battle took place at the head of Las Animas River, this time with the troops. Captain Dawson of the Ninth Cavalry in his pursuit of Victoria was attacked at this place by the Indians who held an impregnable position from which it was impossible to drive them, and after being reenforced by two troops under Captain Beyer of the same regiment the hostiles still had the advantage. The concerted efforts of the troops proved unavailing and that night, after fighting the wily redman in his stronghold all day, it was found necessary to withdraw the troops, whose losses were considerable, five soldiers, two Navajo scouts, and one citizen having been killed, many wounded and thirty-two horses lost.

Victoria then proceeded north, with the troops in hot pursuit, and on the twenty-ninth was overtaken and again attacked by Major Morrow near Ojo Caliente with a force of two hundred men. Two days of fierce fighting ensued in which the soldiers succeeded in stampeding the Indian herds and recapturing sixty horses and mules, among them a number of those captured from Troop E on September fourth. On the second day of the fight the Indians killed and wounded several of Morrow's men and then retreated successfully covering their trail. From a squaw prisoner who was captured on October first Morrow learned the position of the Indians, and by a rapid night-march Victoria's strongly fortified camp was captured and destroyed, the Indians, however, escaping in the dark.

During these three days and nights Morrow's command was without water, and as their rations and ammunition were nearly exhausted, the men and animals were utterly worn out.

Morrow's force, now reduced to less than one hundred available men, continued in pursuit of the fleeing Indians, following them by very hard marches over the mountains, through swollen streams and canyons, dragging their well-nigh exhausted horses after them in a tough foot-climb up the mountain side, or down through the dark ravines, and on October twenty-seventh again overtook Victoria about twelve miles from the Corralitos River, Mexico. Taking about forty men with him, Morrow charged down upon the Indian breastworks in the moonlight, and drove the Indians from them, with a loss of but one scout killed and two wounded.

The soldiers presented a picturesque appearance as they quietly rode toward the breastworks, their felt sombreros with upturned brims, their erect forms and their carbines being sharply outlined in the bright moonlight, and in regular order the men approached the hostiles' camp. When within a short time the fight was fast and furious, the Indians gradually backing off until they could make a dash for the dark ravines, where they secreted themselves. Work was then begun on the destruction of the camp, and in a short time the sky was lighted up by the burning debris of what was a few minutes before Victoria's stronghold.

Further pursuit of the Indians was abandoned and the troops returned to Fort Bayard, New Mexico, reaching there November third.

Joe Grandee

Colonel B. H. Grierson's Victorio Campaign

Frank M. Temple

Midway along in his offical report of the Victorio campaign in West Texas during the summer months of 1880, Colonel Benjamin Henry Grierson mentioned that he had been accompanied by his "son, Robert K. Grierson, who just through school, was out in search of adventure and suddenly found it." For "Grierson's brunettes," the Negro troopers of the Tenth Cavalry, the Victorio campaign was a serious military operation; to the twenty-year-old youngster, it was little more than a summer's outing. Robert jotted down his experiences almost daily, and it is upon a few passages in his journal, as well as other heretofore unpublished materials regarding the campaign, that this paper is based primarily.

Judging by his record, Grierson would have preferred to continue his road-building and telegraph line projects rather than to fight Victorio. But he had learned from experience that such endeavors were futile as long as threats of Indian raids were imminent. With energy equal to that in administering his peaceful activities, therefore, he determined to quell any Indian menace as quickly as possible. He recognized his enemy as a ruthless leader who had been trained in all the refinements of cruelty and elusiveness by the great Mangus Colorado, Victorio, who "reveled in a career of murder and rapine" was the chief of "a hard set of outlaws and horse thieves . . . of a low type,

Reprinted (in excerpted form) through the courtesy of the West Texas Historical Association. The article first appeared in *The West Texas Historical Yearbook*, Vol. XXXV (October, 1959).

having plenty of cunning and audacity, and naturally predatory and murderous."[1] In 1879 Victorio had been ordered onto the San Carlos Reservation in Arizona. Fleeing this despised place, he commenced raiding in New Mexico with tireless energy and ferocity. So skillful was he that by late 1879 the troops of the Ninth Cavalry, under Colonel Hatch, were exhausted and their horses worn out.

In April of 1880, Grierson was ordered to assist Hatch in disarming the Indians at the Mescalero Apache Agency in New Mexico. Nothing went according to plan; the most serious incident was the flight of an estimated thirty to fifty Indians during the operation. For Grierson this was the opening move of the campaign, because he predicted that these warriors would join forces with Victorio and move toward Texas.

During the next two months, May and June, such confused and indefinite orders, suggesting the scattering of troops,[2] were issued to Grierson, that finally he requested and was granted permission to dispose of his men as he deemed best. In order to supervise the movements of his troops in person, Grierson headed west from Fort Concho on July 10 with a small escort. He rode forty-five miles the first day. Robert started his journal that night at Camp Charlotte, noting that "We've got a good supply of beer along. Mr. Millspaugh [the post trader] gave us a dozen bottles, and we had more than that before," [3]

Returning eastward on July 29, Grierson proceeded to Tenaja de los Palmos, called "Rocky Point" by Robert, and made camp at this waterhole twelve or fifteen miles west of Eagle Springs. En route an Indian, thought to be one of Victorio's spies, was seen. Anticipating action, Grierson sent word by the eastbound stage driver to Captain J. C. Gilmore at Eagle Springs to send reinforcements. Shortly after midnight, couriers notified Grierson that sixty or more Indians were camped on the Texas side of the Rio Grande. The couriers were sent on with orders for Captain Nicholas Nolan, at Quitman, to join Grierson at Rocky Point.

Knowing that the only water in the vicinity was at Eagle Srpings and Rocky Point, Grierson determined to hold his position, if possible. His force, Robert wrote, "consisted of ten, including the teamsters, Papa, Lt. Beck and me." The wagon, ambulance, and six-mule team were drawn up on the side of the ridge, and on top two stone breastworks were thrown up hastily, named Forts Beck and Grierson.

About 4 A.M., Lieutenant Leighton Finley arrived with fifteen men to escort Grierson to Eagle Springs. Rather than to abandon his position, however, Grierson ordered Finley to establish himself lower down on the ridge. After the position had been secured and his journal entry written, Robert, with youthful unconcern, lay down and went to sleep. He did not make another journal entry for three days.

Breakfast was at 7:30 A.M. Soon after, in Robert's own words:

> The vedettes holloed: "Here come the Indians!!" We made for our posts immediately. The Indians came through a canyon in the hills S.E. of camp & got within half a mile before we saw them. Their intention was to cross northward. After considering for a while Papa had Lt. Finley and ten men charge after a party of them who'd crossed the road – couldn't tell how many Indians there were at first – they kept coming through the hills. Several Indians hid in a hollow till Lt. F. passed, & then fired on his party – he had them on both sides of him & poured it into them thick & vice versa. The rifles sounded splendidly and you could hear the balls singing. Just as Lt. Finley was about to dislodge the Indians from behind a ledge, Capt. Viele's and Lt. Colladay's companies came & in the smoke and dust took F. for Indians & fired on him. F. thought they were troops at first, but when they fired he thought they were Indians and returned the fire. He concluded that if all those were Indians he'd better get back to our fortifications & ordered his men mounted & charged back to camp & lots of Indians following howling like coyotes. Lt. F.'s party killed two Indians & one of his men had his horse killed and the same man had his finger grazed by a ball. All got back about the same time except the dismounted man – he got along as best he could – the Indians were nearly on him – he turned & fired his revolver & this checked them some. We then let fly from our fortifications at the Indians about 300 yds. off & golly!! you ought to've seen 'em turn tail & strike for the hills. If this man had only got back with the rest we could have waited till the Indians got very close to us before firing and would have played hob with them (they supposed that Lt. F.'s party was the whole force). As it was the sons of guns nearly jumped out of their skins getting away.

In this engagement against numerically greater forces (about four to one), Grierson had no intention of seeking glory. As he made clear in a letter to his wife on August 2, he merely was taking a risk, calculated in terms of military duty and necessity. With considerable pride, Grierson wrote:

> It may seem to have been a very rash and dangerous undertaking to get

> ready to fight Victorio and his hundred Indians with only (at first) seven men, but I had looked the ground over well before going into camp, and saw clearly what a strong position I had, and with what ease it could be fortified. I decided immediately what to do, and it turned out to be the best thing that could possibly have been done under the circumstances . . . . If I had not made my stand as I did, Victorio and his whole outfit would have gotten through without a fight, and we would have had only the uncertain chance of pursuit.[4]

Actually Victorio did get through a day or so later, because Grierson miscalculated the next move. Figuring that Victorio would try to move northward through Bass Canyon, Grierson planned to head him off east of the Van Horn Mountains. Victorio slipped by east of the Van Horns. News of his having outwitted his pursuers came without warning, and Robert, writing by the camp-fire when the couriers came crashing into camp like a party of Indians, feared that he had ruined his boots stamping out the flames. By a forced march of sixty-five miles in less than twenty-one hours, and by concealing his movements from the Indians, Grierson reached Rattlesnake Springs ahead of the Indians. Robert marched with the advance guard. "The walking," he remarked, "was awful – sandy, thorny, bunch grass, and here and there you'd step into a hole and jar yourself." His companion "took nearly every [Spanish] dagger for Indians, and brought his gun to his shoulder to shoot several times." Robert admitted that the "daggers with their fan tops [looked] like an Indian feather headdress," and had a terrifying aspect at night." John Bigelow, Jr., in his history of the Tenth Cavalry, stated that the forced march was the crucial move of the campaign.[5] By preventing Victorio's progress northward through Texas, very probably on his way to pick up recruits at the Mescalero Agency, Grierson forced his adversary to retreat toward old Mexico.

Several days were spent at Rattlesnake Springs, about forty miles south of Guadalupe Peak; and at Sulphur Springs, twenty-two miles north of Rattlesnake. Writing at the latter camp, Robert headed his entry for August 11: "Headquarters, District of the Pecos, in the field, Camp at Sulphur Springs, Gypsum Bottom, Hellfire Flat, between the Sierra Diablo and Devilhoof Mountains, Dagger County, Texas," names, he commented, which were "diabolical," but which did "not misrepresent the place." With the immediate pressure relieved, Robert, and even his father, Lieutenant Beck and the medical officer, whiled away their time making "cactus canes – the wood is tough & when the pitch is dry, they look like basket work." The officers played whist in the evening, and Grierson read occasionally in Harper's *Half-hour Stories.* Newspapers were forwarded to the troops, and Robert noted that "The papers (San Antonio, at least) mangle the news in reference to our fights with the Indians." More of this later.

While at Rattlesnake Springs, Grierson had two visitors. One was Captain W. R. Levermore of the Engineer Corps, for whom the highest peak in the Davis Mountains was named, who was surveying sites for new posts beyond Fort Davis. Robert caustically remarked that Livermore would locate the sites "after the Tenth Cavalry had already selected the places," and that if he had arrived the day before, the "Indians 'd've scalped him," and interjected "O! I forgot that he's bald-headed!!" Commenting on Livermore's remark that he had rushed through from El Muerto, Robert stated that a cavalry train had made a routine journey much quicker and added: "West Point tactics & engineering."

The other visitor was Captain George W. Baylor with fifteen Texas Rangers. After a few days of scouting with the cavalry, the Rangers headed southward toward the Carissa Mountains to continue searching for the Indians who had presumably retreated toward Mexico. Grierson, at the same time, circled west of Sierra Diablo, reached Eagle Springs, and then proceeded toward El Paso. En route he stopped briefly at Rocky Point. Robert noted that "the Indians had been there & knocked down the walls. Papa found a sort of wrap made of calico & red flannel – we stuck it away up on a dagger bush."

The dagger bush draped with calico and red flannel stimulated a mild criticism of Grierson's conduct of the Victorio campaign. Writing thirty-six years later, Captain Baylor who had passed Rocky Point shortly after Grierson's last visit, observed the dagger bush. Baylor recounted:

> He (Victorio) stopped long enough to make a scarecrow on top of the hill. He made a dummy of dagger stalks, with arms extended, and placed a woman's dress on it and a sunbonnet. This was to show him contempt for the general not coming on the plain to fight him.[6]

Of the same encounter, J. J. Byrnes wrote to Congressman Throckmorton on August 6:

> Victorio and his band of three hundred or four hundred Indians are sufficient, not only to escape the vigilance of the Mexican troops, but to cross the river at pleasure, openly taunt and challenge the United States forces to battle, and defy their gallant (?) commander (Grierson), who, on their appearance in the country, retreats to an almost impregnable mountain fortress, and commences fortifying. This is the protection the United States Government is extending to its citizens on the exposed frontier.[7]

Though Byrne was careless with his facts, he was correct in his appraisal of the dangerous situation. Nine days after the fight at Rocky Point, while Grierson was heading off Victorio in Rattlesnake Canyon, Byrne was killed, as was also the stage driver, as they approached the Quitman Mountains. Byrne's widow later wrote to Grierson:

> I am fully aware of the enmity existing between your honored self and my husband, but I did not think it would be carried to the extent of refusing a few Negro soldiers – some of them probably having been slaves of mine – to protect the body of him who was murdered on a frontier that is supposed to be protected by you.[8]

Certainly the most vicious criticism of Grierson's activities arose in San Angelo. Evidence points to its instigation by three men: Judge Allen Blacker, William S. Veck, and Henry Clay Bird. Their dislike of Grierson was quite likely due to the fact that he was an ex-Union cavalry officer in command of a regiment of Negro troops. Furthermore, in 1878, he had strongly opposed the removal of the postoffice from adjacent to Fort Concho across the river to San Angelo. Veck and Bird had undoubtedly sponsored the move to change the location.[9]

Lieutenant Robert G. Smither, regimental adjutant of the Tenth Cavalry dismissed Judge Blacker's remarks appearing in the *San Antonio Express* as being so inaccurate that "they must either emanate from his seedy and alcoholic brain or they are the wild imaginations of a scared man while en route from El Paso."[10]

Concerning Veck and Bird, Smither alleged that Veck first received his misinformation from a stage-station keeper named Reilly, who resided somewhere between El Muerto and Quitman, and then caused Bird to do "his dirty work in the way of letter writing." "These two reputable citizens," continued Smither, "who were situated at a very safe distance, some 260 miles, from the scene of the Indian troubles, take this means of venting their hatred for General Grierson, and thus it will be seen that such characters are only plying their daily vocation which they can do without the least compunction."[11]

The Mexican forces contributed little to Grierson's efforts. Though Victorio had both sought refuge and had raided in Mexico for several months, Grierson reported that "There seems to be a tacit understanding between Victorio and many of the Mexicans, that so long as he does not make war upon them in earnest," he would not be molested.[12] Mention has been made of Valle's hapless condition when met by Grierson at Fort Quitman, and Grierson complained that after Victorio's retreat from Rattlesnake Springs, when the Mexicans were in a position to strike a telling blow, Valle headed for "Chihuahua, ostensibly for reinforcements and supplies, but probably an account of threatened [internal] revolution."[13]

No less disconcerting to Grierson would have been the policy of his own government. Under the provisions of General Order Number 9, of the Department of Texas, dated May 4, 1878, General E. O. C. Ord, commander of the department, was granted the authority to permit United States troops to cross the Rio Grande in pursuit of raiders if, "in the use of his own discretion," the situation demanded such a move.[14] General Ord, in 1879, though undoubtedly aware of Victorio's activities in New Mexico and Arizona, nevertheless implied that Texas was immune to Apache forays and suggested that United States troops no longer would have occasion to cross into Mexico. Furthermore, the Mexican government expressed its displeasure of United States forces on its soil, but at the same time was negotiating for the same privilege for itself. Accordingly the order of June 1, 1877, permitting the United States troops to cross the river, was revoked.[15] Grierson, in turn, was uncertain of the current regulations as indicated in his communication to headquarters in October. Having learned "by telegram from the commanding officer at Fort Bliss" that Colonels Carr and Buell had crossed into Mexico, Grierson inquired "Has the United States ordered troops to cross into Mexico . . .? I am not aware of any such authority . . ."[16]

Equally uncertain, and for much the same reason, was Grierson of the exact limits of his district. This doubt was still further evidence of Ord's disregard for affairs in the Trans-Pecos. In 1879, General John Pope had been advised of Ord's ignorance of the boundaries of his department, and cautioned the latter of his "misapprehension which it seems has misled him in several instances, and which I request be corrected."[17]

In the midst of the campaign, the War Department was informed by Grierson of his opinion of the Indian Bureau. Reporting upon his trip of the previous April to New Mexico, he described the Mescalero Apache Agency as "simply a sort of hospital for old and infirm Indians, and a safe refuge and a convenient place . . . to obtain supplies . . . virtually a supply camp for Victorio's band." Grierson stated that the troops would, however, pursue the Indians and force their eventual surrender "unless the kind friends of the marauders step in and, through their influence with the Interior Department, save the Indians for humanity sake and for the use in future wars."[18] On this occasion Grierson revealed that though he usually regarded the Indians with some sympathy, he regarded Victorio as brutal and degenerate, an animal undeserving of any consideration whatever. His attitude was reflected in his exposure to danger and his relentless driving of his men when circumstances demanded it.

The Battle at Rattlesnake Springs

1880 was the year of decision in the Trans-Pecos. Thirty years of warfare between the Mescalero Apaches and the U.S. Army were drawing to a close, although neither side was yet aware of this.

All those years of ambushes, raids, skirmishes, campaigns, and frustration came to a head in July and August. The dusty mountains looked down that summer on the last cavalry charges across the alkali plains of West Texas. A way of life was ending even though it would take several more years to bury the corpse.

Colonels and chiefs beyond recall had entered this harsh land. They had learned to live with the country but not with each other. Now, the struggle had come down to two men. Each of these two leaders had already carved for himself a niche in the hall of warriors. Each was keenly aware of the other's skills and reputation. Each despised the other. Each was determined to emerge victorious.

Colonel Benjamin H. Grierson, commanding officer of the Tenth Cavalry Regiment, had persuaded his superiors that the enemy could be overcome here in the Trans-Pecos. He argued successfully that there was nothing to be gained by concentrating troops to the north in New Mexico as had first been proposed. He knew the waterholes and springs of West Texas, and he knew the Indians could not pass through the country without using them. He had the troops to guard these sources

Reprinted from an unpublished manuscript at the Fort Davis National Historic Site, Texas, with their permission.

and was sure he could channel the Apaches' movements to where he wanted them.

Victorio, the greatest of all Apache chiefs, waited in the security of his mountain retreat in Mexico. Soon he would have to order his men to ride north across the Rio Grande to raid for supplies and ammunition. He was not alarmed over Grierson's buffalo soldiers. He had not out-maneuvered and outwitted a multitude of Army officers just to become a worrier. As it had always happened, he would cross the river and the dry land beyond to raid the settlements of New Mexico. Grierson was but the thorn of another cactus – to be avoided or, if necessary, to be torn from the hide and cast aside.

In late July, Victorio crossed the river and met Grierson's soldiers at Tinaja de las Palmas, an insignificant waterhole that has not survived on the most detailed of maps. And Grierson stopped the Apache and forced him to retreat to Mexico. Victorio prepared to come again. Grierson waited and watched.

The fight at Tinaja de las Palmas occurred on July 30. After the Indians withdrew and on the same day, Colonel Grierson marched his men – Troops A, C, and G, Tenth Cavalry – to Eagle Springs, eighteen miles to the northeast. Already at the springs were Company H, Twenty-fourth Infantry, and Company H, Tenth Cavalry. For the next few days, pickets and scouts scoured the country searching for signs that Victorio had recrossed the river.

Grierson's knowledge of the country led him to believe that next time Victorio would try to bypass him farther down the river. The most likely trail, the colonel decided, lay beyond the Van Horn Mountains, thirty-five miles to the east. On August 2, leaving part of his command at Eagle Springs – in case he was wrong – Grierson marched to Van Horn Wells.

He was almost right. On August 3, Corporal A. Weaver, Troop H, led his small patrol toward Alamo Springs, a trickle of water between Eagle Mountains and Van Horn Mountains. Corporal Weaver's name entered the dispatches that day, for it was he who discovered Victorio. The Indians had crossed the river about where Grierson had figured they would.

Weaver rose to this mighty occasion and with his handful of men engaged Victorio's band in a running fight. It was a brave but useless gesture. The Apaches disappeared toward the north; Weaver hastened to give the alarm.

Although Grierson had been right about the river crossing, he was wrong concerning Victorio's next move. Victorio did not pass around the east end of the Van Horn Mountains, where the troops lay in wait. He continued to ride north where he and his Apaches melted into the wilderness of the Devil's own country, the Sierra Diablo.

When Grierson heard about Corporal Weaver's adventures, he sat down to study his maps. He saw that Victorio would have to head for the wide valley called Salt Flat. This forsaken area had the region's only springs between the Van Horn Mountains and the Guadalupe range on the New Mexico border farther to the north. Paralleling this valley to the east were the broken escarpments called the Delaware and Apache Mountains. The western side of Salt Flat was dominated by the terrible, thoroughly dry Sierra Diablo. Without access to the springs of the valley, Victorio could not reach the plunder of New Mexico.

Grierson knew his men would have to reach these waterholes first. If they failed, Victorio would be in New Mexico and Grierson would be in disgrace.

Before dawn August 5, Grierson began a desperate race to beat Victorio to Rattlesnake Springs on Salt Flat.

A small spur of hills, Baylor Mountains, penetrates the center of Salt Flat from the south. The cavalry's route was along the east side of this spur. Victorio was somewhere on the west. Grierson, his small headquarters, and his son Robert traveled in two ambulances. With them were several freight wagons carrying food and other immediately needed supplies. For most of the day the cavalry troops rode with them. By sundown, however, the cavalry moved on ahead and reached Rattlesnake Springs at midnight. They had ridden sixty-five miles through some of Texas' most desolate country in just twenty-one hours. It was a strenuous ride and only hardened and experienced men could have done it. The price would be paid later when each captain sadly recorded the great number of horses "broken down" as a result of it. The colonel himself arrived at 3:30 A.M., August 6. Robert Grierson described the march:

> Our mules are very tired, and all of us had to walk . . . except a couple of sick men in Doctor's ambulance. Now and then we got into the

> ambulance or wagon for a minute or so to rest our legs. We had no trouble following the trail, but our mules gave out . . . .
> The [telegraph] operator took every dagger for Indians . . . I confess these daggers with their fan tops, like an Indian feather headdress, have a terrifying aspect at night. The walking was awful – sandy, thorny, bunch grass. . . .

As dawn flooded over the Delaware Mountains and reached across Salt Flat to light the Diablo, the scouts made their reports. Grierson learned he had won the race. Victorio had underestimated the soldiers and had not driven his own men hard enough. His band was camped at Fresno Springs at the south end of the Sierra Diablo. The colonel could now wait for the Apache to appear.

With him and nearby, Grierson had six troops of cavalry and one company of infantry. Not before in the history of the Trans-Pecos had there been so large a concentration of troops. The infantry company, H of the Twenty-fourth, was still to the south. It had left Horn Wells the same time as the rest of the command; but its unrewarding job was to guard the slow-moving supply train that would reach Rattlesnake Springs before the day was out. High on top of the Sierra Diabo, Troop K of the Tenth Cavalry, under Captain Thomas C. Lebo, had been scouting the rough terrain for Indian tracks since August 1. It had discovered what it believed to be Victorio's advance supply camp on August 2. During the next few days it was engaged in chasing this group of Indians that had fled in great disorder, abandoning all the supplies. Troop K was not to come down to Salt Flat until August 7, one day too late for the big show.

Despite the long march there was no rest for the five troops with Grierson on August 6. Immediately, he ordered Captain Nicholas Nolan's Troop A, Tenth Cavalry, to patrol the passes of the mountains. This troop was to ride a total of more than six hundred miles in the next few days. Only then would it get a chance to really rest.

This left the colonel with four troops with which to set his trap for Victorio: Troops B, C, G, and H, all of the Tenth Cavalry. These he formed into a battalion under the command of Captain Louis H. Carpenter.

During the morning, scouts reported in with news of Victorio's warriors. From these reports, Grierson decided the Apaches would come down an arroyo named Rattlesnake Canyon. In this canyon, in carefully selected positions, Carpenter placed Troops C and G under the command of Captain Charles D. Viele. For the time being, Carpenter decided to hold B and H in reserve. For some unstated reason, Grierson, rather than taking a direct hand in the coming fight, remained at Rattlesnake Springs some distance from and out of sight of Viele's position. Grierson was to regret this later.[1]

Early in the afternoon, Victorio and his warriors approached the springs. Young Robert recorded the events:

> Captain Viele "C" Company, and Lieutenant Ayres with "G" Company moved southward in the forenoon, and about 2 P.M. we heard volleys. It was Victorio's main outfit, and seeing there were but two companies charged for the troops, but just at this time . . . Captain Carpenter "H" and Lieutenant Jones "B" reinforced Viele, and the Indians, greatly surprised, fled for the hills and mountains.

This must have been a disappointment to Grierson. After two weeks of forced marches and two engagements, was this all that was to be accomplished? He had succeeded in getting in front of the enemy; he had guessed Victorio's intentions correctly; his men were ready to fight. Surely there should have been more decisive action than merely causing "the disconcerted Indians to flee and again scatter in the hills and ravines."

But there was more to come. Another drama was about to unfold. In that pause following the skirmish, in which both sides pondered what to do next, there occurred what has since become a Western cliché. To the southeast, rounding the Baylor Mountains, the supply train came into view. Guarded by Captain John C. Gilmore's Company H, Twenty-fourth Infantry, and a scattering of cavalry, it snaked its way toward the springs.

The temptation was too much. A group of Victorio's braves, whooping and yelping, roared out of a canyon toward the wagons. But it was a futile attack. The guard poured out a warm welcome and the Indians, carrying off several badly wounded warriors, fled back from whence they came. But they found no shelter. When these Indians had attacked the caravan, Carpenter had ordered his battalion forward and now gave chase to the fleeing figures. He followed the band until the gathering darkness allowed the Indians to make good their escape. Then he returned to the camp at the spring.

Victorio had had enough. Once again he led his people south toward the river. The battle of Rattlesnake Springs was over.

Twice Grierson had stopped Victorio – at Tinaja de las Palmas and now at Rattlesnake Springs. He did not defeat the Apache, but he had stopped him. No one had done that before.

The Apaches remained in the hills for a few days as if it were difficult for them to realize they could not go to New Mexico. But Victorio knew and, dejectedly, he led his warriors back to their mountains in Mexico. During the next week. Grierson's troops scoured the Sierra Diablo and all the springs between there and the river. There was a small skirmish or two but the evidence accumulated that Victorio had retreated.

Colonel Grierson attempted to get permission to enter Mexico. It was he who had hurt Victorio and now he wished to administer the death blow. His request was denied. He took what satisfaction he could in penning his report:

> From the 28th of July, when they first crossed into Texas, until August 12, when Victorio and the last of his badly demoralized band were the second time driven across the Rio Grande, their loss in the fights at Tenaja de los Palmos [sic] and Rattlesnake Spring, and in the several skirmishes, were certainly thirty killed and wounded, very probably fifty, besides the loss of all their supplies, and from seventy-five to one hundred animals.

On October 14 Victorio and most of his followers were killed by the Mexican colonel, Joaquin Terrazas. The Mescalero Apache threat to the Trans-Pecos ceased. Peace came to the bare-bone land. In a certain way, the cavalry colonel had won.

Captain Dodge's Colored Troops to the rescue *Frederic Remington*

The Thornburgh Battle with the Utes on Milk Creek

Elmer R. Burkey

During the first days of October, 1879, the people of Colorado and adjacent states were horrified by the news that Mr. N. C. Meeker, agent of the White River Indian Agency in western Colorado, and several other Agency employees had been killed by the Ute Indians, and the women and children had been carried into captivity; also that the United States soldiers from Fort Steele, Wyoming, who were on their way to the White River Agency, had been ambushed by Indians and many had been killed and wounded. Although trouble with these Indians had been freely predicted during the previous months and great anxiety had prevailed in the Ute Indian country, the news of this tragedy came as a shock to the people of Colorado.

For several months previous to this occurrence the Colorado papers had carried many stories of outrages and depredations which the Ute Indians of western Colorado were alleged to have committed. Also much had been written and reported concerning the administration of the White River Agency by Agent Meeker, and much correspondence had taken place between Mr. Meeker and the War and the Interior Departments relative to his plans and troubles at the Agency.

This article is not concerned with the facts or supposed facts of Mr. Meeker's administration of the White River Agency, nor with the charges and counter-charges made by the various parties concerned in

Reprinted through the courtesy of *Colorado Magazine*, ed. Maxine Benson. The article first appeared in May, 1936.

them. Those who are interested may find in the files of the War Department and the Government Miscellaneous Documents the complete and official reports of the investigating committees who inquired into the causes which led to the calling of the troops, the fight with these troops, and the massacre at the Agency.

The writer, after visiting the battleground and making a study of all available records, will attempt to present only the incidents immediately preceding the fight, the events of the battle, and the rescue of the beleagured soldiers by General Merritt.

After several requests had been made by Mr. Meeker, officials of Colorado, and others, the War Department issued orders for a military expedition to proceed to the White River Agency for the purpose of establishing peaceable relations between the Utes and the white settlers in western Colorado, and to arrest, if necessary, those who were the instigators of trouble.

On September 16, 1879, General Crook, commanding the Department of the Platte, issued orders based on endorsements from army headquarters, to Major T. T. Thornburgh, commander at Fort Steele, Wyoming, "to move with a sufficient number of troops to the White River Ute Agency, Colorado, under special instructions." [1]

Although Mr. Meeker had asked for only one hundred men, Major Thornburgh organized an expedition consisting of Companies D and F of the Fifth Cavalry, commanded by Captain J. S. Payne and Lieutenant B. D. Price, the entire fighting strength being about one hundred and eighty men. A supply train of twenty-five wagons, carrying rations for thirty days and forage for fifteen days, in charge of teamster McKinstry, accompanied the troops. Lieutenant S. A. Wolf, Fourth Infantry, was quartermaster and commissary, and Dr. R. B. Grimes the accompanying surgeon. Mr. Joe Rankin, stableman of Rawlins, who formerly carried mail to the agency on horseback, acted as guide for the troops.

S. A. Cherry, Lieutenant in the Fifth Cavalry, who was stationed at Fort D. A. Russell, was ordered to join Major Thornburgh, and was by him appointed adjutant of the command.

Major Thornburgh's troops left Fort Steele, Wyoming, on the twenty-first of September, 1879, and camped the first night at Rawlins, Wyoming. Leaving Rawlins early on the twenty-second the command followed the military road south and that afternoon reached

Fortification Creek, where camp was made. Here Lieutenant Price and his company of infantry were left to establish a supply camp.

At this place Major Thornburgh wrote the following letter to Mr. Meeker:

> Headquarters White River Expedition,
> Camp on Fortification Creek
> September 25, 1879.
>
> *Sir:*
>
> In obedience to instructions from the General of the Army, I am enroute to your agency, and expect to arrive there on the 29th instant, for the purpose of affording you any assistance in my power in regulating your affairs, and to make arrests at your suggestion, and to hold as prisoners such of your Indians as you desire, until investigations are made by your department.
>
> I have heard nothing definite from your agency for ten days and do not know what state of affairs exists, whether the Indians will leave at my approach or show hostilities. I send this letter by Mr. Lowry, one of my guides, and desire you to communicate with me as soon as possible, giving me all the information in your power, in order that I may know what course I am to pursue.
>
> If practicable, meet me on the road at the earliest moment.
>
> Very respectfully,
> *your obedient servant,*
> T. T. Thornburgh,
> Major Fourth Infantry, Commanding Expedition
>
> To Mr. Meeker, Indian Agent, White River Agency, Colo. [2]

The following day the command resumed its march, following Fortification Creek for eighteen miles, and at two o'clock in the afternoon went into camp at Yampa River.

Here they were met by a delegation of Indians from the Agency, consisting of Jack, an Indian chief, and about ten others. While the actions and demeanor of Jack and his companions were far from hostile, it was very plain to the soldiers that they had come for the purpose of counting the troops and picking up all available information about the expedition. Jack several times asked why the soldiers were going to the agency, and in spite of the assurances by the soldiers of their pacific intentions, he showed a decided distrust. He was very bitter in his denunciations of Agent Meeker.[3]

Major Thornburgh did his best to allay any fears the Indians might have as to the purpose of the expedition, and invited Jack to accompany him to the agency. This Jack refused to do and left that night for the agency.

Of this visit by the Indians Captain Payne writes as follows:

> They came to us, not "as an army with banners," nor by any intimation of their hostile intent, "but with duplicity in their hearts whilst the countenances wore the signals of peace." They visited our camp, professed friendship, and, having learned our force, departed, feeling no doubt assurance of an early massacre.[4]

Even Major Thornburgh was unaware of any hostile intent on the part of the Indians as is evidenced by the following telegram which he sent to his department commander from Yampa River:

> Have met some Ute chiefs here. They seem friendly and promise to go with me to agency. Say Utes don't understand why we have come. Have tried to explain satisfactorily. Do not anticipate trouble.[5]

The next day the troops advanced to William's Fork, where they camped for the night. Here they were met by Colorow, Henry, the interpreter, three other Indians, and Mr. Eskridge, an employee of the Agency, who brought the following letter from Mr. Meeker to Major Thornburgh:

> White River Agency, Colo.
> September 27, 1879
>
> *Sir:*
>
> Understanding that you are on the way hither with United States Troops, I send a messenger, Mr. Eskridge, and two Indians, Henry (interpreter) and John Ayersly, to inform you that the Indians are greatly excited, and wish you to stop at some convenient camping place, and then that you and five soldiers of your command come into the Agency, when a talk and a better understanding can be had.
>
> This I agree to, but I do not propose to order your movements, but it seems for the best.
>
> The Indians seem to consider the advance of the troops as a declaration of real war. In this I am laboring to undeceive them, and at the same time to convince them they cannot do whatever they please. The first object now is to allay apprehension.
>
> *Respectfully,*
>
> N.C. Meeker, Indian Agent
>
> To Major Thornburgh,
> or Commander United States Troops,
> between Bear and White River, Colo.[6]

After Major Thornburgh had conferred with his officers he wrote the following answer to Mr. Meeker and sent it by Henry, the interpreter, who later testified that he delivered the same to Mr. Meeker.[7]

Headquarters White River Expedition,
Camp on William's Fork,

Sir:

Your letter of this date just received. I will move tomorrow with part of my command to Milk River, or some good location for camp, or possibly may leave my entire command at this point, and will come in as is desired with five men and a guide. Mr. Eskridge will remain to guide me to the agency.

I will reach your agency some time on the 29th instant.

Very respectfully
Your obedient servant,
T. T. Thornburgh,
Major Fourth Infantry, Commanding Expedition

Mr. Meeker, United States Indian Agent, White River Agency[8]

The Indians were apprised of the contents of these letters which passed between Mr. Meeker and Major Thornburgh. Although only Henry, the interpreter, could speak the English language, he was told to tell the other Indians what was in those letters, which he purported to do.[9]

Major Thornburgh made it very clear to Henry, the interpreter, that the Indians had nothing to fear, and that he was not going in with the troops, but would stop before reaching the Agency, but no particular point was designated.[10]

Later, at the congressional investigation, Henry testified "that the officer told him that the letters said he was to come on with five more men, but that the officer said he could not do that as his orders were to go on with all."[11]

These Indians were not disposed to be very sociable at first, and Colorow was exceedingly surly, refusing to smoke because the soldiers could not oblige the "Colorado Big Chief" with anything better than a pipe, since "Jack" had helped himself to the last of the Havanas which the officers had with them.[12]

This camp at William's Fork was about thirty-five miles from the

Agency. There was neither a sufficient quantity of grass nor timber to make a longer camp, and besides, "it was a very bad place to camp, surrounded by high bluffs, so that if the Indians had chosen to attack us there, the whole command would have been annihilated at once. That was one of Major Thornburgh's reasons for moving on,"[13] the other being to get closer to the Agency.

On the following day, September 28, the command marched about eleven miles, to a point where spring water and some grass were found. After making camp Major Thornburgh held a council with his officers and told them "that he had been thinking of this matter during the day and that he was satisfied that, under his orders, he had taken a little too much responsibility in consenting to keep his command so far from the Agency, and he asked our advice about it."[14]

Captain Payne expressed the opinion that it was best to continue the march the following day until Milk Creek was reached and to camp there or at some point near it, and that Major Thornburgh with five men should go on to the Agency, either that night or the next morning. Meanwhile "the command would go into camp just as under ordinary circumstances, pitch their tents, and go through all the forms of encampment for the night; then, as soon it became dark, I would take the cavalry column and carry it through the canyon[15] and place it near the agency; that, as the Indians would see him going on into the Agency, they would follow him as if they were on the lookout, supposing that he was carrying out his programme, and we could get through without trouble, and that then the command would be within supporting distance, and yet meet the requirement of the Indians, not to go to the agency."[16]

Another reason for going through the canyon at night was because the guide had told the officers that "it was a very bad canyon, with very steep and precipitous sides, so that the Indians could roll rocks down upon us and annihilate us."[17]

After some discussion it was decided to carry out this plan, and that the major and his party would go on to the agency at night of the following day. A letter informing Mr. Meeker of the changed plans was written by Captain Payne and sent by Mr. Eskridge:

Headquarters White River Expedition,
Camp on Deer Creek,
September 28, 1879

Sir:

I have, after due deliberation, decided to modify my plans as communicated in my letter of the 27th instant in the following particulars:

I shall move with my entire command to some convenient camp near, and within striking distance of, your agency, reaching such point during the 29th. I shall then halt and encamp the troops and proceed to that agency with my guide and five soldiers, as communicated in my letter of the 27th instant.

Then and there I will be ready to have a conference with you and the Indians, so that an understanding may be arrived at and my course of action determined. I have carefully considered whether or not it would be advisable to have my command at a point as distant as that desired by the Indians who were in my camp last night and have reached the conclusion that under my orders, which require me to march this command to the agency, I am not at liberty to leave it at a point where it would not be available in case of trouble. You are authorized to say for me to the Indians that my course of conduct is entirely dependent on them. Our desire is to avoid trouble, and we have not come for war.

I requested you in my letter of the 26th to meet me on the road before I reached the agency, I renew my request that you do so, and further desire that you bring such chiefs as may wish to accompany you. I am

Very respectfully,
Your obedient servant,
T. T. Thornburgh,
Major Fourth Infantry, Commanding Expedition

Mr. Meeker, United States Agent, White River Agency, Colo.[18]

That Mr. Meeker received the above letter is shown by the fact that at 1 P.M. on September 29, shortly before the massacre at the agency, he sent the following reply to Major Thornburgh.

United States Indian Service,
White River Agency,
September 29, 1879–1 P.M.

Dear Sir:

I expect to leave in the morning with Douglas and Serrick to meet you. Things are peaceable, and Douglas flies the United States flag. If you have trouble in getting through the canyon today let me know in what force. We have been on guard three nights and shall be tonight, not because we know that there is danger, but because there may be. I like your last programme. It is based on true military principles.

Most truly yours,
N. C. Meeker, Indian Agent[19]

This letter was never delivered to Major Thornburgh, because Mr. Eskridge, who left the agency with it, was later found dead a short distance from the agency, with the letter in his possession.

From some of the events which had transpired, Mr. Meeker must have been somewhat apprehensive, even though his last communication does not show it. Two days before the fight, the squaws and the children had been moved with their tepees from the Agency to the head of the east branch of Pice-ance Creek, twelve miles south of the Agency, where they made camp, which was known as Squaw Camp. Only four of the former ninety-four tepees were left at the Agency, one of these belonging to Chief Douglas.[20]

At dusk of this same day Mr. Meeker sent Ed Mansfield with an urgent message to Captain Dodge, who with his colored troops had been sent from Fort Garland to Middle Park to establish peace between the settlers and the Indians, asking for immediate aid.

When Charles Lowry, who carried messages from Captain Thornburgh, arrived at the agency a short time after Mansfield left, he found Meeker in a very nervous state. Later in the evening when a band of Utes came to the agency from Milk River and reported the approach of soldiers, the Indians held a council, and then all joined in a wild demonstration of war whoops, fierce yells, and dancing about Meeker's quarters. When Meeker attempted to quiet them he was jeered at by the Indians, and only after Lowry had intervened did they finally become quiet.[21]

Lowry returned to Thornburgh's camp on the night of the Twenty-eighth, with a letter from Meeker which seems to have been lost later, and its contents remain unknown.[22]

It is, however, known that he informed Major Thornburgh of the serious conditions existing at the agency and expressed fear that the Indians would fight the troops.[23]

At 6:30 A.M. on that fateful day, September Twenty-ninth, the command began the march to Milk River and at 9:30 reached the high ground overlooking the river. Captain Payne gives us a graphic picture of the scene before him:

> Descending the hill, a fine landscape lay before us. A small stream running softly down a narrow valley; on the right hand, a mile off, a line of bluffs continuous and inaccessible, with broken ridges nearer the creek; on the left rounded knolls and what our English friends call "downs," furrowed with arroyos and running back to the high hills which form the advance guard of the White River Mountains. The air was soft and balmy as with the breath of the sweet south, and the bright sunshine shooting in broad flashes across the hilltops filled the valley as with liquid gold. Save in the long column which, dismounted, was winding its way down the hill, not a living creature was in sight. Earth and sky were fair to behold, and the pictured calm seemed the very symbol of peace.[24]

Just before the troops reached the stream they passed on the hill a wagon train belonging to the Indian contractor, Mr. France, of Rawlins, in charge of Mr. John Gordon, which was hauling supplies to the Agency. "These train-people informed some of the soldiers that Indians had passed them before we reached them, coming from the direction which we were approaching, and told them to keep out of the way, that there was going to be a fight with the soldiers."[25]

When Milk River was reached "fresh trails and indications of a large body of Indians."[26] were seen, among these being some newly started fires which were still burning.[27] The command was halted at the river and the horses watered, after which the march was resumed, Major Thornburgh having ordered that the troops should move about four miles beyond the river and make temporary camp at "the top of the ridge on this side of the canyon."[28]

One reason for not stopping at the river was that much of the grass there had been burned off by the Indians, and there was no running water in the river, but only in pools.[29]

The troops followed the river for a thousand yards, crossed, and then, instead of following the road which led along Beaver Ravine and into the canyon, took a trail going over the hills to the left. This trail cut off the elbow made by the road, and saved considerable distance. Troop E of the Third Cavalry, and F of the Fifth were in the lead under the immediate command of Major Thornburgh.

Troop D of the Fifth Cavalry remained with the wagons which had been halted several hundred yards north of the river crossing, and which were to follow more slowly.

At this point of the story there is some controversy. Mr. Joe Rankin, who accompanied the expedition as scout and guide, claimed that it was he who informed Major Thornburgh of the trail which led over the hill to the left of the road and that he had strongly urged the major to take this trail rather than the road which led into the canyon, because he was fearful that the Indians would attack the command while in that place.

Newspaper dispatches, which were sent out from Rawlins, Wyoming, also carried this version of the affair, but they were based upon the story as told by Mr. Rankin himself, upon his arrival at Rawlins with the first news of the fight.[30]

Authentic accounts of the battle as told by those who participated in it do not, however, substantiate his claims. Captain Payne, in an article written by him, denied Rankin's story. "A good deal of nonsense," he wrote, "has been written in the newspapers to the effect that the command pursued this route (the trail) by the advice of a guide, who, knowing that the Indians were lying in ambush in the canyon, took us this way to avoid annihilation. Major Thornburgh turned off the road to shorten his march. Neither he nor I were apprehensive of trouble at this time."[31] In further reference to this, Captain Payne, in his testimony before the congressional investigating committee, said: "The old Indian trail crosses the road repeatedly. The road winds in and out among the mountains, and the trail makes a good many cut-offs, and the cavalry column would frequently take the trail while the wagons would follow the road."[32]

Lieutenant Cherry, who as adjutant of the command was familiar with all of Major Thornburgh's orders, in his testimony before the same committee, while speaking of the troops taking the trail, said: "It has been said that it was done by Mr. Rankin's orders, but it was not; it was a mere fortunate circumstance; he happened to take the trail instead of the road and it was providential that he did so."[33]

The first intimation of trouble came from Lieutenant Cherry, who had been placed in charge of an advance guard of several men and ordered to "keep half or three-quarters of a mile in advance of the command and keep on the lookout for Indians, as he expected that there might be trouble."[34]

It has been claimed that Mr. Rankin, the guide, and Frank Secrist, a private soldier, were riding a quarter of a mile in advance of Thornburgh and were the first to see the Indians, and that they returned to Major Thornburgh, who halted the command and called a short conference, in which it is alleged that Rankin urged Major Thornburgh to immediately open fire upon the Indians.[35] There is not, however, anything of an authentic nature to verify this statement, while there are several authorities who agree that Lieutenant Cherry's party was the first to see the lurking Indians.[36] According to Mr. A. M. Startzell, a member of Company E, Third Cavalry, he, Mr. Rankin, and another soldier by the name of William Lewis, were in Lieutenant Cherry's advance party and were therefore merely among those who first discovered the danger ahead.[37]

The trail which Lieutenant Cherry followed passed between ridges of successive heights. On the right there were two ridges lying between the trail and the road which ran through Beaver ravine, one ridge somewhat higher than the other.

When about half or three-quarters of a mile beyond Milk River, Lieutenant Cherry and his party saw three Indians disappear from the nearest ridge lying on the right of the trail, and about five hundred yards in advance of his party. His suspicions aroused, he divided his men, sending part of them to the left, while he with the remainder "went down on the right about two hundred yards and crossed a little stream and got up on the ridge that these three Indians had disappeared behind." He now discovered that the Indians were lying down in ambush on the top of the second ridge with their guns in readiness to fire.[38] He was now within one hundred yards of the Indians who were drawn up in a line of battle which extended for at least four hundred yards and which covered and commanded the road below, and was parallel with it. Every plan had thus been made to attack the troops when they entered the canyon, but, instead, the troops "took them in the rear of their position instead of stringing ourselves out along their front as they expected and wished us to do."[39]

Upon seeing the position of the Indians, Cherry waved his hat to Major Thornburgh and made "signals for the command to retrace its steps just as the leading company (F, Fifth Cavalry) was descending the ridge into the valley beyond."[40]

Major Thornburgh at once realized that the signals meant the presence of Indians and immediately ordered Company F deployed as skirmishers on the left flank, and Company E, Third Cavalry, to the right and on the crest of the ridge, the battle line at this time resembling the letter V, the point toward the Indians. Some Indians had by this time appeared in front, and both Captain Payne and Major Thornburgh now "made efforts to communicate with the Indians by signalling," using handkerchiefs, the only available objects, "and several of the Indians answered these signals."[41]

Lieutenant Cherry, who had meanwhile reported to Major Thornburgh, was sent with orders to Captains Payne and Lawson "to dismount and fight on foot, keeping the horses in the rear, and not to fire a shot until he gave the order."[42]

Lieutenant Cherry was then ordered to take fifteen men from Lawson's company, cross the ravine lower down on the right flank, and, if possible, to communicate with the Indians. When Cherry had gone a distance of about four hundred or five hundred yards from Lawson's company a body of about fifteen or twenty Indians appeared from behind a ridge. Cherry moved out some fifteen or twenty feet in advance of his men and waved his hat "in a friendly manner; not at all in an excited manner, and I was looking toward the Indians, not toward my men." Which action, Lieutenant Cherry thought, the Indians would and did understand as friendly. He was replied to by a shot which came from one of the Indians in this advanced group, and which was evidently meant for the Lieutenant as it wounded a man who was not over ten feet directly behind him. Cherry at once dismounted his men and sent word to Major Thorburgh that he had been fired upon and could hold his position until further orders, also that the Indians were riding around upon the flanks in an apparent endeavor to cut off the troops from the wagon train. In the investigations which were held after the battle and massacre, some Indians said that they did not know who fired the first shot,[43] while others claimed that the soldiers began the firing. Chief Jack claimed that he had come to talk with the soldiers, not to fight, and that the Indians had supposed that the troops would make camp on Milk River and were surprised to see them coming on beyond that point.[44] This story does not, however, explain the established fact that the Indians were hidden in ambush along the expected line of march. Charles Adams, Special Indian Agent, evidently did not believe the story told by the Indian, for in a letter written to Secretary Carl Schurz, on October 25, 1879, he said that after making investigations, and having the Indian version of the affair, he was "satisfied that the attack on Thornburgh was premeditated."[45]

Meanwhile a large force of Indians had gathered about four hundred yards to the left of the troops, while those which were in front were approaching very cautiously, taking advantage of any obstructions in the ground to keep out of range.

Upon hearing the firing on the right of the line where Lieutenant Cherry was, for the first shot had immediately been followed by others, Captain Payne did not wait for any orders, but turned around and directed his men to open fire on the Indians, without waiting to investigate where the shot had come from or who had fired it, his reason being that his "knowledge of Indian affairs was such that I knew we had an Indian fight on our hands then and there."[46] The Indians returned the fire and soon two of Payne's men and several Indians were killed.

Major Thornburgh now realized that it would not be wise to try to hold his ground against a foe so superior in numbers and occupying much better positions. The number of soldiers at Thornburgh's immediate command was less than 150 men including the teamsters, while the number of Indians was estimated at between 300 to 400.[47] Orders were therefore issued to gradually fall back to the wagon train, which had reached a point about 800 yards north of the river crossing, and to concentrate all the forces there.

Lieutenant Paddock, who with his company was guarding the wagons, received orders from Major Thornburgh to form a corral, and the Lieutenant with the aid of wagonmaster McKinstry and others, formed the wagons into a three-quarter elliptical-shaped circle on a flat near the north side of the stream and about twelve feet above its level. The tongues of the wagons were turned toward the inside of the circle, the open space of which bordered on the banks of the stream.[48]

In ordering the retreat to the wagons Major Thornburgh gave orders that Captain Payne was to charge upon a large force of Indians which had passed around the left flank, beyond carbine range, and gathered upon a large knoll commanding the line of retreat, with the obvious intention of cutting off the troops from the wagons. He was directed to sweep the Indians back, "and then at once without attempting to hold the hill, to fall back upon the train and take measures for its protection."[49]

Captain Lawson, whose company was deployed on the right flank, was ordered to hold his line and gradually withdraw to the wagons, while Lieutenant Cherry was given the task of covering Lawson's retreat, "and keep the Indians from getting into the gullies and ravines until the other companies had fallen back," and then he was to fall back slowly.[50]

Becoming short of ammunition, Lieutenant Cherry asked for a volunteer to ride to the wagons, which were about a thousand yards away, for an additional supply. It was a hazardous errand, as the Indians had by this time surrounded the entire expedition and were shooting at the soldiers and wagons from every direction. Sergeant Edward Grimes volunteered his services, and mounting his horse, already bleeding from two wounds in the neck, he heroically performed the task, and thereby made possible an orderly retreat by Lawson and Cherry. For this accomplishment, Grimes was later awarded a Medal of Honor by the War Department.[51]

After giving his orders for the retreat, Major Thornburgh started on a gallop for the wagon corral, with the evident intention of making plans for the defense of his troops. He was shot after he had crossed the river and was within five hundred yards of the corral.[52]

Several conflicting stories have been written of this sad event. One writer says that Thornburgh was killed while leading a charge against some Indians who were between the troops and the wagons.[53]

Another account says that O'Malley, the Major's orderly, who was within fifty yards of the Major when shot, saw an Indian hidden behind a sagebrush do the shooting. O'Malley killed the Indian, but because of other near approaching Indians, he was unable to rescue the body of his commander.[54] Although the body remained within the enemy lines for several days, when recovered it "bore no signs of the customary mutilation," nor had he been scalped. "Within the cold fingers of one hand was a photograph of 'Colorow,' who had probably placed it there."[55]

In regard to the photograph which was said to have been found on Major Thornburgh's body, Captain Payne, in his testimony, gave the following facts which doubtless refer to the same incident.

> I forgot to state one thing in regard to these pictures that have been spoken about. Lowery or Rankin, I forget which, the night before the fight, gave me the picture of an Indian, which I put in my trunk. My trunk was captured, with all my baggage, by the Indians, as was also Major Thornburgh's, Lieutenant Cherry's, and Lieutenant Wolf's. We had all of our property in a light wagon, which followed the column, and the driver had to cut his horses loose to save his life, and the wagon fell into the Indians' hands. When Major Thornburgh's body was recovered, this picture, or at least a picture which I am satisfied is the same, was found upon his body held down by a little stone which had been placed upon it to prevent the wind from blowing it away. I am satisified, from the examination I made of it after it was recovered, that it is the same picture, and was left on Major Thornburgh's body under the impression that it was his property. (The witness exhibited the picture to the members of the committee.) When Ignacio's band were coming here the other day I went into the car and shook hands with them all, and I suddenly drew this picture out of my pocket and said "Sabe"? One of them said, "Yes, it is Toca, an Uncompahgre"; but a few minutes later they denied it. I went down to the Tremont House two or three days ago, and showed the picture to some of the Indians there, and one of them said it was Captain Billy. I don't know what tribe he belongs to.[56]

Another story is that a stray shot apparently wounded Thornburgh and his horse and that he was quickly surrounded by a band of Indians who dragged him from his horse and beat him severely.[57]

Captain Payne, in his testimony before the congressional investigating committee, stated that no one knew just when or how Major Thornburgh was killed, as he was apparently by himself, and that he was probably picked off by a sharpshooter at long range, "because I know there were no Indians close to the position where he was found. I went over the ground myself within five minutes of the time he was killed, either before or after."[58]

The orders for retreat given by Major Thornburgh to his company officers were faithfully carried out. Captain Payne, after driving the Indians from the knoll on the left, which opened the way for the return of the lead horses, made his way to the wagon train and took steps for its defense. He thus describes his work there: "Upon reaching the train I found it parked on the right bank of Milk River, about two hundred yards from the water, the wagons forming the north side of a corral elliptical in shape, its long axis running east and west, and the south side exposed to a fierce fire from the Indians, who, massing in ravines along the river and upon commanding heights, were making a determined effort to capture and destroy the train before it could be placed in position for defense. The animals were crowded within the area indicated, and I at once directed some twenty or more of those wounded to be led out and shot, along the open space referred to, thus making a continuous line of defense, and affording cover for our sharpshooters."

"The wagons now unloaded, and bundles of bedding, grain and flour sacks, and mess boxes were used for the construction of breastworks." During this busy time Lieutenant Paddock and Captain Payne both received wounds, Paddock's being very painful.[59]

As soon as a semblance of order had been restored, Captain Payne sent out a party of ten men under command of Sergeant Poppe to cover the retreat of Captain Lawson and Lieutenant Cherry, who were on foot, the most of their lead horses having come into the corral.[60] After hard fighting to keep the Indians from cutting them off from the wagons these troops had reached the banks of Milk River, which, with the cottonwoods, offered some protection, and after routing the Indians from beneath the benches along the river, they made their way inside the enclosure without any fatal casualties, only Sergeant James Mongomery having been wounded. Donovan, who was with Lawson, brought the news of Major Thornburgh's death to Captain Payne, who, as senior ranking officer, now took command.[61]

No sooner had the troops reached the corral than a new danger threatened. The Indians, determined in their efforts to drive the soldiers into the open, where death awaited, "took advantage of a high wind blowing towards the corral and set fire to the dry grass and sagebrush down the river." At the same time it was observed that the Indian supply train which the troops had passed about a mile back on the road, was parked about seventy-five yards from the corral, and so situated as to command the approach to water. Fearing that the Indians might, under cover of the smoke, make a lodgement in the train, "and with the further purpose of burning the grass on the near side of the corral, so as to present as little surface as possible to the Indian fire when it should approach," Payne gave orders to Sergeant Poppe to get three or four men and set fire to the grass immediately about the corral. "Poppe said he would do it by himself, and springing over the breastworks before I could prevent him, he lighted a match, touched it to a wisp of grass, and going from place to place fired the sagebrush, returning only after the duty had been thoroughly performed. Soon the grass and Gordon's train were in flames."[62]

Meanwhile the fire from below was rapidly approaching the corral, "volumes of black smoke rolling before it, through which the angry, lurid tongues of flames shot high into the air, giving to the scene an aspect appalling and grand."[63] A change in the wind turned the fire somewhat away from the corral, and thereby saved the soldiers from almost certain death.[64] Nevertheless, some of the flames reached the exposed salient of the corral, setting fire to several of the wagons, and the greatest effort was required to extinguish the flames. "At this critical juncture the Indians made their most furious attack. Not one could be seen, but the incessant crack of their rifles dealt destruction to man and beast. In every ravine the red devils were lurking, and from every sagebrush came the messenger of death."[65]

During this time the soldiers were ordered to fire into the smoke, and they thereby kept the Indians at a greater distance from the corral.[66] The men fought the fire with blouses, burlap sacks, and anything that they had, also by digging up dirt with their scabbard knives and spreading it on the flames. Private James Hickman, under fire of the Indians, pulled off a wagon sheet which had caught fire, and thus prevented the destruction of the wagons. For this brave act he was later awarded a medal by the War Department for bravery.[67]

This great peril had, however, been averted at great loss. Wagonmaster McKinstry, Teamster Maguire, Sergeant Dolan, Privates McKee and Mooney had been killed, and less than a dozen men wounded, Captain Payne receiving his second wound.

This fire burned over the entire east end of Danforth Hills, an area of about twenty square miles.

From the time of the fire, about 2:45 P.M., until night, the Indians maintained a furious fight. "They were armed with improved weapons, Winchester, Sharps, and Remington rifles,"[68] and were firing from hills and ravines, which, in some places, were within thirty or forty yards from the corral. The Indians had to rise and fire suddenly, firing at the corral rather than at individual persons. They, however, did a great amount of damage, having killed twelve men, wounded forty-three, and killed all but four horses.[69]

At dark a large body of Indians charged down beyond Gordon's train, firing volley after volley, and coming up to within about forty yards of the corral, but were easily repulsed and suffered the loss of several of their warriors. This was the last serious effort they made to dislodge the besieged either that day or afterwards.[70]

When night came the prospects, though unpleasant, were not discouraging. The soldiers had thirty days' rations and were within two hundred yards of water, and although over a dozen men including the commander had been killed and many wounded, there were about ninety brave men, unhurt and confident of their ability to hold out until help arrived.

During the night the dead animals were dragged down into the bed of the stream, a supply of water sufficient for twenty-four hours was obtained, and the wounded were cared for under direction of Surgeon R. M. Grimes, who was himself severely wounded. Liquor was obtained from the sutler stock, which helped to relieve suffering. Dead men were wrapped in canvas or blankets and covered with dirt from the trenches, which were dug around the circle near the wagons. These were eight to ten feet in length, four feet deep, and four to five feet wide. In the center three large trenches were dug for the wounded.[71]

Near midnight a council was held in which it was decided to send out some couriers with dispatches to the military authorities. Joe Rankin, John Gordon, and Corporals Moquin and Murphy were selected as messengers.[72] One writer names a Sergeant Grimes as one of those sent.[73]

Rankin made a record-breaking ride to Rawlins, Wyoming, a distance of approximately 150 miles in 27½ hours, and gave the world the first news of the fight. Immediate steps were taken by the military authorities to send relief to Captain Payne.[74]

During the following days and nights the Indians kept up an almost incessant fire, killing nearly all the animals, but doing no other damage. On the night of October first, the water party was fired on at short range, and one man was shot in the face.

At daylight, on October second, Captain Dodge and Lieutenant Hughes, with Company D, Ninth Cavalry, reached Payne's command. Captain Dodge, with this colored company, had, in July of this year, been ordered to do scout duty in Middle Park, and to prevent, if possible, "any collision between the Indians and settlers in that region."[75]

Captain Dodge had occupied the time by following his instructions, making many excursions from his base in Middle Park. Upon the return to this base from one of these trips, in the latter part of September, he found orders awaiting him to return "to the White River Agency with the least practicable delay" to force the return of Indians to their reservation and "to act in accord with Agent Meeker and under his directions."[76]

The captain left his supply camp on Grand River on September twenty-seventh, and on the thirtieth camped on a small stream about ten or fifteen miles south of Steamboat Springs. The command had traveled about ten miles on October first, when a piece of paper was found on a sagebrush by the side of the road on which was written: "Hurry up, the troops have been defeated at the agency," and signed, E. E. C. After reading this message Dodge pushed on with speed to Hayden, which he found deserted. There he met John Gordon, one of the couriers who had left Payne's improvised fort in search for help, and, learning from him the exact situation, he marched on with all possible speed, making camp on Yampa River at 4:30 in the afternoon.

After having supplied each soldier with 125 rounds of ammunition and three days' rations, he ordered the wagons repacked and sent with a guard to Price's camp on Fortification Creek. Then guided by John Gordon and a Mr. Lithgow, he started for Milk Creek with only one pack mule and a force which consisted of two officers, thirty-five soldiers, and four citizens. Following the Marapos trail,[77] rather than the road, they reached the Milk River road about five miles from the entrenchments, and shortly afterward came upon the dead bodies of three men and a burned wagon train, and half an hour later arrived near the corral. They had not been molested by Indians, a fact that Dodge could only account for by supposing that the Indians imagined a much stronger force was coming in and they were unwilling to expose themselves.[78]

A short halt was made within five hundred yards of the trenches, shortly before daybreak, and Sandy Mellen and John Gordon advanced toward them. An Indian, lying in a ravine, "called out, as a warning, no doubt, to his copper-colored companions, 'Soldiers coming.' At first the men in the trenches thought this was a ruse to get them to expose themselves, but soon a shout from Gordon, whose voice was recognized, caused great rejoicing by the entrenched men, and the newcomers were greeted with glad hand."[79]

Contrary to some reports, the best evidence shows that Dodge's men were not subjected to any great fire from the Indians while coming into the trenches, the reason being that most of the Indians had gone to their emergency camp one mile south for rest and a change of mounts, and that Dodge and his company had slipped into the trenches at a time least expected by them.[80]

The arrival of the new troops brought cheer to the besieged, and assured them that their couriers had gone through with safety, and that soon they would be rescued from their perilous situation.

The shouts of the soldiers aroused the resting Indians, who now began sending a veritable rain of shots into the trenches. Captain Dodge proposed to charge the Indians on the ridge, but was persuaded that it would only result in a useless loss of men.

The deadly firing of the Indians throughout the day and succeeding night resulted in the killing or wounding of nearly all the horses and mules, only five horses and two mules surviving the siege. The wounded animals were killed by the soldiers to relieve them of suffering.

It was not safe for a man to expose any part of his body above the trenches, and only during the night could any venture outside the enclosure to get the needed water and to gather sagebrush with which to make fire for boiling coffee.

The many surface obstructions, the banks of the river, and the large sagebrush afforded splendid protection behind which the Indians could hide. "Not an Indian could be seen on whom to return the fire; only a puff of white smoke indicated from time to time where the bullet came from."[81]

The soldiers were not permitted to become bored because of monotony or inattention from the Indians. Signal fires at night, yells of the Indians holding their scalp dances, mingled with the howls of hundreds of coyotes, attracted by the dead animals, as well as the meant-to-be-humorous taunts of Indians lying in nearby ravines, furnished plenty of entertainment for those in the trenches, who vied with each other in expressing their feelings, often in original terms, concerning their red-skinned entertainers.[82]

On the morning of the fifth of October, General Merritt arrived at Milk River with his relief command, after making a forced march which has become famous. Within four hours after marching orders had reached General Merritt at Fort Russell, on October first, the relief troops with horses and equipment were on the cars and being carried by rail to Rawlins, Wyoming, a distance of 200 miles, from which point it was necessary to proceed by foot to the besieged soldiers. By daylight, Oct. second, a force of about 200 cavalry and less than 150 infantry had collected at Rawlins, and at 11 o'clock the march of 170 miles was begun. "Without drawing rein, save for a needed rest at intervals to conserve strength for the whole of the work, the command pressed on with advance guard, and at times flankers, to prevent the possibility of ambuscade or surprise."[83] "As night came on the difficulties of marching were much increased by the darkness and rough roads," and from time to time halts were made while staff officers went to the rear to direct the column and see that it kept well closed.[84]

Early on the morning of October fifth, the guide having satisfied himself that the command was near the entrenchments, the bugler was ordered to sound the call known as "officers' call" in the cavalry, which had become a sign of recognition between friends, that there might be no collision, and friends be mistaken for foes.

No better description of the following moments can be given than that of Captain Payne, who wrote as follows:

> Just as the first grey of the dawn appeared, our listening ears caught the sound of "officers' call" breaking the silence of the morning and filling the valley with the sweetest music we had ever heard. Joyously the reply rang out from our corral, and the men rushing from the rifle pits made the welkin ring with their glad cheers. Deliverance had come, and their fortitude and courage had met with reward.
>
> The scene beggared description. Brave men wept, and it was touching to see the gallant fellows hovering around to get a look at the general whose name had been on their lips for days, and who, as they heard from their comrades just arrived, had risen from a bed of sickness to make a march unparalleled in military annals.[85]

J. CISNEROS

The Sioux at Pine Ridge

John H. Nankivell

The participation of Companies C, E, F, and H, under Lieutenant Colonel Van Horne, Twenty-fifth Infantry, in the Pine Ridge Campaign of 1890-91, received but scant mention in the regimental returns, but inasmuch as this was the last important Indian war in which United States troops were engaged, a brief account of the campaign would, no doubt, be of interest and is given herewith.

Many causes are ascribed for the outbreak among the various Indian tribes throughout Montana and the Dakotas in the winter of 1890-91, but there can be little doubt that the condition of destitution among the Indians brought about by reduced rations and the dishonesty and mismanagement of minor government officials had a far-reaching effect. Suffering under a sense, imagined and real, of injustice and oppression the credulous Indians were ready to accept any scheme which promised them relief, and it is little wonder that they were quite willing to believe the promises made them by an Indian who claimed to be their Messiah. The principal tenet of this new religion, or craze, was that the coming of the Messiah would give domination of the red man over the white, and that the white man would be driven from the country and vast herds of buffalo would cover the prairies as in the days gone by. It was also believed that coincident with the disappearance of the white man all dead Indians would be resurrected, and join

Reprinted from John H. Nankivell, *History of the Twenty-fifth Regiment United States Infantry, 1869-1926* (Denver, 1927).

the living and together they would roam the country in unrestrained liberty.

The craze grew apace, and a dance, known as the "ghost dance," sprang into vogue. This dance induced a religious fervor, and added greatly to the prevailing agitation. By November of 1890 there were serious indications of an uprising among the Sioux in the Dakotas, and at some of the agencies there was open defiance of the Indian agents and police. At the request of the Interior Department, who had become convinced that the situation was too serious to be handled without troops, the War Department took action by directing General Miles, division commander at Chicago, to take such measures as he deemed necessary to cope with the situation.

General Miles immediately ordered that all troops at the various stations in the Northwest be put in instant readiness to proceed to the scene of action, and an initial force of cavalry was sent to the Standing Rock Agency where trouble seemed to be most imminent.

Investigations instituted by General Miles and the various Department commanders, prior to and during the outbreak, revealed that a secret conspiracy existed among certain of the prominent leaders of the Sioux to effect an organized revolt against the white race in which the tribes of the Northwest were to unite in common cause. The time set for this revolt was the spring of 1891. This added a grave danger to a situation that was already serious enough and required prompt and decisive action on the part of the military authorities.

General Ruger, commanding the Department of Dakota, made a visit to the Indian Agencies along the Missouri River, and by his tact and the adoption of certain precautionary measures he succeeded in quieting the hostile elements. However, at the Pine Ridge Agency about the middle of November 1890, matters became decidedly threatening, and at daybreak, November 20, General Brooke, commander of the Department of the Platte, arrived at the agency with a force composed of five companies of infantry, three troops of cavalry, and a small battery of artillery. This force was in a rather precarious position inasmuch as they were greatly outnumbered by the Indians, and the situation was rather acute until the arrival of more troops later in the month.

The disaffected and hostile factions at the agency, probably numbering about three thousand, left soon after the arrival of the troops and sought refuge in the Badlands, a region of high peaks and deep gulches, about thirty miles to the north. Sitting Bull at this time was sending his emissaries to urge the Indians to stand firm against the whites, and his attitude was so evidently hostile that it was deemed necessary to effect his arrest. A small body of Indian police was detailed for the task, and in a resulting melee, precipitated by Sitting Bull's followers, the old medicine man was killed. Several of the followers escaped and joined the band of Big Foot, hostile Sioux chief, up the Grand River. Big Foot and about 150 of his band were eventually captured by Colonel Sumner on Cherry Creek, a tributary of the Cheyenne River, on December 22.

On the morning of December 29, 1890, Big Foot's band guarded by the Seventh Cavalry under command of Colonel Forsyth were on a little creek near Pine Ridge Agency called Wounded Knee. It had been decided to disarm these Indians on this date, and as a precautionary measure the cavalry was dismounted and drawn up on three sides of a square with the Indians assembled in front of them. With their usual cunning the Indians had concealed their weapons under their blankets which they put on before leaving their tepees, so that when the detail under Captain Wallace commenced searching very few firearms could be found in the tepees. While engaged in this duty Captain Wallace was treacherously slain by an Indian by a blow on the head with a club. About this time one of the Indians seated in front of the cavalry drew his rifle from beneath his blanket and fired upon the soldiers. This, apparently, was the signal for the attack on the troops by the Indians, and in a few seconds the whole camp was ablaze. The struggle was at first almost hand to hand, and was desperate in the extreme. Eventually the Indians drew off from the vicinity of the troops and made for the gullies and draws which cut up the plain separating them from the foothills to the west. A battery of three Hotchkiss guns that had been placed on a knoll about a hundred yards away from the Indian camp did considerable execution among the Indians as they made their dash for the ravines. The battle lasted intermittently until the afternoon, and at its end the casualties amounted to about two hundred Indians and thirty officers and soldiers killed with several wounded on both sides.

The excitement among the Indians caused by this battle was intense, and a large band left the Pine Ridge Agency soon after receiving news of the fight. This band attacked a supply train, and committed other depredations. Eventually they were rounded up by detachments from the Seventh and Ninth Cavalry.

On January 7, 1891, Lieutenant Casey, commanding a company of Cheyenne scouts, was murdered by a Brule Indian named Plenty Horses. Plenty Horses was afterward tried by a civil court and freed on a technicality.

About the middle of January reports began to come in that all was not in strict harmony among the hostile camps in the Badlands, and that the lives of several Indians who had determined to return to the agencies had been threatened by their recalcitrant brethren. General Miles, who had assumed personal command of the troops in the field, had so disposed his forces that the hostiles were practically surrounded by troops placed at strategic points, and the possibility of their escaping was small indeed. These dispositions finally convinced the Indians that further resistance was useless, and by the end of January practically all had returned to their reservations. Much credit was unquestionably due General Miles for the tact and skill with which he had handled a very delicate situation, and the confidence that he inspired among the more influential chiefs had a marked effect in bringing the outbreak to an end.

In order that the Indians might be given an object lesson and to show them that further hostile efforts were useless General Miles concentrated his forces and marched them in review before the assembled hostiles. The red man acknowledges no argument so readily as force, and there is no doubt that this display of seasoned troops with all the paraphernalia of war has been lasting, and no outbreaks of a grave nature have since occurred among the Indians of these tribes.

The part played by the Twenty-fifth Infantry in this campaign was a minor one, but it played that part well, and to it must go a measure of thanks for the successful termination of our last great Indian War.

L. Bjorklund

The Ninth United States Cavalry in the Sioux Campaign of 1890

Alex W. Perry
(Lieutenant, Ninth Cavalry)

On November 19, 1890, three troops (F, I, and K) of the Ninth Cavalry left Fort Robinson, Nebraska, and on the following day reached Pine Ridge Agency, South Dakota, where they were joined on the twenty-sixth by Troop D of the same regiment, and the whole was organized into the Battalion of the Ninth Cavalry, commanded by Major Guy V. Henry, Ninth Cavalry.

Our duties in camp at the Agency were more like those in garrison than those of a life in the field against an active foe, although our time was taken up in preparing our battalion for any duty that it might be called on to perform.

The first important step was the organization of our pack train, the nucleus of which came from Fort McKinney, Wyoming, under charge of Reemer, the chief packer at that post. Details of five men from each troop were made at once, and, although there were (owing to the scarcity of mules) only five pack mules to each troop, the men were drilled daily, often after dark, in order to familiarize the packers with their duties. Our packers had reached such a state of proficiency that when, about the tenth of December, we were given five more mules to each troop, we found ourselves equipped with a sufficient number of packs to carry eight days rations for the command.

Reprinted from the *Journal of the United States Cavalry Association,* IV (1891), through the courtesy of its editor, Colonel O.W. Martin.

Our wheeled transportation was in an excellent condition, and there was plenty of it, each troop having three six-mule wagons.

In the meantime our commanding officer did not let the troopers be idle, nor was he satisfied with a perfunctory horse exercise. There were daily drills of the battalion, interesting to both men and officers, as they did not confine themselves to the narrow limits of "Close Column," "On First Troop, Right in Front," but were adapted to the principles of the art of attack as taught in our military schools at West Point and Fort Leavenworth, and the best of schools, that of actual warfare; particular attention being paid to rapid deployments. The gaits were rapid, and the commands were generally given by a preconcerted system of blasts on a whistle; the necessity of the latter being daily shown, owing to the high winds and accompanying noises of the drill ground. Drills were always in overcoats and full armament, and held daily, Saturdays and Sundays excepted, in rain, sunshine, warm or cold weather. This was our daily life in camp at the Agency until December 24, 1890, when, without a moment's notice, we were ordered to proceed to the White River.

A telegram was received at the Agency about 1 P.M. December 24, from General Miles, saying:

> I regret exceedingly that "Big Foot" has eluded Sumner and is making south in light order and will probably join those in the Badlands. . . . If a command were to move quickly from Pine Ridge a little northeast and thence down Porcupine (Wounded Knee), or in that vicinity, it might possibly intercept him.

Colonel Henry's battalion was ordered on this duty. At 2 P.M. the order was received in camp, and at 3:30 P.M. the battalion was ready and awaiting further instructions from General Brooke.

We were joined by a detachment of Light Battery E, First Artillery, consisting of a detachment of ten men, two Hotchkiss guns and packs, under Lieutenant Hayden, First Artillery, who remained with us throughout the campaign.

We left the Agency about 2:30 P.M., and traveled with our pack train until about 6:30 P.M., when we reached "White Cow Creek," and there took supper and fed the animals, forage having been brought that far by Moore's Fort Russell pack train. After a halt of about one hour and a half or two hours, we again took the road and marched until we reached the White River, about 2 A.M. Then, after a short halt we pushed on to Cottonwood Creek where we found no water, but nevertheless bivouacked there until daylight. This had been our objective point, but as we found neither wood nor water there, our destination was changed. The next morning we changed our camp to Harney (Iron) Springs and awaited the arrival of our wagon train and further developments. We had traveled fifty-six miles in all, or fifty before we bivouacked, about 3:30 A.M., the morning after leaving the Agency. We moved constantly at a trot and walk, and the results were favorable to both man and beast, as there was not a sore-backed or lame horse in the battalion.

Our duty for the next week was confined to daily scouting. On Sunday, December 28, in compliance with instructions from General Brooke, we moved our camp to White River, forty-four miles below the Agency. That same day orders were received to examine the "table" (Short Bull's camp); so, on the morning of December 29, about 9:30, Colonel Henry with his battalion and the detachment of two Hotchkiss guns left camp on White River and explored the so-called impregnable fortress of the Indians in the Badlands. One troop scouted Porcupine Creek and returned, covering a distance of twenty-one miles each way or forty-two miles altogether. Camp was reached about 4 o'clock, when the usual duties of the camp were resumed.

News had reached us that Major Whiteside, Seventh Cavalry, had corralled Big Foot, and that the campaign would probably be brought to an early close. We had finished supper and had been sitting around talking and had just dispersed to seek our "downy couches" when our adjutant suddenly announced: "Big Foot has attempted to break away; they have had a fight and Wallace has been killed, and Garlington and Hawthorne been wounded;" and then he gave us orders to break camp at once. This was about 8:30 P.M. Our camp was struck, the wagons loaded, and the command was en route to the Agency at 9:30. We were in a hurry, and our gait was a rapid trot. We made three halts and reached the Agency just as reveille was sounding, 5:30 A.M.

One troop (D) had been left behind with the wagon train, which had dropped back about an hour and a half behind us. On arriving at the Agency we went to our old camp ground and had waited about two hours for our wagons when a courier reached us, bringing the news that our train had been attacked and was then parked about two miles from our camp.

"Boots and saddles" was immediately sounded, and we were off to the relief of our wagons. The affair amounted to the exchange of a few shots with the Indians and the loss of one poor trooper, who was shot, in the first volley, by an Indian dressed in the uniform of a cavalry soldier, with the yellow lining of his overcoat boldly displayed over his back. We proceeded to camp and had hardly unsaddled when we were again ordered out with the Seventh Cavalry to the Mission which was reported to be in flames. Colonel Henry obtained permission for us to remain behind and allow the horses time for their morning feed.

About noon a courier from Colonel Forsyth arrived in our camp saying that they (the Seventh Cavalry) were hard pressed, and to come at once. "Boots and saddles" was again sounded, and the battalion proceeded to the Mission as rapidly as our weary horses could travel. On arriving a short distance below the Mission we met the Seventh, and with the deployment of our troops, and under cover of the Hotchkiss guns, the troops of the Seventh were withdrawn, and we all returned to our camps together. The distance traveled on this occasion was about twelve miles.

This much for the marching of our battalion; between 9:30 A.M., on the twenty-ninth, and 4 P.M. on the thirtieth of December, we had marched one hundred and two miles, this in thirty and a half hours, including the several hours rest that we had taken at the Agency and two skirmishes with the Indians. Our gait had been almost constantly the trot.

The advantage of this gait is that the men are kept awake, and lounging in the saddle is impossible. The horses had an unusually heavy load, consisting of blanket-lined horse covers, and two hundred and twenty rounds of carbine and twenty-four rounds of revolver ammunition, weighing about twenty-five pounds, besides the usual pack.

In the battalion there was not a sore backed horse, and the only case of lameness that came to my notice was that of my own horse, which I had had shod for the first time only a week before.

Our casualties among the horses were two; one dropped dead on our return from the Mission, and another two days later, from exhaustion.

THE OFFICERS AND THE ENLISTED MEN

In the four black units the need for good leadership, both black and white, was apparent from the very beginning. If the men were to succeed as soldiers and citizens, there had to be help from responsible leaders within the commands. At the same time, the troops had to do something for themselves, too; they had to achieve the rudiments of at least a basic education in order to carry out *all* of the duties of military life. This meant going to school in the evenings after road building or Indian fighting or patrol riding – and it mean a voluntary attendance. The realization of both good leadership and self-education were to be experienced in time.

Erwin Thompson's very excellent study of the black troopers and their officers extends to an erea of study not usually considered by most writers and historians. In presenting his study he also painted an excellent picture of life in the military and on the frontier, making clear that the exciting episodes that have captured the imagination of millions of people were so infrequent as to cause boredom and desertion in the ranks. More often than not, most patrols chased shadows; and only once in a while did they fight Indians. It nevertheless seems that the Ninth and Tenth Cavalry Regiments and the Twenty-fourth and Twenty-fifth Infantry Regiments came in for more than their share of action.

It would be untrue to suggest that the majority of white officers wished to be assigned to the all-black units. Some came willingly because they thought that these were good assignments where they could earn quick promotions. Some simply came because they were assigned to one of the regiments. And, of course, some came because they wanted duty with the new troops. Whatever the reasons, they came, they served, and most were highly respected by the enlisted men.

But what of those who did not want to come? There are many stories about the officers who bought their way out of assignments, or of those who "traded" assignments with a monetary inducement: and there are those who made it known that they did not want the assignment under any circumstances. Their reluctance stemmed to a large degree from the bitter feelings engendered by the Civil War: There were opinions and attitudes toward blacks that lingered on and were not to be settled simply by the outcome of an armed struggle. One man who turned down a commission was Frederick William Benteen, Brevet Brigadier General, U.S. Army, and Senior Captain of the Seventh Cavalry after the Civil War. He is mentioned because he is probably the best known figure in American history to be involved in a refusal of assignment to one of the black units.

In an exchange of letters with Private T. W. Goldin, long after the Battle of the Little Big Horn, Captain Benteen made known why he had not wanted the assignment to the Tenth Cavalry. This letter, which is but one of several of this very famous correspondence, dated October 20, 1891, and printed here in full for the first time reflects an attitude that was shared by many officers in the service at that time. One cannot help reflecting on the path of Benteen's career had he accepted the assignment with the Tenth and not the one with the Seventh Cavalry under the command of Lieutenant Colonel George Armstrong Custer.

During the daily routines of patrol and shadow-chasing, there sometimes occurred an incident that would cause considerable stir among the American public. Newspapermen and other writers had a field day when Captain Nolan and forty troopers of A Troop, Tenth Cavalry, became lost on the Staked Plains of Texas for a long period of time without water and under conditions that could easily have meant death to all of them. They survived, and the story of how they drank the blood and urine of their horses to stay alive has been the inspriation for dozens of chroniclers of the western scene.

The duties of the black units were not solely characterized by complete boredom alternating with fleeting moments of danger and adventure. The three final chapters in this section illustrate the other types of duties that were sometimes found to be necessary and sometimes distasteful. The article entitled, "Oklahoma," describes the participation of members of the Ninth Cavalry in one of the most colorful episodes in the history of the Southwest and the Indian Territory, that of preventing the Boomers from settling in Indian Territory (Oklahoma) during the initial stages of that land grab. The territory was, of course, eventually opened up to settlers, but not until the Ninth had spent time escorting settlers *out* of the frontier instead of *in.*

The chapter "Our Soldiers In the Southwest" gives a graphic account of the respect and dependence that existed then between the black troopers and their white officers under most adverse conditions. The author writes:

> The military service done by General Miles' troops on the Southwestern border is as onerous and barren of opportunities for achieving renown as ever fell to soldiers in any land. They cannot attack the enemy, whip him, and be done with it. They seldom have the pleasure of a battle, but they may at any time suffer an attack.

"Practice Maneuvers in Arizona" illustrates the military effectiveness of the black troops. The events described took place twenty-one years after the four units had become established by congressional act. They had been through several campaigns and were on the verge of another major conflict. In between engagements, they had become a polished outfit, second to none in the service.

The final selection is an extract from the official history of the Twenty-fifth Infantry Regiment and is intended to make known the varied duties required of these men over a span of time. They were necessary duties but, for the most part, unpleasant. Nevertheless, no matter how unpleasant the assignment, the troops consistently displayed the highest degree of professionalism.

The Negro Soldier and His Officers

Erwin N. Thompson

THE OFFICERS

During the Civil War, Confederate authorities repeatedly threatened to put to death captured white officers who commanded Negro units in the Union army.[1] The U.S. Senate recalled these threats during the debate on the army reorganization bill in 1866. In recognition of the unusual hazards faced by the white officers of Negro units during the war, the Senate provided that they should have preference when the commissions were being given for the peacetime colored regiments, although other veterans were not to be excluded. The bill as it finally passed required that all lieutenants be from the Volunteers, two-thirds of the higher grades be from the Volunteers, and the other third from the regular army. All officers had to have had a minimum of two years service in the war and to "have been distinguished for capacity and good conduct in the field." [2]

In one aspect, the officers in the colored regiments far exceeded those in the white. This was the number who reached the general grades. Of the one hundred officers selected from the Negro regiments for comparison, eleven eventually became brigadier or major generals, while only six out of one hundred in the white units reached the general grades; however, only thirty-one officers in the colored units were promoted to the field grades (major-colonel) as compared to forty-eight for the others.[3]

Reprinted from Erwin N. Thompson, "The Negro Regiments of the U.S. Regular Army, 1866-1900." Master's thesis, University of California at Davis, 1966.

In three aspects the Negro regimental officers fell far behind their peers. Only four received a Medal of Honor, as compared to thirteen in the white units. As few as nine were graduates from the Military Academy, as compared to twenty-seven in the white regiments. In the matter of unsatisfactory service, nine officers in the Negro regiments were dismissed from the army, while only half that number left the white regiments under the same conditions.[4] On the whole, however, the career comparisons tend to show that the officers of the Negro regiments were quite similar in ability and potential to the rest of the commissioned ranks. they were hardly better and probably of a general quality that was no worse than the army at large.

One other statistic that might be noted is the number of officers who transferred between the white and colored regiments. Thirty-six of the hundred officers eventually transferred from the four Negro regiments to white units, while only thirteen moved over to the colored regiments.[5] Whereas too much weight should not be given to these figures, they suggest that most officers did not look favorably upon service in a Negro unit and that many of them in these units were there primarily to have an army career, rather than by choice. Unfortunately very few candid statements by the officers about serving in the colored regiments have been uncovered. But one finds hints and oblique remarks that suggest such service was undesirable. Captain John Bigelow, writing about the eve of the Spanish-American war, said, "For over twenty years I had labored under the disadvantage of serving in a colored regiment. I was now in a position to derive some advantage from it, and was quite set on doing so."[6] Bigelow did not mention what the disadvantages were.

One well-established disadvantage present in the early years of these regiments was the shortage of educated enlisted men to fill the noncommissioned and clerical positions. Consequently the junior officers had to do most of the paper work including calling the rolls and making out the monthly returns.[7] Surgeon William Notson at Fort Concho, Texas, who had an obvious dislike of Negro troops, wrote, "The impracticability of making intelligent soldiers out of the mass of the negroes, is growing more evident to the Post Surgeon every day, and his opinion is concurred in by their own officers when speaking with confidence. . . ."[8]

In a few incidents, the ladies of the garrison disclosed antagonistic attitudes more clearly than their husbands. An officer's wife, on arriving at Camp Supply and seeing Negro soldiers for the first time, allowed that they made good servants, "It did look so funny, however, to see such a black man in a blue uniform." While she was at Camp Supply, segregation was extended to the daily guard mount, and this lady saw it as progress for "it was outrageous to put white and black in the same little guard room, and colored sergeants over white corporals and privates." [9]

None other than the commanding general of the Department of Texas, Brigadier General Edward Otho Cresap Ord, felt that Negro regiments should not be in the regular army at all. Confiding in Colonel Shafter, he wrote, "I had the assurance when I was in Washington that the recently introduced bill would certainly come up and pass – it gradually makes the Col'd Regts. white – (I suppose) as was recommended by myself Gen. Sherman and the president – by scattering the Col'd recruits among all Regts."[10] Ord was not suggesting this integration because of any advanced social theories; in the same letter he referred to "the ruffians in Col'd troops," and in another instance is reported to have asked for the withdrawal of Negro troops from the Mexican border because they could not be trusted "without officers – who are not always available."[11]

Regretably there was no further mention of Ord's scheme. His implication that President Grant and General Sherman were involved in the plan to eliminate the Negro regiments indicated its potential importance. A search in the *Congressional Globe* and elsewhere failed to uncover any bill that would have affected the Negro regiments at this time. Additional research in archival records should establish more fully General Ord's scheme and perhaps illustrate more clearly the attitudes of the officers toward the Negro regiments.

Sex posed more than the usual set of problems for the Negro regiments, particularly at the isolated forts on the frontier. Infidelity on the part of officers' wives probably occurred no more often than in the upper middle class at large. Extramarital relations were not condoned but they were not unknown, including liaisons between officers' wives and enlisted men. The taboos surrounding extramarital relations between the races, however, were very strong – to the point that affairs must have been almost nonexistent. Still, the Negro enlisted men were present, usually without wives, and the folklore about Negro sexual powers and promiscuity was as prevalent then as in more recent times. Not often spoken about, there was always lurking under the surface of the routine garrison life the fear of assault and rape.

This potential problem emerged into the open at Fort Davis in the fall of 1872. Lieutenant Frederic Kendall, Twenty-fifth Infantry, was absent from the post on duty. About 1 A.M., November 21, Mrs. Kendall was awakened by the sound of breaking glass. She discovered a man climbing through the bedroom window. She ordered him to go away but he kept coming. Mrs. Kendall fired a pistol at him, "the ball taking effect on the top of the man's head, the blood spilling into the room, his cap falling into the room, while the man fell back from the window on the porch dead. . . ."[12]

The man turned out to be Corporal Daniel Talliforro, Ninth Cavalry. Immediately it became more than a case of forced entry, it assumed the ugly proportions of a racial incident in which the character of the entire Negro garrison was indicted. Neither the officers nor their families doubted that Talliforro's intentions were rape and that this was to be expected of Negroes. Colonel Andrews wrote:

> It is now seventeen months since I commenced my services with Colored Troops and during that time, attempts similar to the one related above have been made upon the officers quarters at Fort Duncan, Stockton, and Davis, and I think McKavett and Concho. While stationed at Fort Clark, five such attempts were reported to me.[13]

Andrews said that both officers and married enlisted men were "reluctant to leave their families for any purpose after dark and that detached service becomes a positive cruelty." Much of his report was based on the emotions of the moment, yet the colonel was reflecting an attitude that existed, an attitude that might help to explain Captain Bigelow's feeling of twenty years of disadvantages.

Problems, sexual or otherwise, were not necessarily confined to the Negro men. A number of the white officers had no hesitancy whatever in accusing their peers of infidelity or dishonesty. The notorious Captain George Armes, whose proficiency in name-calling was unexcelled, once preferred charges against his fellow officer, Captain George Graham, saying that his "reputation is so notoriously disreputable that no respectable lady can treat him with civility and courtesy due his uniform without incurring a taint upon her fair name. . . ."[14] Although Armes called almost everyone names, the eccentric captain was quite right in this case. Graham soon was dismissed from the army for selling government horses for personal gain.[15] At the time of General Ord's retirement, Armes said that "at least 10,000 signatures could have been obtained requesting his removal from this department. . . ."[16] It may have been with officers like Armes in mind, however, that General Ord wrote, "We must establish a higher moral as well as military standard in the Colored Regiments *among the officers* or I shall not be able to write of them as I desire to."[17]

Had he inquired, Ord would have found support in his concern about the caliber of the officers in Captain T. A. Baldwin. While on the Staked Plains with Shafter in 1875, Baldwin wrote his wife, "It seems that the Tenth Cavalry is particularly blessed with incompetent commanders. If I ever see General Ord, I shall tell him for God's sake to take this command, shoot them but not mutilate them."[18]

Still, such outbursts were fairly rare in the writings of these officers. More often they wrote well of one another. It was a small, tight world in which the members protected one another and, in their physical and professional isolation, they found it wise to get along. The long associations at one small frontier post after another built lasting friendships as well as enduring animosities. Major Anson Mills, Tenth Cavalry, recalled that at the Military Academy before the Civil War one of his classmates was Lieutenant Colonel Wesley Merritt, Ninth Cavalry. At the Academy, "a question of veracity arising between us, our friends decided we should go down by Dade's monument and settle the matter." They had their fist fight. "Although our hearts were not in it, we had one of the hardest fights that took place while I was at the academy."[19] Later, in the West, the two men were always the best of friends.

The younger officers, fresh out of West Point, who joined the regiments in increasing numbers in the 1880s and '90s, rapidly became imbued with a sense of kinship. Lieutenant Frank R. McCoy, who joined the Tenth Cavalry in 1898, reminisced that he met his captain, William Beck, "chasing our transport in Tampa Bay reporting from sick leave in spite of orders to stay sick." Beck, who had served in the Civil War and had been with Grierson at Tinaja de las Palmas in 1880, was still only a captain when the Spanish-American war broke out. McCoy served under him in Cuba and ever afterwards thought of him as his captain and leader. "The last time I saw the old Colonel was when in the War College he sent for me to come to the hospital at Washington Barracks, and I found him propped up in bed smoking a pipe, cheerful and cool as ever, and asked me to stand by him while he had his leg cut off."[20]

Only one medal, the Medal of Honor, was awarded for bravery during these years. Even it was sometimes exchanged after 1888, for the Certificate of Merit which was accompanied by a small increase of pay. Apparently, too, no common policy for making awards existed. Compared to those in the white regiments, these officers fared poorly in the number of medals. During the Indian wars, only seven officers in the four regiments received the award: Ninth Cavalry – four; Tenth Cavalry – two; Twenty-fourth Infantry – one. Deeds of valor and outstanding leadership in combat were also recognized by the award of brevet rank. How many of these honorary promotions were made or how the number compared to the white regiments cannot be determined from the available records. Nonetheless these regiments had their share of courageous leaders. Perhaps their failure to receive as many medals or to be recognized as much as their fellow officers was another of the disadvantages they thought they suffered.

NEGRO OFFICERS

In 1873 a tall, slim young man, Henry Ossian Flipper, entered the United States Military Academy. His arrival caused a stir among the cadet corps, "The rear windows were crowded with cadets watching. . . with apparently as much astonishment and interest as they would, perhaps, have watched Hannibal crossing the Alps." This son of a Georgian slave was to be the first Negro to graduate from West Point and the first to become an officer in the regular army.[21]

When the colored regiments were formed in 1866, there was no thought of having Negro officers. Such an idea was simply inconceivable. Then, radical reconstruction took effect in the southern states, and the freedmen succeeded in some places in sending their candidates to the U.S. Congress. It was then only a matter of time before Negroes would be appointed to the Academy.

Four Negro candidates had preceded Flipper. Only one of these,

James W. Smith from South Carolina, had survived the early days of the rigorous program and was now an upperclassman. There was no mistaking the hostility of the cadets toward the Negroes, and Smith's life at the Academy had proven to be an ugly experience marked with name calling and fights. However, his premature departure, which was to come in 1874, was in part brought on by his own contentious trouble-seeking character. Although Smith was the victim of cruel persecution, his own unpleasant reputation created an additional burden for Flipper to bear.[22]

Flipper endured "the sneer, the shrug of the shoulder, the epithet, the effort to avoid, to disdain, to ignore" during the four years at West Point.[23] Through restraint and patience, and by conducting himself in a "straightforward, self-respecting manner, neither cringing nor meeting trouble more than half way," Flipper gained the respect if not the friendship of his fellow cadets.

In 1877, Lieutenant Flipper journeyed westward to join the Tenth Cavalry at Fort Sill in the Indian Territory. Assigned to Captain Nicholas Nolan's company, Flipper quickly adjusted to the fort's activities. At first "there was a constant stream of colored women, officers' servants, soldiers' wives, etc., to see the colored officer."[24] To his surprise he was readily accepted by some of the officers and their wives and was included in the social affairs of the post. The first time he was invited to a party, "I did not go because I thought it was only a courtesy invitation. I went to bed early, but Lieutenant and Mrs. Maney came to my quarters, roused me out and wanted to know why I had not gone to the party." They persuaded Flipper to get dressed and attend the party where Mrs. Maney made him dance every dance.[25]

There were incidents too when race prejudice was present. On one occasion the officers at Fort Concho decided to have a dinner for Flipper who was visiting the post, but the commanding officer, Major Anson Mills of Flipper's own regiment, forbade the dinner. The junior officers apologized to the lieutenant for this indignity.[26]

Flipper's career came to an abrupt end in 1881 at Fort Davis, Texas. Arrested by Colonel Shafter, then the post commander, for stealing quartermaster funds, he was found guilty of misconduct and dismissed from the army. Flipper maintained he was the victim of Shafter's prejudices and that the charges were wholly false.[27] After he left the army, he became a successful mining engineer in Mexico, and, many years later, was appointed a special assistant to the Secretary of the Interior (U.S.). Despite his short army career, Flipper had established firmly that there could be Negro officers without impairing the army's mission. The presence of the tall, dignified lieutenant in a colored regiment must have had a great effect on the enlisted men who served under him. Regrettably none of them left a record of the event.

Almost unnoticed in history is John Hanks Alexander, the second Negro officer in the regular army. Alexander graduated from West Point in 1887 and joined the Ninth Cavalry, which at that time was stationed in the Dakota Territory. He remained an inconspicuous second lieutenant for seven years with the Ninth, dying in 1894 of natural causes.[28]

When the Spanish-American war came, Flipper offered his services to the government again, but his offer was not acknowledged. An article appeared in the *Washington Post* at the time saying that the War Department was considering the raising of a Negro volunteer cavalry regiment with Flipper as its colonel and Charles Young as its lieutenant colonel.[29] Young was the third Negro to graduate from the Military Academy in the nineteenth century. An outstanding officer, he eventually reached the grade of colonel. He also served in the Ninth Cavalry. In 1896 he set a new precedent by transferring to a white regiment, the Seventh Cavalry, where he remained on the rolls for one year. Young did not get the position rumored in the *Washington Post,* but when the war came he was appointed a major in the Ninth Ohio Colored Infantry, being of course the first regular army Negro to reach field grade.[30]

These were not the only Negroes to live in officers' quarters. The act establishing the colored regiments had authorized a chaplain for each of them. Five of the chaplains appointed before the end of the century were Negroes.[31] Although few posts had a chapel in the sense the word is used today, most of the forts had a building that was suited for religious services as well as being a library, schoolroom, theater, and ballroom for the regimental parties. The army was not an especially religious organization, and the attendance at church was liable to be rather small, often the mainstay being the officers' families rather than the soldiers; however, the enlisted men were likely to come into contact with the chaplain in other ways. He was usually the librarian and the teacher of the classes set up for illiterate soldiers. He might also be the post treasurer, and in all instances he was available as a counselor for those in search of advice. A wise commander could make use of the Negro chaplain as a bridge to understanding the wants and needs and the character of the Negro soldiers.

THE NEGRO SOLDIERS

Published works have spelled out a variety of reasons why the army instituted Negro units in 1866. One writer proposed that it was to slap the South, or to give unemployed Negroes jobs, or perhaps white men were tired of fighting.[32] A sociologist suggested that the reason was to reward valor in the war and that it "was not looked upon as a device for segregation but as a friendly and progressive step."[33] An army officer agreed that in the Civil War Negroes had earned the right to be soldiers. He also thought that the colored regiments were organized to provide positions in the regulars for officers who had served in colored units during the war.[34] Some U.S. Senators had another reason. The original draft of the bill called for Negroes in the infantry only. These senators argued successfully to have colored cavalry regiments because it was a known fact that Negroes did not desert as did the white cavalry, and therefore would be more effective against the Indians.[35]

There was one voice in opposition to the idea of Negro soldiers. James Albert McDougall, California's Democratic senator, exclaimed that officers and soldiers "must belong to the ruling forces and should not belong to inferior forces." He warned that "this undertaking to place a lower, inferior, different race upon a level with the white man's race, in arms, is against the laws that lie at the foundation of true republicanism."[36] Few others publicly joined Senator McDougall in opposition. It would seem that the record of the 170,000 Negroes who saw active duty during the Civil War was overwhelming evidence that they had won the right and the obligation to serve as soldiers.

There was, however, almost complete agreement that the new units be segregated. To most white Americans, Negroes were inferior. Despite their being freed, colored men were limited in what they could accomplish. Captain T. A. Baldwin was not alone in his opinion that "the only thing they care for is someone to look after them, they never will think for themselves."[37]

There were a few individuals who saw the situation in its true light. One of these was Richard H. Pratt, a company officer of the Tenth Cavalry. Recalling a conversation with a fellow officer, Pratt wrote, "In considering the case of the Negro, we were agreed that when the Fourteenth Amendment became a part of the Constitution, the Negro would be entitled to be treated in every way as other citizens, and we were unable to reconcile that two regiments of cavalry and two of infantry then being inducted into the army of the United States . . . would accord with the Amendment which provided that there must be no distinction."[38]

Despite Pratt's uncomfortable feeling about segregation, few of the Negro soldiers themselves seemed concerned about their status. Sergeant Samuel Harris, for example, was quite certain that his reason for joining the regular army was to see the West, when he had completed his hitch he would get a good government job.[39] In his compilation of the reminiscences of the Indian Wars' enlisted men, Don Rickey has concluded that most Negro soldiers joined the army for social and economic betterment.[40] Segregated or not, most of them felt they found these goals. Private Charles Creek summed it up well when he said "I got tired of looking mules in the face from sunrise to sunset, thought there must be a better livin in this world. . . ." so he joined the cavalry.[41] Private George Gently, the illegitimate son of a Negro woman and a white man joined the army simply to get away from his mother and a brother, neither of whom he liked.[42]

It was hardly surprising that in the beginning the educational level of the Negroes was low. Rickey has established that even in the white regiments many of the enlisted men were illiterate and most of them were from the bottom of the economic ladder.[43] The great difficulty as discovered by the company officers was that almost none of the Negro enlisted men possessed the basic skills of writing and keeping accounts. In a white regiment there was usually a handful of men who could be made into clerks, but the shortage in the Negro units was great. The regimental historian of the Ninth Cavalry wrote, "It is difficult nowadays fully to appreciate all the work and labor devolving upon the officers in those early days. The men knew nothing, and the noncommissioned officers but little more."[44] The Twenty-fifth

Infantry experienced the same situation, " I beg to call special attention to the great labor thrown upon the officers of the colored regiments in being obliged to make all rolls, returns, accounts, and keep all books with their own hands."[45]

If the Negro enlisted men had to be closely supervised in these early years, they quickly proved themselves willing, even anxious, learners. Before the end of the 1860s, after-hours schools were established at many army posts to teach enlisted men to read and write, even though the act establishing army schools was believed to be inapplicable west of the Mississippi River.[46] At Fort Davis, the school experienced a series of ups and downs. The first teacher, apparently a civilian, left when the condition of the post fund required that his salary be reduced.[47] Classes were reestablished under Lieutenant Frederic Kendall's supervision and, later, under the Twenty-fifth's chaplain, George G. Mullins.[48]

By the 1890s the officers' complaints of the lack of technicians and clerks had largely disappeared from their accounts. Because of the training the soldiers received in their regiments and the influx of recruits who possessed some education; the problem was considerably alleviated. It was probable however that the majority of the men remained at the lowest levels of formal education.[49]

Aside from formal education, the troops in a frontier post underwent endless drills, parades, and inspections. In these physical aspects of training all the Negro regiments quickly became proficient organizations, which proficiency repaid itself in making these men skilled fighters. Observers noted that these troops seemed especially proud of their uniform and of their profession as soldiers.[50] The soldiers had many opportunities to dress in full uniform and to strut the parade ground. Fort Davis in 1877 had dress parade every evening of the week "Saturday excepted."[51] These dress parades were not taken lightly. The post band played the marches of the day, all the troops not on patrol or guard mount took part, the families from officers row and from soapsuds row came out to watch as the huge garrison flag was slowly lowered. Even thirty years of service did not lessen the attraction of this moment in a fort's day.

In contrast to the formal parades and guard mounts of garrison life was the appearance of the troops while in the field. Lieutenant Bigelow described a column of Negro cavalry men in Arizona during the Apache wars: "Most of the men ride in their blue flannel shirts . . . one big sergeant wears a bright red shirt . . .; some of the men take off their shirts and ride in their gray knit undershirts. There are all sorts of hats worn, of American and Mexican make, the most common being the ugly army campaign hat of gray felt." As for trousers, some wore army blue, others civilian overalls. "There are few trousers not torn or badly worn, especially in the seat. Here is a man with a single spur; here one without any."[52] Supporting Bigelow's description are two pencil sketches of the Tenth Cavalry enlisted men, apparently on the Texas frontier, in the papers of General Shafter. Probably drawn by a Negro soldier possessing a wry sense of humor, both soldiers look a great deal like caricatures of pre-war plantation field hands with their torn shirts and ragged trousers.[53]

The forts themselves were not much to look at, especially in the 1870s. Despite popular conceptions they were rarely stockaded and Indians never attacked them. Most of them resembled run-down villages located in some of the most unpleasant country the West could offer. The enlisted barracks was often a mere hovel in the early postwar years. The Congress resisted authorizing construction funds for forts the army seemed to be closing down every few years as Indian warfare shifted from one area to another. The post surgeon walked through the barracks at Fort Davis one night at ten o'clock and found the squad rooms almost suffocating due to the crowded conditions.[54] When the quartermaster general, M. C. Meigs, inspected some of the Texas forts in 1869-70, "and saw the roughboard, vermin infested bunks in which the men slept, he was horrified. . . ."[55] Even General Sherman on one of his field trips, was repulsed by the enlisted quarters, as he described them "hovels in which a negro would hardly go."[56]

Although the post surgeon at Fort Grant, Arizona, reported as late as 1887 that the barracks were badly ventilated and one set was unfit for occupation, quarters improved vastly throughout the 1800s.[57] Other facilities improved gradually also, such as bathtubs and hot water replacing washing in creeks. Recreation rooms were set up at some of the larger forts. The food remained very much the same throughout the Indian Wars: beef or bacon, potatoes, beans, fresh vegetables from the post garden, bread, and sometimes fruit or jam made up a typical ration. The post surgeon at Fort Davis noted that "colored troops consume much more of their ration than white troops. . . ."[58]

Varying only slightly with the season, the bugle calls regulated a fort's daily life. A typical routine for the waking hours was posted as follows:[59]

Reveille 1st Call	5:20 A.M.
Reveille	5:30
Stable and Police Call	5:40
Breakfast Call	6:40
Sick Call	7:30
Water and Fatigue Call	8:00
Guard Mount Call	8:50
Drill 1st Call	9:20
Drill Call	9:30
Recall from Drill	10:30
Recall from Fatigue	12:00
Orderly Call	12:10 P.M.
Dinner Call	12:30
Fatigue Call	1:00
Drill 1st Call	3:50
Stable Call	4:00
Recall from Stables and Fatigue	5:00
Recall from Drill	5:20
Retreat 1st Call	15 min. before sunset
Retreat	Sunset
Tatoo	8:30

As the trumpeters sounded reveille day in and day out, year in and year out, the colored regiments became ever more an integral part of the professional fighters of the Western army. As the years passed, traditions originated and became ever more deeply entrenched in the regimental memories. No one really knows when the term "buffalo soldiers" originated as a nickname for the Negro soldiers. Some writers would claim it started with the Indians when they first came in contact with the colored troops. Others would rely on the story of the Negro troops serving in the Department of the Platte, where on cold winter marches their black faces would peer out of heavy overcoats of buffalo hides. An officer's wife at Camp Supply in 1872 wrote, "The officers say that the negroes make good soldiers and fight like fiends. They certainly manage to stick on their horses like monkeys. The Indians call them 'buffalo soldiers,' because their woolly heads are so much like the matted cushion that is between the horns of the buffalo."[60]

At some times "buffalo soldiers" was applicable to any Negro soldier, at other times it seemed to have been limited to the cavalry troopers. As time passed, it came to apply more to the Tenth Cavalry than the others. When a regimental coat of arms was designed for this outfit, a buffalo appeared on it. White troops had another name for this regiment however, calling it "Grierson's brunettes." The Negro troopers do not seem to have taken offense at either name, indeed, they developed considerable pride in their being called the buffalo soldiers.[61]

Other distinctive traits of the Tenth that have been recorded include their special vocabulary. These troopers never called a new soldier a recruit, which was the standard term, but throughout his first enlistment he was referred to as a "young soldier." Recruit to them meant a new horse. Another custom they are said to have observed was the repeating of "sir" at least three times in response to an order. An example of this is "Yes sir, Captain sir, it shall be done, sir."[62] Then, as in more recent times, Negroes were supposed to be musically inclined. Captain Stephen Jocelyn described the formation of a band and orchestra at Fort Du Chesne in the winter of 1887-88, "Naturally the trumpeters were easily taught and several of the colored troops from the Ninth Cavalry had the usual excellent negro ear for music."[63]

Holidays were rare on the frontier in the nineteenth century, but the army celebrated July 4 and Christmas whenever possible and however meager the facilities. On July 4, 1882, at Fort Stockton, Texas, Captain Armes had a greased pole set up for climbing, a shaved and greased pig for chasing, wheelbarrows and sack races. The day was climaxed by "several splendid horseraces." This same captain, who had a reputation for poor treatment of his troops, claimed to have spread a Christmas feast for his company consisting of whole sheep, roast pigs, cake and wine."[64]

July 4, 1874, at Fort Davis was marred by an accident. Private John Jourdan, Twenty-fifth Infantry, was ramming home a round in an artillery piece when the gun prematurely discharged. Jourdan lost his sight in one eye and a bad gash in an arm.[65] The post surgeon's reports recorded this and the other accidental injuries and deaths over the years. Private Chambers, Twenty-fifth Infantry, was discharged from the army because of a mule kick in the stomach. Private Wilson, Ninth Cavalry, accidentally shot and killed himself while cleaning his carbine.

Private David Boyd, Ninth Cavalry, was accidentally killed by another soldier.[66] In addition, homicides, suicides, and the various diseases took their toll. A comparison of various Surgeon General's reports shows that the number of cases, pro rata, of illness among Negro troops was somewhat less than among whites. In contrast, the number of deaths was slightly higher among Negroes.[67]

Illnesses and Deaths, Whites versus Negroes

Per 1000

Number of Cases	1868	1869	1870	1871	1872	1873	1874
Negro	3061	2087	1822	1362	1400	1708	1816
White	2908	2589	2156	2163	1974	1963	1790
Number of Deaths							
Negro	56	18	19	19	22	21	15
White	30	13	12	17	15	17	13

Although not prorated, statistics showing the number of homicides and suicides were compiled by the Surgeon General for the period 1869-74. Among white troops there had been a total of 144 homicides and 104 suicides. In the Negro regiments during the same period the number of homicides was 44, suicides, 4. Considering that Negroes composed roughly one-tenth of the army, the number of homicides among them was high whereas the number of suicide victims was extremely low.[68]

The types of illness that hit an army post mirrored the state of medicine at the time. In 1868 scurvy swept through Fort Davis and elsewhere. While the doctors knew the importance of fruits and vegetables as preventatives for this disease, they were not certain about the causes of dysentery and diarrheal infections that were so common. Lung troubles, ranging from bronchitis to tuberculosis were also among the principal illnesses in the sick reports. Alcoholism was another, although the officers believed there was less alcoholism and drunkenness among Negro troops than among the whites, including themselves.[69] The germ theory was still only vaguely understood by most doctors, however widespread the use of vaccines against smallpox.

There were no vaccines against venereal diseases which were prevalent throughout the army.[70]

Wherever the soldiers went in the West, the prostitutes were close behind. This was as true for the Negro units as for the white. The post surgeon at Fort Grant, Arizona, at a time when Negro troops occupied the post, complained that venereal diseases had become an epidemic. He knew the source – two "whiskey ranches" just outside the military reservation where gamblers and prostitutes congregated on payday.[71] A departmental commander, Brigadier General A. H. Terry, in his investigation of a killing, reported that there were two brothels in Sturgis City, Dakota Territory, "catering to the taste and pandering to the passions of the colored troops, for they are 'stocked' with colored prostitutes – negresses and mulattoes."[72]

Laundresses were also commonly seen at the western posts – at least until they were abolished as an institution in 1877. A law of 1802 had authorized each company four laundresses who could accompany the troops, and the Negro companies as well as the white employed these women. The army supplied their rations and transportation, the men had to pay for their laundry. All kinds of women were employed in this occupation. Some were the upright wives of enlisted men who could not otherwise afford to accompany their husbands; others who may have first been employed when single had acquired a husband in the company either through marriage or common law. Most of the laundresses, however, seem to have been a hard-bitten lot who supplemented their incomes through prostitution. Called "spikes" they were usually the source of trouble, fights, and disease.[73]

Although the army did not recognize wives, of either officers or enlisted men, as having any legal status, and rarely considered them or their children in the assignment of quarters, a number of Negro enlisted men managed to have their wives accompany them to the western posts. Other men pursued and won the Negro cooks and servants brought to the forts by officers' wives.[74] The official records have few references to these families, but an entry in a post surgeon's record gives a glimpse, "On the 30th there was a son born to 1st Sgt. John W. Harper Co. H, 25th Infantry and Fanney Harper, his wife. . . ."[75] Only one reference to an interracial marriage was noted. Not too long before Mrs. Kendall killed the soldier trying to enter her quarters at Fort Davis, a musician in the Twenty-fifth Infantry, Martin Pedee, was convicted of attempting to commit rape, "on the white wife of a corporal in the same company."[76]

Despite the absence of families for many of the men, and despite the loneliness and boredom of frontier service, an amazingly small percentage of the Negro soliders deserted. Their small desertion rate is all the more surprising when compared to the amazingly high desertion rate among the white troops. In 1867, twenty-five percent of the aggregate strength of the army deserted. Out of these 13,608 deserters only 570, or 4.2 percent, were Negro. The following year showed a similar pattern; out of 10,939 deserters, only 3.6 percent were from the colored regiments.[77]

No reasons were given as to why the Negro desertion rate was so low. The same conditions that were thought to cause the high rate of desertion among the white troops affected the colored troops: low pay (particularly the reduction in 1871 from $16 to $13 per month for privates), labor work instead of fighting, absence of recreation facilities, and the light penalties imposed on recovered deserters.[78] Two speculative reasons for the low rate might be the difficulty of Negroes disappearing into an all-white community on the frontier and, more positively, the fact that the Negro soldiers were still highly impressed with their elevation in their status by being soldiers. To leave the army would be to drop back into the lower social status they had experienced prior to active duty. By the late 1870s the army's overall desertion rate had dropped to less than seven percent of the aggregate strength. Still the Negroes' rate is thought to have remained proportionately lower although no specific data for the later period was available.[79]

In matters of crime and punishment, the Negro regiments seem to have had about the same percentage of crimes and other offenses as the white regiments. Although not a wholly meaningful set of statistics, the number of courts-martial in the army in 1882 was noted by the Secretary of War that year. The Ninth Cavalry, with 74, had more courts-martial than any other cavalry regiment; the Tenth had the smallest number, 36. The Twenty-fourth Infantry, with 20 and the Twenty-fifth, with 25, had an average number for the infantry regiments in the army.

The types of crime varied from thievery and drunkenness to murder and arson. At Fort Davis in 1873 an arsonist set fire to the post headquarters, injuring slightly the sergeant major of the Twenty-fifth Infantry and threatening the regiment's 1200-volume library.[80] Two murders occurred on the post in 1878. In one case, a fight broke out among the prisoners in the guardhouse, and Private William Grant, Tenth Cavalry, was killed by a fellow prisoner. That same summer, "Corporal Richard Robinson Co. 'H' 25 Infantry while lying asleep on his bunk was assassinated by Sergeant Moses Marshall, by shooting him through the head with a Springfield rifle. . . ." Sergeant Marshall's motivations are not known.[81]

Punishment was swift on the frontier. With little chance of their being reprimanded by higher authorities, the various commanders devised some unusual punishments beyond the ordinary means of confinement, double-timing around the parade ground at post arms, and tying up the offender so that he was suspended by his hands.[82] Captain George W. Graham, who had a pre-army prison record of his own, had two quarreling sergeants take blacksnake whips to each other.[83] Equally erratic was Colonel Miles' "moral suasion horse." When he was stationed at Fort Bridger, after he had transferred from the Negro troops, he made his wayward soldiers ride a large narrow wooden horse, built in such a way that the man's feet could not touch the ground. Besides the torture of sitting on this, the soldier had to carry a six-foot wooden sword and dismount "occasionally to curry and water it with currycomb and water bucket." Miles claimed that the painful punishment worked.[84]

In the mid-1880s a source of many disciplinary problems disappeared when the institution of post trader was abolished. Free enterprise stores, with their ample stocks of liquor, were replaced with army-operated canteens which sold beer under pleasant conditions, providing the enlisted men with a club-like atmosphere. However, temperance organizations took exception to the army's selling beer to its soldiers and succeeded in having the canteens closed down. The soldiers quickly reverted to their old customs of patronizing the unregulated saloons outside the forts.[85] Despite crimes, payday sprees, and other breeches in military etiquette, the discipline of the Negro regiments was relatively good. Many of the examples given were the exception, the more routine entry in the post surgeon's report read, "The discipline of the troops during the month quite good, no desertions, and consequently very little punishment. . . ."[86]

With the exception of the desertion record and perhaps a few other aspects, such as the lack of drunkenness, the Negro regiments must be regarded as being more like the white units than different from them. Generally, on the posts where both races served together there was very little disagreement on racial grounds. Secretary of War William Belknap on a tour of Texas in 1873 noted, "At several of these posts where both white and colored soldiers were stationed, the general good conduct and their fine military appearance of all the troops comprising the garrison were prominent to a marked degree."[87]

Although General Ord wanted full integration in order to get rid of the Negro regiments, and perhaps eventually to rid the army of Negro soldiers, each of these small frontier posts which had companies from both races were, as a result of their smallness, integrated but only in a temporary, limited way. Mrs. Roe noted this, with strong disapproval, at Camp Supply, "This. . .would be all right if there were not a daily mingling of white and colored troops which often brings a colored sergeant over a white corporal and privates."[88] Despite Mrs. Roe's emotions, the two races could and did associate on guard and fatigue duties and, at Fort Robinson, Nebraska, on the post baseball team.[89] Still, the old prejudices died slowly, if at all. Captain Charles King, Fifth Cavalry, described Nicholas Nolan's Tenth Cavalry troop as having an "Ethiopian lieutenant" (Flipper) "and sixty of the very best darkies that ever stole chickens."[90] At Fort Arbukle, Lieutenant Pratt was dressed down by the post commander, who was in the Sixth Infantry, for selecting a Negro over a white soldier as orderly. Still there was very little friction between the two groups throughout these years. In the end, the institution of segregation remained, reflecting the growing separation of the races practiced in the civilian society.

While the Negro and white soldiers were able to cooperate on the army reservations, the colored soldiers found a generally hostile world outside the fort gates. But occasionally there were compliments from the white community. At the time of the 1894 railroad strike when the Twenty-fifth Infantry was called in, the editor of the *Anaconda Standard* of Missoula, Montana concluded, "They are model soldiers when in garrison, and their conduct whenever they have been called into the field has been excellent." More often, the Negro soldier could expect the kind of comment that has been made by the contemporary propagandist, J. Evetts Haley, "The prestige of the Army and the well-being of Texas suffered from the fact that Fort Concho and other frontier posts were garrisoned with Negro troops." Haley believes that the presence of Negro troops in Texas was doubly unfortunate because Negroes were poor frontiersmen and poor soldiers and "the ingrained attitudes, social customs, and prejudices so strong in the South were often violent in Texas."[91]

Haley is right about the violence. Around Fort Concho there assembled a collection of desperados and criminals that was typical of the Texas frontier. The community of saloons, cribs, and gambling houses outside the fort eventually adopted the ironic name of San Angelo. Drunken cowboys, ex-Confederates, pimps, and prostitutes waited to prey on the unwary soldier. An illustration of this environment was a drunken brawl of whites in February 1878 where the participants cut the chevrons and stripes off a Negro sergeant's uniform. Before the night was over, Company D of the Tenth showed up in the village armed with carbines. A riot ensued in which two men were killed and a number wounded.[92] Haley justifies the white outlaws' behavior on the grounds that it was a mistake for the North to put the ex-slaves in uniform.[93]

Three years later, in 1881, a Negro soldier was killed in San Angelo by a professional gambler, and a white private from the Sixteenth Infantry was killed by another civilian. The enlisted men of both regiments got together and secretly printed the following handbill:

Fort Concho, Texas
February 3, 1881

> We, the soldiers of the United States Army, do hereby warn cowboys, etc., of San Angelo and vicinity, to recognize our rights of way as just and peaceable men.
>
> If we do not receive justice and fair play, which we must have, someone must suffer; if not the guilty, the innocent.
>
> It has gone too far; justice or death.
>
> U. S. Soldiers, one and all[94]

Two companies of enlisted men, one from each regiment, then marched into town, arrested the sheriff, and demanded that he turn over the one murderer he had in custody. At that crucial point, Colonel Grierson discovered what was happening and averted a crisis by ordering the troops back to the post.

Such incidents were by no means restricted to San Angelo. They occurred in every collection of saloons outside every army post. At Suggs, Wyoming, in 1892, trouble developed between Negroes and whites over a white prostitute who had solicited among both groups. No deaths occurred in this fray.[95] At Fort Davis the village of Chihuahua was the scene of repeated violence such as in 1876 when a citizen killed Principal Musician Charles Hill with a pistol.[96] The frontier man wanted the army's protection, but he was not particular about associating with soldiers, especially if they were Negroes.

There were exceptions to this attitude. One admirer of the colored regiments was the western artist, Frederic Remington, who felt they were "charming men with whom to serve." Remington knew these to be brave men. "Will they fight?" he asked. "That is easily answered. They have fought many, many times. The old sergeant sitting near me, as calm of feature as a bronze statute, once deliberately walked over to a Cheyenne rifle pit and killed his man."[97]

The Medal of Honor winners among the colored soldiers support Remington's opinion. Although the Twenty-fifth Infantry, for reasons not known, appears not to have made awards to its men during the Indian wars, the other three regiments more than made up for it. The Twenty-fourth Infantry had five medal holders during the Indian Wars – the three men with Bullis in Texas in 1875 and two men who were in the paymaster fight in Arizona in 1889. These last two were Corporal Isaiah Mays, Company B, and Sgt. Benjamin Brown, Company C., whose citation read, "Although shot in the abdomen, in a fight between a paymaster's escort and robbers, did not leave the field until again wounded through both arms."[98] At least one enlisted member of the Tenth Cavalry received a Medal of Honor during the Indian Wars, but the Tenth's real moment of recognized glory came in the Spanish-American war. After the battle of San Juan Hill, the old Confederate General, Joseph Wheeler, recommended nine Tenth troopers for the medal, and at least five others from the regiment received the decoration.[99] No fewer than ten Ninth Cavalry troopers were awarded the Medal of Honor during the Indian Wars. Some of these have already been noted but one who has not is First Sergeant Moses Williams, Company I. When Nana led his renegade Indians across New Mexico in 1881, Sergeant Williams' company was one of the many in the pursuit. His citation describes the event:

Rallied a detachment, skillfully conducted a running fight of 3 or 4 hours, and by his coolness, bravery, and unflinching devotion to duty in standing by his commanding officer in an exposed position under a heavy fire from a large party of Indians saved the lives of at least three of his comrades.[100]

Recruit in Full-Dress Uniform (1885) **Paul Rossi**

The Bentin-Goldin Letter

P.O. Box 118
Atlanta, Georgia
Oct. 20th, 1891

Dear Mr. Goldin,

Yr. favor of 12th inst. recd. to-day.

It is very gratifying to know that my efforts while belonging to the 7th Cav. were appreciated by the rank and file; – i.e. the enlisted men, – and your letter of today tells me that they were.

I was with the regiment from its organization to December 1882, and – of course can look far behind the date you came to me, and the backward glance is as full of memories – many of them glorious, and all pleasant – as from the point where you first drew sabre.

Captain Owen Hale was the last of our old "Mess" – of seven – to bite the dust; and I alone remain to think of them – I mean the "Mess" associations – and cherish their memories in that regard.

In 1866 I could have gone into the 10th U.S. Cav. as a Major, but I preferred a captaincy in the Seventh. Fate, however, after being a captain 17 years – "threw" me into a negro organization of cavalry anyhow; and being well off in this world's goods, and feeling it was not proper to remain with a race of troops that I could take no interest in – and this on account of their "low down," rascally character – and having served my 30 yrs. – there seemed nothing left for me to do but to commence looking after my property interests.

It costs me $10,000, more than my pay came to, to follow the trumpet calls of the United States; and this amount – was not thrown away – or wasted either. Now, as a retired Major, I am getting along comfortably and am looking after my flocks and herds – city blocks in prospective – and the interests of Fred, my only child – I lost four children in following that brazen trumpet around.

I am pleased my dear Sir at having heard from [you], and I wish you an uninterrupted run of everything that is good.

Very truly yr. friend,
F.W. Benteen
Brevet Colonel
U.S. Army

T.W. Goldin, Esq.

US
H. D. Bugbee

Captain Nolan's Lost Troop on the Staked Plains

Colonel M. L. Crimmins

Many stories have been told about Captain Nicholas Nolan and Troop A, Tenth United States Cavalry being lost on the Staked Plains in mid-summer, 1877. They were without water for nearly four days and nights and managed to keep alive by drinking the blood of their dying horses. In an article which came to the writer's attention recently an old Texas Ranger stated that half of Captain Nolan's men died of thirst in the Staked Plains during the summer of 1876.[1] I, therefore, looked up the records in the Old Records Division of the Adjutant General's Office in Washington, D.C., and make the following report on the evidence found there:

> The Commanding General, Department of Texas, received on August 4, 1877, the following startling telegram from Brevett Brigadier General John Wynn Davidson at Fort Richardson, Texas: "Just received the following telegram, Concho August 3rd. Captain Nolan, Lt. Cooper & twenty-six enlisted men are lost on Staked Plains near Sand Hills – men of the Command have come in tonight saying that men and animals were dying for water and the Command was scattered in all directions – Indians were in the vicinity. The men who came in straggled from the

Reprinted through the courtesy of the West Texas Historical Association. The article first appeared in the *West Texas Historical Yearbook*, Vol. X (October, 1934).

> Command and found water 20 miles from where Nolan was last seen with a few of his men . . . when they returned to the place where Nolan was last seen about 25 miles from Yellow House.
>
> (Signed) Smithers
>
> 1st Lt. and Adjutant Robert G. Smithers, Tenth United States Cavalry.

The records reveal that on July 10, 1877, Captain Nicholas Nolan, Lieutenant Charles L. Cooper, and sixty men of Troop A, Tenth United States Cavalry, left Fort Concho, at San Angelo, Texas, for a two months scout. They planned to establish a supply camp near the base of operations and patrol the country in search of hostile Indians and pursue them if found. Their object was to protect the settlers, who were rapidly populating the country, due in a large measure, to the favorable report of Colonel William Rufus Shafter, Twenty-fourth Infantry. This report was published by me in the West Texas Historical Association *Year Book* for 1933. Colonel Shafter had spent the last half of 1875 carefully exploring West Texas and reported on the soil and climate and water and its suitability for stock raising and farming.

Captain Nolan marched with his troop about 140 miles in a northwesterly direction and scouted around Double Lake and Cedar Lake. When he reached Bull Creek, seven miles northeast of Moo-cha-ko-way mountain he ran into a bunch of twenty-eight buffalo hunters who were in pursuit of Indians, who had stolen some of their stock. Captain Nolan decided to establish his supply camp at Bull Creek and leave twenty men in charge and with the balance, forty men and Lieutenant Cooper and eight pack mules, joined the buffalo hunters. They had a good Mexican guide, named "Jose," who was supposed to know all the waterholes; and many of the buffalo hunters also knew the country and would be most useful in the pursuit of the Indians and greatly increase his chance of overtaking and attacking them.

On July 19, 1877, the expedition set out reenforced with twenty-one buffalo hunters and the Mexican guide, Jose. It was a dry year and water was scarce, for the first few days, until they reached Double Lake on the Staked Plains. Here they rested until July 26, while the guide Jose and some of the buffalo hunters scouted for water towards Dry Lake, seventeen miles to the west.

At 11 A.M., July 26, two of the hunters returned with the news that there was no suitable water in Dry Lake, but that that morning, about 8:30, forty Indians were seen, traveling leisurely and hunting game and acting as if unaware of the pursuit.

Nolan saddled up, fed and watered his men and horses, and at 1 P.M., July 26, 1877, started in pursuit. It was a hot day and the men had emptied their canteens by the time they got to Dry Lake. The water at the lake was so alkaline, that neither men nor beasts could drink it. The guide and buffalo hunters followed the Indian trail as long as there was any light. They were so intent on the trail that landmarks were not noted; so when it was dark, the guide could not find water, and on the night of July 26 Captain Nolan and his party made a dry camp. On the morning of the twenty-seventh they took up the Indian trail, as soon as it was light enough to see. They followed without stopping until dark and made the second dry camp the night of July 27. Two men were sunstruck that day and a sergeant and a few men were left with them, with orders to follow as soon as they could. The Indians must have known of the pursuit, for they scattered and their main trail could not be followed in the sand. The men had been dropping from their horses through exhaustion, as this was the second day without water since leaving camp. The country was gently undulating and the soil very dry and of a reddish color, with short grass and stunted mesquite and scrub oak about a foot high. The horses needed water as badly as the men. So Captain Nolan gave the guide his spare horse, which was in better condition than the others, and accompanied by eight men with the canteens of the command, the guide went in search of water. He searched every valley and gully, and the men were spread out searching too, when last seen. They were not seen again for ten days.

On the morning of July 28 they tried to pick up the trail of the guide and eight men, without success. Captain Nolan marched all day in a northeasterly direction. He and Lieutenant Cooper then conferred; and, as they could not find water or overtake the guide, they decided to fall back on Double Lake, where they were confident they would find water. They believed the distance was between seventy-five and one hundred miles toward the southeast. Their agony was intense as they could not eat. The saliva in their mouths had dried and they could not swallow food. They marched until dark and then waited for the moon to guide them, as they could not afford to lose their way and live.

The party had now been reduced to two officers, eighteen soldiers, and one buffalo hunter. The men had started dropping out one by one unable to keep up; nor were the others able to assist them. Their tongues and throats were swollen. Sugar put in the mouth would not dissolve and could not be swallowed. They marched till daylight, for they must have water and could not stop and live. By noon the intense heat was unbearable. The hard bread they tried to masticate accumulated between their teeth and in the palate. They had to scrape it out with their fingernails, as it would not go down their throats, nor could they spit it out. They tried to chew mesquite beans, but could not swallow them. The mouths by that time had no feeling. Vertigo and dimness of vision affected all. They could hardly speak, and when they did they did not recognize their own voices. They were troubled with deafness, and their minds were so dull that questions would have to be repeated several times before they could comprehend them. They were feeble, delirious, and tottered when they walked, like a horse with "blind staggers." They started to drink the blood of their dying horses. The blood coagulated so quickly that it could not be swallowed, except when taken hot. They were wild and hard to control and fought over the blood like hungry wolves. The heart and other viscera that had any moisture was grasped and sucked. The blood made them sick, and they drank their urine sweetened with sugar, and some drank the urine of the horses. They felt faint and suffocating. The sides of their tracheas felt as if adhering, so they closed their mouths and breathed through their noses as slowly as possible. Their lips were pale, like those of the dead. Their fingers and palms were pale and shriveled. Some removed their boots from their swollen feet and legs. The horses were dying one after another. The sun was terrific, and as a horse died his saddle blanket was sometimes put over his body and the soldier would lie in the shade alongside his horse, or put the blanket over a mesquite bush, for the same purpose. This was the third dry camp; and they started out again at 11 P.M. July 28 and kept going until 10 the next morning. This then was the start of the third day without water.

Lieutenant Cooper told his men that the only chance of their getting out alive was to stand together and obey orders like true soldiers. They must stop fighting and trying to take more than their share of the horses' blood, and they only had a few horses left. There were rain clouds in sight, and they might get some rain and yet be able to reach some streams to the East or be picked up by a relief party from the supply camp of Fort Concho. Some of the buffalo hunters might have gotten through and were getting them help. They then abandoned all their rations and every unnecessary article, only keeping their pistols and carbines, to protect themselves from hostile Indians and enable them to kill buffalo, if encountered, for their blood. Before they left the last camp, every horse they had was dead except two. Captain Nolan and Lieutenant Cooper then mounted pack mules, for as the leaders they must conserve their strength as much as possible. It was necessary that they guide and direct their men. There were only eighteen men of the troop left. They left camp at 8 P.M. July 29, the fourth night without water, and marched until 3 A.M. the thirtieth. At each halt the men would lie down, hoping to snatch a few minutes sleep, but their agony prevented it.

At 3 A.M. they struck an old wagon trail, and after following it Lieutenant Cooper got his bearings. You can imagine the delight of his men when he told them the good news that now there was hope of living. By 5 A.M. some of the men had marched the five miles to Double Lake. A number of men were missing, for they could not help those who fell out.

When Captain Nolan reached Double Lake, he found six of the men who had been absent for several days. He had them fill their canteens with water and take their horses and go back on his trail to help the survivors. Captain Nolan, Lieutenant Cooper, and his eighteen troopers had been without water for eighty-six hours or three days and four nights. When they got the water they were so exhausted it did them very little good. They vomited it and also vomited any food they tried to take. Finally they found they could retain hot coffee.

It must be remembered that the system normally loses through evaporation from the lungs and perspiration through the skin, about 3½ pounds of moisture a day, so these men in the intense heat, had probably lost 15 or 20 pounds of moisture in four days. This had to be gradually replaced by absorption not only by the stomach but by the system.

Captain Phillip Ludwell Lee, Tenth Cavalry, and eleven Tonkawa scouts, who had been sent out looking for them, arrived in camp next day and rendered valuable assistance.

On August 1, Captain Nolan received the good news, that fourteen of his men reached the supply camp safely. After resting a few days he marched to the supply camp, reaching there August 7, 1877.

The loss of the expedition was, four soldiers, one civilian, twenty-three horses and four mules died of thirst, out of forty soldiers and twenty-one civilians.

Frederic Remington

Oklahoma

The "Oklahoma boomer" has come to be a familiar name of late. At present there are one thousand or more Oklahoma boomers. They are encamped on Cheeota Creek, six miles from Arkansas City, on the southern border of Kansas. To the south of them lies the Indian Territory. Nearly in the center of that Territory stretches the Oklahoma country, an exceedingly fertile and attractive area. The boomers wish to march upon it, to settle it, and to possess it. The United States government says that they must not do this; and that the land is pledged to the Indians. The boomers declare that they will do it. United States troops are posted opposite the camp of the boomers, on the opposite side of Cheeota Creek. They have orders not to permit the boomers to set foot in the Indian Territory. Other United States troops are posted in the Territory – in the Oklahoma country – to guard it against the boomers. From the accounts that come to us there is likely to be an outbreak and bloodshed at any moment.

In November last died Captain David L. Payne, known better as Oklahoma Payne. He was the originator and first leader of the Oklahoma boomers. He was a man of obstinate convictions. He contended that the Oklahoma lands were public property, upon which he and his followers had the right to settle. These lands, as has been said, are fertile and desirable. They lie a little to the east of the center

Reprinted from *Harper's Weekly Magazine*, March 28, 1885.

of the Indian Territory. They cover about eighteen hundred square miles. From north to south at their longest part they measure sixty miles, and they stretch forty miles at the point of their greatest breadth. They are bounded on the north by the Cherokee strip of land lying west of the Arkansas River; on the east by the reservations of the Pawnee, Iowa, Kickapoo, and Pottawattomie tribes of Indians; on the south by the Canadian River; and on the west by the reservation of the Cheyenne and Arapahoe Indians. In these limits are included 1,887,800 acres, half a million acres more than are comprised in the State of Delaware. Colonel Boudinot, a Cherokee, gave the name of Oklahoma to the country. It is a word of the Cherokee language, and signifies "the home of the red man." The shortest way into the Oklahoma country from Kansas is from Caldwell, on the Kansas border, along a stage road and cattle trail that runs to Fort Reno, on the western border of Oklahoma.

Captain Payne made his first raid into the Oklahoma country in July, 1880. President Hayes had issued a proclamation declaring an invasion of Oklahoma an offense against the law, and ordering interlopers out. Payne and his party were arrested by United States troops. He was tried civilly at Fort Worth, Texas; the court decided against him, and he was warned by Secretary Teller to keep out of the Indian lands. In 1882, with twenty-nine followers, he again pushed across the border and settled in Oklahoma. The troops again drove him out. Again he went back, and in August last two squadrons of the Ninth United States Cavalry (colored) arrested him and the whole community which he had established at Rock Falls, and escorted them, with their personal property to the Kansas line. It is said that Payne at his death was worth $60,000.

Captain Couch succeeded to the command of the boomers on the death of Payne in November last. On the 15th of January last, General Hatch, in command of the United States forces opposing the boomers, sent word to Couch from his headquarters at Camp Russell, Indian Territory, warning him not to proceed in his scheme of colonization. Captain Couch, then at the head of four hundred men, defied the United States officer. On January 23, General Hatch sent Lieutenant Day, with forty-two soldiers, to Captain Couch at his encampment at Stillwater. Lieutenant Day requested the boomers to quit. Captain Couch ordered them to prepare for battle, and Lieutenant Day retired.

On January 25, General Hatch visited Couch's camp in person and offered him twenty-four hours in which to retreat. The general had at hand four companies from Fort Leavenworth, one from Fort Gibson, Indian Territory, one from Fort Lyon, Colorado, three from Fort Wingate, and three troops of cavalry from Fort Riley. After a parley, Couch made a conditional surrender, and on January 26 left the Territory with the honors of war. Troops and boomers fraternized immediately after the surrender.

The troops escorted the boomers to Arkansas City. There the boomers were received with applause by the citizens. A public meeting passed resolutions condemning the action of the government and declaring the intention of an early renewal of the attempt to colonize the Oklahoma country. Captain Couch, H.H. Stafford, George W. Brown, and Colonel S.E. Wilcox were imprisoned in Arkansas City on a charge of conspiracy and rebellion against the United States government. They were arraigned at Wichita, Kansas, before United States Commissioner Sherman, and bound over in $1000 each for a hearing on February 10. While awaiting trial, Captain Couch presided at the boomers' convention at Topeka, which assembled on February 3. Delegates from sixteen Oklahoma colonies were present. They declared that they represented twenty thousand boomers. A committee was appointed to prepare and publish an address to the people of the United States defining the position of the boomers, and also to present the case to President Cleveland, and to protest against interference with American citizens who contemplated settling on such lands in the Oklahoma country as did not belong to any Indian tribe. Arrangements were also made to send Sidney Clark, an ex-member of Congress, and S.N. Wood, an editor of Topeka, East to present the case of the boomers more clearly to the President.

There was not sufficient evidence to convict Captain Couch and his associates at the trial on February 10. They are now at liberty, and Captain Couch is in command of the encampment of boomers on Cheeota Creek. It is said that many of the boomers are old soldiers, and that most of them are frontiersmen accustomed to arbitration by bullet.

On March 13, General Hatch telegraphed from Caldwell, Kansas, to the Secretary of War that there were then no trespassers upon the Indian Territory, though the boomers on Cheeota Creek were threatening to go over the line. Troops, he said, were stationed in the Territory and would drive out any invaders.

On the same day President Cleveland issued a proclamation warning the boomers that they would be met by the troops if they attempted another raid upon the Oklahoma country.

The boomers again protested when they heard of this proclamation. They passed resolutions declaring that "a large number of cattle men and cattle syndicates" were occupying the Oklahoma country with permanent improvements for farming and grazing purposes. The resolutions were telegraphed to the President. On the same day Captain Couch announced that he would break camp on Monday, March 16, and move south into the Indian Territory. He called upon those who would follow him to be prepared with agricultural implements and sixty days' rations, as he was going to stay. On the same day General Hatch announced that the boomers could not get through his line. He had six companies of the Ninth Cavalry (colored) directly opposed to the boomers, and plenty of other troops near by. He said they could successfully contend with 3,000 or 4,000 men.

The government at Washington says that the whole of the Indian Territory is guaranteed by the United States to the use of friendly Indian tribes forever. Squatters may not light upon it. If there are cattle men there, they are not permanent, and may be driven off at any moment.

The rescue of Corporal Scott

Our Soldiers in the Southwest

If the present or any other controversy of our government with Mexico should ever bring our soldiers in the Southwest prominently and critically into public attention, they would have no need to fear judgment of their bravery. But their manner of life would not excite envy. Their uniform would attract attention, but it would hardly be regarded as a model of military dress. Whether or not they do "thirteen dollars' worth of fighting" every month, no other men in the government's service so well earn their pay. The military service done by General Miles's troops on the Southwestern border is as onerous and as barren of opportunities for achieving renown as ever fell to soldiers in any land. They cannot attack the enemy, whip him, and be done with it. They seldom have the pleasure of a battle, but they may at any time suffer an attack. They have to do a sort of police service, which may on a sudden become warfare over a large area. The marauding Indians have no homes, no base of operations, no supplies to be cut off, no military code, no purpose or plan more definite than to wander about the mountains, to take their revenge, and to gratify their passion for cruelty. But while the Apaches can desist from fighting at any time, and retreat to renew their supplies by plunder, the soldiers must be always on guard, must subsist on scanty fare, must camp without tents, where there are no trees, and as far removed from the luxury of life in

Reprinted from *Harper's Weekly Magazine*, August 21, 1886.

the least attractive garrison as an explorer is from civilization.

The individual troopers. . .are men who are never safe from death by an Apache surprise. Their camp may any night be their burial place. But they can never be surprised out of a heroic mood. Their personal careers may have been uneventful except for their fights, but they are as far from being commonplace men as they are from being refined. Their biographies, if condensed after the fashion of the biographies of "our prominent citizens," would contain nothing more notable than such notes as these: Jack Hayward, a tall young fellow, born in Connecticut, became bankrupt in New York, did not know what else to do, so he enlisted and discovered that he was born with uncommon capacity for Apache warfare. The grizzly veteran, who looks like a pirate, has enlisted five times. Of course he swore every time that he would never enlist again; but he was not happy out of the army. Another is a scarred soldier who got his military training in the Prussian service; and another is an Irishman who kept going West without knowing why, and who tried to earn a living one way and then another for the same reason, and without being able to explain it any more than he could foresee it, he found a soldier's life on the frontier not only a tolerable but an ideal life. The play-day soldiers have all been rejected, or have deserted before this severe test of endurance and bravery has been reached, and if you were to ransack your whole philosophy for an explanation why these men endure such hardships without hope of military glory, and without chance of reward in money or in renown, you would find no better explanation than their own – "Oh, we like it!" The military vanity surely is not gratified by dress parades or impressive accouterments. General Miles himself wears buttons that do not glitter, boots that do not shine, a uniform the color and weight of which have been changed by many undisturbed deposits of dust. One spur is missing, and his trousers have been reenforced with buckskin, his hat is battered, and a soldier never had a better suntanned face.

The Indian "trailers" from San Carlos, who are employed by the government, are as savage in appearance for Indians as the troopers are for white men. They belong to one tribe of Apaches, but they are as unlike the stolid Indians of the Northwest as if they were of a wholly different race. They have quick motions, are runners of uncommon swiftness and of almost incredible endurance, and they are as cruel as they are alert. The Mexican, José Marie, who is their interpreter, has won a certain authority over them by his vocal energy. He was captured by them when a child and adopted into the tribe, by whom he is considered as respectable an Apache as a Yaque mongrel can become.

The personality of many of these soldiers never passes beyond the sergeant's knowledge, and many deeds of heroism in this fitful and long war with the Apaches is never heard of beyond the campfires of their comrades. The brave conduct of Lieutenant Clark, of the Tenth (colored) Cavalry, in rescuing, under fire, the wounded Corporal Scott, was such conduct as makes military history interesting. But for Corporal Scott's telling of the story, while he lay in the hospital, it might never have been heard outside General Miles's camp. One of Lieutenant Clark's troopers, who saw him expose himself to the fire of the enemy in an open space to rescue the wounded man, then found expression for his admiration in the most vigorous language of the camp vocabulary: "De Injuns jes fairly ploughed up de groun' wid bullets, when he run, an' never tuk no notice what was gwine on no more'n if de man 'd jes fell down in a fiel' anywhar. He'd 've fairly dusted 'way fum dar to save he own hide whole if he wa'n't a – fightin' man – fightin' man, I tell you, an' it jes do 'im good ter see a ––– Injun. An' he don't forgit a man in his stress." It is deeds of unselfish bravery like this, when done on battlefields that whole armies are watching and war correspondents see, that make heroes of men for all the world to admire. But the admiration of his comrades is as sweet to the trooper as praise in print could be; and sweeter than either is the feeling of having done a soldier's duty. The love of such service and the satisfaction that comes of doing a dangerous duty bravely and generously are the same to the born soldier in the Southwestern mountains as on a battlefield that will become historic; and this must be why these men love this hard life.

Practice Maneuvers in Arizona

Lieutenant Carter P. Johnson, Tenth Cavalry, operating in command of a raiding party during the field maneuvers of last autumn, eluded all the efforts made during many weeks to capture him, and at last, under the rules of the maneuvers, was adjudged – as a note of the artist informs us – to have surprised and captured with his small force Fort Bowie and Fort Huachuca.

The novel system of field practice of which Lieutenant Johnson's raid forms an incident was established in the autumn of 1887 by General Nelson A. Miles, then commanding the Department of Arizona. Its chief feature is that of sending out a raiding party, well mounted and provided with extra horses, who are to be pursued after a fixed time. while all the post commanders near the probable line of march are notified to be on the alert and to endeavor to discover, surprise, and capture the raiders. The first half of the month of September, 1887, was occupied in preparing for this practice by making the troops and their officers as well acquainted as possible with the region in which they were serving, and establishing outposts and signal and heliograph stations. Then a party of two officers and twenty men, with pack animals carrying equipage, clothing, etc., started from Fort Huachuca for Fort Apache. In the military game thus to be played there were careful rules to determine whether pursuers or pursued had gained the

Reprinted from *Harper's Weekly Magazine*, December 22, 1888.

advantage. Thus the route prescribed for the raiding party was to be east of Fort Bowie, west of Fort Grant, east of Fort Thomas, and west of Fort Apache; and on the return a like limitation of the route was prescribed. Again, after the first day, the raiding party was limited to marching between noon and midnight of each day, but within these limits the commanding officer could select his own line of march and conceal his men and camps. The pursuers from the various posts were instructed to communicate with each other and with Department headquarters on discovering any clue to the raiders, and the latter, or any portion of them, were to be regarded as captured when another command of equal numbers should get within hailing distance or bugle sound. Similar raiding parties were sent out from Fort Wingate to Fort Bayard and back, and from Fort Stanton around Fort Bayard. When one party was captured, another was sent out.

When General Miles, near the end of December, reviewed the operations which had thus been conducted through September and October, he found that ten distinct field maneuvers, covering an area of hundreds of miles, had been carried out. In five instances the raiders were overtaken, although they had adopted such devices for escape as temporarily dispersing, or driving cattle across their trail. In the other five instances the raiding detachments misled their pursuers, but were discovered and captured sooner or later by troops lying in wait for them in advance. The most successful of these raids was one in which the whole outward march had been made, and a part of the homeward, before it was checked.

Early in the autumn of the present year General Miles directed a renewal of this sort of field practice, with such improvements in the preparations and the rules as experience had suggested.

Without repeating the details, it will be enough to say that the most noteworthy performance was that of Lieutenant Johnson, already referred to. Starting out early in October with thirty men of his troop, he circled the posts near his route without discovery, and about November 20 reached Fort Huachuca, having eluded all his opponents through that period. His capture of the post during the absence of a part of its garrison followed. These, it should be understood, are only unofficial memoranda of his exploit, but from the official reports any needed corrections and fuller accounts can in due time be ascertained. Lieutenant Johnson, a native of Virginia, enlisted in the army twelve years ago. Promoted to be corporal and sergeant in the Third Cavalry, he received his commission as second lieutenant of the Fourth Infantry early in 1882, after a successful examination, and the next year was transferred to the Tenth Cavalry. He has had much experience in Indian campaigning both in Arizona and elsewhere during his twelve years of service. Mr. Remington [the artist, Frederic Remington] says that he once questioned a man of the troop (colored) of which Johnson is a lieutenant, and received this answer: "Oh, he jus' make dem gray hosses sweat blood when he get on de warpath; he's terrible bad man to foller, 'cause he don't neber get tired."

The training and experience derived from these annual maneuvers in Arizona and New Mexico must be valuable, supplemented as they are by detailed reports and suggestions from all detachments that take part in them, either as pursuers or pursued.

Frederic Remington

Some Duties of the Twenty-fifth

John H. Nankivell

During 1871 and the first four months of 1872, the regiment remained at its original stations in West Texas with but few changes. The period was employed in building and repairing roads and telegraph lines, scouting for hostile Indians, escort duty, and the everyday humdrum of garrison life in a frontier post of the day. In fact, with the exception of a few consoling skirmishes with the Indians, this was the daily work of the regiment during its ten years of service in Texas.

Scouting for Indians and escort duty entailed long and arduous marches in all kinds of weather, and the regimental returns of the period reveal that quite frequently a company or a detachment would march two to three hundred miles in a month while performing these duties.

General Forsythe, in his intensely interesting book, *The Story of the Soldier* (D. Appleton and Company, New York), has given us a very graphic picture of escort duty in those early days of the great Southwest; he says in part:

> Escort duty was always distasteful, and of all escort duty, that with a "bull" or "ox train" was the worst. Man was subordinated to the beast, because the distance made, the time of starting, the length of the stops, the situation of camps, everything connected with traveling, depended upon grass, the animals' sole food. If a fine grazing place was

Reprinted from John H. Nankivell, *The Twenty-fifth United States Infantry, 1869-1926* (Denver, 1927).

reached a halt was called, and the stock turned out with a blissful indifference to everything else, even to water. The stock did not require it, and the men must be satisfied with the water kept in little kegs which were fastened to the wagons. Those kegs were supposed to be freshly filled at the streams upon which the command had last encamped, though this important detail might possibly have been forgotten. It was kept only for cooking and drinking, lavation not being the "bull-whacker's" strong point.

Oh! The tedium of it all! The starting twice a day in the small hours of both meridians; the diurnal journey of from seven to twelve miles in a trip of one or two hundred miles and return. The train, numbering from twenty to fifty wagons, rolled out in the matutinal twilight to an accompaniment of cracking whips, of yells, and teamsters' oaths, the officer commanding the escort, bored and sleepy, riding a few yards ahead of the leading wagon, the escort scattered about where it could do the most good in the event of sudden need. At the end of the first mile up gallops a wagon master.

"Leftenant," he says, "Hunk Hansen has shed a tire, and we'll have to put it back." Everything stops, fir it will not do to separate the train. The tire is put on, and a fresh start made. Half an hour later a wagon master is at the escort commander's side again. "That idiot Doby Dave," he exclaims, "never told me he had a split yoke before we left camp, and now it comes apart, blast him! and I've got to go through the wagons or bank the yoke." "Which can you do more quickly?" asks the lieutenant patiently. "Band her." "Do it then." Another halt, another half hour or hour lost, and so it goes through the day, day after day, in rain and shine, always in heat, for freighting is possible only when the grass is green, and there is ever a steady strain of responsibility on the officer. He well knows that he is followed and watched, and should he be caught napping, he will surely have to pay the penalty, for the stock is a prize that the Indians will risk much to secure. They know the route, the length he will be on the road, and his destination, and he must act accordingly. The men, naturally enough, become weary of the slow progress, the short halts, and the mighty hard guard duty. They do not care to affiliate with the teamsters, and get tired of each other, and, in fact, it is a dreary business all around. As the train is groaning and cracking its slow way over a bit of rolling country a cry of "Indian!" "Indian!" suddenly comes from the flankers, and the band of Indians dashes rapidly forward out of a hollow towards the wagons, yelling and firing as they advance. The soldiers spring quickly to their stations and promptly return the fire, and the drivers instantly begin to form a park by turning their teams. So the Indians, seeing that the attempted stampede is a failure, fired a volley and disappeared. They had hoped to surprise the train and run off some of the cattle. A day or two later an attempt will be made to wile away the herd while it is grazing, but the guard will be on the alert, and expecting such an effort, will frustrate it. However, the Indians were not always unsuccessful; wagon trains were bereft by them of every animal they possessed, and the mollified losers compelled to wait ingloriously for relief to arrive from some adjacent fort or else go after it on foot.

"Another unpopular duty was escorting Government and contractors' mule trains. It was similar in many ways to escorting ox-trains, but free from the tediousness incident to the slow daily progress. The mule train traveled from twenty to thirty miles a day, without a break. The escorts were larger and the work harder on account of the greatly increased responsibility. A herd of horses or mules was to the Indians, free booters of the plains, what the golden laden galleons of Spain were to Howard and his cutthroats on the Pacific. From the moment the mule train entered the hostile Indian country and until it left there raged a contest of wits between the officer in charge and the wiliest, shrewdest, most cunning horse thieves that ever the sun shone on. The Indians, more eager than when on the track of an ox-train, were untiring in the pursuit of their prey.

The careful commandant had his escort posted before daybreak, the most dangerous time of all, in readiness for whatever might happen; and afterward, during the preparations for the early start, he exercised great care and vigilance against surprise from any quarter. Getting away from camp was the first and almost the greatest of the day's anxieties.

The train moved with advance and rear guards, while the rest of the escort was distributed along the sides of the wagons. This formation was regularly maintained while the train was on the road, except when crossing wide open reaches. It did not prevent the making of sudden dashes by the Indians, but it kept them, as a rule, from being successful. Camp reached, the animals were watered and turned out to graze. A number of mounted "mule skinners," as the drivers were called, went with them as herders, and always all the soldiers, except the cooks, were also sent out with the herd. A good commanding officer took no unnecessary risks.

After dinner the camp was at rest. Toward sunset, guard mount caused a flurry of excitement, and shortly afterward retreat ended the day. By the time the evening was fairly under way back in the East, "at home," the camp was asleep.

Such work as this was easy enough. There was no great hardship about it; rather the contrary. One would be difficult to please if he could not find enjoyment in traveling with a column of soldiers. But there were marches of all sorts. It is one thing to cross a country leisurely, knowing that every night's rest will be comfortable; it is another to struggle through the deadly cold of midwinter with a

> rampant blizzard driving the snow in one's face, knowing that when the entire journey is ended, a bit of canvas will be the only shelter for the remainder of the intensely cold weather until spring comes.
>
> A column going to the relief of others in dire straits or making forced marches in a pressing emergency, travels in much the same manner, except that there is no camping from noon to daybreak, but a constant pressing onward, stopping only for food, and when necessity compels a halt to keep the command from giving out.

The greater part of this escort duty was necessarily done by the cavalry, but the infantry was frequently called upon to assist, and the regimental records of the time show that the Twenty-fifth Infantry was given its share of this irksome duty.

Scouting after the wily and elusive Apache and Comanche, more often than not, entailed long, arduous marches on short rations with only now and again a fight or a skirmish to enliven the tedium of the march. Occasionally, . . . the Indian himself did a little attacking, and then, to use a frequent expression of one of the old-timers, "Business began to pick up."

Along the main routes of travel throughout West Texas and New Mexico in the "sixties" and "seventies" were stage and mail stations. These stations, usually a collection of adobe huts and corrals where drivers and animals were changed and meals (such meals!) as travelers required were served, were, more often than not, at some lonely spot on the plains invitingly open to attack by marauding Indians or outlaws. To guard the mails and the more important stations, small detachments of the regiment were posted at these stations, and frequent mention is made in the regimental records of such places as Melvin Station, Centralia, El Muerto, Barilla Springs, etc., important points on the mail routes of the Texas of those days. A soldier usually rode on the stage between stations because it was found that the Indians rarely attacked the stage when it had a soldier escort. The "stage" was ordinarily a two-mule buckboard carrying only the mail, but a four-mule, covered "mud-wagon" ran at infrequent intervals for the accomodation of passengers.

West Texas owes much to the road building activities of the army in the years immediately succeeding the Civil War, and the Twenty-fifth Infantry can at least claim that it did its share. No doubt these roads were built primarily to connect the various posts and camps, but in the process of time, as the country became more settled, they were used by the incoming settlers and emigrants, and today many a well traveled highway in West Texas had its inception in an old army post road.

Some Heroic Individuals

The deeds of those individuals who are singled out as heroes are usually inflated out of all proportion as time passes. These figures become larger than life, some even become caricatures of their former selves, and, as such, historically suspect. Perhaps that is why it is a pleasure to discover an individual who appears in history in an unspoiled, original form.

Almost hidden in history are the Seminole Negro-Indian scouts who played an important role during the hostilities in the Trans-Pecos area. They were a unique group, physiologically and genetically, part Indian and part black. They lived in Mexico by choice, but their original home had been Florida. Persuaded to serve in the United States Army as scouts, they personally accounted for four Congressional Medals of Honor. Their fate after the cessation of hostilities was a disgraceful and undeserved reward for years of loyal service.

Dr. Porter, in his article on these scouts, gives a very thorough picture of their history, function, service and denial. He draws no conclusions but tells the tale in a very straightforward manner, offering an exciting and long overdue exposé of a little-known part of American history.

Although marred by the author's racial prejudice, Jacob Wilks' personal narrative of his experiences while a member of the Ninth

Cavalry is an exceptional discovery. This first-person account provides a vivid "on the scene" memoir of daily life in the saddle. Among other things, it is very interesting to note here that Wilks disclaims the theory that many of the Negro-Indian scouts were part Indian.

Another first-person narrative is the one by Sergeant Horace W. Bivins written about his experiences while on frontier duty. This account was written while the sergeant was on duty in Cuba during the Spanish-American War. His story is told with a great deal of attention to detail: He recalls, for instance, that the black troopers who returned from the West, where they had served side by side with white troops, were astonished to see signs in public places in the South that read: "White waiting room," and "Niggers not allowed inside."

The best known of all the blacks represented in this section is Lieutenant Henry Ossian Flipper. Flipper's place in history is assured: Being the first to do anything is an automatic passport to historical fame. It is unfortunate that most historians give him credit for being the first black graduate of West Point and pass over the rest of his career; after being forced to leave the army, he achieved success as a mining engineer and an assistant to a Cabinet officer.

Isaiah Dorman, the last black man to be presented in this section, was not a soldier; he served with the military as a translator and guide. Married to a Sioux woman and fluent in the Sioux language, he was known and accepted by the Indians of the northern plains. He lost his life at the Little Big Horn with Lieutenant Colonel Custer and several hundred others.

There are many references to Dorman in the volumes of literature that have been published about the battle that was known as Custer's Last Stand. Before reading Robert Ege's story, it would be appropriate to review some of the references to Isaiah Dorman. The sources have been arranged in chronological order.

> Not least important was Isaiah, or Teat, Dorman, a Negro interpreter, who had spent many years in the Indian country. Having come up the Missouri River some time before 1871, he is said to have married an Indian woman and to have become an intimate friend of Sitting Bull. The Sioux apparently had great affection for him and had given him the name "Teat" because the Sioux word for it sounds very much like the name Isaiah. He had served as a government courier or mail carrier, and apparently accompanied the Custer expedition at his own request because he loved the wild country and wished to see the western land

again before he died. (Edgar I. Stewart, *Custer's Luck* [Norman]: University of Oklahoma Press, 1957, p. 182)

The morning of the 17th of May we prepared to make a move. . . . The Cavalry passed in review through Fort A. Lincoln, where a great many officers and enlisted men took a last look at their wives and sweethearts. In marching through the fort first came the scouts under command of Lt. Varnum, with Chief Bloody Knife and Charlie Reynolds and Fred Girard, two white scouts, and Izar [sic] Dorman, the negro interpreter from Fort Rice. (W.A. Graham, *The Custer Myth* [Harrisburg, Pa.: The Stackpole Co., 1953], p.239.)

. . .Dorman threw the body [a dead Indian from a burial scaffold, by order of Custer – ed.] in the river, and when he was later seen fishing at that same spot, the Arikaras [Custer's Indian scouts] not unnaturally suspected that he was using the corpse as bait. (Stewart, *Custer's Luck,* p.231).

A leetle [June 25] later whilst I was eatin' my own breakfast the nigger scout, Isaiah Dorman, come to me from whar Varnum was posted with the Ree scouts. He 'peered considerable excited. "Whar's General Custer?" he asked me. I told him the General was restin' and couldn't be disturbed. The nigger said, "This is important, Boss. I got a message from Varnum fur the General." So I pointed to the brush whar Custer was laying, and Isaiah went over to him. I didn't hear what they said . . . . (G.D. Wagner, *Old Neutriment* [Boston: Ruth Hill, 1934], p.148.)

I think some of our men were captured alive and tortured. I know the colored scout Isaiah was, for he had small pistol balls in his legs from the knees down, and I believe they were shot into him while alive. [quoted from the statements of Scout Herendeen]. (Graham, *The Custer Myth,* p.260.)

. . . We passed a black man in a soldier's uniform and we had him. He turned on his horse and shot an Indian right through the heart. Then the Indians fired at this one man and riddled his horse with bullets. His horse fell over on his back and the black man could not get up. I saw him as I rode by. I afterwards saw him lying there dead [quoted from the statement by Chief-Runs-The-Enemy]. (Stewart, *Custer's Luck,* p. 370).

Isaiah Dorman, a nigger, was one o' our scouts. He fell with Custer in the last charge. When he was found his body was mutilized and pinned to the ground with arrows. (Wagner, *Old Neutriment,* p. 89.)

I went riding over the ground where we had fought the first soldiers [the Major Reno fight] during the morning of the day before. I saw by the river, on the west side, a dead black man. He was a big man. All of his clothing was gone when I saw him, but he had not been scalped nor cut up like the white men had been. Some Sioux told me he belonged to their people but was with the soldiers. (Thomas Marquis, *A Warrior Who Fought Custer* [Minneapolis: The Midwest Company, 1931] p. 261.)

Three different soldiers among all of the dead in both places of battle attracted special notice from the Indians. The first was the man wearing the buckskin suit and who had the colored writing and pictures [tattoos] on his breast and arms. Another was the black man killed among the first soldiers on the valley. The third was one having gold among his teeth. We did not understand how this metal got there, nor why it was there. (Marquis, *A Warrior Who Fought Custer*, p. 263.)

... On the prairie dog village at the end of the bushes they found the negro, Isaiah, lying dead; he was a Dakota [Sioux – ed.] interpreter enlisted at Fort Lincoln. The Dakotas had left a kettle full of his own blood close by his head and the body was much mutilated. (*The Arikara Narrative,* edited by O. G. Libby, as stated in the narrative of Young Hawk, p. 110.)

As he [Sitting Bull – ed.] approached the end of the brush near the prairie-dog town, he came upon the Negro, "Teat" Isaiah Dorman. Two Bull, Shoots-Waling, and several others rode up at the same time. "Teat" was badly wounded, but still able to talk. He spoke Sioux, and was well-liked by the Indians. . . . And now, when he saw the Sioux all around him, he pleaded with them, "My friends, you have already killed me; don't count *coup* on me." He had been shot early in the fight. . . . Immediately after [having been given a drink of water by Sitting Bull] Isaiah died. The warriors rode away. Afterward, some spiteful woman found the Negro's body and mutilated it with her butcher knife. (Stanley Vestal, *Sitting Bull* [Norman: University of Oklahoma Press, 1957], p. 165.)

The only arguable point is the mystery surrounding Dorman's death and what happened to his body immediately afterwards. Dorman's death will remain as much of an enigma as the "real" story of the battle itself and of its leading characters.

J. CISNEROS

The Seminole-Negro Indian Scouts 1870-1881

Kenneth Wiggins Porter

The Seminole Negro-Indian Scouts never at any time mustered more than fifty men but, operating on both sides of the Rio Grande during the Indian fighting period of the 1870s and early 1880s, were effective far out of proportion to their numbers. Although frequently referred to merely as "Indian scouts" and "Seminole scouts," their official designation was a more accurate, if somewhat cumbrous, description.

Although a good many were undoubtedly of part-Indian ancestry, the scouts were hardly distinguishable racially from the soldiers of the colored infantry and cavalry regiments with whom they frequently served[1] and with whom they shared some of the distinctive cultural traits of the southern Negro. The older men, at least, spoke a broken plantation English, sometimes with a Gullah twang. Despite twenty years' residence in Catholic Mexico, young as well as old were mostly staunch Baptists. The older Seminole who had been brought up in the United States wore their native garb by preference and spoke Hitchiti or Muskogee. Some had achieved such a blending of the two principal elements of their culture that in their Baptists praisehouses they even prayed in "Injun."[2] What was most important as frontier scouts,

Reprinted from *The Southwestern Historical Quarterly*, LV (January, 1952), No. 3, by permission of the Texas State Historical Association.

whether born in Florida, Alabama, the Indian Territory, or Mexico, all were Indian in their trailing, hunting, and fighting skills. Their Indianism, however, was not that of the wild, nomadic, predatory Comanche and Apache but rather that of the sedentary, semi-civilized Seminole and Creek, with whom hunting was subordinate to stock raising and farming and who usually took the warpath only in self-defense.

How the Seminole Negroes came to be available for service as United States scouts is a long story. Their ancestors were for the most part runaway slaves who had taken refuge among the Florida Seminole. Though referred to by some white observers as slaves to the Indians, General Edmund P. Gaines described them more accurately as "vassals and allies." They lived in separate villages; had their own fields, flocks, and herds; habitually carried arms; went into battle under their own captains; and, except for an annual tribute in corn to the chiefs who were their protectors, were as free as the Indians themselves. In fact, their knowledge of the English language and of the white man's ways and their superior industry and prosperity gave them such influence that some observers styled them the real rulers of the Seminole nation.[3] They took a leading part in the resistance to the annexation of Florida and to the Seminole removal[4] but were finally transported, along with the Indians, to the Indian Territory,[5] where they were exposed to the danger of kidnapping by whites and Creeks.[6]

Many Seminole Indians were also disgusted with the Creek domination to which they were subjected, and in 1849 and 1850 several hundred Seminole Indians and Negroes, under the command of the Indian chief Wild Cat and the Negro chief John Horse, crossed to Mexico and were settled on the border as military colonists, where they did good service against Indians and Texas filibusters.[7]

The Indians returned to the United States following Wild Cat's death in 1857; because of slavery, the Negroes stayed in Mexico and were joined by other Seminole, Creek, and Cherokee Negroes and also by runaway slaves, free Negro settlers, and refugee Biloxi Indians. The need for their services against hostile Indians, the disturbed situation of Mexico, and the abolition of slavery in the United States resulted in the Seminole Negroes' becoming scattered. By 1870 head chief John Horse and the main body of 150 Negroes were in Laguna de Parras in southwestern Coahuila; John Kibbitts, the second-in-command, and one hundred others were at Nacimiento, Coahuila, not far from Eagle Pass, Texas; several families were at Matamoros across from Brownsville, Texas; and a band of Creek Negroes under Elijah Daniel were on the Nueces River in Uvalde County, Texas.[8]

The Comanche and Apache Indians, who had long been making raids into the United States from bases in Mexico and vice versa, had been emboldened in their expeditions into Texas by the abandonment of many of the frontier posts during the Civil War. Even after the reoccupation of these forts the raids continued. Parties of Indians would stealthily cross the Rio Grande on foot, conceal themselves, and wait for the full moon to give them light enough for their operations, which consisted principally of rounding up horses and cattle and driving them across the river but which readily included murder and arson if the opportunity presented itself. The officers commanding posts on the border were rarely able to detect or intercept these thieves and murderers either in their comings or goings, so skillful were they in concealing their tracks.[9] Scouts were desperately needed, but a few Tonkawa and renegade Lipans were the only ones available.

The Seminole Negroes at Nacimiento in the meantime were becoming discontented with Mexico and wanted to return to the Indian Territory. Major Zenas R. Bliss of the Twenty-fifth United States Cavalry (colored), commanding at Fort Duncan, authorized Captain Frank W. Perry to visit Nacimiento and invite the Seminole Negroes to return to the United States to serve as scouts. The Seminole's understanding of the agreement finally arrived at between Captain Perry and John Kibbitts, which the Negroes call "de treaty" or sometimes "de treatment," was that it provided that the government would pay the able-bodied men's expenses to the United States and would furnish them pay, provisions for their families, and grants of land in return for their services as scouts.[10] If the agreement was ever reduced to writing, it has long since disappeared.

The Kibbitts band crossed over to Fort Duncan on July 4, 1870.[11] A month later, on August 16, the first contingent of scouts – Sergeant John Kibbitts, also known by the Seminole name of Sit-tee-tas-to-nachy (Snake Warrior).[12] and ten privates – were enlisted for six months at the pay of cavalry soldiers.[13] The duties of the Seminole Negro-Indian scouts during their first two or three years were largely of a routine nature. Recruiting was a principal activity. During the summer and fall of 1871, twenty scouts were enlisted from Elijah Daniel's band and the Matamoros families; most of these were transferred to Fort Clark, near Brackettville, Texas, the following summer and were soon joined by several others.[14] During the latter part of 1872 and the spring of 1873, a dozen or so recruits, mostly Seminole from John Horse's Laguna band, were enlisted at Fort Duncan.[15] Half a dozen of the recruits, however, were apparently either Texas Negroes who had intermarried with Seminole and Creek women or were time-expired soldiers from colored regiments.[16]

The Seminole scouts were supplied by the government with arms, ammunition, and rations. They were equipped at first with Spencer carbines, for which Sharps carbines were soon substituted[17] – a welcome exchange for the old muzzle-loaders of their Mexican days.[18] The scouts furnished their own horses, for which they received compensation, and seem to have dressed in a modified Indian style. Their appearance and manner were probably a source of exasperation to young officers brought up in the spit-and-polish West Point tradition. One report reads: "Discipline, Fair; Instruction, Progressive; Military Appearance, Very Poor; Arms, Spencer Carbines – Good; Accoutrements, Good; Clothing, Fair." Another report concludes: "Clothing, Good enough for Indians." Some indeed, were so Indian that they sported buffalo-horn warbonnets.[19]

The scouts had not, however, been employed as military fashion plates. Major Bliss described them as "excellent hunters, and trailers, and brave scouts. . . . splendid fighters."[20] Their trailing skill in particular was almost uncanny.[21] Conspicuous among their other useful qualities were the lack of any language barrier between their officers and themselves, their ability to speak the "Mexican" which was the *lingua franca* of the border,[22] their knowledge of the country and of the ways of the Indians against whom they were operating, and their thorough dependability.

The Seminole scouts in the spring of 1873 were about to begin nearly a decade of fierce border warfare under an officer exceptionally well-qualified for such a command. Lieutenant John Lapham Bullis had entered the service in 1862 at the age of twenty-one as a corporal of the 126th New York Volunteer Infantry and in 1864 had been commissioned a captain in a Negro infantry regiment. He had been mustered out in 1866 but had reenlisted the following year as a second lieutenant; two years later he had been transferred to the Twenty-fourth Infantry (colored), serving on the Texas frontier. On September 1, 1871, with four privates of the Ninth Cavalry (colored), he had attacked a party of twenty-eight Indians, maintained the fight for over half an hour, and had taken with him a herd of stolen cattle when he finally had been forced to retire.[23] A fellow officer describes Bullis as "thin and spare, . . . a small, wiry man with a black mustache, . . . his face burned red as an Indian."[24] Commander and men were to participate in the nine-year period from 1873 to 1881 in twenty-six expeditions, ranging in duration from a few days to several months;[25] they were to prove well worthy of one another in hard-fought combat, sometimes with foes outnumbering them six or eight to one.

Elijah Daniel's band at Fort Clark was the first to see important action. Sixteen scouts under Lieutenant Bullis accompanied six troops of the Fourth Cavalry on Colonel R. S. Mackenzie's expedition against the Lipan and Kickapoo camps at Remolino, Mexico, on May 18, 1873, an encounter which resulted in the destruction of three villages, the killing of nineteen warriors, and the capture of forty prisoners. Among the Lipan captives was the aged Chief Costillitto, who was lassoed by Scout Renty Grayson,[26] and his daughter Teresita, who later married Scout James Perryman, the ceremony being performed "with a Bible" by Lieutenant Bullis himself.[27]

Twenty-one Seminole scouts accompanied Colonel Mackenzie on his 1874 expedition against the stronghold of the Cheyenne, Comanche, and Kiowa Indians in Palo Duro Canyon in the Panhandle of Texas, the principal result of which was the capture and slaughter on September 30 of fourteen hundred Indian ponies. One of the scouts distinguished himself in a skirmish on the way to the canyon by the nonchalance with which he swung from his saddle to shoot the horse of a charging Comanche.[28]

The expeditions to Remolino and to Palo Duro had given the scouts comparatively little opportunity to display their trailing skill and their capacity for daring, quick-thinking action. These qualities were, however, conspicuously manifested on April 25, 1875. Lieutenant Bullis, with Sergeant John Ward, Trumpeter Isaac Payne, and Trooper Pompey Factor, struck the trail of about seventy-five stolen horses, followed it to the Eagle's Nest Crossing of the Pecos, and came upon the Indians as they were attempting to cross to the western side.

Tethering their mounts and creeping up to within seventy-five yards, the members of the little party opened fire and kept it up for about three-quarters of an hour with such effect that they killed three warriors, wounded a fourth, and twice forced the raiders to retire from the horse herd. Eventually, however, the Indians – twenty-five or thirty Comanches mostly armed with Winchesters – discovered the small numbers of their attackers and worked around until they nearly succeeded in cutting the scouts off from their horses. Bullis and his men had to run for it.

The scouts had reached their horses, mounted, and were getting away when the sergeant, glancing back, saw that Bullis' mount, a wild, badly-trained young animal, had broken loose, leaving him dismounted among the Indians who were rapidly closing in with yells of triumph. "We can't leave the lieutenant, boys," Sergeant Ward cried. Wheeling his mount, he dashed back, closely followed by his comrades. The Indians opened a tremendous fire on the rescue party, particularly on the sergeant. A bullet cut John Ward's carbine sling; as he reached the lieutenant and helped him to mount behind, a ball shattered the stock. Factor and Payne meanwhile had been fighting off the swarming savages; now, firing right and left, the three scouts and the rescued officer rode again through the hostiles and, as Bullis wrote, "saved my hair." It was an episode which should have been immortalized by Frederic Remington; it did win the three scouts the Congressional Medal of Honor.[29]

The two hundred or more Seminole Negroes at Forts Duncan and Clark[30] had in the meantime become impatient for the land grants which had been a principal inducement in causing them to return to the United States. After three years they were still squatting with their families on the military reservations. It now developed that the War Department possessed no land for their permanent occupancy, and the Indian Office declared that the rolls of the Seminole tribe had been closed in 1866, shutting out those who were in Mexico. The Indian commissioner added that they should not have left the United States in the first place or should have stayed in Mexico. To add to their difficulties, the rations previously issued were cut off from those who were not regularly enlisted scouts. The whole community was thus forced to live on the wages of about fifty scouts, most of whom were married men with from three to six children, supplemented by what little work the women could find in the border communities of Eagle Pass and Brackettville and such scant crops as could be raised on the military reservations. In their destitute condition some had to forage for stray cattle for food.[31]

John Kibbitts and John Horse appealed to Brigadier General C. C. Augur, commander of the Department of Texas, in San Antonio, but the general, although convinced of the justice of their case, could do nothing for them.[32] Ironically enough, on December 10, 1873, the day that Seminole chiefs were vainly pleading for their people, nine Seminole scouts participated with forty-one men of the Fourth Cavalry in an action near Kickapoo Springs, in which nine hostile Kiowa and Comanche were killed and sixty one horses were captured.[33]

A special Indian commissioner reported about a year later, however, that the Indian Bureau was under obligation to remove the Seminole Negroes to the Indian Territory and to provide for them.[34] Lieutenant Bullis emphasized in their favor that they were "fine trailers and good marksmen"; Colonel Edward Hatch of the Ninth Cavalry characterized them as "brave and daring, superior to the Indians of this region in fighting qualities"; and both Colonel Mackenzie and Lieutenant General Philip H. Sheridan endorsed their claims to land but to no avail.[35]

A few discouraged Seminole families returned to Mexico[36] and a couple of scouts deserted, but most remained stubbornly confident that somehow, sometime, justice would be done. New scouts enlisted during the latter part of 1873, in 1874, and in 1875; some of them were direct from Mexico,[37] some were from families already represented on the muster roll, while others were American Negroes, many of whom had intermarried with the Seminole, or were discharged soldiers, or both. One was a Mexican. Of German and mulatto parentage, William Miller, who "looked like a white man and acted like an Indian"[38] was a non-Seminole recruit who proved well worthy of his new title.

In 1875[39] and again in 1876 and 1877, Lieutenant Bullis and the Seminole scouts were principally engaged in accompanying Colonel W. R. Shafter on various large-scale expeditions into the Indian country. When Indian signs were encountered, the scouts would be detached to follow up the trails and inflict such damage as they could on the hostiles. They were sometimes accompanied by detachments of the Eighth Cavalry and of the Tenth Cavalry (colored) but generally operated independently.

The Seminole scouts' method of campaigning was such that it was a severe ordeal for soldiers from other commands to keep up with them. Their effectiveness, aside from their unrivaled trailing skill, was due in large measure to their rapidity of movement and their ability to stay on the trail for months at a time, both of which qualities were derived from their lack of dependence on the commissariat. They could subsist indefinitely on half-rations and, when necessary, live off the country – eating rattlesnakes if no other game was available. Bullis, "a tireless marcher" whom the hostile Indians for obvious reasons called the Whirlwind and the Thunderbolt, could endure the same hardships and eat the same food as his men; it is said that if he wished to be really luxurious on a march, he would put a single can of corn into his haversack. According to another story, when he did have rations, he made it a rule to live on one can of food a day, whether it was corned beef or peaches.[40]

Bullis and his scouts were quite close personally. They were more like a large partriarchal family than an ordinary cavalry troop, and Bullis' relationship to the scouts was more that of a war chief to his braves than the conventional officer-men relationship. Within two or three days of the birth of a child to any of his scouts, Bullis would appear at the Seminole camp on Las Moras Creek to inspect the infant; if the baby was a male, the lieutenant would lift him up and remark that he would make a "mighty fine scout some day."[41] This relationship of mutual affection and confidence was inestimably important to the scouts' effectiveness as a fighting organization.

Only a few of the more interesting or more important of the scouts' expeditions and actions during the years 1875-1877 can even be mentioned. On the night of October 16, 1875, for example, Lieutenant Bullis and Sergeant Miller, the white-appearing, Indian-acting mulatto, crept into an Indian camp at Laguana Sabinas and stole upwards of thirty horses and mules. Sergeant Miller also started off the military season of 1876 for the scouts by boldly entering an Indian camp in Mexico, presumably in disguise, and remaining five days.

During the summer of 1876, Bullis and his scouts were almost constantly on the march or in action and several times entered Mexico.

On July 29, Bullis, with twenty Seminole scouts, twenty Negro cavalrymen, and one other officer, was sent south on the trail of Lipan Indians; the men covered 110 miles in twenty-five hours and reached the San Antonio River, near Saragossa, Mexico, at 3 A.M. At daybreak they succeeded in locating the enemy village of twenty-three lodges, mounted under cover of the threes, and charged into the sleeping camp. After the first volley, Bullis' men were involved in a wild, confused melee in which the two parties were so intermingled that the fighting was chiefly hand-to-hand – clubbed carbines against long Lipan lances. The struggle raged for a quarter of an hour; when it ended, fourteen Indians lay dead, and four squaws were prisoners. Three of Bullis' men had been cut, but none was killed or badly wounded.[42]

It is worthy of comment that in a dozen actions with hostile Indians, occurring over a period of eight years, not a single Seminole scout was killed or even seriously wounded. The older generation of Seminole today confidently ascribe this immunity to divine protection. "The old people in those days were so loving with one another," says Penny Factor. "That's why things went the way they did in the fighting; the old people were doing some powerful praying." Bill Daniels adds: "When you are fighting for the right and have your trust in God, he will spread his hand over you." The Seminole, however, were not so fortunate in their encounters with the Texas citizenry.

While the scouts had been fighting to defend the frontier, their personal situation had on the whole been deteriorating rather than improving. Despite their services against the hostiles and their generally orderly, law-abiding, and industrious character,[43] they had incurred the enmity of some of the Texas borderers. One of their enemies was the notorious "King" Fisher, who liked to boast that he had killed a man for every year in his life. "not counting Mexicans," and whose outlaw band dominated the Eagle Pass area.[44] About Christmas, 1874, King Fisher and his gang and some of the scouts had engaged in a barroom gun battle in which the outlaw leader had narrowly escaped death from a bullet that creased his scalp and in which Corporal George Washington, Chief Horse's nephew, had received a stomach wound. Corporal Washington had died after lingering several months.[45]

This episode may have contributed to the decision to remove the rest of the scouts to Fort Clark on the wooded banks of the cool-flowing Las Moras, which had been carried out by 1876. The Fort

Clark reservation was a much pleasanter location than Fort Duncan,[46] but the Seminole were no nearer than before to obtaining a permanent land grant. Here, too, the scouts encountered hostility. Certain residents of Kinney County accused them of "constantly preying on the property of citizens" and giving shelter to horse-thieves. The heart of the difficulty seems to have been that some of the Seminole who were trying to raise crops on the reservation came into conflict with local citizens who were interested in the same land. On the evening of May 19, 1876, Chief John Horse and Titus Payne were fired on near the post hospital. Payne was killed instantly, and the chief was badly wounded, but the strength and courage of his horse American, which was also wounded, and the chief's own horsemanship enabled him to escape from the ambush and reach the Seminole camp. Members of King Fisher's band were credited with being the hired triggermen. This assassination produced another spasmodic effort to find a permanent home for the Seminole. Brigadier General E. O. C. Ord suggested that the scouts be sent to a reservation occupied by recently hostile tribes, where he believed "their simple manners and religious tendency" would be a God-sent good influence.[47] But nothing came of this suggestion.

The culmination of these difficulties came on New Year's morning of 1877, just after midnight. A former scout named Adam Paine, who was wanted in Brownsville for knifing a Negro soldier, was at a dance in the Seminole camp when a sheriff blasted him from behind with a double-barrelled shotgun at such close range that his clothes were set on fire. Five scouts and former scouts, including Pompey Factor, were so exasperated by this second killing within a year – the third in less than two years – that they washed the dust of Texas from their horses' hooves in the waters of the Rio Grande. In Mexico they again fought Indians, under Colonel Pedro Avincular Valdéz, known as "Colonel Winker,"[48] whom Major Bliss characterized as "one of the bravest men I ever knew."[49]

The majority of the scouts, however, remained loyal – if not to the United States, at least to Lieutenant Bullis. Other scouts were found to replace the deserters, but of the scouts enlisted for the first time during the five years following the shooting of John Horse and Titus Payne, only four were of the original Seminole-Creek-Cherokee Negro stock from Mexico;[50] two were Indians, and no less than a dozen were Mexican.

Among the Mexicans was a former *comanchero,* or trader with the Comanche, name José Pieda Tafoya, whom General Mackenzie had induced to guide the 1874 expedition to Palo Duro Canyon by threatening to hang him to the tongue of a wagon.[51] Another Mexican scout was Julian Longorio, who had been brought up among the Indians and who, to obtain a $500 reward offered by Colonel W. R. Shafter for the capture of a Mescalero Indian, went into Mexico, lassoed one, and brought him back. Unfortunately Longorio broke the captive's neck in the process.[52]

During 1877 the scouts were again almost constantly on the trail and several times crossed into Mexico. The enemy was growing wary, and it was hard to bring him to bay. The scouts trailed Apache horse-thieves for two weeks deep into Mexico without other success then the incidental recovery of two or three hundred head of cattle. They trailed another large party into Mexico, crossing the Rio Grande on a raft of logs, surprising the Indian camp, and killing one Indian, wounding three, and capturing twenty-three of their horses.[53] In a running fight with Lipans, also in Mexico, the scouts captured three women, two children, fifteen horses, and two mules.[54]

Near the end of the year on an expedition which lasted two months, Bullis and his scouts were caught on a narrow ledge in a deep canyon of the Big Bend by Mescaleros; greatly outnumbered, the scouts were "severely handled," but by their "skill and courage" succeeded in extricating themselves without loss. They sent for reinforcements, picked up the trail again, although it was twenty-three days old, and followed it for several days. By leaving their horses and walking over a mountain nearly a mile high, the scouts and cavalrymen succeeded in surprising the enemy camp but were unsuccessful in trapping the Indians, although they killed two warriors, including the chief, wounded three, and captured thirty horses and mules, with all camp equipment.[55]

The campaigns of 1876 and 1877 so put the fear of God – or of Bullis and the scouts – into the Lipan and Mescalero raiders that although the scouts went out on expeditions as before and at least once entered Mexico,[56] they encountered no Indians. They did, however, perform one of their greatest feats of trailing and endurance. On January 31, 1879, Bullis, thirty-nine Seminole, fifteen cavalrymen, three friendly Lipans, and the former *comanchero* José Tafoya set out in pursuit of Mescalero raiders, whom they trailed across the desert for thirty-four days. At one time the Bullis party was nearly perishing from thirst, when Sergeant David Bowlegs displayed uncanny desert craft by discovering a "sleeping spring" which the hostiles had stopped up and hidden; by the greatest care and skill, he made the spring flow freely again. Although they trailed the raiders to within two miles of the Fort Stanton, New Mexico, reservation, the agent refused to give them up, and the scouts had to return empty-handed. They had been gone eighty days and had covered 1,266 miles.[57]

The scouts' last Indian battle.[58] followed the last important Indian raid on Texas soil. A small band of Lipans killed a Mrs. McLauren and a boy named Allen Reiss on April 14, 1881, at the head of the Rio Frio. Lieutenant Bullis, two weeks later, was ordered to take thirty scouts and to pursue the raiders. The Indians had "killed a horse and made shoes out of the rawhide so they wouldn't make tracks,"[59] but despite this device and the elapsed time, the scouts picked up the trail and pursued the raiders "over the rugged, precipitous mountains and canyons of Devil's River, where the marauders killed thirty of their horses." The scouts followed them across the Rio Grande and trailed them into the Sierra del Burro, where on May 2 the Seminole discovered the hostile camp. They surrounded it and attacked at daybreak, killing four warriors and capturing a squaw, a child, and twenty-one animals. Only the chief, San Da Ve, escaped, and he was mortally wounded.[60]

In the following year twelve expeditions from Texas posts covered 3,662 miles, but not the slightest trace of Indian raiders was found.[61]

The Seminole scouts and their leaders were not, of course, by any means wholly responsible for achieving permanent cessation of Indian raids on the Texas frontier. Regular United States troops had played an important part, but without the scouts the work of the regular troops would to a large degree have been futile. The scouts alone could follow a weeks-old trail across hundreds of miles of desert and mountains and could so locate and surround a hostile camp that the enemy could be overwhelmed and terrorized by a surprise attack when it was feeling most secure. Indian campaigns along the Texas-Mexican border would otherwise have been a series of games of hide-and-seek on a large scale, in which the hostiles, except by rare accident, probably would have been the winners. It was to the trailing skill, the endurance, the desert craft of those hard riders, dead shots, and fierce hand-to-hand fighters, the Seminole scouts,[62] that Texas in large measure owed her final exemption from such Indian raids as had plagued her borders from her earliest history.

J. L. Bullis, in recognition of services which would have been impossible except as commander of the Seminole scouts, was most deservedly dubbed "The Friend of the Frontier," presented with two handsome swords,[63] breveted as captain and major, promoted to captain and, eventually, to brigadier general;[64] he was even acclaimed as "the greatest Indian fighter in the history of the United States Army."[65] The scouts themselves, however, were rewarded by the gradual reduction and ultimate disbandment of the organization,[66] followed by the eviction of the survivors and their successors and kinsmen from their homes on the Fort Clark reservation.[67]

Frederic Remington
Sierra Bonitas

A Negro Trooper of the Ninth Cavalry

John W. Hunter

The reminiscences of soldier life on the border, as given below, were related to John Warren Hunter at San Angelo, Texas, in 1914 by a Negro – a plain old time darkey, whose politeness, humility, and respectful bearing towards his superiors commanded the respect and confidence of the white people of San Angelo, among whom he had resided many years. Only a Negro, he had had a military record of which any man might be proud, a record substantiated by valuable documents in his possession and by honorable scars that he bore upon his war-battered anatomy.

Jacob Wilks was born a slave, in Kentucky, about thirty miles south of the Ohio River. While yet in infancy, his father and mother gathered their two children in their arms and fled under cover of darkness to the Ohio River, where they found concealment in the jungle until they could attract the attention of a group of fishermen on the north bank of the river. These fishermen, so it chanced, were connected with the "Underground Railroad," of which we have so often heard mention, and of the which Mrs. Harriet Beecher Stowe had much to say in *Uncle Tom's Cabin,* and being on the alert for runaway

Reprinted with permission of the editor from *Frontier Times Magazine,* Vol. IV (April, 1927), No. 7.

Negroes, these fishermen soon caught the signal, and during the night, the second out from old Mastah Wilks' plantation, the refugees were taken across the river and landed in the free state of Ohio. A Mrs. Waddell stood ready to receive them and on her farm they were given food, shelter, and employment. A year or so later the parents died and their last request was that their benefactress take charge of Jake and care for him until old enough to take care of himself. Jake grew to manhood in the Waddell family and when the war came on he was among the first to join the army. He enlisted in the 116th regiment colored infantry at Camp Nelson, Ky., and served three years and nine months, during which time his regiment saw hard service under Grant in his Virginia campaigns. Wilks had been promoted to a sergeancy during this time and was present at Lee's surrender at Appomattox, after which his regiment was sent to New Orleans and disbanded. The Ninth Cavalry, colored, was being organized and immediately after receiving his discharge from the infantry he enlisted in the Ninth, which was ordered to Texas via Galveston. When the regiment reached San Antonio, the companies were detached and sent to various posts along the border, mainly Forts Concho, McKavett, Stockton, Clark, Davis, Quitman, and Fort Bliss at El Paso. Sergeant Wilks' company was stationed on diverse occasions at posts in New Mexico and Arizona, where they saw hard service while campaigning against Indians.

"In 1873," said Sergeant Wilks, "I was sent with a detail of twelve men of my company to carry the mail to Fort Bliss. Each man carried a mail sack strapped to the cantel of his saddle, and we were armed with seven-shooting Spencer rifles. At Eagle Springs we were attacked by about one hundred Apaches. The fight lasted several hours, during which the Indians made repeated charges. We were on an open plain without any protection whatever, but we dismounted, held our horses by the halter-reins, kept close together, and withheld our fire until the Indians charged up within close range. Our rapid fire from long range guns wrought such havoc that in the evening they drew off, after killing one of our men. During the fight they made six charges, and it was after a repulse of one of these charges that our man Johnson was killed. Contrary to orders, he mounted, dashed away calling us to follow him, and charged right in among the Indians and was killed. When the Indians drew off they went in a direction that convinced me that they were going to ambush us in Buss Canyon, through which our route lay and several miles ahead. I decided to thwart their scheme and with the body of Johnson strapped on the horse, we hit the road and struck out through the mountains for the Rio Grande below Fort Quitman. Five or six miles out where we had the fight we came to a small valley of loose sandy soil where with our butcher knives and tin cups we scooped out a rude grave and buried our comrade. When we reached the Rio Grande we came up with a mule train belonging to Adams and in charge of a Mr. Naile, which was heavily laden with army supplies and stores for Fort Bliss. We told him that the Indians were near and that we had been fighting them all the day before and for him to corral his wagons at once. He did as directed and had scarcely finished preparations when the Indians appeared in large numbers and a furious attack followed. They were driven off and crossed into Mexico, and after they were gone Mr. Naile said to me: 'Sergeant, you have saved my train.'

"It was while I was stationed at Fort McKavett in 1874 that orders came for six companies of the Ninth Cavalry to march to Fort Concho, where we were joined by several companies of infantry and a large supply train. General McKenzie was in command, and the object of the expeditions was the destruction of several Indian villages far out on the Staked Plains. We went by way of Fort Griffin where other forces joined us, and after long and weary marches we came upon the main village, situated in Tule Canyon. The Indians discovered us long before we reached this canyon and employed every strategy to draw us away from the locality of the village, but General McKenzie was not so easily deceived but kept his column moving towards the canyon. The battle that ensued has been so often described that it is needless that I should go into detail here. We destroyed everything destructive in their village. They had many guns, mostly citizens' rifles, and a good supply of ammunition besides bows, arrows, quivers, lances, etc. These we destroyed. We found a vast amount of buffalo robes, of which each man made choice of the best – the rest were destroyed. Their tents were made of poles over which hides were stretched, and these were all burned. We also captured a vast store of dried turkey and buffalo meat; also a considerable amount of peculiar food made in the form of a paste from mesquite beans and other ingredients and put up in the maw of deer and buffalo. In this fight the squaws fought like demons, and many of them were killed who otherwise would have been spared. We captured 112 prisoners, mostly women, children, old "bucks," and three or four of the younger warriors. They were brought to Fort Concho and held six or eight months and finally taken to the Fort Sill reservation. While on the march to Fort Concho, three of the younger "bucks" committed suicide by butting out their brains, preferring a violent death to captivity.

"You ask me to tell you of the fight at White Sand Mountain. We were stationed at Fort Davis when scouts reported a large body of Mescalero Apaches passing on towards Mexico. Lieutenant Bullis with a part of two companies immediately took the trail. We followed them four days over a fearfully rough country and while passing their camping places, every sign showed that they had held a big war dance. Late one evening the scout came in and stated that just across the mountains in our front, the Indians had encamped for the night. This scout was ordered to return and watch the camp and report about midnight. Meantime our pack animals and extra stock were driven into the head of a narrow canyon, while a detail set to work to build a wall at the entrance in order that the stock might be secure. At about the hour of midnight our scout and trailer came in and reported to Lieutenant Bullis. He said the Indians were holding a big war dance and that they seemed to have no apprehension of impending danger. He also described the position of their horse herd and the approaches to their camp, which was in a small valley with very little timber growth. We were ordered to mount and instructed to move with the utmost silence. The guide led us by a very circuitous route, and at dawn we rode out of the valley, where the enemy lay in camp. The Indian in charge of the horse herd was the first to discover us and give the alarm, but too late. We charged pell mell into the encampment, killing old and young and but few escaped. Several prisoners were taken among whom was an old chief – the most ancient looking individual I ever saw. He might have beein feigning extreme decrepitness, but he gave us the impression that he was utterly helpless. He was too old and venerable in appearance for us to kill; we did not care to be encumbered with him as a prisoner, so we placed a ham of venison and an olla of water near him and left him alone to fare the best he could. We gathered up the spoils, such as we wanted to carry away, destroyed the rest, and with the large herd of captured horses, we started on our return to Fort Davis. Among the prisoners taken was a beautiful Apache girl whose age we took to be about seventeen years. She proved to be a most vicious, intractable prisoner and sought every occasion to inflict injury on her captors. She was mounted astride behind one of our troopers who was continually exposed to her sly means of insult and torture. As was the custom, each cavalryman carried a six-shooter in a scabbard or holster the flap of which was buttoned down. Several times this girl was foiled in the act of reaching forward and trying to seize the trooper's pistol and would have succeeded but for the difficulty in releasing the flap from the button. The men reasoned and agreed among themselves that it was better to kill this prisoner than to take the risk of having one or more of their number killed by her, and the morning following this agreement, she made another attempt to get possession of the trooper's pistol and was promptly shot, and nothing was said about it, although it was expected that the offender would have to face courtmartial.

"I have often been asked about Bullis' Seminole scouts, and the general impression went abroad to the effect that these scouts were Seminole Indians, but this was a mistaken idea. Bullis' scouts were all Negroes from Mexico. A number of them were ex-slaves who before and during the war, had run off from their masters in Texas and got into Mexico, while the most of them were sons of Negro parents who had been adopted into the tribe of Seminole Indians in Florida and went with a branch of that tribe into Mexico when driven from Florida. Many of these were part Indian. They all spoke Spanish; only a few of them, the Texas ex-slaves, spoke any English, and were considered to be the best body of scouts, trailers, and Indian fighters ever engaged in the Government service along the border. Their efficiency was due wholly to the skill and military genius of Lieutenant Bullis."

Frederic Remington '88
Arizona-

Sergeant Bivins' Narrative

It is fortunate that the average Negro in the regular army is intelligent and fairly well educated.

Horace Wayman Bivins, son of Severn S. and Elizabeth Bivins, was born in Pungoteague, Accomack County, Virginia, May 8, 1862. He spent his early childhood on his father's farm. At the age of fifteen he was put in charge of an eight-horse farm one mile from Keller Station, Va. His father is a farmer, but has spent much of his time in religious and educational work. He advanced money in 1862 to build a church and schoolhouse at Pungoteague. These were the first buildings erected on the eastern shore of Virginia, for that purpose. Prejudice was so great in that section that the day the schoolhouse was completed it was reduced to ashes before 10 o'clock that night, and a notice was placed upon his father's door notifying him to leave the country within five days or else he would be hanged by his d–d neck until dead. The following day the old gentleman received information that the Yankees were at Drummondtown, but twelve miles away. He rode to headquarters and reported the transaction to the division commander. He at once sent a part of his staff to investigate the matter. The result was in

Reprinted from Herschel V. Cashin, *Under Fire with the Tenth Cavalry* (New York, 1899).

Mr. Bivins' favor, and he was successful in establishing a school and had it opened the following Monday.

The following narrative was written by Sergeant Bivins while in the Cuban campaign, and it shows that he is a careful observer and faithful historian:

"I entered Hampton School, June 13, 1885, at which place I received my first military training. Having a very great desire for adventure and to see the wild West, I enlisted in the United States army, November 7, 1887, at Washington, D. C. Ten days later I was sent to Jefferson Barracks, Missouri. After receiving a few lessons in mounted and dismounted drill I was assigned to Troop E, Tenth Cavalry. Major Kelley was then captain of the troop. I joined my troop at Fort Grant, Arizona Territory, June 19, 1888. In a few days my troop was ordered to take the field. It was reported that some Indians had left the San Carlos Reservation and were *en route* to Old Mexico.

"We scouted along St. Pedro River east and west. For thirty days we were searching for Indian trails, but found none. We then returned to the post. On February 22, 1889, my troop was ordered to San Carlos, Arizona Territory. We arrived there after four days' hard march. Our camp was established on the north side and along the Gila River. I was detailed as lineman. I had to ride and keep the telegraph line in good repair between Camp Carlos and Globe, a mining camp about thirty-five miles from San Carlos.

"There were two troops of the Tenth Cavalry, F and E; G Troop of the Fourth Cavalry; and companies C and G of the Twenty-fourth Infantry. There were several thousands of Indians on this reservation. I often had to ride the line alone, and had to pass within two miles of a band of hostile Indians who had entrenched themselves on the heights opposite Benson's Camp, within twelve miles of Carlos.

"Churchana, an Indian chief, had established his headquarters near Benson's Camp and defied the government to arrest him. We kept a detail of twelve men and one noncommissioned officer at Benson's Camp, two miles from the hostile entrenchment. It was a very unpleasant duty that I had to perform, as often I had to pass this camp in the night.

"April 9, 1889, Lieutenant (now Captain) Watson, Lieutenant Dade, and Lieutenant Littebrant of the Tenth, with three troops and sixty Indian scouts, surrounded the hostile camp and demanded their surrender, which was accepted on conditions. The Indian chief was to identify and turn over all the murderers and the government was not to prosecute him. When the fact became known among the Indians that the chief was going to surrender they mutinied, and in the fight four were killed, and the chief was stabbed in several places and was admitted in the government hospital. Lieutenant Watson at daybreak planted two Hotchkiss guns, six hundred yards east of their fortified position, and trained the guns on their works, and thus effected the surrender.

"These same guns helped to form our battery before Santiago, and of which I was gunner.

"After the surrender of the Indians my troop was ordered to change stations with troop I of our regiment. We arrived at Fort Apache, Arizona Territory, October 17, 1889, after a seven days' march over a rough and rocky road. I was detailed as clerk in the regimental adjutant's office, November 10, 1889, and served until made corporal, June 15, 1890. My first target practice with the rifle was at San Carlos. I stood number two in the troop of sixty men although it was the first time that I had ever shot a rifle. I was made sharpshooter in that year, 1889, and have ever since led my troop in marksmanship. I represented my troop in 1892, '93, and '94, winning eight medals and badges at the department competition. I also in 1894 won three gold medals when I represented the Department of the Dakotas at the army competition at Fort Sheridan and carried off the first gold medal.

"Our regiment was ordered to Chickamauga, April 14, 1898. My troop, G, at this time, was in the field. First Lieutenant W. H. Smith and Second Lieutenant Johnson and thirty-eight enlisted men had been ordered to do patrol duty in the Blackfeet Reservation, which the government had announced would be thrown open for settlement on the fifteenth of April, 1898.

"When the order came for us to go South, General Henry sent a telegram for the troop to report at the post as soon as possible. The troop arrived at post at 2:30 P.M. on the eighteenth looking very much fatigued, having patroled the Canadian line, a portion of the Rocky Mountains, and St. Mary's Lake, a part of the time wading through mud and water from two to three feet deep and more than half of the time without anything to eat.

"We left Fort Assinniboine, Montana, April nineteenth. We were delayed near a little town in Wisconsin about twenty-two hours on account of the burning of a bridge just before we reached it. It was thought that it was burned on purpose to have us lie over there.

"We received great ovations all along the line. Thousands of people were thronged at the places where we would stop and we were treated royally; at Madison, Wisconsin, we were presented with enough flags to decorate our train and were given cigars and many other pleasantries. Our band would play in response to the ovations that were given us from time to time.

"After reaching Illinois we received both flags and flowers from the ladies and schoolgirls. I planted one of the flags given me on the crest of San Juan Hill, July 1, 1898. As we neared the South the great demonstrations became less fervent. There were no places that we entered in which we were courteously treated.

"The signs over the waiting room doors at the southern depots were a revelation to us. Some read thus: 'White waiting room.' On the door of a lunch room we read: 'Niggers are not allowed inside.' We were traveling in palace cars, and the people were much surprised that we did not occupy the 'Jim Crow' cars, *the curse of the South.*

"At Nashville, Tennessee, we were met by thousands of people, both white and colored. Our band played in response to the cheers that went up from the great multitude. After leaving Nashville we were soon in Chickamauga, and our regiment, notwithstanding the fact that we had just come from the extreme cold of the Northwest, began the routine duties of camp life and put in several hours at hard drill. We soon became well-seasoned warriors under the discipline required in war. Not a word of complaint was heard in the lines as our men were marched and countermarched under the hot sun in preparing them for the hardships of the campaign in Cuba. General Wheeler, when first visiting our regiment at Lakeland, Florida, was much impressed by the appearance of our men and said that we looked like fighters. And there were in our lines many Indian fighters who were anxious to get a whack at the Spaniards."

J. CISNEROS

Lieutenant Henry Ossian Flipper

John M. Carroll

Henry Ossian Flipper, the first black graduate of West Point, was born in slavery on March 31, 1856, in Thomasville, Georgia. With all due respect to this remarkable man, he was not the first black to be admitted to West Point, rather the first to graduate. Nonetheless, his was an achievement that signaled triumph over the worst of odds.

Flipper's mother was Isabella Buckhalter, a mulatto owned by the Reverend Reuben H. Lucky. His father, Festus Flipper, was a skilled shoemaker belonging to Ephraim G. Ponder, whose various activities included dealing in slaves. The two slaves met, fell in love, and, with the necessary permission of their owners, married and began a family. From their union five boys were born, Henry being the oldest. Each of the brothers made his mark in this world. One, Joseph, was ordained a bishop of the African Methodist Episcopal Church; another, Festus, Jr., became a wealthy and respected farmer and land owner in Thomasville; Carl became a professor in Savannah; and E. H. earned his medical degree and became a physician in Jacksonville, Florida. But it was Henry Flipper who entered the history books.

To prevent his family from being broken up when Ponder decided to move his slaves from Thomasville to Atlanta, Festus purchased his wife and the two sons born by that time from the Reverend Lucky. This purchase was made possible by the many contradictions that existed in the institution of slavery. Once the Flippers became a united family, the parents lived and worked for only two things: the attainment of freedom for themselves and their children, and an education for their children. After the Civil War, Festus brought his entire family – all free now from bondage – to Atlanta, where he set himself up as a shoemaker. From all indications he began to prosper almost at once. It now began to seem as if the second of their two dreams would come true.

Before the end of the Civil War, Henry had learned to read. Only eight years old at the time, he showed an intense desire to learn. Although his early instruction in reading was casual, coming from another slave who himself knew how to read, Henry's formal education began when the war ended and his father became established as a tradesman. He attended some of the many schools that had been established by the American Missionary Association for the new freedmen. The last of these was Atlanta University which had first opened its doors in 1869; and it was while a student there that Flipper received his appointment to West Point.

James Crawford Freeman of Griffin, Georgia, an elected member of the House of Representatives, considered the appointment of Flipper to the military academy along with the applications of many other native Georgians, but his choice was soon narrowed down to the one who had impressed him the most with his sincerity and potential.

When Flipper entered the Academy he roomed with another black who already had been at the Academy for three years before Flipper's arrival, James Webster Smith, an octoroon from South Carolina, who had arrived there on May 30, 1870. Michael Howard, a black with no mixed blood, was also enrolled in the Academy when Flipper arrived but when, upon examination, Howard was found to be lacking in a fundamental working knowledge of all academic subjects, he was sent home. Smith spent three volatile years at the Academy before being discharged for alleged academic deficiencies. He found some degree of success thereafter as commandant of students at the South Carolina Agricultural Institute where he remained until his death in November, 1876.

The future was different for Henry Ossian Flipper. There were, of course, the usual racial and social slurs at the Academy. That was, unfortunately, still to be expected. He did find, however, that his treatment by peers as a peer was more the rule than the exception. When he graduated in June, 1877, fiftieth in a class of seventy-six, Lieutenant Flipper became famous almost overnight as the first black West Pointer. The newspapers hailed the event as a milestone in race relations, and he was feted in the large cities of the North and the South. Though some papers made uncomplimentary references both to him and to his first regimental assignment, the Tenth United States Cavalry, these were mostly southern papers and obviously prejudiced.

Flipper's first assignment was at Fort Sill; later he served at Fort Elliott and Fort Concho. Fort Sill was in Indian Territory, later to be designated the Oklahoma Territory before becoming a state. Fort Elliott was in the Texas Panhandle, and Fort Concho was the site of what is now San Angelo, Texas. Flipper's military activities consisted mainly of a series of engagements and near-engagements with the Comanches and the Kiowas on whose lands these forts had been built. But in November, 1880, when he arrived at a new station, Fort Davis, he gained a new kind of fame.

His first commanding officer there was Colonel W. R. Shafter, the noted military leader who had commanded several all-black units in the Civil War, notably the Seventeenth United States Colored Infantry. Lieutenant Flipper was assigned to Fort Davis as post commissary. Slightly less than a year after he was posted there, Flipper was placed under military arrest for violation of the Sixtieth Article of War, which involved embezzlement of government funds, and for conduct unbecoming an officer of the United States Army. He was charged with embezzling a total of $3,791.77 while serving as post commissary, with offering false testimony to his commanding officer about the post accounts, and, further, with offering to make good the deficit by writing a check on a bank at which he had no account.

(At this point a credibility gap develops. I was priveleged to see, some four or five years ago, a letter written by an officer in the same command which stated categorically that the charges against Flipper were trumped up and that Flipper was really charged with these crimes because he had been "too familiar" when speaking to the wife of another officer on the post. The letter went on to state that "too familiar" meant that Flipper spoke to her at all. According to the letter-writer, the woman's husband, a violently jealous man, was a southerner who opposed any extension of rights to blacks, and he made the simple greeting appear to be more that what it really was. From this grew the charges of embezzlement. It all smacks of collusion. Some might argue that Colonel Shafter would surely not have been privy to such a thing, for, after all, he had been, at his own request, the commanding officer of many all-black units. This may be true, but although Shafter may have thought well of black enlisted men, no one knows his attitude regarding black officers. It is debatable that this letter would carry any weight in a court-martial hearing of vindication, but unfortunately it was lost in a fire that destroyed the owner's entire library. It is interesting to know, however, that it did exist and that it was written, apparently, without Lieutenant Flipper's knowledge.

In any case, the ruling of the court-martial that tried Flipper was that of not guilty on the count of embezzlement but guilty of the second charge. One must ask how is one guilty verdict possible without the other? Why would Lieutenant Flipper attempt to cover up with a bad check a deficit that did not exist? The Commander of the Department of Texas must have recognized these anomalies because he reversed the first decision and upheld the decision on the second charge. This verdict was changed by the Judge Advocate General of the Army, who finalized the original decisions of the court-martial.

My own reading of the pages and pages of the trial proceedings microfilm reveal nothing substantial or really incriminating against Flipper. The various testimonies really appear to be trumped up, and it is doubtful that they would have been taken seriously had it been a white officer on trial. Today the case might never even have reached trial. In his diaries, which have been annotated and published under the title, *Negro Frontiersman,* by the Texas Western Press at El Paso, Flipper explained everything most satisfactorily. In fact, he seems to go out of his way not to incriminate the perpetrators of those charges.)

Henry O. Flipper was not a man to waste time in finding use for his talents. At West Point he had studied Spanish and become fluent in the language. He had also studied for a degree in Civil Engineering at the Academy. Now, both of these were combined to provide his new occupation, and within a short time he was working on both sides of the U.S.-Mexican border. His primary contribution during this period was validating Spanish and Mexican land grants in the United States. In addition he translated the mining laws of Mexico into English, and in time he completed the prodigious task of translating *Spanish and*

Mexican Land Laws into English, an important contribution to international law.

When Flipper's services became a matter of record, he was asked to join various professional societies, among them the National Geographic Society, the Archeological Institute of America, and the Arizona Society of Civil Engineers. All these honors vindicated his name as a gentleman and a professional.

When the Spanish-American War began in 1898, Flipper offered his services as an officer to the army. Several influential men in both houses of Congress took up his cause, notably Representative Griffin of Wisconsin and Senator Baker of Kansas. Newspapers rallied to his side. But even though all these forces worked toward restoring him to his military rank, and to his rightful dignity, it all came to naught. The congressional bills relating to Henry O. Flipper died on the desks of the responsible men in Washington. Some historians have suggested that Flipper did not receive restoration of rank because there was no recruitment of all-black regiments for this war, and thus no openings. What they fail to remember is that the Ninth and Tenth Cavalries and the Twenty-fourth and Twenty-fifth Infantries, each an all-black unit, participated in great strength and with heroism in Cuba. And the Tenth Cavalry was Flipper's old unit.

After this second humiliation, he took a job as a resident engineer of the Greene Gold-Silver Company at Ocampo. Chihuahua, Mexico. After this, he worked as a mining engineer for several American-owned mines in Mexico. He also held the relatively prestigious position of translator on a subcommittee of the Senate Committee on Foreign Relations. Following this he was an assistant to the Secretary of the Interior. And from 1923 to 1930, he served as a consultant to Pantepec Oil Company in Venezuela.

During the U.S. Punitive Expedition of 1916 against Pancho Villa in Mexico, Flipper was working as an engineer in El Paso. Since he was known by many people on both sides of the border, moving freely from one side to the other in the performance of his duties, and since he spoke Spanish fluently, some were led to believe that he was serving in the capacity of a spy – or, if you will, military observer – for the U.S. Government. It was certainly possible for him to have functioned as such, but despite newspaper allegations, he vehemently denied having engaged in any such activities.

During his last years of inactivity and retirement, he lived with his brother, Bishop Joseph Flipper, in Atlanta, Georgia. When he died in 1940, at the age of eighty-four, his brother completed the death certificate. When he came to the question, "Occupation," he wrote: "Retired Army Officer." This was a fitting tribute.

Some day, some organization may have Flipper's court-martial reopened, just as the case of Major Marcus Reno, who was condemned for his role in the Battle of the Little Big Horn, was reheard many years later. Just as Major Reno was vindicated – and his position was far less tenable than that of Flipper – so should Flipper receive the same consideration.

J. K. Ralston

Braves of All Colors: The Story of Isaiah Dorman Killed at the Little Big Horn

Robert J. Ege

Figuratively speaking, mountains of material have been written about June 25, 1876, and the historic events popularly known to history and fiction as "Custer's Last Stand" and "The Custer Massacre." Brevet Major General George Armstrong Custer, for more than a century, has endlessly trod the literary gamut in terms ranging from "abject fool" to "zealous" to "heroic tactician." Historians, pro and con, have been tireless in their efforts to chronicle the deeds of Reno, Benteen, Keogh, Weir and others. Battle buffs of the Indian Wars have credited close-mouthed "Lonesome" Charley Reynolds with more words than he was probably ever heard to utter. Hero and heel alike have attained their niche in the ever-expanding archives of Custeriana.

But this is the story of a man – not a fighting man – but one who was courageous, sober, of proven dependability, and possessed of the unique ability to converse with the Sioux Indians in their native tongue. It has little to do with all that has been written or said.

At about 3:00 P.M. on June 25, 1876, Major Marcus A. Reno's abortive attack on the southern perimeter of the great Sioux and

Reprinted from *Montana, The Magazine of Western History*, XVI (Winter, 1966), No. 1, with permission of the editor and author.

Cheyenne camp had been repulsed. A number of young warriors had faced the half-hearted Reno assault and the Major had led, what he later deemed a charge, away from his objective to the apparent safety of some bluffs on the east side of the bloodied Little Big Horn. The hasty "charge" resulted in several wounded, and a number of those who failed to comprehend Reno's garbled orders were left behind.

The fighting then in this particular area – the flat bottom land on the west bank of the river – had ceased. As was their custom, the Sioux (and a few Cheyenne noncombatants) were edging along the timber between the flat and the water's edge, in search of any wounded – as well as spoils of the victory – that might be there for the taking. The squaws were very adept at this maneuver. A short distance behind them, but for a different reason, rode the great Hunkpapa medicine leader, Sitting Bull. He was there to appraise the progress of the fight. His Hunkpapa camp circle was located at the southern end of the huge village, and his lodges had already borne the brunt of Reno's short-lived, futile ambuscade. That proximity had also resulted in Sitting Bull's young men being the first to return the fire.

Upon his approach to a dense growth of timber, the great Medicine Man was brought quickly to attention by a squaw's excited cry.

"AI-eeee – Come quickly, *a wasicum sapa,* and he is still alive!" The Sioux word means "black white man." Sitting Bull quickly dismounted. There on the ground, clad in bloody buckskins, was indeed *a wasicum sapa* – one of the few Negroes he had ever seen. The big, elderly colored man seemed mortally wounded. One bullet had entered near his right shoulder. Upon emerging, the slug had also torn a gaping wound in his dark chest. Sitting Bull also noticed that one of the man's boots was missing and that there were still more wounds in his lower leg and foot.

Sitting Bull waved away the enraged squaws. The famed Sioux knelt beside the dying Negro. As their eyes met they conversed briefly in the gutteral Sioux tongue. Sitting Bull ordered one of the squaws to the river for water. She returned quickly with a dripping shawl and squeezed water into the medicine leader's horn cup. The Negro drank a small amount, smiled faintly at Sitting Bull, and slumped over dead.

Sitting Bull explained to the curious group which now surrounded them:

"This is *Azimpi.* I do not know why he is here with the soldiers. He was always one of us. I knew him as a friend, and once he was afraid of the white soldiers. His woman is Sioux. When she learns that he has gone to the Sand Hills she will mourn as the women of our lodges also mourn for their braves killed today."

Following Sitting Bull's departure, squaws quickly stripped the bloody buckskins from the man's body. One old Indian suddenly became the owner of a white straw hat worn by the dead Negro. His watch and a few other possessions were stolen, but the desecration ended on this note. Out of respect for Sitting Bull's friendly gesture to the dying man, they did not scalp or otherwise mutilate his corpse. Instead, they vented their pent-up fury by viciously hacking the bodies of other soldiers found nearby.

In Sioux history and lore, there are many stories of a large "black white man" who roamed their lands, and who was welcome in their villages as early as 1850. He was known as *Azimpi* or "Teat." In the spoken Sioux dialects, *Azimpi,* meaning teat or nipple, also sounds like Isaiah. This frontiersman had sustained himself by small-scale trapping and trading, the story went. He traveled with a horse and also a mule. He seemed to prefer the hospitality of the isolated and roving bands of Plains Indians to that of white settlers. This gives birth to the thought that possibly *Azimpi* was hiding from something – or at least was content to cast his lot away from the white man.

Little is known of *Azimpi.* One finds veiled references to the loss of several male slaves by the D'Orman family of Louisiana and Alabama in the late 1840s. A search through old "wanted" posters indicates that a Negro named Isaiah was one of these. But other leads were in vain. It is notable, however, that Dorman first appeared at a white settlement in 1865, following the cessation of hostilities between the North and South, which brought automatic reprieve for many runaway slaves, North and South.

By this time, Dorman had definitely married a young woman of Inkpaduta's band of Santee Sioux. Perhaps weary of the roving life, and surely safe from those who sought his bounty, he built a small cabin at Fort Rice, Dakota Territory, near present-day Bismarck, North Dakota. He supported himself and his Indian bride by cutting wood for the fort. Soon he became known to the officers of that garrison as a jovial, sober, and trustworthy individual. Inordinately fond of tobacco,

Dorman abstained from the jug that ruined so many civilian employees on the frontier. In the early fall of 1865 he was hired as a wood cutter by the trading firm of Durfee & Peck. Due to his size and strength, it was said that "Old Teat" could cut a cord of wood faster than a helper could stack it.

When the post commander and his quatermaster learned of Dorman's ability with the difficult Sioux language, as well as his vast knowledge of the land, he was promptly destined for better things.

On November 11, 1865, according to military records, Dorman was hired by Lieutenant J. M. Marshall to carry the mail between Fort Rice and Fort Wadsworth. He made the 360-mile round trip only once that year. But his reputation for dependability was established. His terms of employment were of short duration and he was hired when needed. Between trips he continued employment with Durfee & Peck, and occasionally worked for Major Charles E. Galpin at the Standing Rock Agency.

On April 22, 1867, Isaiah was rehired as a mail carrier by Lieutenant F. E. Parsons, then serving as quartermaster at Fort Rice. He again made the Wadsworth trip when Indian troubles made it unsafe for a soldier to attempt the journey. Subsequent trips to James River and other military installations were made by Dorman during this hectic period. His income averaged perhaps $50 per month. Yet these wages were comparable to those of a lieutenant in the army and were supplemented by extra earnings as a wood cutter. Isaiah Dorman fared rather well as an emancipated wage-earning employee of the white man.

As a result of his now proven ability Dorman, on September 9, 1871, was hired by Capt. Henry Inman to serve as guide and interpreter in the field for an army column escorting a party of engineers participating in the Northern Pacific Railroad Survey. He was paid $100 per month. Inclement weather cut short the duration of the project. Dorman was scheduled to be out of a job on October 20, 1871.

On the day prior to the termination of his services, or October 19, 1871, the Commanding General of the Military Department of the Dakotas issued Special Order No. 149, whereby Isaiah Dorman was to be hired as post interpreter at Fort Rice and paid at the rate of $75 per month. His immediate superior was Lieutenant William Van Horne. In February, 1874, a reduction in budget caused all civilian employees of the army to be reduced in pay. The interpreter's salary was cut to $50 per month. By all existing standards, Dorman was still very well fixed. Lieutenant Van Horne left Fort Rice in 1872, and from that time until he assumed his duties with General Custer Dorman served under Captain J. W. Scully. He continued to be a valuable employee whose understanding of the Indians and their language helped avert many incidents at Fort Rice. Dorman's service record is impressive; there are no notations of any disciplinary action ever taken against him.

The trading firm of E. H. (Hicks) Durfee and Campbell K. Peck, with headquarters at Leavenworth, Kansas, enjoyed virtually a monopoly in the Indian and military trade in large sectors of the Dakotas and Montana during the years of 1870-74. They were contracturally obligated to supply cattle, wood, lumber and hay for the military installations and Indian agencies in the territory. The firm, however, was bankrupt and apparently dissolved in 1876, when the government refused them a license to continue their operations.

Refusal of the government to relicense Isaiah Dorman's former employers was not a result of failure to fulfill obligations to the Interior Department. It was necessary for a trading firm to post a $5,000 bond with the Secretary of the Interior in order to do business. Columbus Delano occupied the office at that time. Delano and President Grant's younger brother, Orvil, were reputedly involved in an operation in which a "kickback" was expected from those in the trading business. Durfee & Peck honestly refused to cooperate; hence their bond was refused in 1875.

The national trading post scandal and investigation began in 1875. Delano was found guilty of negligence and incompetence, and resigned. George A. Custer, in newspaper and magazine articles and through other unofficial channels, hinted strongly regarding Orvil Grant's involvement. Both Custer and Campbell K. Peck were summoned to testify before the Indian Affairs Committee by Chairman Heister Clymer in March, 1876. Custer's testimony resulted in a harsh rebuke by President Grant. It was only through intervention by Generals Alfred H. Terry and Phil Sheridan that Custer was allowed to lead his Seventh Cavalry in the summer campaign of 1876.

Upon his belated return to Fort Abraham Lincoln, Custer began assembling the contingent of civilian employees, scouts, packers and interpreters that would accompany the military. The following order was issued:

Hq. Middle Dist.
Dept. Dak.
Ft. A. Lincoln, D.T.
May 14, 1876

Special Order No. 2

The commanding office Ft. Rice, D. T. will order Isaiah Dorman, Post Interpreter, to proceed to this post and report for duty to accompany the expedition as Interpreter – During his absence he will still be borne on the rolls of the Post Quartermaster at Fort Rice.

By order of Brevet Major General Custer.

W. . Cooke
1st Lt. Adjt. 7th Cavalry
AAA Gen.

Pursuant to this special order, Isaiah was officially hired as interpreter for the regiment by Lieutenant Henry J. Nowlan, Regimental Quartermaster of the Seventh. He was to assume his duties on May 15, 1876 at the rate of $75 a month.

Dorman was pleased to accept the position. He was now about fifty-five years old, and most of the past twelve years had been spent in and around the frontier forts in the Dakotas. It wasn't that he wanted to make war on his old friends, the Sioux. He expressed a keen desire to see once again the wonderful Montana land to the west. To him, this wasn't a mission of war, but a chance to renew old acquaintances.

Enough has already been written about Custer's march to the Little Big Horn. At noon on June 25, when "Long Hair" made the fateful division of his command, the entire column was at the Crow's Nest on the divide separating the Rosebud from the Little Big Horn. Most of the scouts and several civilian personnel had been assigned to accompany Troops M, A, and G in the Reno battalion. Reno's orders were to cross the river and attack the Indian encampment from the south.

Reno did this. He led his battalion across the river and proceeded at a brisk pace toward the village. However, when faced with an unexpected, brutal opposition, his attack fell short and he formed his command in a dismounted skirmish line across the valley. The late Dr. Charles Kuhlman describes that line in his excellent text, *Legend Into History:*

> . . . the skirmish line was formed near the site of the present headstone for Lieutenant McIntosh. Its right rested on a narrow strip of timber running parallel, or nearly so, to an old riverbed 150 to 200 yards from the line. Troop G under McIntosh held the right; A under Moylan, the center; and M under French, the left. For a few minutes a mixed group of scouts and civilians, under Varnum and Hare, stood about 200 yards to the left of French. Among them were, besides the Arikara and several Crows, the two Jackson brothers, half-breed Blackfeet, Reynolds, Girard, Reno's orderly, Davern, Herendeen and probably the Negro Dorman . . .

In this position, the command was relatively exposed. The strength of their opposition at this particular point is highly controversial. In reality, the enemy was in such force, that, after ten or fifteen minutes of long-distance sniping, Reno ordered the command to a more sheltered position in the timber on the west bank of the river.

It was here that a closely formed group of soldiers and civilians drew a concentrated fire from the Indians. A well-placed hostile bullet splattered the brains of Custer's favorite Indian scout, Bloody Knife, into Reno's face. Dripping with gore, but unharmed, the major panicked. Lieutenant Benny Hodgson was wounded. Two enlisted men and the chief white scout, "Lonesome" Charlie Reynolds, were killed. It was also in this place that Dorman received his mortal wound. He had renewed no old acquaintances nor had he the opportunity to use his particular skill in palaver with the Sioux. Isaiah, along with others, was left to die in Reno's disorganized exodus.

Some time prior to 1930, Wooden Leg, the famous Cheyenne warrior, told his friend and biographer, Dr. Thomas B. Marquis, that he viewed the body of Isaiah Dorman on the morning of June 26, or the day following his death. The Cheyenne related that at this time the body had been stripped of all clothing, but was otherwise unmolested. There is no reason to doubt Wooden Leg's story. Although he often ranged far afield in typical Indian fashion in relating the battle in narrative style, when queried about specific details, as he was about Dorman, Wooden Leg's answers were truthful, and a great deal of useful history has been gleaned from his keen memory.

When the troopers under Generals Terry and Gibbon came to the relief of Reno's beleaguered command on June 17, a search was immediately made for possible survivors. The picture then had been altered considerably. Isaiah's body when found had indeed been horribly mutilated. In addition to slashing wounds, more than a dozen arrows had been shot into his chest – even a cavalry picket-pin had been driven through his lower abdomen. This desecration was probably the parting gesture of enraged, savage squaws, or of the Cheyennes, who did not know him.

Isaiah Dorman remains essentially anonymous. No photograph of him is known to exist. The location of his grave – like many others on the west side of the Little Big Horn – has been lost. No marker was ever erected to his memory, nor has there been any effort to makr the approximate location where he fell.

At the time of Dorman's death, there was $102.50 due him for services rendered to the army – $40 for the month of May and $62.50 for the days in June of 1876. A recent search of old records in the Treasury Department revealed that on May 23, 1879, a person named Isaac McNutt claimed to be the assignee of Dorman's pay voucher and attempted to collect the money. McNutt, known as a "hanger on" around Fort Rice who worked sporadically as a wood hauler and carpenter, never collected Isaiah's money. His claim was disallowed on September 25, 1879. Dorman's Santee Sioux widow apparently never applied at all.

Along with many other ironies in the story of Isaiah Dorman is the fact that the only reference to his color was made by Major Reno in his report of the battle. War department records of that period required no such information. Out of what was probably haste or oversight, Reno omitted Isaiah's last name in his report. Someone, at a later date, penciled "Dorman" beside the Major's entry. That sparse entry is followed by the words: "Killed by Indians."

THE MEDAL OF HONOR WINNERS

The period of the Indian Wars saw many heroes rise from the ranks of the black regiments. There were eighteen Congressional Medal of Honor recipients in all, two in the infantry and the others in the two cavalry units.

Most of the following fourteen excerpts are eyewitness accounts of those heroic moments which prompted congressional recognition. The others are based on the official reports by the officers who made the citations. The recipients were proud to receive their medals, not least because their regiments were being honored as well.

The Battle of Cuchillo Negra Mountains

FIRST SERGEANT MOSES WILLIAMS
Born: Carroll County, Pennsylvania

PRIVATE AUGUSTUS WALLEY
Born: Reisterstown, Maryland
Citations: For Valor in Battle

A band of [Apache] Indians under the notorious Chief Nana in the month of July, 1881, had committed a number of outrages, killed several women and children, and stolen considerable property along the San Andreas Mountains in New Mexico, and Colonel E. Hatch with eight troops of the Ninth Cavalry and eight companies of infantry was sent to punish the savages and recapture the plunder.

The command started in pursuit at once and in a number of encounters drove the hostiles persistently from one point to another.

A notable engagement occurred on August 12 near Carrizo Canyon, in New Mexico. Nana's band was struck by a detachment of nineteen men under Captain Parker. In the ensuing fight the troopers were outnumbered three to one by the hostiles and lost one killed and three wounded, while one soldier was captured. The Indians, however, also lost heavily and were finally forced to withdraw. That the affair had such a successful ending and was not turned into a serious defeat

Reprinted from Beyer and Keydel, *Deeds of Valor,* Vols. I & II (Detroit, 1963).

was due largely to the extraordinary courage of Sergeant Thomas Shaw, of Company K, Ninth Cavalry, who with his few men stubbornly held the most advanced position and refused to yield an inch of ground. He was an excellent shot, his bravery so dismayed the Indian that they gave up the attack and retreated. A still larger engagement followed a few days later.

On August 16, Troop I, Ninth Cavalry, First Lieutenant Gustavus Valois in command, and Second Lieutenant George R. Burnett on duty with same was lying in Camp Canada Alamosa, New Mexico, recuperating from an arduous campaign in quest of hostile Apaches, when about 9:30 or 10 o'clock in the morning a Mexican whose ranch was a few miles down the canyon came charging into the town shrieking at the top of his voice that the Indians had murdered his wife and children and were coming up the canyon to attack the town; in an instant all was excitement, men, women and children ran hither and thither screaming, crying, cursing, and piteously calling on the "Good Father" to have mercy on them and save them.

In the cavalry camp orders were at once given to "saddle up," and in an incredibly short time this was accomplished. Lieutenant Burnett requested and received permission to make the first detachment ready and proceed toward the scene of trouble. The ranch referred to was soon reached and the ranchman's story corroborated in the finding of his dead wife and a number of small children, all horribly mutilated.

The trail was taken up and followed across the creek and up over the "Mesa," where the Indians were sighted about a mile off, heading toward the Cuchilla Negra Mountains, about ten miles distant. They were heavily encumbered with a large quantity of stolen stock and other plunder that they were endeavoring to get away with.

At the ranch Lieutenant Burnett had been joined by a number of mounted Mexicans, bringing his force up to about fifty men. The Indians, as nearly as could be estimated, numbered between eighty and one hundred. Immediately on sighting the Indians Lieutenant Burnett deployed his command, placing his First Sergeant, Moses Williams, in command on the right and one of the Mexicans on the left, remaining in the center himself. As soon as the advance was begun the Indians dismounted to make a stand, and commenced firing. Favored by the rolling country, the fire of the Indians soon became so warm that Lieutenant Burnett was obliged to dismount his command and to send a part of it under Sergeant Williams to flank the Indians from their position. This the sergeant succeeded in doing, and as soon as he signaled that the Indians had broken and were on the run Lieutenant Burnett mounted the balance of his command and charged them, keeping up a running fight until the Indians came to the next ridge, when they dismounted again, compelling the command to do likewise and to repeat the former tactics of flanking them out of position and then charging.

The fight was continued for several hours, the Indians fighting hard and contesting every foot of the ground in order to save as much of their stock and plunder as possible, but so closely were they pressed that they lost a number in killed and wounded, and were obliged to abandon a large quantity of their stuff and a number of their ponies and to shoot others to prevent their capture.

Finally the foothills of the Cuchilla Negra Mountains were reached, and here the Indians made a determined stand. Being unable to flank them on their right, Lieutenant Burnett decided to make an effort to get around their left flank and if possible keep them out of the mountains. In working this detour he was accompanied by only about fifteen soldiers. The Indians observing his movements and apparent purpose, and his small force, offered no opposition for some time, when suddenly they found themselves in a pocket and surrounded on three sides by a heavy fire, and to make matters worse the Mexicans in the rear were firing into the bank against which the men were seeking to shelter themselves. Fortunately the pocket of basin-shaped formation was so deep that all shots passed just overhead and among the rocks and did no harm except to wound some of the horses. The Indians kept crawling nearer, their shots striking dangerously close, and the situation was growing desperate for the little detachment, unless they could get relief. Orders were given to reserve their revolver fire and fight to the last man.

It was at this juncture that Trumpeter John Rogers, at the suggestion of Lieutenant Burnett, volunteered to carry a message to Lieutenant Valois, whom he knew must be somewhere in the vicinity. Rogers endeavored to crawl out, but getting discouraged with his progress ran to where his horse was picketed and quickly mounting him rode to the rear amid a hailstorm of bullets, miraculously escaping harm, although his horse was wounded.

Rogers found Lieutenant Valois and delivered Lieutenant Burnett's message, which was to take a large hill to the right which commanded the position. Lieutenant Valois endeavored to comply with the request, but the Indians anticipated his purpose, and leaving Lieutenant Burnett's position got there first, greeting him with a volley that dismounted ten men, Valois among their number. From Lieutenant Burnett's position the Indians could be seen rallying from all points toward the hill, and divining the cause he proceeded to withdraw for the purpose of reenforcing Valois. Mounting his men and taking about thirty Mexicans who had then joined him, he started to the right and rear. On coming up over the little rise he saw Lieutenant Valois's entire command on a slight ridge about a quarter of a mile distant, dismounted and seeking shelter behind some prairie dog mounds, about the only thing in sight, and it looked as if the Indians, only a few hundred yards off, were just about to charge them. Without halting an instant, the command being deployed and at a gallop, Lieutenant Burnett ordered it to charge. This was done in a magnificant manner, the command charging splendidly up to and beyond Lieutenant Valois's line; and, dismounting, held the Indians in check until Lieutenant Valois was enabled to get his wounded and disabled men to the rear, when the whole line was ordered to fall, as its position was untenable.

Lieutenant Valois had commenced the backward movement before the charge was made, and in doing so had left four of his men behind unobserved, in places of comparative shelter. When the general order to fall back was given, one of the men called out: "For God's sake, Lieutenant don't leave us; our lives depend on it."

At this time Lieutenant Valois and most of his command was well to the rear and apparently did not hear the cry. Lieutenant Burnett seeing the position these men were in called for volunteers to go to their rescue. Two men only, First Sergeant Moses Williams and Private Augustus Walley, responded to the call. Lieutenant Burnett directed his men to crawl to the rear while he, with Williams and Walley, behind such shelter as they could find, would try to stand off the Indians, who, emboldened by the troops falling back, were making a desperate effort to kill or capture those remaining behind. The marksmanship of the trio, all being good shots, caused the Indians to pause, and two of the soldiers were enabled to get to a place of safety, a third, who made no effort to escape was apparently wounded. This man was Walley's "bunky," so he asked for permission to go to his assistance. Going back to where his horse was picketed he mounted, rode rapidly up to where the man was lying, assisted him in the saddle, got up behind him and galloped safely to the rear.

Strange as it may appear, the Indians made no apparent effort to get Walley, but seemed to concentrate their efforts on Lieutenant Burnett whom they readily recognized as an officer among the colored troopers, and his solitary companion First Sergeant Williams. Finally the fourth man who was left behind was seen wandering off in the direction of the enemy, or rather away from his own lines, and acting very strangely. He was apparently badly rattled. Indians could be distinctly seen making an effort to cut him off. Lieutenant Burnett, realizing that if this man was to be saved no time must be lost, ran to his horse, mounted him, and galloping toward the soldier managed to place himself between him and the Indians and finally drove him to the rear. All the while the Indians kept up a concentrated fire on Lieutenant Burnett, to which he replied with his revolver, but in their excitement they shot wildly and only succeeded in recording two hits, both on his horse.

Lieutenant Valois had in the meantime taken up a new position and assisted by some Mexicans the fight was continued until nightfall. Many horses were recaptured or prevented from falling into the hands of the Indians. The ammunition being about exhausted the command fell back to camp, and at daybreak started on the trail again and followed it until obliged to turn back at the Mexican border.

Medals of Honor were awarded to Lieutenant Burnett and his colored troopers, Williams and Walley, for their courageous conduct and rescue of life under such perilous circumstances.

J. CISNER

The Battle of Canyon Blanco

PRIVATE ADAM PAINE
Born: Florida
Citation: For Bravery and Invaluable Service to the Commanding Officer at the Battle of Canyon Blanco.

Colonel R. S. Mackenzie was moving his command of the Fourth Cavalry towards the Red River, Texas, from the south. The torrents which follow the dry season made the roadbeds almost impassable for wagons and impeded the progress of this column seriously. In spite of the difficulties of the march and the many privations which resulted therefrom, the troops preserved a most excellent spirit and easily repulsed two determined attacks made by the Indians. After crossing the head of the Tule Canyon Colonel Mackenzie located five camps of Southern Cheyennes and their allies at Canyon Blanco, a tributary of the Red River, and immediately proceeded to attack them.

In the subsequent fight, which lasted two days, September 26 and 27, 1874, the Indians were put to utter rout, leaving their entire camp outfits and their herds of ponies, some 1400 animals, in the possession of the victors. The Indians lost four killed and several wounded, while of the troops but one was wounded, and he only slightly. Corporal

Reprinted from Beyer and Keydel, *Deeds of Valor,* Vols. I & II (Detroit, 1903).

Edwin Phoenix and Privates Gregory Mahoney and William McCabe, of Company E, were especially conspicuous for their gallantry in this conflict and received the Medal of Honor in consequence. A like honor was conferred upon Private Adam Paine, who as a Seminole-Negro scout rendered invaluable service to Colonel Mackenzie.

J. CISNEROS

The Battle at Tularosa

SERGEANT GEORGE JORDAN
Born: Williamson County, Tennessee
Citation: For Bravery in Battle.

On the second day of January, 1880, Victoria and his band of Indians were reported raiding and murdering in Southern New Mexico, whereupon all the cavalry in that section of the country were sent out at once to round up this noted chief and his thieving band.

The Mescalero Agency at the Fort Stanton Reservation had largely served as a base of supplies and recruits for the raiding parties of Victoria, and it was determined to disarm and dismount the Indians then on the reservation and thus cut off the supplies of the raiders. Generals Pope and Ord, commanding the Departments of the Missouri and Texas, arranged that a force under Colonel E. Hatch, Ninth Cavalry, numbering 400 cavalry, 60 infantry, and 75 Indian scouts, should arrive at the Mescalero Agency simultaneously with Colonel Grierson and a force of the Tenth Cavalry and Twenty-fifth Infantry. These two forces set out early in January and marched toward each other, each having, on the way, several encounters with the Indians.

Reprinted from Beyer & Keydel, *Deeds of Valor,* Vols. I & II (Detroit, 1903).

While Grierson was moving north and engaging the hostiles Hatch's force was driving Victoria south toward the Mescalero Agency. In this manner both forces worked ahead over a rough country until they met at the Mescalero Agency, where, on the sixteenth of April, Colonels Hatch and Grierson made the attempt to disarm and dismount the Indians, but they put up a brave fight and made a desperate effort to escape. This effort, however, proved futile and the hostiles, numbering about 250, were captured, only about 40 escaping. The captured Indians were disarmed and dismounted and taken into the agency.

Major Morrow, with a portion of Colonel Hatch's force, then pursued the escaping Indians and overtook them in Dog Canyon, where he killed 3 warriors and captured 25 head of stock.

After disarming and dismounting the Indians at the agency Colonel Hatch began again the pursuit of Victoria, assisted by troops from the Department of Arizona, but the campaign resolved itself into a chase of the hostiles from one range of mountains to another, with frequent skirmishes but no decisive fights, until the Indians again escaped into Old Mexico. One fight took place at Tularosa on the fourteenth of May which is described by Sergeant George Jordan, Troop K, Ninth Cavalry, as follows:

> On the eleventh of May I was ordered to Old Fort Tularosa with a detachment of twenty-five men of the Ninth Cavalry for the purpose of protecting the town of Tularosa, just outside the fort. Besides our own rations we had extra rations for the rest of the regiment which was pursuing Victoria's band of Apaches. On the second day out we struck the foothills of the mountains, where our advance guard met two troops of Mexican cavalry. The captain of one of them told me that it would be impossible for me to get through with the small body of men I had and advised me to return to the regiment. I replied that my orders were to go through and that I intended to do so, notwithstanding the fact that large bodies of hostiles were still roaming about outside the Mescalero Agency. After leaving our Mexican friends we pushed along with our wagon train bringing up the rear, until that evening we struck the Barlow and Sanders stage station, where we went into camp. At the station all was excitement. The people were throwing up breastworks and digging trenches in the expectation of an attack by the Indians. My command, being dismounted cavalry, was pretty well exhausted from our day's march over the mountains and we were all ready for a good night's rest; but within an hour after our arrival at the station, and just before sundown, a rider from Tularosa came in and wanted to see the

commander of the soldiers. He told me that the Indians were in the town and that he wanted me to march the men the remainder of the distance to save the women and children from a horrible fate.

My men were in bad condition for a march, but I explained to them the situation as the rider had put it before me, and that I would leave it to them whether they wanted to continue the march that night or not. They all said that they would go on as far as they could. We then had supper, after which each man bathed his feet so as to refresh himself, and at about 8 o'clock we started to the rescue. But our progress was slow. Besides the poor condition of the men we were hampered by our wagon train in that rough country. Once one of the wagons was upset as the train was coming down a steep hill and we lost valuable time righting it. About 6 o'clock in the morning we came in sight of the town, and I deployed the men and advanced quickly toward it, believing that the Indians were already there. We stealthily approached the town and had gotten to within a half mile of it before the people discovered us. When they recognized us as troops they came out of their houses waving towels and handkerchiefs for joy.

Upon our arrival in the town we found that only a few straggling Indians had gotten there ahead of us and had killed an old man in a cornfield. The people gave us shelter, and after we had rested up a bit we began making a stockade out of an old corral, and also a temporary fort close to the timber.

On the evening of the the fourteenth while I was standing outside the fort conversing with one of the citizens, the Indians came upon us unexpectedly and attacked. This citizen was telling me that the Indians had killed his brother that very morning and wanted me to go out and attack them. I could not do this, as my orders were to protect the people in the town. It was then that the Indians surprised and fired fully one hundred shots into us before we could gain the shelter of the fort. As the Indians' rifles began to crack the people rushed to the fort and stockade, all reaching it in safety except our teamsters and two soldiers who were herding the mules and about five hundred head of cattle. The bloodthirsty savages tried time and again to enter our works, but we repulsed them each time, and when they finally saw that we were masters of the situation they turned their attention to the stock and tried to run it off. Realizing that they would be likely to kill the herders I sent out a detail of ten men to their assistance. Keeping under cover of the timber, the men quickly made their way to the herders and drove the Indians away, thus saving the men and stock. The whole action was short but exciting while it lasted, and after it was all over the townspeople congratulated us for having repulsed a band of more than one hundred redskins.

Our little detachment was somewhat of a surprise to the Indians,

> for they did not expect to see any troops in the town, and when we repulsed them they made up their minds that the main body of the troops was in the vicinity and would pursue them as soon as they heard of the encounter. The remainder of the regiment did arrive the next morning, and two squadrons at once went in pursuit, but the wily redskins did not stop until they reached the mountains. There they had encounters with the troops and were finally driven into Old Mexico.

Two other important fights took place in this chase of the hostiles after the engagement at Tularosa, one of them on the twenty-fourth of May at the head of the Polomas River, New Mexico, where fifty-five Indians were killed in one of the hardest fought battles of the pursuit. The other took place on June fifth. In this action Major Morrow, with four troops of the Ninth Cavalry, struck the hostiles at Cook's Canyon killing ten and wounding three of them. Among those killed was the son of the fleeing chief, Victoria.

In August of the following year Sergeant Jordan was commanding the right of a detachment of nineteen men at Carrizo Canyon, New Mexico, in an action with the Indians. He stubbornly held his ground in an extremely exposed position and gallantly forced back a much superior number of the enemy, thus preventing them from surrounding the command. His bravery in this action and his skillful handling of the detachment and also his fearlessness in the engagement at Tularosa won for Sergeant Jordan his Medal of Honor.

J. CISNEROS

The Battle of Milk River

SERGEANT HENRY JOHNSON
Born: Boynton, Virginia
Citation: For Valor in Action.

During the latter part of August and the early part of September, 1879, frequent reports came in to General Pope, commanding the Department of Missouri, that the White River Utes had started several extensive fires in the mountains west of Hot Sulphur Springs, Colorado, that they had fired on an agency employee, attacked his house, driving him out and injuring him, and that the lives of the people at the agency were in great danger.

Satisfying himself that the reports were true, General Pope informed the War Department of the state of affairs, and orders were at once received for the nearest military commander to send a force to the White River Agency to protect the agent and arrest the ringleaders in the outrages reported. Accordingly General Crook, commanding the Department of the Platte, sent Troops D and F, Fifth Cavalry; E, Third Cavalry; and Company E, Fourth Infantry, under command of Major Thornburgh, to the scene of the trouble.

Reprinted from William A. DuPuy and John W. Jenkins, *World War and Historic Deeds of Valor,* 6 Vols. (Chicago, 1919.)

This force, numbering about two hundred officers and men, left Fort Steele, in southern Wyoming, on the twenty-first of September and by rapid marches through rugged mountain passes and over barren plains, reached Fortification Creek, in upper Colorado, where the infantry company was left to establish a supply camp, while the cavalry pushed on to Bear Creek. On the afternoon of the twenty-sixth, while the command was at Bear Creek, several prominent Ute Indians came into the camp and talked with Major Thornburgh about the troops coming to the agency, and being assured of the mission of the troops the Indians left in apparent good humor. This conference, however, did not satisfy the Indians at the agency, and the next day several other prominent Indians carried a letter to Major Thornburgh from the Indian agent, to the effect that the Indians at the agency were greatly excited and begging that the troops advance no farther, but that the major and five soldiers should come to the agency for the consultation.

Major Thornburgh replied that he would meet the agent and five chiefs on the road some distance from the agency, after he had marched his command to a suitable camping place.

Two days later, on the twenty-ninth, a courier brought a letter from the agent saying he would leave the agency with several chiefs on the morning of the thirtieth to meet Major Thornburgh.

It looked now as if the difficulties could be amicably settled and Major Thornburgh, who had by this time reached Milk River, left Troop D to continue the march along the road with the wagons, while he with the rest of the troops turned off from the road and took up a trail leading to his left.

The troops with Major Thornburgh had gone scarcely a mile when, in crossing a high bridge, they came suddenly upon the Indians in large force.

This was less of a surprise to the troops than their hostile attitude, in view of the proposed meeting between the major and the Indian agent on the morrow. Major Thornburgh immediately dismounted and deployed his men, at the same time endeavoring to open communication with the Indians. His efforts were in vain and drew forth a volley from the redskins, whereupon a hot engagement began, in which the Indians had the advantage in both position and numbers. Slowly did they drive the troopers back toward the wagon train, which had "parked" near the Milk River, the soldiers leading their horses and firing back into the Indians with deadly aim. Again and again the Indians attempted to break the skirmish line, but each time they were driven to cover, and only when they realized that the troops were not in precipitate rout did they attempt to get between them and the wagon train. They succeeded in gaining a strong position on a knoll commanding Thornburgh's line of retreat, but a desperate charge by about twenty men under Captain Payne routed the Indians and opened the way to the wagon train.

Sergeant Edward P. Grimes, of Troop F, Fifth Cavalry, had covered the left flank of the troops with a party consisting of two noncommissioned officers, one trumpeter, and seven men. Grimes's company commander ordered his troop to mount and charge. While the men ran to their horses Major Thornburgh came riding along, countermanding the order and directing Grimes to keep his position of defense on the bluffs. Grimes could only get the trumpeter and two men, as the others had already mounted and followed the rest of the troop. These few men defended their position with the greatest bravery until ordered by their company commander to mount and withdraw to the wagon train.

About the same time Lieutenant Cherry, Fifth Cavalry, called for volunteers to cover the retreat of the command to the wagon train. Grimes was again the first one to follow the summons of the lieutenant. With him Corporal Edward F. Murphy and Blacksmith Wilhelm O. Philipsen, of Troop D, Fifth Cavalry, jumped off their horses, and other men of both the Third and Fifth Cavalry followed their gallant example. The heroic band fought with unflinching devotion; their ammunition was running short, the Indians had them nearly surrounded, and some of these brave volunteers were already wounded—Lieutenant Cherry immediately saw that their position was becoming desperate, and that their chances of escaping were growing fewer, with all the wounded to care for and protect. The officer called for a volunteer to make his way to the wagon train for ammunition and support. Grimes realized that the effort was well-night hopeless, but fearlessly informed the lieutenant that he would attempt it. He mounted his horse, for what he fully believed to be the last time, and started on his mission. The Indians seemed to divine his purpose, and at once started in pursuit. His horse, being stronger and speedier than the ponies of his pursuers, carried him safely to the wagon train, where the desired ammunition and support were obtained.

The daring ride was made in full view of all the Indians and soldiers, and the encouraging shouts of the latter cheered the intrepid rider on his daring and dangerous mission.

In the meantime Major Thornburgh, trying to supervise the arrangements for protecting the wagon train, had himself started for it, but was shot and instantly killed when within five hundred yards of it. The wagons were formed into an elliptical corral, about two hundred yards from the river, the side toward the stream being exposed to a furious fire from the Indians, who were now making determined efforts to capture or destroy the train. The horses were rapidly falling under the unerring fire of the hostiles. The wounded were quickly laid in sheltered places within the corral, while the wounded horses were led to the exposed side of the huddled group of men, wagons, and horses and shot there, to form a defense for some of the men who were acting as sharpshooters.

The contents of the wagons were then quickly piled on top of the horses, and behind this meager shelter the troopers kept up their fire – but against one more deadly from the screeching, half-frantic redskins. Not content with the advantage they had over the small corral, the wily Indians set fire to the tall grass and sagebrush down the valley. The flames, fanned by the high wind, spread rapidly toward the troops, igniting bundles, grain sacks, wagon covers and other combustible material, adding the horrors of fire to the rain of lead and arrows. The entire train was threatened with destruction. The troopers, besides being compelled to withstand a fusillade of bullets from the hostiles, were obliged to cease firing and exert their energies to extinguish the flames and care for their wounded, whose cries and moanings added to the weirdness of the scene. The sun was rapidly sinking behind the mountains, and as twilight set in the Indians redoubled their efforts to dislodge the men; but the troopers took courage in the thought of approaching darkness and fought with renewed vigor, picking off a redskin every time he silhouetted his head and shoulders against the deepening gloam. Thus the fight was kept up from 3 o'clock in the afternoon until darkness put an end to the desperate struggle. In a final effort a large party of the reds had charged down upon the corral, firing volley after volley into the huddled-up mass of men, horses, wagons and debris.

With the cessation of hostilities a new difficulty presented itself. Water and ammunition were needed. The command was surrounded by the enemy on three sides, making it almost suicidal to attempt to leave the entrenchment. The command was not to be left in this predicament, however, without an attempt, at least, to obtain water and ammunition, and Sergeant E. P. Grimes and Corporal H. M. Roach volunteered to make the effort. They stealthily crept out of the entrenchments toward the river, and at almost point blank range secured water, going back and forth until a sufficient supply had been obtained. Grimes then crept to a supply wagon some distance away from the corral and secured enough ammunition to last another day. Roach bravely repeated his mission on the two succeeding nights, and luckily escaped the vigilance of the wary hostile guards.

During the first night of their camp, while Grimes and Roach were obtaining water and ammunition, those of the troopers who were not wounded dug better entrenchments, cared for the wounded, dragged away the dead animals and ate lightly of their rations; and at midnight couriers, among them Sergeant John S. Lawton and First Sergeant Jacob Widmer, of Company D, slipped away toward the railroad with dispatches reporting what had occurred and asking for aid.

On the following day, September thirtieth, the Indians kept up an incessant fire, killing all of the remaining animals excepting fourteen mules. The troopers, being comparatively well protected now by their entrenchments, held their fire except when a good opportunity presented itself to pick off an unwary Indian. At nightfall the Indians again gave the weary troopers a rest, but after that they worried them unceasingly with all the tricks known to them, all the time firing with a seemingly inexhaustible supply of ammunition.

The couriers who had slipped away traveled through a region infested with hostiles until they met Captain Dodge and Lieutenant Hughes with Troop D, Ninth Cavalry, late in the afternoon of the first of October, who were scouting in that section of the country. Captain Dodge immediately went into camp for the purpose of deceiving any Indians who might be in the vicinity, issued 225 rounds of ammunition and three days' rations. Then, under cover of darkness, he broke camp and pushed to the relief of the men at Milk River, with his two officers, thirty-five men, and four citizens.

The beleaguered troopers in the trench, waking from their restless slumbers on the morning of the second, were greeted with the sight of advancing cavalrymen, who with some difficulty made their way between the Indians and joined the almost encircled men. It was Captain Dodge's command; and immediately after they entered the trenches the Indians opened fire. With these reenforcements the troops kept up a vigorous attack, and the battle waged for the next three days. The troopers never lagged or flinched under the terrific fire of the Indians, who were now infuriated by the renewed vigor with which the troops fought. Many a brave fellow seemingly exposed himself needlessly in his ardor to get a better shot at the red man, many helped the wounded to places of safety, but among those whose daring, almost sheer recklessness, was most conspicuous in the narrow confines of the corral were Sergeant John Merrill, who, though severely wounded, remained on duty and rendered gallant and valuable service; Corporal George Moquin, Corporal Edward Murphy, and Sergeant John A. Poppe. Sergeant Henry Johnson, on the night of the second, voluntarily left a sheltered position and under heavy fire at close range made the rounds of the pits to instruct the guards; and also, on the next night fought his way to the river and back to bring water to the wounded.

The couriers who went out on the night of the twenty-ninth, after meeting and informing Captain Dodge of the trouble at Milk River, pushed on and succeeded after many hairbreadth escapes in reaching headquarters with their requests for aid. Colonel Wesley Merritt with Troops A, B, D and M, Fifth Cavalry, was immediately dispatched from Fort D. A. Russell to the relief and in a short time was on a special train for Rawlins, a few miles west of Fort Steele, Major Thornburgh's starting point when he went to the relief of the White River Agency. From Rawlins the remainder of the distance had to be made over the mountains, and by a march of almost unparalled rapidity, in something over forty-eight hours Colonel Merritt's column, consisting of 350 men, one half of whom were infantry following in wagons, marched 170 miles over an almost impassable road and reached the command at Milk River at 6 o'clock on the morning of the fifth of October.

Upon the arrival of Colonel Merritt's column at Milk River the crippled and exhausted command gave as hearty a cheer as they could muster in their pitiful condition, after which they were tenderly cared for, given rations, and then sent back to the railroad at Rawlins. The Indians retired from their concealed places when the relief column came within sight, but were followed by Colonel Merritt's command, which had been reenforced by other troops. Merritt pushed on to the White River Agency, the Indians having all disappeared before him, and upon his arrival there he found that they had burned and utterly destroyed the agency, had killed the employees and agent, and had carried off all the females. The bodies were buried and preparations made for the continuance of the pursuit when orders were received to suspend operations at the request of the Indian Department, which was negotiating with the Utes for the release of the captive females and the surrender of all the ringleaders in these outrages.

During the cessation of hostilities various reconnoitering parties were sent out from Colonel Merritt's command; and one of these on the twentieth, consisting of five men under Lieutenant W. P. Hall, Fifth Cavalry, was attacked by thirty-five Indians about twenty miles from the White River. They defended themselves behind some sheltering rocks, Lieutenant Hall several times exposing himself to draw the fire of the enemy, thereby giving his small party an opportunity to respond with telling effect. They kept up the unequal fight until night, when they succeeded in returning to camp with the loss of Lieutenant W. B. Weir, of the ordnance department, and Chief Scout Humme, both of whom were killed.

The loss sustained by the command at the Milk River fight from September 19 to October 5, when it was relieved by Colonel Merritt, was Major Thornburgh, Fourth Infantry, and nine enlisted men, Wagonmaster McKinstry, Guide Lowry, and one teamster, killed; Captain Payne and Second Lieutenant Paddock, Fifth Cavalry, Sergeant Grimes, forty enlisted men, and two teamsters wounded.

The Indians who numbered 350 and were well supplied with ammunition, admitted a loss of thirty-seven killed. The number of wounded, which must have been large, was never known.

All the noncommissioned officers and enlisted men herein mentioned for conspicuous acts of courage and gallantry were awarded the Medal of Honor.

J. CISNEROS

THE BATTLE ON PECOS RIVER

PRIVATE POMPEY FACTOR

TRUMPETER ISAAC PAYNE

SERGEANT JOHN WARD

Citations: For Bravery in Action.

During the early part of the year 1875, campaigns were being prosecuted against the Indians in various parts of the western country for the purpose of rounding up those who would not remain on their reservations.

The expedition against the Kiowas and Comanches, in the Department of Texas, under Colonels Mackenzie, Davidson, and Buell, in cooperation with the column under Miles, was prosecuted with such energy that these two tribes gave up the unequal contest and went into Fort Sill, first in small parties and then in larger numbers, surrendering there, and by June the last of the bands absent from their agencies, the Quehada Comanches, also came into the fort and surrendered themselves, with large numbers of ponies and mules, to Colonel Mackenzie, commanding at that post. Colonel Davidson had in the meantime made an important capture on the Salt Fork of the Red River. He met a band of Kiowas at that place, and in a sharp fight with them he captured 65

Reprinted from William A. DuPuy and John W. Jenkins, *World War and Historic Deeds of Valor*, 6 Vols. (Chicago, 1919).

warriors and 175 women and children, with 375 ponies and mules. The prisoners, including Lone Wolf, Red Otter, and Lean Bull, three most dangerous characters, all surrendered unconditionally with their arms and ponies.

Many small engagements and skirmishes marked these expeditions, among the more important of which were the following:

Lieutenant Bullis with a detachment of three men of the Twenty-fourth Infantry was out scouting on the twenty-sixth of April and came upon a band of about twenty-five Indians, on the Pecos River, Texas. The lieutenant and his three men approached the Indians unseen, and when within close range they attacked the redskins, killing three and wounding one. This little quartet of soldiers fought bravely during the short time the engagement lasted and then retreated safely to their command. Sergeant John Ward, Trumpeter Isaac Payne, and Private Pompey Factor, all [Seminole-Negro] Indian scouts of the Twenty-fourth Infantry, constituted Lieutenant Bullis's detachment, and they were rewarded with the Medal of Honor for their exceptional bravery in standing by their officer against those twenty-five Indians.

L.F. BJORKLUND
1970

The Battle of Clay Creek Mission

CORPORAL WILLIAM O. WILSON
Born: Hagerstown, Maryland
Citation: For Bravery in the Sioux Campaign of 1890.

In December of 1890, the last of the major Indian battles with the U. S. Army on the Plains occurred. It was and is called the Battle of Wounded Knee Creek and took place between elements of the Seventh Cavalry and Chief Big Foot's band of Indians.

Following this battle, reports of which had aroused the hostiles to the highest pitch of excitement, came an attack on the Catholic Mission at Clay Creek, December 30. The Seventh Cavalry had just gone into camp after having repulsed an attack on its supply train, when a courier brought the news of a fire at the Catholic Mission and a massacre of the teachers and pupils. Within twenty minutes the exhausted and worn-out cavalry were once more in motion on the way to the scene of action, a few miles distant. The Indians, 1800 in number, under Little Wound and Two Strike, were found about a mile beyond the mission.

The fighting commenced at once, but on the part of the Indians peculiar tactics were followed, squads of forty warriors fighting at a time and the main body slowly retreating. Colonel Forsyth expected

Reprinted from Beyer and Keydel, *Deeds of Valor* (Detroit, 1903).

another ambush and refused to be drawn into dangerous ground. The Indians became cognizant of the fact that their ruse would not work and thereupon began to close in upon the regiment. They greatly outnumbered the troops and were already drawing their characteristic circle preparatory to a charge, when Colonel Henry, with the Ninth United States Cavalry, appeared on the scene and attacked the Indians in the rear. This forced the whole band to flee.

In this engagement Captain Charles A. Varnum, Troop B, Seventh United States Cavalry, performed an act of great bravery, and thereby gained the Medal of Honor.

The order to retire had been given and was being carried out in the face of the steadily advancing Indians. Captain Varnum realized that a further retreat would result in the cutting off of one of the troops, so disregarding orders he took the lead of his company and made a dashing charge upon the Indians, driving them back and gaining a commanding position, which he held until the Ninth Cavalry came to the assistance of the regiment.

First Sergeant Theodore Ragnar and Sergeant Bernhard Jetter, Troop K, Seventh U.S. Cavalry; Corporal William O. Wilson, Troop I, Ninth U.S. Cavalry; and Farrier Richard J. Nolan, Troop I, Seventh U.S. Cavalry, also displayed on this occasion, as throughout the campaign, qualities of the most conspicuous bravery and gallanty, for which they were granted the Medal of Honor.

The Battle of Carrizo Canyon

SERGEANT THOMAS SHAW
Born: Covington, Kentucky
Citation: For Valor in Carrizo Canyon.

Prior to the Battle at Cuchillo Negra Mountains, a brief encounter occurred which earned Sergeant Thomas Shaw his Medal of Honor.

It all started on July 17, 1881, when Nana struck a pack train of Company L, Ninth Cavalry, near the entrance to Alamo Canyon. One trooper was wounded and several mules were stolen. Lieutenant John Guilfoyle with twenty men of that company and a group of Apache scouts left at once in pursuit of the Indians. The pursuit led them through Dog Canyon to and then across the burning White Sands at which point the renegades slew three Mexicans. Then they fled into the San Andres Mountains. Lieutenant Guilfoyle caught up with the renegades on the twenty-fifth of July and attacked. The Indians, being unprepared, fled the combat area.

Nana rode west across the Rio Grande River and made straight for the San Mateos Mountains. Residents of the area formed a vigilante posse and took up the pursuit of Nana and his band. Without practicing too much military caution, they rode into an ambush which left one

Reprinted from Beyer and Keydel, *Deeds of Valor* (Detroit, 1903).

rancher dead, seven wounded, and all their mounts captured by the Indians. Lieutenant Guilfoyle once more caught up with them on the third of August at Monica Springs, captured eleven horses, wounded one warrior, but could not contain the rest of them who got away.

It was over a week later before the Ninth found Nana again. Captain Parker and nineteen troopers of Company K made contact with him about twenty-five miles west of Sabinal. Captain Parker, though outnumbered two to one, wasted no time in attacking. The battle which lasted only one and one-half hours ended by Nana beating off the army once more and escaping. But in this encounter, Sergeant Thomas Shaw was cited by his troop commander for displaying extraordinary courage under fire, and as a result of this commendation he was awarded the Congressional Medal of Honor.

Stanley M. Long

The Battle of Gavilan Canyon

SERGEANT BRENT WOODS
Born: Pulaski, Kentucky
Citation: Distinguished Himself as a Brave and Gallant Fighter.

Following the Battle at Cuchillo Mountains, another engagement occurred August 19 [1881] about fifteen miles from McEver's ranch, New Mexico. This still involved Nana and his band of Apaches.

Lieutenant Smith with a detachment of twenty men, after a severe fight, defeated the hostiles, but the lieutenant and four of his men were killed. At the most critical moment of the combat a party of citizens joined the military forces and rendered valuable services. In this encounter Sergeant Brent Woods of Company B, Ninth Cavalry, distinguished himself not alone as a brave and gallant fighter, but also by the heroic manner in which he went to the succor of his wounded comrades and injured citizens saving them from falling into the hands of the savages. Nana's band was finally driven across the Mexican border, when the chase, under from the government, was abandoned.

For his gallant action under extreme danger of his own life, Sergeant Woods was recommended for the Congressional Medal of Honor and was easily awarded it.

Reprinted from Beyer and Keydel, *Deeds of Valor* (Detroit, 1903).

The Battle of Kickapoo Springs

SERGEANT EMANUEL STANCE
Born: Carroll County, Louisiana
Citation: For Valor in the Battle of Kickapoo Springs.

On the morning of May 20, 1870, Sergeant Emanuel Stance, of F Company, Ninth Cavalry, stationed at Fort McKavett, left that fort to scout some twenty miles to the north near Kickapoo Springs. About ten miles out, a party of Indians was spotted driving a herd of horses. He formed his men in a charge line and advanced at a dead gallop. Their surprise charge caught the Indians off guard. The troopers managed to capture nine of the horses. From that encounter, the troopers continued on to Kickapoo Springs and went into camp for the night.

The next morning, Sergeant Stance made the decision to return to Fort McKavett with the captured horses, but they were not too far out when they spotted an Indian war party making preparations to attack a small wagon train. Sergeant Stance charged these Indians, and once more, with the element of surprise on his side, managed to rout the enemy, this time capturing five more horses. The Indians only made a tactical maneuver and attacked the sergeant and his men from the rear. Again, he acted quickly and "turned my little command loose on them

Reprinted from Beyer and Keydel, *Deeds of Valor* (Detroit, 1903.)

. . . and after a few volleys they left me to continue my march in peace."

Sergeant Stance had now successfully encountered Indians for the fifth time in two years. For his coolness and quickness of command, Sergeant Stance was awarded the Congressional Medal of Honor.

Stanley M. Long

The Battle of Florida Mountains

CORPORAL CLINTON GREAVES
Born: Madison County, Virginia
Citation: For Valor in the Battle of Florida Mountains.

In late January of 1877, the Chiricahua Apaches began a stepped-up campaign of raids of the countryside. Many young men from the Warm Springs and Mescalero tribes managed to escape from their reservations to join in on these raids. Word was received at Fort Bayard that a party of about fifty Chiricahuas had had an engagement against a detachment of six cavalry units in Arizona and were moving toward New Mexico. Lieutenant Henry H. Wright, with six men of Company C of the Ninth Cavalry and three Navaho Indian scouts left at once to find them.

The renegades were discovered on the morning of January 24 in the Florida Mountains. Since the small detachment was greatly outnumbered, Lieutenant Wright tried to talk the Indians into surrendering. All their talk was in vain, and by the time he had decided to conclude the talks he discovered he was completely surrounded by Indians. He ordered his men to force a path through the ring of Indians, but upon their carrying out his command, a vicious hand to hand fight broke out. The men fired their rifles and then used them as clubs

Reprinted from Beyer and Keydel, *Deeds of Valor* (Detroit, 1903).

against the enemy. Corporal Clinton Greaves "fought like a cornered lion and managed to shoot and bash a gap through the swarming Apaches, permitting his companions to break free." The Indians broke off the fight when they discovered that five of their number were dead and fled the area. Suffering only minor and superficial wounds, the troopers collected six Indian ponies and returned to Fort Bayard. Because of his courage and strength in battle, Corporal Greaves was awarded this nations' highest recognition for valorous acts.

Stanley M. Long

The Battle of Membres Mountains

SERGEANT THOMAS BOYNE
Born: Prince George County, Maryland
Citation: For Bravery in the Battle of Membres Mountains.

On 29 May 1879, Lieutenant Henry Wright was in charge of a small detachment escorting a wounded soldier to Fort Stanton. One of the escorts of this detachment was Sergeant Thomas Boyne. At one point they were in the Membres Mountains of New Mexico. This was an area particularly suited for a surprise attack so they moved cautiously. Suddenly, they were met by a volley of shots and war whoops. They were under attack by Victorio and his renegades.

When the Indians, with the element of surprise on their side for a change, scattered the detachment, they were flushed with what appeared to be a sudden victory. But Sergeant Boyne, not to be done in, flanked the small attacking party and charged them with such ferocity and precision of riding and shooting that they were driven off and the attack ended as suddenly as it began.

For his heroic behavior under fire, Sergeant Boyne was awarded the Congressional Medal of Honor.

Reprinted from Beyer and Keydel, *Deeds of Valor* (Detroit, 1903).

US
© Paul A Rossi

The Battle of Las Animas Canyon

SERGEANT JOHN DENNY
Born: Big Flats, New York
Citation: For Removing a Wounded Comrade to a Place of Safety While Under Heavy Fire.

The Ninth Cavalry finally had Victorio and his band apparently trapped at Las Animas Canyon. Even though the Apaches were terribly outnumbered, they were so well entrenched in their mountain and canyon fortress they could not be driven out.

The Apaches, protected by the natural terrain, took a heavy toll of the troopers, led by Lieutenant Colonel N. A. M. Dudley and Captain Charles D. Beyers; within a short period of time, five enlisted men, two Navaho scouts, and one civilian scout were killed by snipers. Many more soldiers were wounded. In addition, thirty-eight horses were killed, crippled, or otherwise immobilized.

A retreat was ordered by Captain Beyers, but it was not to begin until after dark. In that dangerous move, all but one man was saved. Private Freeland had been shot in the leg and was thrown to the ground some four hundred yards from the soldiers' new position. Private Freeland was unable to make it to his own lines because the Indians kept him pinned down by rifle fire.

Reprinted from Beyer and Keydel, *Deeds of Valor* (Detroit, 1903).

At one point when there was a lull in the fighting, Sergeant Denny looked over into the area where Private Freeland was being held down by snipers. He saw his comrade pulling himself with his hands, painfully, inch by inch toward the new entrenchment.

Sergeant Denny leaped to the rescue of his comrade and dashed toward him through a hail of bullets. He reached Private Freeland and allowed him to climb onto his back and then raced back to the safety of the rocks.

Fifteen years later, Sergeant Denny was stationed at Fort Robinson where he received the Congressional Medal of Honor for "an act of most conspicuous gallantry."

L.F. BJORKLUND '70

THE WHAM PAYMASTER ROBBERY

SERGEANT BENJAMIN BROWN
Born: Virginia

CORPORAL ISAIAH MAYS
Born: Carter's Ridge, Virginia
Citations: For Gallantry During an Attempted Robbery in Arizona.

On the eleventh of May, 1889, at a spot fifteen miles northwest of the town of Pima, in Graham County, Arizona, one of the most baffling and bizarre crimes of the West was perpetrated, known as the Wham Paymaster Robbery.

Twenty-nine thousand dollars, which made up the entire payroll of the soldiers at three army posts in eastern Arizona, namely, Fort Thomas, Fort Apache, and San Carlos, was taken off the stage of Major Joseph W. Wham after a gun battle that disabled his escort of eleven colored soldiers.

Although many men were examined in one of the largest and longest drawn-out trials in the history of the Southwest, no one was ever convicted for the crime and not one dollar of the stolen money was ever recovered.

Sergeant Benjamin Brown and Corporal Isaiah Mays, of the Twenty-fourth United States Infantry, were the ranking enlisted men on that day of the robbery. It happened when the paywagon was

Reprinted from Beyer and Keydel, *Deeds of Valor* (Detroit, 1903).

stopped between Cedar Springs and Fort Thomas. There was a huge boulder in the center of the road, halting the whole convoy. Sergeant Brown ordered all the men except those guarding the paywagon to help move the boulder. Before they could reach the boulder, a command to leave the boulder alone was heard. The command was followed by a volley of gun shots.

The wagon driver, Private Lewis, was hit in the stomach and he fell from the driver's seat. The volley of shots caused the mules to bolt, pulling the wagon with them, but it was halted when one of the horses was killed, making it impossible for the wagon to move.

The shooting from concealed positions began to take its toll. One by one the trooper escorts fell with bullet wounds.

Corporal Mays placed himself near the wagon, firing his carbine all the while. When the bullets got too thick he dove underneath the wagon, still firing.

Sergeant Brown was caught in the open, and most of his men lay near him wounded. At this moment he caught a bullet in his stomach. When he fell to the ground he grabbed one of the wounded men's rifles and continued to fire at the robbers until he was wounded in the arm.

At this moment, the robbers, estimated to be twenty in all, left their areas of concealment and descended on the soldiers and the paywagon. Major Wham ordered his remaining command to retreat to an area of safety. Their retreat left the money unguarded.

In the meantime, however, Corporal Mays made the decision to get help. He alternately crawled and walked two miles to the Cottonwood Ranch and asked the owner, Barney Norton, for help. By the time they got back to the beleaguered troops, the robbers had already fled with the money.

In his report to Washington, Major Wham cited many of the escort for the certificate of merit, but Sergeant Brown and Corporal Mays were awarded the Medal of Honor for their devotion to duty.

J. CISNEROS

THE WINNING OF THE MEDAL OF HONOR BY SERGEANT McBRYAR

SERGEANT WILLIAM McBRYAR
Born: Elizabeth, North Carolina
Citation: For Bravery in an Engagement Against Apache Indians in Arizona.

All the official recognition, in the form of the Congressional Medals of Honor, went to members of the Twenty-fourth Infantry or the Ninth Cavalry, except one. Sergeant William McBryar of the Tenth Cavalry was the only member of that regiment to win it during the twenty-eight year fight against the Indians.

Company K of the Tenth Cavalry had departed Fort Thomas, Arizona, on 7 March 1890. As they entered a canyon on their patrol in search of the last band of renegade Apaches, the Indians attacked. The conflict was a short but decisive one for the troopers. It has also been recognized as the last engagement during the Apache campaigns. Three days after this fight, the campaign against the Apaches was officially declared closed, but not in time to prevent the Tenth Cavalry from installing a member in that "hall of fame."

First Lieutenant J. W. Watson had the honor of nominating Sergeant McBryar for this medal. In his letter of nomination Lieutenant Watson said, "Sergeant McBryar demonstrated coolness,

Reprinted from Beyer and Keydel, *Deeds of Valor* (Detroit, 1903).

bravery, and good marksmanship under circumstances very different from those on the target range.

BLACK-WHITE RELATIONS ON THE FRONTIER

The relationships between the members of the four black regiments and the white settlers on the frontier were often uncomfortable and strained. It is difficult – very difficult indeed – to discover any incident in which the troopers were the instigators of trouble. More often than not, any improper action on their part was really a *reaction* to the attitudes and behavior of the local citizens.

Although the military often received its share of praise, military-civil relations were not always as smooth as they could have been. This was partly due to civilian resentment of many specific duties that had been made army responsibilities, such as having to serve as a police force in areas marked by civil strife and labor unrest. The government must be declared at fault in cases caused by this kind of animosity for not having insight into basic human psychology, even though the signs of potential trouble were there all along. Take the case of the Twenty-fifth Infantry and their unpopular assignment in quelling the labor unrest at Coeur D'Alene, Idaho, or the Coxey's "Army" affair in Montana. The troops did not make themselves very popular while serving as policemen during the military control of the Northern Pacific Railroad in Missoula, Montana, either. They executed their responsibilities in the best military manner but won nothing but the dislike and distruct of the civilians – in a situation which was strained to begin with because the troops were black. One wonders if the same attitude would have been exhibited by the civilians had the troops been white rather than black? Whatever, these duties did nothing to enhance the popularity of the black soldiers. The story of these incidents is told in chronological order in the first excerpt appearing in this section.

By contrast, however, there follows the excerpt which tells of an incident in which the Twenty-fifth Infantry won praise for swift action in bringing a raging fire under control and at the same time acting as policemen to protect an area from looters. This only helps prove the old adage that no one likes a policeman (or any figure of authority) except when he is needed.

Despite all the racial discord that existed on the frontier, the story of Private Bentley proves that it *is* possible for different races to live together without color barriers. In fact, this short report reveals more about local racial attitudes at Fort Davis than it does about Private Bentley's discharge.

The cavalry also came in line for some unpleasant duty during one of the famous range wars that hit the West at intervals throughout the latter part of the nineteenth century.

"Racial Troubles On the Concho" gives an outstanding example of the kinds of problems the black troops faced on the frontier. In an area where there were still dangers from marauding Indians, and in an era when there still was safety in numbers, the black troops often found themselves faced with two enemies, the Indians and the white settlers. Indeed, the troopers found they frequently needed protection from the very civilians they had been sent to protect. The author presents a factual, although racially biased, report on those troubles.

It would be impossible to cut through all the cloudy issues surrounding the Brownsville (Texas) Affray, an incident which occurred in 1906. As a result of a court of inquiry, President Theodore Roosevelt had all the men in three companies of the Twenty-fifth Infantry dishonorably discharged even though the evidence was inconclusive. No actual circumstantial evidence was brought forth – except shell casings and clips. None of the rifles were produced, and no fingerprints belonging to any member of the Twenty-fifth were found; all evidence was made by oaths of persons claiming to have been shot at, but none could positively identify the assailants.

Since the guilty individuals could not be found, President

Roosevelt felt they would presumably be caught up in the mass punishment when they were discharged along with their whole companies! Had it not been for the intervention of the NAACP, this national embarrassment, virtually an unconstitutional act, would have gone unchecked. After the affair was settled, many of the discharged men were able and willing to reenlist in their old regiment.

In retrospect, one can see that the "glory years" peaked at the turn of the century. For better or worse, the four black regiments had been created to aid in the pacification of the West. It was a Herculean task that was undertaken with hard work, sacrifice, and bravery. The black soldiers of the Ninth and Tenth Cavalry and the Twenty-fourth and Twenty-fifth Infantry earned their honored place in American history.

J. Cisneros

Police Duty on the Frontier

John H. Nankivell

The year 1891 was rather a quiet one for the regiment. Early in 1892, trouble had developed between the mine owners and labor unions in the Couer D'Alene mining district of Idaho, and during the spring the unions declared open war on the mine owners. Scenes of disorder and anarchy followed, and on the Fourth of July, 1892, the American flag was riddled with bullets and spat and trampled upon by a mob of strikers and union sympathisers. By July 11 a condition of absolute anarchy prevailed, and several mines were blown up with much loss of life. The aid of the federal government was invoked, and on July 12, United States troops were on their way to the scene of the disturbances. A provisional battalion of the Twenty-fifth Infantry from Fort Missoula, Montana, was among the troops sent to the Coeur D'Alene, and the following cryptic entries from the "Record of Events" for July, 1892, tell the story of the battalion's activities during its stay in Idaho.

> *July:* Companies F, G and H, 7 officers and 148 enlisted men, left Fort Missoula, Mont., at 8:30 P.M., July 12, 1892, to report to Colonel

Reprinted from John H. Nankivell, *History of the Twenty-fifth Regiment United States Infantry, 1869-1926* (Denver, 1927).

> W. P. Carlin, Fourth Infantry, commanding U. S. Troops in Idaho operating in the Coeur D'Alene mining district. Arrived at Mullan, Idaho, at 6:30 A.M., July 13th, and found the track of the Northern Pacific Railroad blown up in two places; reported by telegraph to Colonel Carlin and received orders from him to join him at Wardner Junction, Idaho, via the Coeur D'Alene City, Harrison, and Union Pacific Railroad. Arrived at Wardner Junction at 6:30 P.M., July 14, and made camp there. Assisted in guarding trains, furnishing escorts, scouting, and making arrests. Relieved from further duty in the Department of the Columbia and ordered to proper station in Department of Dakota per S. O. 8, Headquarters, U. S. Troops in the Field, Wardner, Idaho, July 26, 1892. Left Wardner at 3:00 P.M., July 27, and arrived at Fort Missoula, Mont., 8:30 A.M., July 28. Distance traveled by rail about 722 miles. Captain W. I. Sandborn, Twenty-fifth Infantry, commanded battalion during its operations in the Coeur D'Alene.

The presence of the regular troops had a distinctly pacifying effect on all actions, and when the celebrated "bull pen" was built and the arrest of the disturbers accomplished, law-abiding citizens began to breathe easier.

The year 1893 was another "quiet" year for the regiment, and the only incident of note was the march of ninety miles made by Company F from November 10 to 24 in the Clearwater Country, Idaho, in an unsuccessful attempt to find and relieve a party of hunters known as the Carlin party, who were snowbound in the mountains.

"Events" for the year 1894 commenced with the movement of Company B from Fort Buford, North Dakota, to Fort Missoula, Montana, on May 6. During the same month Company G left Fort Missoula for Arlee, Montana, to assist United States marshals in controlling the members of Coxey's "Army" who were under arrest at that place. The company returned to Fort Missoula on June 5.

During July and August, 1894, labor troubles were rife among the employees of the Northern Pacific Railroad, and the situation became serious enough to again call forth federal troops to prevent disorders and to guard the trains and the mail. A considerable portion of the regiment was engaged on this duty, and the movements of the various companies are shown in the following extracts from the regimental returns for the months of July, August, and September, 1894.

July: Company A left Fort Custer, Montana, July 8, 1894, en route to Custer Station, Montana, where it arrived at 12:30 P.M., July 9th; distance marched thirty-four miles. Company left Custer Station at 8:15 P.M., July 9 guarding passenger train, west bound, on N.P.R.R. Reached Livingston, Mont., at 4:30 P.M., July 10th; Company remained at Livingston guarding railroad property from strikers.

Company B was guarding property of the Northern Pacific Railroad at Missoula, Montana, from July 8-15, 1894.

Company D left Fort Custer, Montana, July 8, 1894, per telegraphic instructions Headquarters Department of Dakota, enroute to Custer Station, Montana, where it arrived at 2:00 P.M., July 9. Distance marched thirty-four miles. On July 9 at 4:30 P.M., the Company left for the west on passenger train No. 1, N.P.R.R.; arrived at Billings, Mont., at 8:00 P.M., same date. Left Billings at 9:00 A.M., July 10, as train guard on passenger train No. 1, N.P.R.R., and arrived at Livingston, Montana, 2:00 P.M. same day, since which time it has performed duty guarding trains and railroad property.

Company F left Fort Missoula, Montana, at 2:30 P.M., July 8, 1894, en route to O'Keefe's Canyon, Montana, there to guard the two iron trestles on the N.P.R.R. Two camps were made, Lieutenant Caldwell and twenty-six enlisted men at O'Keefe's Trestle, and Captain Andrews and twenty-six enlisted men at Marent Trestle. Later, thirty-one enlisted men were sent, by order Department Commander, to report to Commanding Officer of the camp at the railroad workshops at Missoula, Montana. On July 29 Captain Andrews was ordered to return to Fort Missoula, and Lieutenant Caldwell and seventeen enlisted men were retained on guard at the trestles.

Company H left Fort Missoula, Montana, at 5:30 P.M., July 8, and marched to Missoula, Montana, distance four miles. On duty to date guarding property of the N.P.R.R. against strikers.

August: Company A, guarding workshops, rolling stock, bridges and tunnels of the N.P.R.R. between Big Timber and Muir, Montana, during the month.

Company D, guarding and protecting railroad trains from Livingston to Cokedale, Montana, and protecting railway property at Livingston, Montana, during month.

Company F, Lieutenant Caldwell and detachment relieved from duty guarding N.P.R.R. trestles near O'Keefe's Canyon, Montana, and returned to Fort Missoula, Montana, August 15, 1894. Distance marched sixteen miles.

September: Company A returned to Fort Custer from Livingston,

Montana, 12:00 noon, September 2, 1894. Distance marched thirty-five miles.

Company D returned to Fort Custer, Montana, from Livingston, Montana, September 3, 1894.

Referring to the services of the Twenty-fifth Infantry during the strike the *Anaconda Standard,* Missoula, Montana, under date of August 6, 1924, had this to say:

DID THEIR WORK WELL

MISSOULA HAS NO CRITICISM TO OFFER OF THE COLORED TROOPS

THEY MAKE GOOD SOLDIERS

During all the time the Northern Pacific was under military control the men acted with wisdom.

Missoula, August 6 – The military control of the Northern Pacific Railroad is at an end except for the detachment under Captain Andrews, which is guarding the Marent and O'Keefe trestles. The sentries, who had become a familiar sight about the depot and yards, have vanished, and the visitor at these points no longer runs against a bayonet when he attempts to mount the platform steps, or walk to the roundhouse. It is no longer necessary to dig up a passport to gain admittance to the headquarters building, for every walk and path is free and open. The troops are once more quartered at the post, and Captain Hodges, who was in command of the detachment in camp, has resumed his duties on the governor's staff in connection with the state militia.

Leaving out of consideration the question of the advisability of ordering out the troops, it is generally admitted that the conduct of the soldiers, during the time that they were on duty here, was exemplary, and demonstrated beyond a doubt the excellence of the Negro as a soldier. During the entire period that the guard was on duty, no act the troops was open to criticism, and there was not a single instance of an unjust exercise of authority. There were several instances when a blunder might have led to serious results, but at these critical times the conduct of the men was admirable. The railroad authorities are naturally loud in their praise of the troops, and the majority of the strikers admit that if the soldiers had to be called out there could have been none better than the companies of the 25th Infantry who were encamped here.

The prejudice against the colored soldiers seems to be without foundation, for if the Twenty-fifth Infantry is an example of the colored regiments there is no exaggeration in the statement that there are no better troops in the service. During the strike, opportunity was afforded to compare them with the white soldiers and in no instance did the Twenty-fifth suffer by the comparison. When asked by a *Standard* reporter the other day as to the disciplinary measures necessary to handle his command, Captain Hodges replied, "There are none. The men are soldiers because they like the life, and during the time that we have been in camp here there has not been an instance of insubordination and not a man has been punished, simply because it wasn't necessary." This is considered by army men to be a remarkable record and is indicative of the excellent spirit which prevails among the men.

Of the life of the colored troops at the post the *Standard* has previously made mention. They are model soldiers when in garrison, and their conduct whenever they have been called into the field has been excellent. Twice within a year they have been in active service, the first time in the attempt to rescue William C. Carlin and his party in the Clearwater and again to guard the railroad property. The men are orderly and quiet, and all who have visited the post and studied the existing conditions involuntarily share the pride which Colonel Burt and his officers feel in the Twenty-fifth Infantry. It is a splendid regiment and worthy of unstinted praise.

GEN. MOSE
J. CISNEROS

Fire Fighting

John H. Nankivell

Department of the Interior
United States Indian Service
Fort Belknap Agency
Harlem, Montana, October 9, 1910

The Honorable Secretary of the Interior
Washington, D.C.

Sir:

I deem it only proper that I should call your attention to the splendid work done by the troops fighting fires in Glacier National Park last summer.

I had one company of the Twenty-fifth Infantry (colored) stationed at Essex, under the command of First Lieutenant W. S. Mapes. I doubt if I can say enough in praise of Lieutenant Mapes and his Negro troops. The work performed by them could not be improved upon by any class of men. To their lot fell the worst fire in the park and they went at its extinguishment with snap and energy, built roads and trails and miles and miles of fire guard trenches without the least sign of discontent. Personally, I believe that it is only fair to the officers

Reprinted from John H. Nankivell, *History of the Twenty-fifth Regiment United States Infantry, 1869-1926* (Denver, 1927).

and men of the U.S. Army who participated in the fire-fighting in Glacier National Park, that you call the War Department's attention to the splendid work performed by them, as they certainly deserve commendation.

I am,

Very respectfully,

W. R. Logan,
Superintendent

The appalling nature of these fires, and the hazardous duty performed by those who were involved in fighting them may, in some measure, be gauged from the following extracts from a newspaper and a magazine published at the time:

> The hurricane had seized upon the small fires, fanning them furiously, scattering them abroad through miles of forest, each falling spark to kindle a raging firestorm of its own. Since early in May no rain had fallen in the Bitter Root Mountains. The Coeur D'Alene timber reserve, in the panhandle of Idaho; the Cabinet, Clearwater, and Lolo reserves in Western Montana, were like so many open magazines of powder. Resinous spines, steeped in the drippings of pitch and turp from the overhead branches, lay many inches deep around the holes of the trees and beneath cluttering trunks and fallen brushwood – the accumulation of years. Man never laid the foundation for a fire more completely or carefully than nature had done in the great national forests of the Northwest last August.
>
> All was ready for the hurricane, all so nicely pitched, oiled, and dried, that in six hours' time this tidal wave of fire spread over 2,000 square miles of splendid forest. When it finally burned out, it left – in charred, prone, and riven trunks of pine, fir, and cedar – billions of feet in timber, worth at the lowest estimate, a hundred million dollars – wasted, cruelly wasted. And strewn in shriveling heaps here and there along the black trail of this flood of fire huddled the remains of scores of brave men who had gone out to match their courage against its might.
>
> There never was a forest fire like this since men have been keeping a chronicle of events. District Forester W. B. Greeley, in command of the fire district – in which the burned region lies – says such a fire has not swept the forests of the Northwest in perhaps a thousand years. The history of forestry, he declares, contains no parallel. Its destructive force and the speed with which it traveled were marvelous. The ordinary forest fire travels slowly, at the most but a few miles a day. This one, according to an official of the Chicago,

Milwaukee and Puget Sound Railway, who timed its advance over a known area, was traveling seventy miles an hour – a speed beyond anything known in wild fires, even upon the prairies. Imagine a prairie with grasses from 150 to 200 feet tall, and flames proportionally high beating over it at seventy miles an hour, and you will be able to conceive in some measure the magnitude of the August fire in the timber reserves of the Northwest.

Avery was one of the last places in the Couer D'Alene reserve to be reached by the fire. While the flames were pressing down upon it, the women and children were removed on a special train. They were given just thirty minutes to get ready. Already the roar of the approaching fire could be heard. Four passenger coaches were loaded, and the train set out for St. Joe under command of Sergeant John James of Company G, Twenty-fifth United States Infantry, from Fort George Wright, Washington – a Negro company, which, under the command of Lieutenant E. E. Lewis, had been detailed to patrol the burning district and preserve order. Privates Chester Gerrard, William Hogue, Roy Green, and G. W. Bright were stationed on the platforms of the cars. "They stuck to their posts like men," said Ranger Debitt. The forests all along the way were on fire, the heat so intense that the varnish on the coaches blistered and the windows cracked. These Negro soldiers stood on the platforms through this bath of fire and kept the doors closed, holding back the heat-crazed women and children, many of whom would have leaped off and been lost if they had not been restrained.

Another train of boxcars carried most of the men away from Avery, the Negro soldiers remaining to the last. (G. W. Ogden, "A World Afire," *Everybody's Magazine*, December, 1910.)

Penned in by fire while trying to get out of Avery Sunday night, Company G of the Twenty-fifth Infantry, under Lieutenant Lewis, with sheriff H. D. McMillan and Depty C. J. Sullivan, narrowly escaped being entombed with their train. The fire closed both ends of the line, leaving the train only a few miles of clear track between burned culverts. For seven hours they backed up and down the track, each time within a shorter space, while the fires kept eating inwards.

With the cessation of the gale which destroyed two national forests Sunday, they were enabled to get back into Avery. The houses in the town were looted after the soldiers left by a few hoboes, though chance of escape seemed small for those who remained. (*The Spokesman-Review*, Spokane, Washington, August 26, 1910.)

Retired Tenth Cavalryman

Private Bentley's Buzzard

Erwin N. Thompson

As he promised he would, Judge Scobee visited Fort Davis last Sunday with Mr. and Mrs. George Bentley in tow. Scobee had been urging Bently to donate his father's buzzard (Army discharge certificate) to the nation, and Mr. Bentley had finally agreed that the time was ripe to do so.

Still strong of back and steady of hand at sixty-five, Mr. Bentley possesses a quiet dignity, a warm but controlled and very deep voice, a patriarchal touch of pride, and an honest friendliness that "betters the breed of men." Mrs. Bentley is of that older generation of Mexican ladies that is becoming all too rare in this noisy world. Shy, a trifle nervous, silent, and full of deference to her husband she remained slightly but deliberately in the background. Her still-pretty but slightly sad face was framed by her best jewelry which she wore especially for this formal and important visit.

Mr. Bentley carefully opened a parcel that had been wrapped in newspapers and held up a framed picture of his father and mother. This was the first George Bentley, ex-private of the Ninth Cavalry, one of Fort Davis's earliest permanent settlers, half Negro and half white.

Reprinted from an unpublished manuscript at the Fort Davis National Historic Site, Texas, with their permission.

Then Mr. Bentley took out an envelope. On it, in pencil, was written "my father's Army discharge." He opened it and removed the folded certificate. The ink is faded on this AGO Form No. 98, but it is still in excellent condition. It begins: "Army of the United States. To all whom it may concern: Know Ye, That George Bentley a Private of Captain J. Lee Humfreville's Company K of the Ninth Regiment of Cavalry who was enlisted the eighth day of December one thousand eight hundred and sixty-six to serve Five Years, is hereby discharged from the Army of the United States in consequence of expiration of term of service."

When Fort Davis was reestablished in 1867, the first postwar troops were the Ninth Cavalry Regiment, one of the first Negro units in the Regular Army. However, Company K did not arrive at the Post until April 1868. Along with Private Bentley there were sixty-one enlisted men and one officer in the company. The officer was Frederic William Smith who was to be placed under arrest and to die the next year.

Bentley probably saw Second Lieutenant James Edgar who was with the company briefly that summer. Edgar was awaiting news as to the outcome of a general court-martial. The news arrived and Edgar was cashiered.

According to family tradition, Bentley was a company baker during part of his Fort Davis assignment. If he had that assignment in September 1868, he may have missed going on a chase with Lieutenant Patrick Cusack. Cusack's patrol, which included parts of both Company K and Company F, was one of the more decisive undertakings carried out by Fort Davis troops. Some twenty Indians were killed, two hundred head of cattle captured, Mexican captives freed, and the foundations for the legend of Indian Em'ly were formed.

In April 1869 Bentley witnessed the arrival of another lieutenant to Company K, Louis H. Rucker. Like Bentley, Rucker had joined the Army as a private; unlike Bentley, he was to retire a general. For the time being it must have been pleasant to have a leader who was not undergoing a general court-martial.

Another major Indian fight involving Company K occurred shortly after Colonel Edward Hatch took command at Fort Davis. The post return for January 1870 described it thus:

> Two officers and seventy men from Companies C and K Ninth Cavalry formed a part of an Indian expedition organized by Brevet Major General Edward Hatch, Colonel, Ninth Cavalry, commanding the Sub-District of the Presidio, which had an engagement with the Apache Indians in the Guadalupe Mountains, January 20, 1870. The Indians left ten killed, and thirty dead horses in our hands; the total loss to the Indians in killed and wounded is estimated at fifty. Two enlisted men were slightly wounded.

This report is quoted at length for it must have been a sharp and bloody incident such as this that gave rise to a rather frightening story about Private Bentley that is told farther on.

In July 1870, the post quartermaster was promoted to captain and transferred to Company K. This was Jacob Lee Humfreville who was to write in a character rating on Bentley's discharge. Then in May 1871 Company K transferred to Fort Quitman. Thus Bentley's military days at Fort Davis came to an end. That December, however, he returned to Fort Davis as a civilian and settled down to establish a flourishing dynasty.

The discharge certificate continues: "Said George Bentley was born in Danville in the State of Kentucky, is 26 years of age, 5 feet 8½ inches high, Mulatto complexion, Black eyes, Black hair, and by occupation, when enlisted a laborer."

The Bentleys today are neither proud nor ashamed of being partly Negro. It is just a simple fact that needs no artificial supports. When race is so much of a problem for everyone else these days, Mr. Bentley's philosophy on it seems calm indeed. He frankly notes that his father was the illegitimate son of a white man and a Negro woman. He joined the Army simply to get away from his mother and a brother, neither of whom he liked.

But the Bentley case is not an isolated case in this old Army town. An old crotchety doctor, I.J. Bush, who once practiced here (1891-92) wrote in a letter,

> ... Fort Davis became a regular melting pot. Foreigners [immigrants in the Army] married Mexican women; Negroes married Mexican women; and occassionally a white man who forgot that his skin was white [—married Mexican women (?)]. Mexicans do not draw the color line. I knew one Mexican woman who married a white man ... while her aunt was married to a very black Negro. An Irish girl

> married a Jew, and her brother a Mexican girl. Fort Davis had a regular crazy quilt population.

Perhaps that quotation explains the rather relaxed attitude on racial issues that many native Fort Davis people still display today.

This same doctor also told a rather alarming story about Private Bentley:

> There lived in Fort Davis at that time [1891] and [sic] old mulatto negro named George Bentley who had a Mexican wife and seven children ranging in age from two months to seventeen years. Every one of them died. At that time there were living in Fort Davis ten or twelve old ex-Tenth cavalry Negroes and when the trouble came on Bentley all of them declared that it was a judgement of heaven sent on him for his cruelty to an Indian baby some years before when he was in the army.

According to the doctor's story, Bentley had cruelly bayoneted an Indian baby that was found when a party of Indians were being hotly pursued by a patrol. There is nothing by which to verify or to disprove the story. Perhaps it should be regarded as just a story, for as the doctor himself wrote, "It is absolutely astounding how people can get things so mixed up in just a few short years."

In any case, Bentley was regarded as a good soldier by his captain: "Character, Good, s/ J. Lee Humfreville." And written in ink, crosswise in a corner of the document, "Paid in full Dec 22 '71." Below that are the figures 147.15. And that is the story of Private Bentley's buzzard.

L. Bjorklund

The United States in the Aftermath of the Johnson County Invasion

Robert A. Murray

The year 1892 stands about midpoint in the decade and a half in which Northern Wyoming's livestock industry evolved from the transitory open-range phase toward a land-use pattern essentially like that of today.

The army ended effective Indian occupation of this region in the decisive campaigns of 1876-77 and settled down to slow-paced years of intermittent police action against tribal fragments straying from the reservation. The vast grazing land attracted first and briefly, the buffalo hunter,[1] then the cattlemen who had already filled the range of southern Wyoming and adjacent states.[2]

Open-range cattle ranching found its basis in the idea that a stockman could use public owned grazing lands free of charge and up to the full extent that he could stock them. A belt of such open-range stockmen formed one of the westward-moving layers of the frontier from the American Revolution on. These stockmen followed the hunter and the soldier and occupied any given tract only until the land began to fill with legitimate settlers, and then moved on to new pastures. Conflicts over land use did not ordinarily arise, since land law and

Reprinted with permission from *Annals of Wyoming* (Cheyenne: Wyoming State Archives and Historical Department), XXXVIII (April, 1966), No. 1.

tradition were clearly on the side of the settler, and since more and better grazing land lay ahead to the west. . . .[3]

During the winter of 1892, belligerent defenders of "free grass" organized and planned a raid into Johnson County. Ostensibly this was to be a punitive expedition against "rustlers" of cattle from corporate herds. This approach gained them the sympathy and in some cases the financial support of men and corporations not willing to participate directly. The size and the extra-legal nature of the expedition belie the assertion that the few "rustlers" of the region were their goal. It seems equally unrealistic to assume that they planned a complete reign of terror. Rather it appears they aimed to do in a number of alleged "rustlers" plus enough of the "guilty-by-association" (or rather by lack of association with the corporate interests!) to discourage not only rustling, but any influx of small landholders into the region. The expedition failed miserably to achieve its objective. The general facts and many details of the "Invasion" and subsequent events have been widely publicized.[4] The role of the U.S. government in general, and in particular that of the U.S. Regular Army have not. Federal correspondence on the topic is particularly valuable in that it contains the largest surviving volume of continuous contemporary correspondence on the subject. Most of it, too, is the writing of persons who were not among the contenders, but who had the uncomfortable and difficult role of peace-keepers in those tense times.

The army had fairly substantial forces scattered through the northern plains in 1892, largely because of the recent Ghost Dance trouble on the northern reservations in 1890-91.[5] Fort D.A. Russell, with eight companies from the Seventh and Seventeenth Infantry Regiments, stood just outside Cheyenne.[6] Near Buffalo was Fort McKinney, with Headquarters and three companies of the Eighth Infantry and three companies of the Sixth Cavalry.[7] Fort Custer, Montana, and Fort Robinson, Nebraska, were but a short distance from the state's boundaries.

There was little real legal reason for federal intervention in Wyoming's cattle troubles. The "Invasion" was planned and executed in violation of Wyoming law. The Invaders on April 9 killed Nathan D. Champion and Nick Ray and burned the KC Ranch. Sheriff W.G. Angus soon assembled a legally-constituted posse and surrounded the invading party some thirteen miles from Buffalo. That numerous members of

Wyoming's state government sympathized with the Invaders has been abundantly proven by other writers, whose contentions are borne out by subsequent justice department investigations some months later. . . .[8]

Meanwhile several events occurred to lend support to the cattlemen's assertions of lawlessness in northern Wyoming. On May 12, 1892, the remains of Deputy U. S. Marshall George Wellman were brought to Buffalo.[9] The death of Wellman complicated the local situation. He was a foreman at the Hoe ranch, whose employers had been involved in the Invasion. He was however, well thought of personally in Buffalo. His funeral took place in St. Luke's Church on May 13 and was attended by members of the local Masonic lodge.[10] There are widely divergent theories about Wellman's death, some seeing it as a cattleman's plot to discredit Johnson County,[11] others holding that "rustlers" were responsible.[12] Whatever the truth, the incident did create dissension in Johnson County and was used as argument by the cattle companies in seeking Martial Law for the region.[13]

The second incident occurred May eighteenth, when a disastrous fire destroyed the post exchange and several barracks at Fort McKinney. A second smaller fire several days later was of definite incendiary origin and it was generally supposed that both were.[14]

Now the Invaders and their supporters struck a new political blow. They sent the following demand to Senator Carey in a telegram on June First:

> We want changes of troops made as follows: Headquarters of Eighth infantry and three companies of that regiment now at Fort McKinney ordered to Sidney. Major Egbert and Seventeenth Infantry and three companies of that regiment ordered from Russell to McKinney. This gives us commanding officer. We want cool level headed man whose sympathy is with us. Order Major Fechet and the two companies of the Sixth Cavalry from McKinney to Niobrara, anywhere else out of that country. He and his men have relations with the sheriff and his gang that make the whole command very undesirable for us. Send six companies of Ninth Cavalry from Robinson to McKinney. The colored troops will have no sympathy for Texan thieves, and these are the troops we want. See General Manderson who understands situation and will assist in carrying out this plan. It is important that action should be taken at once. We urge that time is everything. This is preliminary to declaration of martial law. Advise us when order is made.[15]

Senator Warren sent a telegram from Cheyenne to Senator Carey the same day, stating:

> Declaration of martial law seems inevitable. Please direct attention Department of Depredations at Fort McKinney. Facts show and Flagg's *People's Voice* twenty-first instant acknowledge twenty carbines stolen from cavalry and incendiary fire at post buildings attempted by rustlers. Very latest information I saw matters Chicago, Burlington officials Omaha, late letters from Mayor Burritt, Buffalo, also merchant Munkres, banker Thom, editor Bouton, manager Winterling, all asserting in the most positive terms that nothing less than immediate drastic measures from the authorities outside and above county officials can reduce present state of almost if not complete anarchy Johnson County. Parties writing send letters in private hands over part of route, asserting mails tampered with at small intervening offices. Northern letters implore martial law. Perry Organ tonight emphatically urges martial law. Exhibit, but do not file this dispatch because I am only permitted to use northern names secretary, they fearing distruction of their property and assassination if publicity given their names and views.[16]

Cary forwarded these on June second to Secretary of War Elkins, with this comment:

> I enclose you copies of dispatches which I desire you to read and hand back to Mr. Morris, as it is not well to file them at present.
>
> I had a very satisfactory talk with the President yesterday, and also with General Schofield. I dislike to leave here; but I cannot well do otherwise, so I go to Minneapolis.
>
> General Schofield believes in concentrating troops in the disturbed district in Wyoming immediately. This would be a good move, and would be carrying out the plans heretofore adopted at the army headquarters with reference to summer encampments.[17]

General Schofield asked General Brooke's opinion on June 3, 1892,[18] and received this reply:

> Replying to your telegram of today I would say that a cavalry camp can be established near where the Burlington and Missouri Railroad will cross Powder River—the cavalry from Robinson and Niobrara to be sent there. From present information and to accomplish the purpose referred to, I think it would be better to establish two camps—one to be between Douglas and Casper, at such point as may be found best. In this case, the cavalry from Robinson should be at Powder River

> Crossing and that from Niobrara at the other place. The troops to be moved as circumstances may require. The garrison at McKinney should not be disturbed. Rail transportation should be used as far as practicable owing to the heavy rains having made the country very difficult.[19]

Schofield approved Brooke's suggestion,[20] and the troops were in motion by June seventh,[21] six troops of the Ninth Cavalry going into camp near the point where the Burlington Railroad was to cross Powder River, and six troops of the Sixth Cavalry camping near old Fort Fetterman northwest of Douglas.[22]

Major C. S. Ilsley, commanding the contingent of the Ninth Cavalry found the small but typical end-of-track town Suggs occupying his projected camp site. He preferred to go on to Clear Fork, to find better campgrounds and to avoid contact between his colored troops and the citizens of this hard-looking little town. His orders seemed to preclude crossing Powder River, so he moved the column upstream some four miles and went into camp.[23] This "camp-of-instruction" was designated Camp P. A. Bettens.[24]

Conditions at Suggs were ready made for trouble. There were a number of saloons in the town. Troops of Ilsley's command were colored regulars, steady and well proven in combat, but sometimes inclined to be a bit turbulent in camp.[25] Citizens in the town were generally resentful of the presence of troops. Some, especially the businessmen, were at least civil to the troops. Others, a collection of miscellaneous drifters, unemployed cowboys and the like, were belligerent and insulting to white officers and colored enlisted men alike when these were in town on business.

The command had as a civilian guide one Philip du Fran, who had been sent to Major Ilsley by General Brooke, and represented as one who knew the Powder River country thoroughly. This was the same Phil du Fran captured as a member of the Invaders at the TA Ranch, and at the time was supposed to be in confinement at Fort D. A. Russell awaiting trial. Du Fran's presence led the citizens to believe the troops would be used in a federally sanctioned raid on the region. Du Fran himself said that when "his friends in Cheyenne" were free he would come back with a commission as a deputy U.S. Marshall with warrants for over forty citizens of the Powder River country and a regiment to back him up. He agitated among the soldiers and openly aired his views to junior officers.

Just one spark was needed, and a lady of easy virtue supplied this on June sixteenth. The unnamed woman had formerly lived at Crawford, Nebraska, near Fort Robinson, and at other points down-track, and with other girls also now in Suggs "had been in the habit heretofore of dispensing their favors regardless of color." Private Champ, of G troop, in town without permission, somehow found the girl was in town and went to call on her. She, now living with a white man, styled a "rustler," refused to let Champ in the house. After a few ineffective kicks at the door he drifted down town to a bar, and was joined there by Private Smith of E company, in town on an official errand. Moments later, the "lady's" white lover stalked in, pointed a cocked revolver at Champ and cursed him unprintably. Private Smith drew his service revolver and covered the "rustler." Bystanders in turn drew their revolvers and covered Private Smith. The bartender intervened, got all to holster their guns, and showed the soldiers a good route out of town. As they rode out, mounted double on Smith's horse, a fusillade burst from a house behind them, one bullet passing through Smith's hat. They returned the fire with their revolvers and sped off to camp.

Their arrival created great excitement, but prompt action by Ilsley and his officers and N.C.O.'s prevented a mass foray to the town. Anticipating trouble the next night, the Seventeenth, Ilsley doubled the guard around camp and ordered two nighttime check roll calls. Even so, during the early evening hours, Private Smith, Champ, and eighteen others slipped out of camp, armed, and assembled near the town.

They moved in a body to near the stage station and fired a volley into the air to attract attention, then commenced firing at stores, houses, and at a saloon they called "rustler headquarters." Townsmen swarmed out and opened a heavy fire with their repeating rifles and a general melee ensued. Women and children rushed out in their night clothes and headed out the other end of town to hide in the sagebrush. The soldiers retreated toward camp under a brisk fire from the town, leaving Private Willis Johnston dead in the street and bringing their wounded, Privates Champ and Thompkins with them. One citizen received a slight wound in this foray.

When officers in camp heard the firing, they formed up the

command. Captain Jonathan Guilfoyle and companies I and A were sent to town to investigate. On the way they met and arrested the absentees straggling back to camp. Guilfoyle threw a picket screen around the town to protect it, and spent the night calming the citizens and conferring with officials and prominant citizens to restore the peace.

A series of investigations followed. Du Fran's role exposed, he was escorted to Gillette by a company of cavalry. Investigating officers thought Private Willis Johnston might have been killed by the fire of his comrades. The army was extremely embarrassed over the entire affair.[26]

General Schofield instructed the adjutant general to issue the following order:

> . . . your troops should be kept out of the town and away from the people. The military commander has no functions whatever to perform there respecting the civil authorities, and no duty in respect to the preservation of the peace. Under the present state of feeling the troops should be kept in their camps and entirely separated from those who may entertain hostile feelings.[27]

Thus ended the direct involvement of the army in Wyoming's affairs. The troops at Camp Bettens and Camp Elkins continued their field training and were withdrawn to their respective posts early in November.[28]

Through that summer and fall, other federal intervention tapered off. A presidential proclamation at the end of July pleased the cattlemen and reassured some of Johnson County's worried citizens. Behind the scenes, U.S. Marshall Rankin, once assured of the support of the assistant U. S. Attorney and the federal district judge, calmly let Johnson County simmer down, without provoking further incidents, and with confidence restored, sent in three good men to arrest and/or run off the mere handful of actual outlaws believed to be in Johnson County's back country.[29] A justice department investigation upheld Rankin, sharply criticized the role of the U.S. Commissioner Churchill, and of certain state officials, and stated that the federal government should never have intervened in the situation at all.[30]

Through the closing months of 1892 at the state level, the Invaders politicked their way to freedom, having lost their "battle" and their "war" and infinitely complicated Wyoming politics for many years.

Racial Troubles on the Conchos

J. Evetts Haley

Unfortunately the wisdom shown in the strategic location of Fort Concho did not carry over to the choice of garrisons. Military history too often discloses that wise conception is one thing, while outstanding execution on the field is genius of a different order. The prestige of the Army and the well-being of Texas suffered from the fact that Fort Concho and other frontier posts were garrisoned with Negro troops. It was unfortunate on the one hand because colored troops were neither apt frontiersmen nor good soldiers, and doubly unfortunate on the other because the ingrained attitudes, social customs, and prejudices so strong in the South were often violent in Texas.

In view of the harsh antipathies that inevitably follow devasting war, it is likely that Negroes were designedly garrisoned in the South as further humiliation for its people. But when they were placed there in the role of military police and protectors of the peace, bitter insult was added to apparently irreparable injury. It was like rubbing salt into the wounds of fiercely proud, rebellious, and individually unconquerable people. Recent history reiterates the tragic lessons that are apparently never learned, at least lessons quickly forgotten in the passions of war. Thus Negro troops came to be garrisoned amoung the resentful frontiersmen in the most important posts in Texas.

Under military occupation, the warlike spirit of Texas erupted into violence. Everywhere men unshucked their six-shooters and pulled down their cap and ball rifles to rectify affronts to their dignity and their rights. Violence became as common as pig tracks in the Piney Woods and many of the "best people" organized themselves into extra-legal riders known as the Ku Klux Klan, or salved their souls with personel killings and then took refuge in outlawry.

Trouble within the military service developed almost at once. Vigorous protest was made to the *San Antonio Express* in May, 1867, after a violent outbreak in the Ninth Colored Cavalry under Colonel Edward Hatch. One officer was killed and another wounded before the "murderer" was shot and ten mutineers arrested. It was bootless for a rebel to protest the practice. But a Southern Unionist wrote of the rashness of a policy of inducting recently-freed Negroes into the service with insufficient officers to control them.[1]

With the founding of new posts and the reoccupation of the old ones, this policy was at once extended to the frontier. Dr. William Notson, no prejudiced Southerner but a remarkably observant and astute patriot from the North, made acid comment on the situation at Concho, repeatedly recording his grave doubts of the policy and even the use of Negroes as soldiers. He left his observations in the *Medical History* of the posts:

> The peculiarities of Negro troops in contrast with the white garrison [he wrote], deserves probably some notice. . . . As individual agents, as sentinels, they are not reliable; too liberal in their application of instructions; given to understandings usually incapable of appreciating them. Lying and thieving are the principal vices. As malingerers they are not so successful as the white troops confining their efforts to rheumatism, "miseries," and stiff limbs . . .

A little later he added:

> The impracticability of making intelligent soldiers out of the mass of the Negros is growing more evident to the Post Surgeon every day, and his opinion is concurred in by their own officers when speaking with confidence invited by the freedom and intimacy of garrison life. The discipline and police of the post is too poor to decently condemn. . .

Still later, July 3, 1870, as the last of the Ninth Cavalry started off for Fort Davis, Dr. Notson devoutly hoped that it marked "the end" of his "service with such troops." [2]

So much for an unbiased appraisal of the troops that the Army commands, in gross stupidity if not in pure cussedness, chose for the occupation in Texas. Little wonder that the frontier should fly into flames at the smallest spark.

The lack of settlers in the Concho country at the same time of the founding of the post deferred the outbreak of troubles there, but in the San Saba region to the immediate east the explosive tensions were quickly set off, even as the post surgeon there warned against the same policy, saying:

> As a rule Negro troops yield to all impulses both mental and physical and 'tis almost impossible to teach them that mind is superior to matter.[3]

In that section the charming San Saba valley attracted a few settlers before the war, and with the reoccupation of Fort McKavett, April 1, 1868, and the introduction of colored troops, trouble began. The worst centered around an old southerner named John M. Jackson, noted for his sturdy character and a distorted back that gave him the nickname of "Humpy."

"Humpy" Jackson was a native of Georgia who had come to Texas from Arkansas, settled on the San Saba, and built his log cabin near what came to be called the Five-mile Crossing, below where the village of Menardville started a little later. During the dreary years of the Civil War, Jackson stuck by his guns on the frontier. When McKavett was reinvested, opening a ready market for the produce of the hard-living settlers and offering a little protection against the raiding Indians, Humpy seemed in a fair way to enjoy a measure of prosperity.[4]

The buildings at McKavett were badly in need of repairs, and the Army set up a sawmill to cut the native timber near Humpy's home. The fort was garrisoned with Negroes, and in keeping with the use of military labor a detail was sent to run the mill. There, they were frequently observed by Humpy's family. Among the Jackson children was a daughter named Narcissus who attracted the eye of one of the Negro soldiers, a mulatto sergeant called Lanky Jim, evidently a sort of a pioneer progressive on notions of social equality.

One day Lanky Jim wrote a love letter to Narcissus. When old Humpy got the news, his southern rage knew no bounds. He pulled his rifle off the doorsill and headed for the sawmill. He took a stand behind a pecan tree nearby and waited for his quarry to appear, though one account indicates that he simply walked up and shot the first Negro that ambled into sight.

At any rate, Humpy drew a deadly bead and then took to the tall uncut. Unfortunately he did not pick the right victim. This slight slip of justice never altered the pattern that fate was tracing, and Private Boston Henry was just as dead as if he had deserved to be. The news was carried, as only Negroes can, into McKavett. On June 9, 1869, Lieutenant John L. Bullis was detailed to apprehend a man named Jackson, who on the military records, immediately assumed the standing of "a horse thief and murderer." [5]

Bullis, an able and zealous soldier, mounted and headed down the river with six men. But Humpy Jackson, who knew the recesses of the San Saba valleys and hills, had not for years been dodging Indians for nothing. He could not be found. After four days and sixty miles of riding, Bullis returned to report his fruitless quest, while a party from Concho under Lieutenant George E. Albee covered four hundred miles with the same result.[6]

Humpy dodged in and out of his home place as the chase continued for months, and he managed to raise a good corn crop on the side. He improved his time and his chances of continued evasion by digging a cellar under his house and connecting it by tunnel with the river bank. When surprised in his cabin, he ducked into the cellar and emerged out of sight along the river.

An older daughter named Henrietta, mounted on a sidesaddle on a good horse, rode the country at times as a sort of picket to warn her father of approaching danger as he worked in the field. On one occasion Humpy fell sick. He took to his cellar while Henrietta, armed with her pistol – for Indian raids were still common – rode into Menardville to watch for soldiers who were continually on the prowl for Humpy. She found the village full of them. They at once placed her under surveillance and she was hard put to figure a ruse for escape. She confided her problem to John Finley, a young clerk in Tull Smith's general store, who suggested she ride leisurely from town, until near home, and then put the whip to her pony and beat the troops in if they followed her.

Finley walked with her to the hitching rack, tightened the saddle cinch, and helped her mount. She casually jogged out of the shady town and headed her horse toward home, aware that a detail of Negroes had fallen in behind her. When within running distance, she turned her horse loose and laid on the quirt, with the troopers in pell-mell pursuit. Her two little sisters, Sallie and Susie, were playing in the yard when they looked up and saw the cavalcade coming. They ran into the house in terror, screaming:

"Oh, Mother, they'll get Pap this time. Henrietta is coming at top speed and about a hundred niggers are right behind her."

Instead of stopping at the house, Henrietta raced past. When alongside the corn field she drew and shot her gun, and pulled her horse to a halt. The furious white officer in charge drew up and said:

"I suppose that is a signal, Miss!"

"It answers every purpose," she replied, and headed her dripping horse for the cabin at a walk while the officer ordered his men to tear down the rail fence and search the field. When they found no freshly worked land, they hurried to Humpy's home, searched the house, and found the hideout in the cellar. But the ailing Humpy was up and gone.[7]

After that, Humpy could rarely figure on feeling safe at home. He kept on the move while the chase continued under the ruthless resolve of Colonel Ranald S. MacKenzie, then in command at McKavett. On February 1, 1870, Humpy was passing along the Menardville road below the Peg-Leg Stage Station, riding one horse and leading another, when he bumped into a detail of Negro soldiers. He whirled his horse and took to the timber. The troops gave hot pursuit. He was about to get away until the lead horse rim-fired or circled a tree and jerked Humpy's mount under a limb. The old man was swept from the saddle and violently thrown on the ground. The soldiers surrounded him before he was able to move.

He rolled in misery and complained that his back was broken, as well it might have been, and its excessive hump, unfamiliar to his captors, was to them positive proof of his complaint. The white officer in charge—Negro troops were, by general order, commanded by white officers—told them to pick him up and take him home. Three soldiers were left as guards until an ambulance could be sent from Fort McKavett. At once the news spread far and wide among the hot-blooded sons of the frontier who would always accommodate a worthy neighbor, even to commendable homicide. Plans were drawn and the appointed minute set.

Meanwhile Humpy's wife slipped him a six-shooter beneath the covers. The ambulance from McKavett was momentarily expected on the night of February second, and the ready men of Menardville reached there first. Three well-armed Texans dropped into the place and Humpy came out from under the covers with remarkable alacrity for a man with a broken back, six-shooter spitting fire. Two of the soldiers, Corporal Albert Marshall and Private Charles Murray, were killed, while the third, at first thought to be accounted for, later escaped by making it to the river bank.

He hit a trot up the river, to Paddy Fields' place, six miles west of Menardville, where he managed to get a horse. Then he loped into McKavett and reported to Colonel Mackenzie, who at once ordered the stubborn young Bullis to take the trail. With John DeLong as scout and guide and a detail of Negro cavalry, Bullis struck down the river. He was unable to find the elusive Jackson, but placed his wife and children under arrest and burned their home to the ground.

Mackenzie, by then aroused, ordered a general roundup of the men of the whole countryside. He imprisoned Jackson's family in the guardhouse at the post and paraded the men before the escaped soldier in an attempt to identify Humpy's allies, though these worthies were out in the hills beyond the reach of the military.

Yet the army is a permanent and a persevering machine, especially in the hands of an officer like Mackenzie. Relentlessly the search went on. On February 15, 1870, Mackenzie reported that Stephen Cavaness, Peter Crane, George E. Harvey, and Charles Owens had helped Jackson kill his guards. Mackenzie posted large rewards for their capture and sent implicating affidavits to Judge David Sheeks at Mason, April 12, 1870, and again put his scouting parties into the field.[8]

At the same time he arrested William Epps and B. P. Smith as possible accomplices and kept Mrs. Jackson and Henrietta under arrest. Captain Henry Carroll and Lieutenant Bullis were sent out with a detachment of the Ninth Cavalry. Carroll left the post and headed into the hills, south by west to Copperas Creek, and marched down it to camp on the North Llano.

From that point he detached Bullis with a guide and nine men to scout out the Bear Creek country in search of the fugitives. Bullis caught sight of Cavaness working in a field on Moore's Ranch on Bear Creek but failed to catch him. Bullis rejoined the command on report, and they made camp. Next morning Carroll sent Bullis back to Bear Creek, where he was lying in wait with his men concealed in the brush when Cavaness returned to Moore's field, tied his horse, and walked out to see the men at work. When Bullis attempted his arrest, the fight started. The nine soldiers in ambush shot the fugitive down and returned with his horse, saddle, bridle, spurs "and a pair of Colts pistols," while Moore's men buried the body in the field.[9]

Mackenzie turned Mrs. Jackson and her daughter over to the district judge at Mason in response to a civil summons, April 13, 1870, while the doughty Humpy lived the elusive life of an Indian in the San Saba hills. The sympathies of the settlers were on his side, and they had their ways of helping him without making themselves liable for collusion. Of a sudden he would show up and cut a slab of bacon off the hook in a familiar smokehouse, or pick up a flour sack full of fresh biscuits mysteriously swinging from a mesquite near a friendly cabin.

His confederates drifted on to more tolerant environments, and Owens, after other stirring experiences in the Lincoln County War, died as a highly respected citizen of southern New Mexico. As for Humpy the civil law eventually had its way. He made bond in Menardville, June 14, 1871, for $2000, stood trial in a court of Texans and, as Mrs. A.W. Noguess, pioneer of Menardville reports with positive finality, "of course came clear."[10]

The racial problem that stirred the San Saba county was soon felt along the conchos. Dr. Notson's pleasure upon seeing the colored troops removed was of short duration. Other companies were sent to take their place and the volatile feelings of the frontiersmen–buffalo hunters, cowboys, freighters, and adventurers–flocking into the Concho country were frequently stirred by some untoward incident that transgressed their dignity, their pride, and their taste.

White troops were requested by General D. O. Ord for the Mexican border in place of the colored troops because, as he pointed out, the army "cannot trust their detachments without officers–who are not always available."[11]

At Concho the colored laundresses were a special source of trouble, and in the summer of 1875, Dr. W. F. Buchanan, Dr. Notson's successor, asked for a detail to remove one from the vicinity of the hospital whom he had fired for "theft, disqualification to tell the truth, and general imprudence." Two weeks later Captain Nicholas Nolan filed his brief of particulars against three others because of their "utter worthlessness, Drunkness [sic], and Lewdness." Complaints were general, partly because the Negroes compounded their troubles by taking up the white folks' personal quarrels, which they were inclined to do in an excess of loyalty and through cooperation.[12]

Of a more intimate nature was the outraged complaint of a colored private who addressed the commander of the Post at this time:

> Sir General I private William Bulger . . . Respectfully have the honor to make this application so I may be justified in my undertaken sir the are a woman hear sir that I am Lawfully married to her and she is living with another man . . . Sergeant Brown . . . and sir I Respectfully request of this woman be Put out of the Post why sir she has been keeping up a destrubments between me and this man ever sence she had been hear she run away and come to this Post exspecting not to find me hear when she got hear.

And so in outraged dignity this properly incensed soldier signed his mark, May 10, 1875. The captain to whom it was referred endorsed the complaint with commendable wisdom. He noted that the wench had "taken up with another man (as she terms it), but that he "could respectfully state that it is similar to numerous cases which are taking place daily in most any post . . . " It was a condition that could not "be obviated except by cleaning them all out which would at the same time be the means of depriving officers of servants." Obviously, he continued, "the man is very Jealous . . . which under the circumstances is correct," adding, judiciously, that "it is a very hard matter to correct the morals of these people and I can therefore recommend nothing in the case."[13]

Thus, the Negroes, in post and out, at Concho stayed on until, under General B. H. Grierson's command, an all-time high was reached in general resentment. In the Fort Griffin country to the north the colored troops were called "buffalo soldiers," while around Concho they were derisively known as "Grierson brunettes."[14]

Meanwhile the village of Saint Angela, as it was first called, came to anything but innocent life across the river, and its uninhibited and wide-open diversion contributed no more to peaceful racial relations than to sedate social life generally.

Its beginnings were noted in the *Medical History* of the post in February, 1870, when Dr. Notson wrote:

> An effort is being made to establish a town or village on the north side of the North Concho River. The pioneer in the venture is Mr. B. DeWitt, one of the traders of the Post. Two hackel [jackal] or picket houses are in process of erection.[15]

Bart DeWitt, the founder of the town, had arrived from San Antonio. In September, seven months later, the name St. Angela first appears in the *Army Records,* and the observant post surgeon commented further on its beginnings:

> The question of the sutlers . . . is interesting. . . . Mr. James Trainer, the first post trader, who was on duty in that capacity when the post surgeon arrived here in January, 1868, had purchased land adjoining the post and erected thereon a substantial stone building. Messrs. Wickes & Newton, have started another establishment with the consent of the Commanding officer, within what is supposed to be the Post limits. . . . The history of the various trading establishments of the vicinity may some day form an item in the history of this section. The village of St. Angela, across the North Concho, is almost entirely made up of traders who have been appointed or welcomed by one post commander, and ejected by his successors.[16]

By November, 1870, Dr. Notson was able to write that:

> The village across the North Concho – is attaining an unenviable distinction, from the numerous murders committed there. This condition of society [the surgeon continued, philosophically] seems to be almost necessarily a concomitant with the advance of American civilization, but it is certainly fostered by the residents themselves and the short-sightedness of the state authorities. From the heavy tax laid by this state (Texas) upon stores, especially where liquors are sold, (and all Texan stores sell liquors) the interest of each storekeeper is enlisted in keeping away such civil authority as takes from his sales so large a proportion of his profits, even at the risk of not having the same protection for the remainder of his stock. While the military, tied hand and foot, through the jealousy of civil powers, dares not assume any control, lest like Sheridan at Chicago it be charged with usurpation. The result of this condition of society is increased lawlessness. Within the last six weeks there have been seven murders in a population of less than a hundred, men, women and children, all told, and during the

> residence of the Post Surgeon over one hundred murders have taken place within a radius of ten miles from the adjutant's office, in a population which has never at any time exceeded two hundred and fifty.
>
> The last murder gives some indication of having broken upon the apathy of the community. On Sunday week a man called another a louse, and refusing to retract, was for this grave offense shot dead with four balls from a revolver. On the Tuesday following the body of the murderer was found on the prairie, about a quarter of a mile from the Post with a bullet hole through his breast. Was it a "Vigilance Committee" or merely vendetta?

Dr. Notson, after this interesting commentary on the local death rate, added, without humor, that "the health of the command has been good. . . ."[17]

Obviously the Concho country placed a commendable restraint upon loose and undignified personal talk, but the penalties still seem a little generous just for calling a man a louse, especially when subsequent action seemed to prove the allegation. And as Dr. Notson suggested, "over one hundred murders" out of a population that never exceeded 250 and then totalled only about a hundred, counting all resident noses, in a brief period of two years and eight months, does seem a little excessive.[18]

Organization of Tom Green County and the local administration of civil law helped matters some. Yet Saint Angela continued to be a center of bucolic nature where a generous admixture of colored soldiers bent on recreation in her dives further inflamed the volatile feelings of healthy men responsive to pride, passion, and liquor. Yet no really disturbing incident seemed to alter the rather orderly procession of her homicides until the late seventies.

By then Saint Angela was not only a convenient point on the Goodnight Trail, but it was the southern center for the buffalo hide trade – that vast slaughter by bold and greasy meat-eaters from all over the Western world.

As such it was running in high and wide open, if anything but handsome, in its 'dobies, dugouts, and picket *jackals.* As a sort of damper on its most dangerous men, the Texas Rangers scouted by once in a great while. Captain John S. Sparks came with his company from an expedition into the buffalo range in the fall of 1877 and camped nearby. On the night of arrival his rough and ready boys piled into Sarge Nasworthy's saloon and dance hall for drinks and social diversion. As they swirled through the evening with the Mexican girls, they suddenly waked up to the fact, in the dim lights, that six or seven Negroes were likewise waltzing around the place.

According to Noah Armstrong, veteran Ranger who was there, the boys pulled their guns and broke up the dance by getting "kinda rough." Next day the sore-headed soldiers reported the incident. The commander of the post called on Sparks and demanded an apology. In typically Texan rage Sparks responded to this studied insult from federal authority by saying that he and his little company could whip the whole colored garrison at Fort Concho. Grierson never called the bluff and so the matter seemed to pass. That night the Rangers camped on the Concho a few miles below the post. But the outraged Negroes slipped back to Nasworthy's while festivities were at their height, and, thinking the Rangers were again on the floor, opened fire on the milling dancers, killing an innocent hunter.[19]

The commanding officer reported the incident to Adjutant General Steele at Austin, and Sparks went out of the Ranger service to make way for a hotter firebrand, Captain G. W. Arrington.

Early in February, 1878, a festive party of cowboys and hunters cut the chevrons off a sergeant's blouse and ripped the stripes off his pants. After some preliminary fighting, so one story goes, they ran the Negroes out of Jim Morris's saloon. The troops of Company D got their guns from the post and returned by the side door to take the whites by surprise. The shooting became general as Fred Young, a buffalo hunter, and a soldier named Brown were killed, and another soldier seriously wounded. Two white men were also wounded.[20]

On hearing of the trouble Captain Arrington came in with his men and marched across the parade ground in search of Sergeant George Goldsbury, who had apparently permitted the troops to get their guns. Colonel Grierson rushed out to challenge Arrington's appearance on the federal domain. Further trouble appeared imminent while nine Negroes were indicted by Issac Mullins' grand jury at Benficklin, and William Mace was given the death penalty. Goldsbury jumped his bond of $750 and never came to trial.[21]

Thus it went with discordant variations but no sensible revision of federal policy for many years, until in 1881, when a considerable settlement was sprawling up the slope on the north side of the Concho. The buffalo hunt had frazzled out but other vital movements were in full force. The Texas and Pacific Railroad was rushing west from Weatherford; sturdy British capital in the hands of sensitive Englishmen was hunting lands and cattle; freighters were steadily stirring the dust between Concho and San Antonio; and the dynamic nature of free men and venturesome money held the land enthralled. The trend was westerly and the tolerant town across the river from Fort Concho was the focal point for those with business, and the lodestar of fun and frolic for all.

Hence one Thomas McCarthy, "a tall, black-haired, black-eyes, manly and prepossessing person," according to the record, rode into San Angelo on diversion bent. Originally he came from Syracuse, New York.[22] After work for the Pullman Palace Car Company at Houston as assistant superintendent, he had gone into the sheep business near Austin. Then with a brother John, and the financial backing of a cousin, Dave McCarthy, a drygoods merchant of Syracuse, he made his way to Brady Creek and established a ranch there. When Dave came down to visit him, they struck out for San Angelo to see the sights.

Horse racing and related sports made January 31, 1881, a lively day; and after taking in the races, everybody very properly took in the town, the McCarthys merrily among them. Late that night they wound up at Charlie Wilson's saloon where a Negro trooper, William Watkins, Company E of the Tenth Cavalry, was entertaining those still in an appreciative mood by singing to his banjo. From here on until one o'clock next morning the accounts are, understandably, somewhat conflicting and confused.

According to John A. Loomis, who was just then making his way to the McCarthy ranch on his first trip into the Concho country, and who attended court at Benficklin, McCarthy claimed the Negro kept bothering him. He was so insistent on additional pay for his entertainment that McCarthy finally pulled his gun to move him on his way. The Negro grabbed the gun, a peculiar English revolver with a set or hair-trigger. In trying to take it from McCarthy, according to the Loomis story, Watkins simply shot himself.[23]

Yet the newspaper accounts of the time reported that the Negro was standing outside the saloon eating his lunch when McCarthy just drew his six-shooter and "shot him in the head." This may be biased too since all immediate news to the outside world was over the military telegraph line, and it is a notorious fact that government agencies are loath to disseminate information unfavorable to their cause, and the army shortly became involved. In fact, a few days later, the *Dallas Herald* apologized for its lack of details because, it claimed, "the military operator at Concho is afraid to telegraph them."[24]

Yet according to Ranger Jeff Milton, who got there soon after the killing McCarthy had carelessly bowled Watkins over while innocently shooting up the town. Sancho Mazique, veteran of the colored forces, recalled that the whole shooting match was drunk and that McCarthy's party, in sheer high spirits, took over the saloon and put everybody else out. Watkins, likewise drunk, kept trying to get back in until McCarthy pulled his gun and stopped him.[25]

But after all it does not really matter. Two facts are obvious and important. McCarthy was not a murderous gunman, as has been claimed, but Private Watkins was just as dead as if he had been.

It should also be noted in justice to the people generally that a substantial number of drinking men had been killed by other fighting along the Conchos, without raising the blood pressure of the community generally. When one white man killed another white man in a local brawl, nobody seemed particularly to care. But with the Negro troops it was different. Nothing but the gentle Concho and the color line separated the high-spirited men on the north side of the river from a military mass on the south side that is too often divided from a mob only by the thin line of prestige and authority.

To make matters worse, some ten days earlier another colored soldier had been killed in Sarge Nasworthy's saloon by a gambler named P. G. Watson, when he interfered with a fight that Watson had matched with a Negro cavalryman. Watson left town on a good race horse while the temper of the Negro garrison rode high.[26]

The stage was already set for real trouble when McCarthy rushed out of Wilson's saloon in apparent bewilderment. He staggered into a sentinel on the post reservation where he was challenged and taken in charge. He was thrown into the post guardhouse but properly surrendered to Sheriff Jim Spears by Colonel B. H. Grierson about one o'clock on the afternoon of February 1, 1881.

Feeling ran high in the garrison, and Colonel Grierson ordered a guard about the soldiers and established check rollcalls that night. The first check of the barracks after taps showed that the arms racks had been pried into and a great many troops were absent. The "long roll was sounded," and the officer of the guard trotted off with a detachment to round up the missing soldiers from the village across the river.

He found that hell was already poppin'. The troops had taken Sheriff Spears in charge, surrounded the Nimitz Hotel, where they thought McCarthy was being held, and were demanding that McCarthy be surrendered to them. They scattered and straggled back to the post when the officer of the guard arrived.[27] Meanwhile, McCarthy was being held for his own safety in the Benficklin jail, at the Tom Green County seat, about four miles up the river.

The affairs at the post suggest a lack of rigorous discipline by Grierson and his officers. The troops got out inflammatory circulars on a hand press at the post. As leaves had not been canceled, they scattered the handbills about San Angelo as they walked the streets in angry, muttering groups. One of these posters, dated, "Fort Concho, Feb. 3, 1881," read:

> We soldiers of the United States Army, do hereby warn for the first time all citizens, cowboys, etc., of San Angelo and vicinity to recognize our right of way as just and peaceable men. If we do not receive justice and fair play, which we must have, some one will suffer, if not the guilty, the innocent. It has gone far enough. Justice or death.
>
> U.S. Soldiers.[28]

McCarthy's preliminary hearing got under way at Benficklin. Grierson claimed that Sheriff Spears had notified him on the fourth that McCarthy's friends were gathering to release the prisoner by force, and had appealed to the post for protection, though there is nothing in the scanty civilian records to substantiate the claim. Grierson claimed, with discretion, that he could not comply "without violation of the law" and without such action's being interpreted as "an attempt to overawe the civil authorities." [29]

He did send a "discreet officer" to talk with Spears, and claimed he "held a company in readiness to move promptly," apparently in case of an outbreak, while he sent another to Benficklin to arrest any soldiers who attempted to enter the county seat. Then, apparently in an attempt to appease the rebellious troops, who were still threatening to burn and pillage San Angelo, he ordered a company to fall in behind

Sheriff Spears at the river crossing and help him escort the prisoner to the Benficklin jail. To a disciplinarian or a careful student of human nature, this seems not only ridiculous in an army man, but a downright foolish concession inclined to promote mutiny. What was really needed was the cancellation of all post leaves and an arrest of the rebellious leaders.

Instead the Negroes were left free to roam the village streets in muttering and threatening groups. Citizens sent their families scurrying to refuge on the surrounding ranches, while the local officials thought of the Texas Rangers. The Frontier Battalion, as that fighting organization was then known, had a company stationed at Hackberry Springs, on the extreme frontier in Mitchell County, eighty miles to the north. From there its tiny force ranged back and forth across that open world from Monument Spring in New Mexico, to Horsehead on the Pecos, hunting vagrant Indians from the reservations and white fugitives from justice.

This company was under the hot-headed command of Captain Bryan March, a Confederate veteran with an immense contempt for the federal forces. The late war had left him short of one arm and several fingers on the remaining hand, a bitter reminder—while prowling for Indians who eluded the federal forces—to nurse his wrath against the Yankees and keep it powerfully warm.

San Angelo was the point of supply for his company, and Ranger Johnnie Miles happened to be there when the trouble broke out. As things really got hot, Sheriff Spears pushed a petition signed by himself, the district judge, and the district attorney into Johnnie's hands, and begged him to hit a high lope for March's camp.

Eighty miles is a long ride, but Johnnie spared neither himself nor horseflesh. By sundown next day Captain March and twenty-one eager men were shaking out their reins on the trail to Fort Concho while Jim Werner, their Negro cook, followed in a wagon loaded with their beds and rations.[30]

Even as Johnnie left town, the shooting started and became promiscuous. Justice of the Peace Billy Russell "experienced a miraculous escape from death" when a bullet came through his window and lodged in a copy of *The Revised Statutes* that lay on his table. After all, the printed statutes of Texas had to be good for something in San Angelo.

Unfortunately just at this point McCarthy's brother rode into town and stopped at the Nimitz Hotel. He was seen by a Negro woman who on account of the resemblance spread the report: "Tom McCarthy's out of jail." That rumor hit the post with a bang, and certainly the fat was out of the pan and in the fire.

Grierson claimed a party of five men fired on the post guard that afternoon. That night "between tatoo roll call and taps" a mob of soldiers made a rush through the barracks. They put out the lights, tore open the arms racks, and in the confusion took off for the town. The newspapers claimed there were some hundred and fifty of them in all.

Captain Marsh thought they were, "both black and white, some fifty or more strong." Grierson claimed there were only "thirty to forty." Anyway, the mob marched into town, fired "several hundred shots in rapid succession," and wounded one man in front of Sterling C. Robertson's store. But they centered most of their shots on "the destruction of the Nimitz Hotel, completely riddling the building with bullets." Jeff Milton recalled that when the mob approached the Tankersley Hotel, Mrs. Frank Tankersley stepped out with a double barreled shotgun, saying:

"Cut it out. The first nigger that shoots a hole in my hotel, I'm going to kill him." And they shot no holes!

"She was quite a lady," praised the gentlemanly Milton.[31]

At length the officers of the post appeared and the mob dispersed. Next day Marsh and his rangers rode into town. The old warrior pitched camp in Sarge Nasworthy's wagon yard, took two quick shots of liquor, and began thirsting for war. He sent J. M. Sedberry and a detail to guard the jail at Benficklin and threw others out over the town. Then with several men he headed straight for the post and Grierson's office. He sent a guard to a convenient roof to watch the approaches, and taking his youngest ranger, Jeff Milton, with him, he said:

"Get your Winchester. Throw a shell in it! Kill the first man that bothers me!" The firm and eager hand of a completely fearless young man pressed the lever down and slipped a shell into the polished chamber, appreciatively guarding this fire-eater from the Confederacy and the frontiers of Texas as he read the riot act to the commanding symbol of military power. Much of Marsh's talk was not calculated for print. But the expurgated substance of the message that crackled from the tongue of the rough old Texan to the neat man with the polished eagles on his shoulders may be reduced to this:

"I am going to kill the first man that comes across the river without a pass—nigger or anybody else. Keep these troops on this side. If they cross we'll kill every one of them."

"What do you mean?" spluttered Grierson. "You have only a handful of men."

"Yes," snapped Marsh, "but enough to kill every one of these niggers if you don't obey my orders." As Marsh turned to go, it was an obvious fact that a powerful compulsion flows from strong hearts and dominant personalities. Even with the power and prestige of the United States Army behind him, Grierson knew that in this one-armed man with the mangled hand he had certainly met his match.

Discipline was at last invoked, and that peace which is the concomitant of tolerance came again to the banks of the Conchos. But the official story of the riot of the Negro troopers was not quite over.

A few days after Marsh's arrival McCarthy's preliminary trial was completed. He was sent to the settlements for safekeeping under guard of Ranger John Hoffar and lodged in jail at Austin pending his trial.

News of the riot quickly spread over the state. Governor O. M. Roberts approved the movements of the rangers and wired the general in command of the military district, at San Antonio, reminding him of the invasion of the civil authority of the arrest of Sheriff Spears and the riot that followed. Grierson had never even reported the outbreak. On February 8 the Commanding General of the Department relayed Governor Roberts' wires in a tart message to Grierson, wondering "if it can be possible that the statements are true, and if so, why you have not reported the matter to these headquarters." That day Grierson filed his special pleading in answer.[32]

He detailed the history of the trouble from his point of view. He emphasized his periodic checks of the barracks, claimed he had enlarged the guard, observed that Captain Marsh was cooperating with him, and pointed out the series of incidents that had helped infuriate the Negroes.

He did not offer this to excuse "the wrongs done by soldiers," he added, "but simply to show under what difficulties the officers are placed to control men, when their comrades are shot down without any punishment being inflicted upon the guilty parties." In spite of his bumptious brass and lack of ability in coping with a situation that a more courageous man would have prevented, herein Grierson assayed the fundamental fault in the whole business. It was one of policy. The Texas frontier was not a proper place for colored soldiers.

Grierson's official report occupied seven foolscap pages in the *Army Records* at Washington. Marsh made his report to Adjutant General John B. Jones, and it may still be read in telegraphic form in the State Library at Austin. It consists of seven words:

"Arrived here Saturday with company all quiet."[33]

On February 14, 1881, with that sense of discipline, propriety, and character that has usually justified our pride in the American army in time of test, the commanding general served orders on Grierson. Grierson was to remove the companies involved in the trouble from Fort Concho to his outposts. He was told to court-martial the mutinous individuals because "such conduct on the part of the troops, whatever the provocation, cannot but react unfavorably upon the army and must be emphatically rebuked." Then in high regard for the limitations of a Constitution that should rigidly steer our conduct in dire emergency even more than in social quietude and calm, the Commanding General continued:

"Any attempt on the part of the troops to influence the civil authorities . . . by threats or intimidation must be checked by the most effective measures. A failure on the part of the civil authorities to do their duty will in no way justify or palliate any interference by the military. It is our duty to see that the army is right, whoever else may be wrong. Let us see that the duty is fully performed." The penalty for a renewal of the troubles, he advised, "will insure the breaking up of the whole command."[34] Thus spoke traditional military honor and character.

McCarthy made a favorable impression on all who met him and was released from the Travis County jail on $6000 bond late in the month. He was indicted for murder at Benficklin. The case was transferred to Kimble County where it came to trial in November. The jury was out just long enough to write its verdict: "Not Guilty!"[35]

Anywhere else in Texas it would undoubtedly have been the same. The moralists may contend that the Texans were all wrong. But neither defeat in the terrible war they had just fought, nor more than three-quarters of a century of peaceful development since, have convinced them that they were.

The world may disagree. But after all it is impossible to condemn an entire race for fierce pride and strong tradition. When mistaken policy runs counter thereto, the policy runs into trouble and usually fails. It is a lesson of history that has continuous application, though unfortunately for the peace of the world is too rarely applied.

The troops, too, evoke their share of sympathy. Those recent slaves, pushed to the frontier, where individualistic men daily flirted with danger and flaunted death, under the supposition that they were qualified soldiers, were also the unfortunate victims of mistaken policy at the hands of those who had freed them. Though they broke the tradition of the United States military by mutiny, the blame was not on them. Historically, it rests on the white men in authority who, through ineptitude or vindictiveness, set the policy and sent them here.

L. Bjorklund

The Brownsville Affray

Report of the Inspector-General of the Army

War Department,
Office of the Inspector-General,
Washington, October 22, 1906

Sir:

I have the honor to submit the following report of an investigation made at Fort Sam Houston, Texas, and Fort Reno, Oklahoma.

I proceeded from Washington to the headquarters of the Southwestern Division, Oklahoma City, Oklahoma, to consult with Major A. P. Blocksom, inspector-general, who had, under orders from the commanding general Southwestern Division, made an exhaustive investigation of the affair at Fort Brown, Texas, of August 13, 1906, and who had submitted on August 29, 1906, a full report of the circumstances connected therewith (1157577). As a result of this consultation nothing new was developed beyond the fact that on October 4, 1906, Lieutenant Colonel Leonard A. Lovering, inspector-general Southwestern Division, made an investigation at Fort Reno, Oklahoma, into certain collateral circumstances connected with the trouble at Fort Brown, by direction of the commanding general Southwestern Division. No material facts germane to the main issue were developed by this investigation.

I then proceeded to the headquarters, Department of Texas, Fort

Reprinted from the Report of the U.S. Inspector General, 60th Cong., 1st Sess., Sen. Doc. 389

Sam Houston, Texas, for the purpose of examining the men of the Twenty-fifth Infantry confined in the guardhouse at that place, for whom warrants had been issued at Brownsville immediately after the affair of August 13. On the eve of my departure from Washington I had received papers informing me that the grand jury in Brownsville, Texas, had failed to find true bills against these prisoners. I examined each of the prisoners very carefully, first, in the form of general conversation, referring to the personal history of the man, including the place of birth, home, former occupation, and relations in civil life. I found several of them had lived in localities with which I was more or less familiar, one having lived at my own home, and then subjected them to a rigid examination. As soon as the subject of the trouble at Brownsville was introduced the countenance of the individual being interviewed assumed a wooden, stolid look, and each man positively denied any knowledge of the circumstances connected with or individuals concerned in the affair. Under close inquiry it was admitted by each man that he knew of the discrimination made by saloon keepers against the enlisted men of the Twenty-fifth Infantry; that he knew Newton had been hit by a revolver in the hands of a citizen of Brownsville, and that Reed had been pushed into the mud by another citizen.

Each man admitted that these occurrences had been talked of and discussed within their hearing in the barracks of their respective companies, but I could extract no admission from any man that this discrimination and these acts of violence had caused any feeling of animosity on the part of the enlisted men of the Twenty-fifth Infantry against citizens of Brownsville. When this attitude on the part of the enlisted men under examination was developed, it became apparent that I could get no information from them that would assist me in locating the men actually guilty of the firing on the night of the thirteenth of August, 1906. I spent several hours in this interview with the men, taking each separately and immediately afterward separating him from the rest of the prisoners, so that there might be no communication between them during the examination. The next morning I called the men before me again, four at a time, beginning with the men of the longest service. I again talked with them, endeavoring to elicit information, and upon failure to succeed I notified them of the orders of the President in the case and gave them until 5 o'clock that afternoon to consider the matter. At the time set I received nothing from them.

The men confined in the Fort Sam Houston guardhouse were the noncommissioned officers holding the keys of the arm racks of the respective companies, the sergeant of the guard, and the sentinel on post in rear of company barracks on the night of the thirteenth of August, 1906; an enlisted man, part owner of a saloon in Brownsville; a man whose cap was alleged to have been found in the city on the night of the thirteenth of August (not substantiated); Private Newton, who had been assaulted; Private Reed, who had also been assaulted, and the men who were with him at the time.

From Fort Sam Houston I proceeded to Fort Reno, Oklahoma. I called together the officers present at the station who were on duty with the Fort Brown battalion on the night of August 13, 1906. I discussed with them the means and methods employed by them, contemporaneously with the occurrence and subsequently, to locate the guilty individuals. I found that absolutely nothing had been discovered; that they had found no enlisted men who would admit any knowledge of the shooting or of any circumstances, immediate or remote, connected with the same.

I then called before me, individually, a number of the enlisted men, noncommissioned officers, and privates, of long service in the Twenty-fifth Infantry, ranging from twenty-six years to five or six. I proceeded with them practically along the same lines as with the prisoners at Fort Sam Houston and found the same mental attitude on their part; could discover absolutely nothing that would throw any light on the affair, and received the same denial that any feeling of animosity or spirit of revenge existed among the enlisted men of the Twenty-fifth Infantry against the citizens of Brownsville on account of discrimination against them in the way of equal privileges in saloons or on account of the two acts of violence against their comrades. Each man questioned admitted that he knew of these acts of violence; each had heard it talked of in his barracks; but each denied that any feeling was displayed at any time by individuals of the respective companies or by the enlisted men of the companies as a whole. I could get no explanation of this apparent indifference to the indications of hostility that such acts on the part of citizens of Brownsville disclosed, except in one instance where a sergeant of the company to which Private Newton belonged, said: The fact that Newton had been assaulted made no special impression upon him, because Newton was liable to get into a row almost any time and had been battered up on previous occasions at Fort Niobrara.

The uniform denial on the part of the enlisted men concerning the "barrack talk" in regard to these acts of hostility upon the part of certain citizens of Brownsville indicated a possible general understanding among the enlisted men of this battalion as to the position they would take in the premises, but I could find no evidence of such understanding. The secretive nature of the race, where crimes charged to members of their color are made, is well known. Under such circumstances self-protection or self-interest is the only lever by which the casket of their minds can be pried open. Acting upon this principle, the history and record of the regiment to which they belong, the part played by these old soldiers in this record, were pointed out and enlarged upon. The odium and disgrace to the battalion and to its individual members by this crime was indicated. The future effect upon the individuals and upon the battalion as a whole was referred to; and, finally, the concern of the President of the United States in the matter, his desire and the desire of the War Department to separate the innocent from the guilty were explained; all without effect.

The next day the battalion was paraded without arms, every officer and enlisted man being present except two men sick in hospital. The battalion was formed in convenient arrangement. I then addressed them, stating who I was, namely, the Inspector-General of the Army, sent there by order of the President of the United States to afford the men of the Twenty-fifth Infantry an opportunity to give such information as might be within their power that would lead to the detection of the few men guilty of the crime of firing during the night upon citizens of a sleeping town, and talked to them along the same lines as I had done to the old soldiers; and, in conclusion, read to them the orders of the President and of the Acting Secretary of War in the premises. I informed them that they would be given until 9 o'clock the next day to consider the matter, and that I would be accessible during that limit to any soldier who possessed information and had a desire to make it known. Only one man presented himself, and that was *not* to give information, but to urge his own case for exemption from the penalty imposed by the President, but still disclaiming any knowledge of the affair, and stating his inability to make any discovery connected therewith. This was First Sergeant Mingo Sanders, Company B, Twenty-fifth Infantry – a man with twenty-six years' service.

I decided upon a short period for the consideration of the ultimatum given because I thought it more probable to bring results. Two months had elapsed since the occurrence on the very day I made the ultimatum known, and it appeared to me that further time for reflection was unnecessary and that the time limit set by me would be more likely to convince the men that the penalty in case of failure was sure to follow; whereas if a longer period had been given it might have impressed them with the idea that it was made more in the nature of a threat for effect. . . .

I recommend that orders be issued as soon as practicable discharging, without honor, every man in Companies B, C, and D of the Twenty-fifth Infantry, serving at Fort Brown, Texas, on the night of August 13, 1906, and forever debarring them from reenlisting in the Army or Navy of the United States, as well as from employment in any civil capacity under the Government. In making this recommendation I recognize the fact that a number of men who have no direct knowledge as to the identity of the men of the Twenty-fifth Infantry who actually fired the shots on the night of the thirteenth of August, 1906, will incur this extreme penalty.

It has been established, by careful investigation, beyond reasonable doubt, that the firing into the houses of the citizens of Brownsville, while the inhabitants thereof were pursuing their peaceful vocation or sleeping, and by which one citizen was killed and the chief of police so seriously wounded that he lost an arm, was done by enlisted men of the Twenty-fifth Infantry belonging to the battalion stationed at Fort Brown. After due opportunity and notice, the enlisted men of the Twenty-fifth Infantry have failed to tell all that it is reasonable to believe they know concerning the shooting. If they had done so, if they had been willing to relate all the circumstances – instances preliminary to the trouble – it is extremely probable that a clue sufficiently definite to lead to results would have been disclosed. They appear to stand together in a determination to resist the detection of the guilty; therefore they should stand together when the penalty falls. A forceful lesson should be given to the Army at large, and especially to the noncommissioned officers, that their duty does not cease upon the drill ground, with the calling of the company rolls, making check inspections, and other duty of formal character, but that their responsibilities of office accompany them everywhere and at all times; that it is their duty to become thoroughly acquainted with the individual members of their respective units; to know their characteristics; to be able at all times to gauge their temper, in order to discover the beginning of discontent or of mutinous intentions, and to anticipate any organized act of disorder; that they must notify their officers at once of any such conditions. Moreover, the people of the United States, wherever they live, must feel assured that the men wearing the uniform of the Army are their protectors, and not midnight assassins or riotous disturbers of the peace of the community in which they may be stationed.

No absolutely accurate verification of the rifles and men of the battalion was made on the night of the thirteenth of August in time to account for all the rifles or all the men at the beginning of the firing or immediately upon its conclusion. This failure is explained as follows: The commanding officer and his associates, when the alarm was sounded and they heard the firing, assumed that it came from the city of Brownsville, and that the guns were in the hands of civilians; in other words, that the garrison was being fired into from the outside by civilians. It does not appear to have occurred to any of them that certain enlisted men of the Twenty-fifth Infantry had possession of their arms and were committing the crime of firing into the houses and upon the citizens of Brownsville until the mayor of the city came into the garrison and informed the commanding officer, Major Penrose, that one man had been killed and another wounded by his soldiers.

I return herewith all the papers in the case.

Very respectfully,

E. A. Garlington,
Inspector-General

BROWNSVILLE AFFRAY

The Military Secretary, *War Department.*

THE PRESIDENT'S ORDER

The White House
Washington, November 5, 1906

The Secretary of War:

I have read through General Garlington's report, dated October 22, submitted to me by you. I direct that the recommendations of General Garlington be complied with, and that at the same time the concluding portion of his report be published with our sanction as giving the reasons for the action.

Theodore Roosevelt

PRESIDENT'S MESSAGES

Message From the President of the United States, Transmitting Certain Documents, Correspondence, etc. – to the Senate:

In response to Senate resolution of December 6 addressed to me, and to the two Senate resolutions addressed to him, the Secretary of War has, by my direction, submitted to me a report which I herewith send to the Senate, together with several documents, including a letter of General Nettleton and memoranda as to precedents for the summary discharge or mustering out of regiments or companies, some or all of the members of which had been guilty of misconduct.

I ordered the discharge of nearly all the members of Companies B, C, and D, of the Twenty-fifth Infantry by name, in the exercise of my constitutional power and in pursuance of what, after full consideration, I found to be my constitutional duty as Commander in Chief of the United States Army. I am glad to avail myself of the opportunity afforded by these resolutions to lay before the Senate the following facts as to the murderous conduct of certain members of the companies in question and as to the conspiracy by which many of the other members of these companies saved the criminals from justice, to the disgrace of the United States uniform.

I call your attention to the accompanying reports of Major

Augustus P. Blocksom, of Lieutenant Colonel Leonard A. Lovering, and of Brigadier General Ernest A. Garlington, the Inspector-General of the United States Army, of their investigation into the conduct of the troops in question. An effort has been made to discredit the fairness of the investigation into the conduct of these colored troops by pointing out that General Garlington is a Southerner. Precisely the same action would have been taken had the troops been white – indeed, the discharge would probably have been made in more summary fashion. General Garlington is a native of South Carolina; Lieutenant-Colonel Lovering is a native of New Hampshire; Major Blocksom is a native of Ohio. As it happens, the disclosure of the guilt of the troops was made in the report of the officer who comes from Ohio, and the efforts of the officer who comes from South Carolina were confined to the endeavor to shield the innocent men of the companies in question, if any such there were, by securing information which would enable us adequately to punish the guilty. But I wish it distinctly understood that the fact of the birthplace of either officer is one which I absolutely refuse to consider. The standard of professional honor and of loyalty to the flag and the service is the same for all officers and all enlisted men of the United States Army, and I resent with the keenest indignation any effort to draw any line among them based upon birthplace, creed, or any other consideration of the kind. I should put the same entire faith in these reports if it had happened that they were all made by men coming from some one State, whether in the South or the North, the East or the West, as I now do, when, as it happens, they were made by officers born in different States.

Major Blocksom's report is most careful, is based upon the testimony of scores of eyewitnesses – testimony which conflicted only in nonessentials and which established the essential facts beyond chance of successful contradiction. Not only has no successful effort been made to traverse his findings in any essential particular, but, as a matter of fact, every trustworthy report from outsiders amply corroborates them, by far the best of these outside reports being that of General A. B. Nettleton, made in a letter to the Secretary of War, which I herewith append, General Nettleton being an ex-Union soldier, a consistent friend of the colored man throughout his life, a lifelong Republican, a citizen of Illinois, and Assistant Secretary of the Treasury under President Harrison.

It appears that in Brownsville, the city immediately beside which Fort Brown is situated, there had been considerable feeling between the citizens and the colored troops of the garrison companies. Difficulties had occurred, there being a conflict of evidence as to whether the citizens or the colored troops were to blame. My impression is that, as a matter of fact, in these difficulties there was blame attached to both sides; but this is a wholly unimportant matter for our present purpose, as nothing that occurred offered in any shape or way an excuse or justification for the atrocious conduct of the troops when, in lawless and murderous spirit, and under cover of the night, they made their attack upon the citizens.

The attack was made near midnight on August 13. The following facts as to this attack are made clear by Major Blocksom's investigation and have not been, and, in my judgment, can not be, successfully controverted. From 9 to 15 or 20 of the colored soldiers took part in the attack. They leaped over the walls from the barracks and hurried through the town. They shot at whomever they saw moving, and they shot into houses where they saw lights. In some of these houses there were women and children, as the would-be murderers must have known. In one house in which there were two women and five children some ten shots went through at a height of about 4½ feet above the floor, one putting out the lamp upon the table. The lieutenant of police of the town heard the firing and rode toward it. He met the raiders, who, as he stated, were about 15 colored soldiers. They instantly started firing upon him. He turned and rode off, and they continued firing upon him until they had killed his horse. They shot him in the right arm (it was afterwards amputated above the elbow). A number of shots were also fired at two other policemen. The raiders fired several times into a hotel, some of the shots being aimed at a guest sitting by a window. They shot into a saloon, killing the bartender and wounding another man. At the same time other raiders fired into another house in which women and children were sleeping, two of the shots going through the mosquito bar over the bed in which the mistress of the house and her two children were lying. Several other houses were struck by bullets. It was at night, and the streets of the town are poorly lighted, so that none of the individual raiders were recognized; but the evidence of many witnesses of all classes was conclusive to the effect that the raiders were Negro soldiers. The shattered bullets, shells, and clips of the Government rifles, which were found on the ground, are merely corroborative. So are the bullet holes in the houses, some of which it appears must, from the direction, have been fired from the fort just at the moment when the soldiers left it. Not a bullet hole appears in any of the structures of the fort.

The townspeople were completely surprised by the unprovoked and murderous savagery of the attack. The soldiers were the aggressors from start to finish. They met with no substantial resistance, and one and all who took part in that raid stand as deliberate murderers, who did murder one man, who tried to murder others, and who tried to murder women and children. The act was one of horrible atrocity, and, so far as I am aware, unparalleled for infamy in the annals of the United States Army.

The white officers of the companies were completely taken by surprise, and at first evidently believed that the firing meant that the townspeople were attacking the soldiers. It was not until 2 or 3 o'clock in the morning that any of them became aware of the truth. I have directed a careful investigation into the conduct of the officers, to see if any of them were blameworthy, and I have approved the recommendation of the War Department that two be brought before a court-martial.

As to the noncommissioned officers and enlisted men, there can be no doubt whatever that many were necessarily privy, after if not before the attack, to the conduct of those who took actual part in this murderous riot. I refer to Major Blocksom's report for proof of the fact that certainly some and probably all of the noncommissioned officers in charge of quarters who were responsible for the gun racks and had keys thereto in their personal possession knew what men were engaged in the attack.

Major Penrose, in command of the post, in his letter gives the reasons why he was reluctantly convinced that some of the men under him – as he thinks, from seven to ten – got their rifles, slipped out of quarters to do the shooting, and returned to the barracks without being discovered, the shooting all occurring within two and a half short blocks of the barracks. It was possible for the raiders to go from the fort to the farthest point of firing and return in less than ten minutes, for the distance did not exceed 350 yards.

Such are the facts of this case. General Nettleton, in his letter herewith appended, states that next door to where he is writing in Brownsville is a small cottage where a children's party had just broken up before the house was riddled by United States bullets, fired by United States troops, from United States Springfield rifles, at close range, with the purpose of killing or maiming the inmates, including the parents and children who were still in the well-lighted house, and whose escape from death under such circumstances was astonishing. He states that on another street he daily looks upon fresh bullet scars where a volley from similar government rifles was fired into the side and windows of a hotel occupied at the time by sleeping or frightened guests from abroad who could not possibly have given any offense to the assailants. He writes that the chief of the Brownsville police is again on duty from hospital, and carries an empty sleeve because he was shot by Federal soldiers from the adjacent garrison in the course of their murderous foray; and not far away is the fresh grave of an unoffending citizen of the place, a boy in years, who was wantonly shot down by these United States soldiers while unarmed and attempting to escape.

The effort to confute this testimony so far has consisted in the assertion or implication that the townspeople shot one another in order to discredit the soldiers – an absurdity too gross to need discussion and unsupported by a shred of evidence. There is no question as to the murder and the attempted murders; there is no question that some of the soldiers were guilty thereof; there is no question that many of their comrades privy to the deed have combined to shelter the criminals from justice. These comrades of the murderers, by their own action, have rendered it necessary either to leave all the men, including the murderers, in the Army, or to turn them all out; and under such circumstances there was no alternative, for the usefulness of the Army would be at an end were we to permit such an outrage to be committed with impunity.

In short, the evidence proves conclusively that a number of the soldiers engaged in a deliberate and concerted attack, as cold-blooded as it was cowardly, the purpose being to terrorize the community and to kill or injure men, women, and children in their homes and beds or on the streets, and this at an hour of the night when concerted or effective resistance or defense was out of the question and when detection by identification of the criminals in the United States uniform was well-nigh impossible. So much for the original crime. A blacker never stained the annals of our Army. It has been supplemented by another, only less black, in the shape of a successful conspiracy of silence for the purpose of shielding those who took part in the original conspiracy or murder. These soldiers were not schoolboys on a frolic. They were full-grown men, in the uniform of the United States Army, armed with deadly weapons, sworn to uphold the laws of the United States, and under every obligation of oath and honor not merely to refrain from criminality, but with the sturdiest rigor to hunt down criminality; and the crime they committed or connived at was murder. They perverted the power put into their hands to sustain the law into the most deadly violation of the law. The noncommissioned officers are primarily responsible for the discipline and good conduct of the men; they are appointed to their positions for the very purpose of preserving this discipline and good conduct, and of detecting and securing the punishment of every enlisted man who does what is wrong. They fill, with reference to the discipline, a part that the commissioned officers are of course unable to fill, although the ultimate responsibility for the discipline can never be shifted from the shoulders of the latter. Under any ordinary circumstances the first duty of the noncommissioned officers, as of the commissioned officers, is to train the private in the ranks so that he may be an efficient fighting man against a foreign foe. But there is an even higher duty, so obvious that it is not under ordinary circumstances necessary so much as to allude to it – the duty of training the soldier so that he shall be a protection and not a menace to his peaceful fellow-citizens, and above all to the women and children of the nation. Unless this duty is well performed, the Army becomes a mere dangerous mob; and if conduct such as that of the murderers in question is not, where possible, punished, and, where this not possible, unless the chance of its repetition is guarded against in the most thoroughgoing fashion, it would be better that the entire Army should be disbanded. It is vital for the Army to be imbued with the spirit which will make every man in it, and above all, the officers and noncommissioned officers, feel it a matter of highest obligation to discover and punish, and not to shield the criminal in uniform.

Yet some of the noncommissioned officers and many of the men of the three companies in question have banded together in a conspiracy to protect the assassins and would-be assassins who have disgraced their uniform by the conduct above related. Many of these noncommissioned officers and men must have known, and all of them may have known, circumstances which would have led to the conviction of those engaged in the murderous assault. They have stolidly and as one man broken their oaths of enlistment and refused to help discover the criminals.

By my direction every effort was made to persuade those innocent of murder among them to separate themselves from the guilty by helping bring the criminals to justice. They were warned that if they did not take advantage of the offer they would be discharged from the service and forbidden again to enter the employ of the Government. They refused to profit by the warning. I accordingly had them discharged. If any organization of troops in the service, white or black, is guilty of similar conduct in the future I shall follow precisely the same source. Under no circumstances will I consent to keep in the service bodies of men whom the circumstances show to be a menace to the country. Incidentally I may add that the soldiers of longest service and highest position who suffered because of the order, so far from being those who deserve most sympathy, deserve least, for they are the very men upon whom we should be able especially to rely to prevent mutiny and murder.

People have spoken as if this discharge from the service was a punishment. I deny emphatically that such is the case, because as punishment it is utterly inadequate. The punishment meet for mutineers and murderers such as those guilty of the Brownsville assault is death; and a punishment only less severe ought to be meted out to those who have aided and abetted mutiny and murder and treason by refusing to help in their detection. I would that it were possible for me to have punished the guilty men. I regret most keenly that I have not been able to do so.

Be it remembered always that these men were all in the service of the United States under contracts of enlistment, which by their terms and by statute were terminable by my direction as Commander in Chief of the Army. It was my clear duty to terminate those contracts when the public interest demanded it; and it would have been a betrayal of the public interest on my part not to terminate the contracts which were keeping in the service of the United States a body of mutineers and murderers.

Any assertion that these men were dealt with harshly because they were colored men is utterly without foundation. Officers or enlisted men, white men or colored men, who were guilty of such conduct, would have been treated in precisely the same way; for there can be nothing more important than for the United States Army, in all its membership, to understand that its arms can not be turned with impunity against the peace and order of the civil community.

There are plenty of precedents for the action taken. I call your attention to the memoranda herewith submitted from the Military Secretary's office of the War Department, and a memorandum from the Military Secretary enclosing a piece by ex-Corporal Hesse, now chief of division in the Military Secretary's office, together with a letter from District Attorney James Wilkinson, of New Orleans. The district attorney's letter recites several cases in which white United States soldiers, being arrested for crime, were tried, and every soldier and employee of the regiment, or in the fort at which the soldier was stationed, volunteered all they knew, both before and at the trial, so as to secure justice. In one case the soldier was acquitted. In another case the soldier was convicted of murder, the conviction resulting from the fact that every soldier, from the commanding officer to the humblest private, united in securing all the evidence in their power about the crime. In other cases, for less offense, soldiers were convicted purely because their comrades in arms, in a spirit of fine loyalty to the honor of the service, at once told the whole story of the troubles and declined to identify themselves with the criminals. . . .

So much for the military side of the case. But I wish to say something additional, from the standpoint of the race question. In my message at the opening of the Congress I discussed the matter of lynching. In it I gave utterance to the abhorrence which all decent citizens should feel for the deeds of the men (in almost all cases white men) who take part in lynchings, and at the same time I condemned, as all decent men of any color should condemn, the action of those colored men who actively or passively shield the colored criminal from the law. In the case of these companies we had to deal with men who in the first place were guilty of what is practically the worst possible form of lynching – for a lynching is in its essence lawless and murderous vengeance taken by an armed mob for real or fancied wrongs – and who in the second place covered up the crime of lynching by standing with a vicious solidarity to protect the criminals.

It is of the utmost importance to all our people that we shall deal with each man on his merits as a man, and not deal with him merely as a member of a given race; that we shall judge each man by his conduct and not his color. This is important for the white man, and it is far more important for the colored man. More evil and sinister counsel never was given to any people than that given to colored men by those advisers, whether black or white, who, by apology and condonation, encourage conduct such as that of the three companies in question. If the colored men elect to stand by criminals of their own race because they are of their own race, they assuredly lay up for themselves the most dreadful day of reckoning. Every farsighted friend of the colored race in its efforts to strive onward and upward should teach first, as the most important lesson, alike to the white man and the black, the duty of treating the individual man strictly on his worth as he shows it. Any conduct by colored people which tends to substitute for this rule the rule of standing by and shielding an evil doer because he is a member of their race, means the inevitable degredation of the colored race. It may and probably does mean damage to the white race, but it means ruin to the black race.

Throughout my term of service in the Presidency I have acted on the principle thus advocated. In the North as in the South I have appointed colored men of high character to office, utterly disregarding the protests of those who would have kept them out of office because they were colored men. So far as was in my power, I have sought to secure for the colored people all their rights under the law. I have done all I could to secure them equal school training when young, equal opportunity to earn their livelihood and achieve their happiness when old. I have striven to break up peonage; I have upheld the hands of those who, like Judge Jones and Judge Speer, have warred against this peonage, because I would hold myself unfit to be President if I did not feel the same revolt at wrong done a colored man as I feel at wrong done a white man. I have condemned in unstinted terms the crime of lynching perpetrated by white men, and I should take instant advantage of any opportunity whereby I could bring to justice a mob of lynchers. In precisely the same spirit I have now acted with reference to these colored men who have been guilty of a black and dastardly crime. In one policy, as in the other, I do not claim as a favor, but I challenge as a right, the support of every citizen of this country, whatever his color, provided only he has in him the spirit of genuine and farsighted patriotism.

Theodore Roosevelt

The White House, December 19, 1906 Message from the President of the United States, Transmitting Additional Testimony in the Brownsville Case – to the Senate:

In my message to the Senate treating of the dismissal, without honor, of certain named members of the three companies of the Twenty-fifth Infantry, I gave the reports of the officers upon which the dismissal was based. These reports were made in accordance with the custom in such cases; for it would, of course, be impossible to preserve discipline in the Army save by pursuing precisely the course that in this case was pursued. Inasmuch, however, as in the Senate question was raised as to the sufficiency of the evidence, I deemed it wise to send Major Blocksom, and Assistant to the Attorney-General Purdy, to Brownsville to make a thorough investigation on the ground in reference to the matter. I herewith transmit Secretary Taft's report, and the testimony taken under oath of the various witnesses examined in the course of the investigation. I also submit of various exhibits, including maps of Brownsville and Fort Brown, photographs of various buildings, a letter from Judge Parks to his wife, together with a bandoleer, thirty-three empty shells, seven ball cartridges, and four clips picked up in the streets of Brownsville within a few hours after the shooting; three steel-jacketed bullets and some scraps of the casings of other bullets picked out of the houses into which they had been fired. A telegram from United States Commissioner R. B. Creager, at Brownsville, announces that six additional bullets – like the others, from Springfield rifles – taken from buildings in Brownsville, with supporting affidavits, have since been sent to the Secretary of War.

It appears from the testimony that on the night of the thirteenth of August, 1906, several crimes were committed by some person or persons in the city of Brownsville. Among these were the following:

(a) The murder of Frank Natus.

(b) The assault with intent to kill the lieutenant of police, Dominguez, whose horse was killed under him and whose arm was shot so severely that it had to be amputated.

(c) The assult with intent to kill Mr. and Mrs. Hale Odin, and their little boy, who were in the window of the Miller Hotel.

(d) The shooting into several private residences in the city of Brownsville, three of them containing women and children.

(e) The shooting at and slightly wounding of Preciado.

These crimes were certainly committed by somebody.

As to the motive for the commission of the crimes, it appears that trouble of a more or less serious kind had occurred between individual members of the companies and individual citizens of Brownsville, culminating in complaints which resulted in the soldiers being confined within the limits of the garrison on the evening of the day in question.

The evidence, as will be seen, shows beyond any possibility of honest question that some individuals among the colored troops whom I have dismissed committed the outrages mentioned; and that some or all of the other individuals whom I dismissed had knowledge of the deed and shielded from the law those who committed it.

The only motive suggested as possibly influencing anyone else was a desire to get rid of the colored troops, so strong that it impelled the citizens of Brownsville to shoot up their own houses, to kill one of their own number, to assault their own police, wounding the lieutenant, who had been an officer for twenty years – all with the purpose of discrediting the Negro troops. The suggestion is on its face so ludicrously impossible that it is difficult to treat it as honestly made. This theory supposes that the assailants succeeded in obtaining the uniform of the Negro soldiers; that before starting on their raid they got over the fence of the fort unchallenged, and without discovery by the Negro troops opened fire on the town from within the fort; that they blacked their faces so that at least fourteen eyewitnesses mistook them for Negroes; that they disguised their voices so that at least six witnesses who heard them speak mistook their voices as being those of Negroes. They were not Mexicans, for they were heard by various witnesses to speak in English. The weapons they used were Springfield rifles; for the ammunition which they used was that of the Springfield rifle and no other, and could not have been used in any gun in Texas or any part of the Union or Mexico, or in any other part of the world, save only in the Springfield now used by the United States troops, including the Negro troops in the garrison at Brownsville, and by no other persons save these troops – a weapon which had only been in use by the United States troops for some four or five months prior to the shooting in question, and which is not in the possession of private citizens.

The cartridge used will go into one other rifle used in the United States, when specially chambered – the Winchester of the '95 model – but it will rarely if ever go off when in it; and, moreover, the bullets picked out of the buildings show the marking of the four so-called "lands" which come from being fired through the Springfield, but not through the Winchester, the latter showing six. The bullets which I herewith submit, which were found in the houses, could not therefore have been fired from a Winchester or any other sporting rifle, although the cartridges might have been put into a Winchester model of '95. The bullets might have been fired from a Krag, but the cartridges would not have gone into a Krag. Taking the shells and the bullets together, the proof is conclusive that the new Springfield rifle was the weapon used by the midnight assassins and could not by any possibility have been any other rifle of any kind in the world. This of itself establishes the fact that the assailants were United States soldiers, and would be conclusive on this point if not one soldier had been seen or heard by any residents in Brownsville on the night in question, and if nothing were known save the finding of the shells, clips, and bullets.

Fourteen eyewitnesses, namely, Charles R. Chase, Amado Martinez, Mrs. Kate Leahy, Palerno Preciado, Ygnacio Dominguez, Macedonio Ramirez, George W. Rendall, Jose Martinez, J. P. McDonald, F. H. A. Sanborn, Herbert Elkins, Hale Odin, Mrs. Hale Odin, and Judge Parks, testified that they saw the assailants or some of them at varying distances, and that they were Negro troops, most of the witnesses giving their testimony in such shape that there is no possibility of their having been mistaken. Two other witnesses, Joseph Bodin and Genero Padron, saw some of the assailants and testified that they were soldiers (the only soldiers in the neighborhood being the colored troops). Four other witnesses, namely, S. C. Moore, Doctor Thorn, Charles S. Canada, and Charles A. Hammond, testified to hearing the shooting and hearing the voices of the men who were doing it, and that these voices were the voices of Negroes, but did not actually see the men who were doing the shooting. About twenty-five other witnesses gave testimony corroborating to a greater or less degree the testimony of those who thus saw the shooters or heard them. The testimony of these eye and ear witnesses would establish beyond all possibility of contradiction the fact that the shooting was committed by ten or fifteen or more of the Negro troops from the garrison, and this testimony of theirs would be amply sufficient in itself if not a cartridge or bullet had been found; exactly as the bullets and cartridges that were found would have established the guilt of the troops even had not a single eyewitness seen them or other witness heard them.

The testimony of the witnesses and the position of the bullet holes show that fifteen or twenty of the Negro troops gathered inside the fort, and that the first shots fired into the town were fired from within the fort; some of them at least from the upper galleries of the barracks.

The testimony further shows that the troops then came out over the walls, some of them perhaps going through the gate, and advanced a distance of three hundred yards or thereabouts into the town. During their advance they shot into two hotels and some nine or ten other houses. Three of the private houses into which they fired contained women and children. They deliberately killed Frank Natus, the bartender, shooting him down from a distance of about fifteen yards. They shot at a man and woman, Mr. and Mrs. Odin, and their little boy, as they stood in the window of the Miller Hotel, the bullet going less than two inches from the head of the woman. They shot down the lieutenant of police, who was on horseback, killing his horse and wounding him so that his arm had to be amputated. They attempted to kill the two policemen who were his companions, shooting one through the hat. They shot at least eight bullets into the Cowen house, putting out a lighted lamp on the dining-room table. Mrs. Cowen and her five children were in the house; they at once threw themselves prone on the floor and were not hit. They fired into the Starck house, the bullets going through the mosquito bar of a bed from eighteen to twenty inches above where little children were sleeping. There was a light in the children's room.

The shooting took place near midnight. The panic caused by the utterly unexpected attack was great. The darkness, of course, increased the confusion. There is conflict of testimony on some of the minor points, but every essential point is established beyond the possibility of honest question. The careful examination of Mr. Purdy, assistant to the Attorney-General, resulted merely in strengthening the reports already made by the regular army authorities. The shooting, it appears, occupied about ten minutes, although it may have been some minutes more or less. It is out of the question that the fifteen or twenty men engaged in the assault could have gathered behind the wall of the fort, begun firing, some of them on the porches of the barracks, gone out into the town, fired in the neighborhood of two hundred shots in the town, and then returned – the total time occupied from the time of the first shot to the time of their return being somewhere in the neighborhood of ten minutes – without many of their comrades knowing what they had done. Indeed, the fuller details as established by the additional evidence taken since I last communicated with the Senate make it likely that there were very few, if any, of the soldiers dismissed who could have been ignorant of what occurred. It is well-nigh impossible that any of the noncommissioned officers who were at the barracks should not have known what occurred.

The additional evidence thus taken renders it in my opinion impossible to question the conclusions upon which my order was based. I have gone most carefully over every issue of law and fact that has been raised. I am now satisfied that the effect of my order dismissing these men without honor was not to bar them from all civil employment under the Government, and therefore that the part of the order which consisted of a declaration to this effect was lacking in validity, and I have directed that such portion be revoked. As to the rest of the order, dismissing the individuals in question without honor, and declaring the effect of such discharge under the law and regulations to be a bar to their future reenlistment either in the Army or the Navy, there is no doubt of my constitutional and legal power. The order was within my discretion, under the Constitution and the laws, and can not be reviewed or reversed save by another Executive order. The facts did not merely warrant the action I took – they rendered such action imperative unless I was to prove false to my sworn duty.

If any one of the men discharged hereafter shows to my satisfaction that he is clear of guilt, or of shielding the guilty, I will take what action is warranted; but the circumstances I have above detailed most certainly put upon any such man the burden of thus clearing himself.

Theodore Roosevelt

The White House,
January 14, 1907

BROWNSVILLE AFFRAY

Message from the President of the United States Relating to the Extension By Act of Congress of Time Limit for Reinstatement of Soldiers Discharged Without Honor from Companies B, C, and D, Twenty-fifth Infantry.

To the Senate:

On December 12, 1906, the Secretary of War by my direction issued the following order:

> Applications to reenlist from former members of Companies B, C, and D, Twenty-fifth Infantry, who were discharged under the provisions of Special Orders, No. 266, War Department, November 9, 1906, must be made in writing and be accompanied by such evidence, also in writing, as the applicant may desire to submit to show that he was neither implicated in the raid on Brownsville, Texas, on the night of August 13, 1906, nor withheld any evidence that might lead to the discovery of the perpetration thereof.

Proceedings were begun under this order; but shortly thereafter an investigation was directed by the Senate, and the proceedings under the order were stopped. The Senate committee entrusted with the work has now completed its investigation, and finds that the facts upon which my order of discharge of November 9, 1906, was based are substantiated by the evidence. The testimony secured by the committee is therefore now available, and I desire to revive the order of December 12, 1906, and to have it carried out in whatever shape may be necessary to achieve the purpose therein set forth; any additional evidence being taken which may be of aid in the ascertainment of the truth. The time limit during which it was possible to reinstate any individual soldier in accordance with the terms of this order has, however, expired. I, therefore, recommend the passage of a law extending this time limit, so far as the soldiers concerned are affected, until a year after the passage of the law, and permitting the reinstatement by direction of the President of any man who in his judgment shall appear not to be within the class whose discharge was deemed necessary in order to maintain the discipline and morale of the Army.

Theodore Roosevelt

The White House,
March 11, 1908

A New Breed Of Frontier Soldier

World War I, and the events leading up to it, garnered most of the newspaper space and general interest during the second decade of the new century. Around 1910, however, various incidents began to focus some attention south of the border. One such incident was the murder of Francisco Madero by Victoriano Huerta – done, it is said, on the assurances of U. S. recognition of the Huerta regime by the U. S. Ambassador Henry Lane Wilson. Other incidents that electrified Americans were the arrest of U. S. Marines in Tampico and then the U. S. naval seizure of Veracruz in 1914. Some of the newspapers specializing in "yellow journalism" maintained reporters in the area most of the time, while the more reputable news agencies had reporters there only part of the time. Reportage was frequently fictionalized and always romantic in nature. Military dispatches were often suspect in terms of their authenticity. The most newsworthy items seemed to be those based on the leading characters of the drama, with General Pershing and Pancho Villa receiving the most play.

The Punitive Expedition of 1916 involved high drama, to be sure. One such drama was the controversial military order issued to Captain Charles T. Boyd by General Pershing which resulted in the damaging defeat at Carrizal, an incident reported fully in one of the chapters to follow. The order has been called one that had "no meaning as a tactical military maneuver"; yet the carrying out of it caused the death and capture and humiliation of many soldiers from the Tenth Cavalry. Another dramatic note is the fact that this war records the last major cavalry charge by American troopers on this continent. There is the drama also of having U. S. soil invaded by an enemy – not once, but several times.

The situation had its roots in the revolutionary opposition to Venustiano Carranza, a *de facto* President of Mexico who had gained that office through revolution. Pancho Villa was the main antagonist as far as both the United States and Carranza were concerned. Villa and his men had willfully and knowingly killed eighteen American engineers who had been asked by Carranza to come into Mexico to help reopen the mines. In addition, Villa was responsible for raids into Texas and New Mexico, the raid on Columbus, New Mexico, on March 9, 1916, being the most noteworthy. In that raid, seventeen Americans were killed. As a result of this raid, and because of American interests in Mexico, President Wilson felt called upon to abandon his "watchful waiting" policy and ordered a punitive expedition of 15,000 men into action. General Pershing was appointed the commanding officer of the entire operation. In addition to those regulars, 150,000 militia were ordered to duty and stationed along the border. There was a common purpose of action, and Carranza stood to benefit greatly from this help: The pressures would be taken off his government, since the Villistas would be forced to combat American forces rather than engaging the Carranzitas.

However, pressure from the people of Mexico led Carranza to object to the incursion by American forces, an almost foreseen reaction. Anti-American feeling ran high in Mexico. In an effort to combat this feeling, a joint but independent guarding of the border was suggested to Carranza, but he rejected the plan almost at once. Now, instead of receiving support, the American forces found themselves fighting both the Villistas and the Carranzitas in Mexico as well as countering strong criticism in the United States.

The threat of World War I was responsible for the final withdrawal of our troops from the border, but not before the climax of the drama had been played, the Fight at Carrizal. Sometime after this battle and the subsequent withdrawal of our forces, a new Mexican constitution was proclaimed and Carranza was officially elected to office to head a

government to which the United States government paid *de jure* recognition.

Carrizal was not to be the last border incident, but it was to be the last time that a major expeditionary force was assembled at the Mexican border. New border incidents – of different origins and consequences – occurred. Formal history books, papers, and studies of this period do not explore these incidents as fully as necessary; attention has been focused instead on the war, on peace negotiations, on President Wilson, and the League of Nations. All during this era black troops were involved in a sometimes peaceful, sometimes not so peaceful, existence on the Mexican border. For example, the popular news stories completely overshadow the Nogales fight, a drama which could have had far more serious consequences had it not been for the extraordinary coolness of the Tenth Cavalry and the Twenty-fifth Infantry.

The last Indian fight with the United States Cavalry took place after World War I – in 1918. This encounter involved the cavalry and the Yaqui Indians. This story is an appropriate one to conclude this presentation of the black military experience in the American West.

L. Bjorklund

The Cavalry Fight at Carrizal

Captain Lewis S. Morey (Tenth Cavalry)

Henry C. Houston was my first acquaintance among enlisted men of the United States Army. Upon reporting to Captain Harry LaT. Cavenaugh of the Tenth Negro Cavalry, who commanded Troop K at Fort Ethan Allen, Vermont, he told me that he had picked Private Houston to serve as my striker who would clean my quarters and my horse equipment and who would groom and saddle my troop horse. Houston was a bright, friendly young soldier, hardly more than a recruit himself at that time, and for several months he attended perfectly to my needs until he was promoted to the grade of corporal. After our regiment was transferred to Arizona in 1913 and Troop K was posted to Forrest, a watering station of the Southern Pacific Railroad, I took charge of training a squad in flag signaling. Corporal Houston acted efficiently as squad leader.

Within a few months, Troop K was ordered to join three troops of the regiment at Naco where trouble from Mexican insurgents threatened. I had by then obtained two mounts of my own, one a strong young pony, sired by a Morgan from a dam of mustang breed, that I hoped to train for polo. After the march to Naco I had no opportunity

Reprinted from Jerome W. Howe, "Campaigning in Mexico, 1916" (Arizona Pioneers Historical Society: 1968), with permission.

to exercise my pony for a few days. At last I mounted the little rascal with intent to give him plenty of gallop over the prairie and to take some of the mischief out of him.

I was alone as I rode quickly away from the camp and raced through uninhabited country with mesquite and cactus fringing the trail I had discovered. I was soon several miles distant, still at full speed, when suddenly a barbed-wire fence blocked my way unexpectedly. It was too close to allow me to change course or check my pony or gather for a jump. I plowed into it and lost consciousness.

In an hour or two I was found by two women, I suppose from the ranch that owned the treacherous fence. I judge that my pony, probably tripped by the lowest wire, broke through and fell, on me, and left me by the fence while he raced on to the ranch where he was recognized as an army horse, which led to my discovery. I had a moment of consciousness later when I believe the women came again after sending word about the accident. I think they tried to make me more comfortable, but there was not much help they could give. I was completely incapacitated, and continuously unconscious. I had a rough ride back to camp in a springless escort wagon.

The next day I was sent by train to Fort Huachuca and the Fort Hospital, where it was determined that I had suffered an impacted fracture of the neck of the femur. After a few weeks in hospital, I was invited by Major Ellwood W. Evans to occupy his vacant quarters, not far from Sam Kee's restaurant. And Captain Cavenaugh permitted Corporal Houston to come in to the Post to be my nurse. My former striker was wonderful in his attention, and I grew quite fond of him.

The post and regimental commander, Colonel W. C. Brown, remembered his earlier acquaintance with heliographic signaling. He obtained some instruments from the Signal Corps and invited me, who could then get about with crutches, to train a squad in their use so that we could maintain communication with Naco in case the wire contact should be interrupted. I was glad to have this experience and of course I utilized Houston's assistance to advantage, for he was well trained in Morse code. The Arizona climate and mountainous topography is ideal for such signaling, and we were very successful.

Houston's term of enlistment expired and he took his freedom for a while, but the lure of the cavalry brought him back to K Troop which he rejoined at Lochiel. When the troops marched into Mexico, he was attending a musketry course at the Fort Sill School of Fire; but at its termination he was sent back to Troop K, then in camp at Ojo Federico. There I found him again, after General Dodd was retired and I had returned to K Troop. That was only a short time after the disaster of Carrizal, and since Corporal Houston had been one of the men who had particiapted and whose recollections of it were still very fresh, I asked him to write a letter to my sister and relate his experiences. This is the letter he wrote, which long afterward I recovered.*

Down in Mexico
Sept. 11, 1916

Miss Howe,

As I have been asked by Lieutenant J. W. Howe to write you an account of the little engagement at Carrizal, I shall write all my memory recalls.

On the 18th day of June, 1916, "K" Troop of the Tenth Cavalry was notified[1] that they were to pack and saddle up for a march of 5 days and to be ready as soon as possible, we were ready and leaving Ojo Federico at 10 A.M., we rode 18 miles and arrived at a town called Sabinal at 2 P.M., camped all night and left next morning at about 7, rode 33 miles across a desert to Rio Santa Maria, the day was very hot and we were awfully thirsty when we completed that hike (and the water was the worst water I ever drank) after camping all night we hid some rations for us and feed for our horses in a large mesquite bush where they were not likely to be found by anyone else, for the wagon that had been with us was unable to proceed further because of bad ground we had to cross, our intentions were to recover the rations on our return to the Rio Santa Maria.

Next day which was the 20th of June we rode 50 miles to Santa Domingo ranch where we joined "C" Troop under command of Capt. [Charles T.] Boyd who was superior to our Capt. [Morey] which placed Capt. Boyd in command of both troops. Camped at the ranch that night and was called at 3 A.M. the 21st of June. We cooked and ate our breakfast, fed our horses, packed and saddled up our mounts and left at 4:15.

We traveled about 2 miles to a ditch where we watered our horses, oiled and loaded our rifles and automatic revolvers.[2] After everything was ready we left the ditch and rode 5 miles to the outskirts of Carrizal. Both troops after water were dismounted, and our guide (a

*This letter is now in the possession of the editor of this book, and it is considered one of the prized historical additions to his library.

Mexican named José) was dispatched with a message to General Gomez[3] from Capt. Boyd. After about half an hour's wait a column of Mexican cavalry was seen coming from the town. They deployed in line of skirmishers about 1500 yds. from us and their Col. and his staff held a council with Capt. Boyd half way between the two lines (our line and the Mexicans' line). After the council both commanders returned to their organizations and Capt. Boyd addressed our troops as follows: Quote, "Men, we have orders to go East and reconnoiter Villa Ahumada and in order to do that we shall have to go through this town (Carrizal) and the Mexican Col. told me just now that the Gen. refused us permission to pass through the town but when I told him I was determined to pass through anyway he said for me to wait a few minutes and he would send for the Gen." About that time our Mexican guide returned with an answer to our message from the Gen. which also refused us permission to pass through the town but before we had time to form any plans the General himself was seen coming with his staff. Capt. Boyd then rode forward again and he and the Gen. held a council for about half an hour. After the council split up Capt. Boyd rode back to us with his head bowed and when he got back to where we were he raised his head and said, Quote, "Boys, this looks fine, the General says the only direction we can travel is North, my orders are to travel East to Villa Ahumada which is 8 miles on the other side of this town and I am going through this town and take all you men with me."

When Capt. Boyd made the last remark all of our boys cheered and began singing phrases of spirited songs to show their willingness to accompany Capt. Boyd in his charge through town and to show their contempt of the Mexicans as foemen.

Then our commander gave his orders for our advance which were for the 1st platoon of "C" Troop and the 2d Platoon of "K" Troop to pass through town driving all Mexicans in front of them and for the 2d Platoon of "C" Troop to protect the left flank and for 1st Platoon "K" Troop to protect the right flank.

We started forward deployed in line of foragers, moved forward until we were within 500 yards of the enemy, then we dismounted and our horses moved to the rear and we moved forward, the Mexican cavalry started riding around both flanks and when we were about 200 yds. from the enemy we received a heavy volume of fire from rifle and machine guns and we knew that the ball was opened then.

We then received the order to lie down and commence firing, using the battle sight (which is the way we aim our rifles when we are fighting at close range). All of our men were taking careful aim, and Mexicans and horses were falling in all directions but the Mexican forces were too strong for us as they had between 400 and 500 and we only had 50 men on the firing line, so even though we were inflicting terrible execution they outnumbered us too greatly for us to stop their advance around our right flank.

At this stage of the game the Mexicans were so close that it was almost impossible to miss them, they were even so close that it was possible to hit them with stones had we desired. After about 1½ hours hard fighting they were about 30 yds. from our right flank, I tried to swing the left half of our platoon (of which I was in command) around so as to help out our platoon on the right but it was impossible, about that time our Capt. (Capt. Morey) yelled out to Sergt. Page, Quote "Sergt. Page! Good God man, there they are right upon you," and Sergt. Page responded, "I see them Capt. but we can't stop them and we can't stay here because it is getting too hot." By that time bullets were falling like rain and the Capt. ordered all of us to look out for ourselves and our men moved off the field by our left flank. No one can truthfully say that our men ran off the field because they did not, in fact they walked off the field stopping and firing at intervals.

At the edge of the field is an irrigation ditch and upon arrival at this I saw our Capt. who had been shot, trying to get across with the aid of two men. I assisted them in helping him across and we sat him in a dry ditch. Then I gave him a drink of water out of my campaign hat. Next I satisfied my own thirst. By that time the men were rallying for a final stand but our Capt. said, "I am done for Boys, You had better make your getaway."

And then we scattered each for his own self. One bunch started to go N.W. the direction from which we came and another bunch went S.W. but as I knew a person had a better chance for escape by himself than he would have with a bunch, I decided to go directly West to a chain of mountains which seemed to be about 12 miles away.

I had only gone about 200 yards when a bullet hit close behind me. I stopped and looked around to see if I could find the one who fired the shot and instead of finding an enemy I discovered Corp. Queen, a corporal of my troop about 100 yards in my rear. I waited and Corp. Queen joined me. Then we started for the mountains.

I cautioned Queen to evade all soft places on the earth so as not to leave a track for the Mexicans to trail us by. We left the battlefield about 10 A.M. and reached the mountains about 1:30 that afternoon and it was the hottest day I have ever witnessed. We were both craving for a drink of water but there was none in sight.

We continued our march across the mountains all the rest of that afternoon and a little before dusk we arrived at the top of the last mountain we had to cross and to our joy we saw a group of trees which looked to be about 18 miles away, it was just in time too because a few miles more and we would have lost all reasoning and began to wander aimlessly around and we would have died of thirst there in the mountains.

But after seeing the trees (any place in this country one can find trees there is almost sure to be water also) we were refreshened with new energy so we continued on at a much faster gait.

Some time during the night Queen and myself were parted, how I do not know, because both of us were staggering along half unconscious with only one thought in our minds and that was to keep going in the direction of the trees.

I wandered on by myself for a few miles further and then dropped from exhaustion and there I remained until daylight. By that time I had gathered enough rest to continue. After standing up I was very much refreshened to see that the trees were only 4 or 5 miles away.

After arriving at the trees which proved to be the La Salado Ranch I again found Corp. Queen. I was fortunate enough to have some money in my possession with which we bought some food and a horse.

The distance we had covered on foot without water was between 50 and 60 miles in 24 hours. After resting a few hours we continued our journey to Ojo Federico. Queen was leading the horse which was packed with our rations and water and in this manner we hiked until 11 P.M. when we found that we had lost the road so we decided to camp right there until morning and then find the road, for not only had we lost the road but there were three animals which we took for cows about 400 yards from us and anywhere there is cows it is a good sign for water.

Next morning while Queen was packing up I went over to investigate the cows and instead of cows found three "C" Troop horses. We rode them to Rio Santa Maria and had been there about one hour when "M" Troop arrived, and escorted us back to Ojo Federico where we made our report.

As the story is finished with your permission I shall close.

Sincerely,

Corp. H. C. Houston,
Troop "K", 10th Cav.

I will add that later, during my command of K Troop at Ojo Federico, Sergeant Page and a squad was sent out to recover some strayed horses. He got drunk instead and had to be punished. Page, who was first sergeant, had to be stripped of his chevrons, and feeling that

Houston, though only a corporal, was the best man in the troop for that duty, I recommended his promotion. With the approval of the squadron commander it was done. He filled the position effectively to the end of the campaign and for months afterward.

When the National Army was being raised to fight the Germans in 1917, and a division of Negro troops was organized, the four colored regiments of the Regular Army had to send many of their best noncommissioned officers to a training camp to be fitted for company commands. Houston and Queen were among those to be selected. They were sent to France as captains in the 92nd Division. Howard D. Queen also served in World War II in Europe as colonel of a colored regiment, and after the war became a high school principal in Parkersburg, Pennsylvania.

Border Fight at Nogales

Colonel H. B. Wharfield

Nogales, Sonora, for a number of years had been the object of contending Mexican political and bandit factions. It was a port of entry town and therefore attractive as a source for such loot as the customs house might provide.

The twin towns of Nogales had grown up around a trading post of 1880 established on the boundary of the 1853 Gadsden Purchase land. The adjacent settlements developed importance after 1882 when the Southern Pacific Railroad laid a track from Benson, on its main line, down the valley to near Guaymas, Sonora. The Nogales of Mexico became a lusty place of excitement, engendered by its local inhabitants, outsiders from across the line, and armed bands from the interior.

Yaqui Indians in 1897 raided the place, and guerrilla bandits were there in 1910. Obregon and others fought for possession in 1912, chasing the federal troops across the line.[1] In 1915 there were frequent shootings at the Tenth Cavalry patrols all along the border from Lochiel, climaxed by the siege of Nogales by contending revolutionary forces. The Twelfth Infantry, camped on the outskirts of Nogales, Arizona, also did their share of returning the fire when out on patrols.

Reprinted from Colonel H. B. Wharfield, *Tenth Cavalry and Border Fights* (El Cajon, California: 1964), with permission.

Nogales, Sonora, of 1918 was under control of a Mexican federal garrison. The local situation was complicated by agitation aroused through German agents and an accompanying rising dislike for us – the Gringos. On the American side the people were on the alert. Most of the householders had a Winchester or other weapon in a convenient location.

During the latter part of August 1918 the Thirty-fifth Infantry at Camp Stephen D. Little was completing its movement to an eastern staging area for overseas war duty. Only Companies G, F, and H remained, awaiting relief by the Twenty-fifth Infantry (Negro). The cavalry camp had Troop A (Tenth U.S. Cavalry) Captain Roy V. Morledge, Troop C [2] under Captain Joseph D. Hungerford, and Troop F with Captain Henry C. Caron.[3] Troop M of Captain John Lee and First Lieutenant Herbert W. Farrand were at Arivaca, and Loehiel was occupied by Troop B commanded by Captain Edgar R. Garlick with Lieutenant Shuman.

Manning the international guard station in Nogales were details from the Thirty-fifth Infantry. And patrolling east and west along the border were cavalry detachments. Lieutenant Colonel Frederick J. Herman, Tenth Cavalry, was with the cavalry troops and also acting Nogales subdistrict commander.

Military intelligence developed information that the Nogales situation was becoming critical. The Mexican garrison were digging some trenches in the hills overlooking the American side. Groups of mounted Mexicans, some in uniforms, were seen moving along the trails into town, and the Sonora border guards at the crossing gate had adapted a changed and officious attitude. Such an explosive condition seemingly only awaited an incident for ignition.

At 4:10 P.M. on August 27, 1918, a Mexican coming from the American side tried to walk through the guarded international gate without interrogation. When the U.S. customs inspector ordered "Halt!," the man kept moving toward the other side. Then the government official drew his revolver and went after the person. Private W. H. Klint of Company H, Thirty-fifth Infantry, followed for protection. A Mexican custom guard fired at the American official, missed him but killed Private Klint. Instantly Corporal William A. Tuckere of Company H shot the Mexican officer. More Mexican guards came running and started shooting. The corporal opened fire with his Springfield and killed three more. The U. S. Inspector gunned down one. A civilian at the gate phoned to the Thirty-fifth guard detail at the West Coast Company warehouse about the emergency. Another cranked up his truck and sped to the place, returning with Lieutenant Fanning and the soldiers. They arrived amidst a fusilade of lead from the Mexican side. That was the beginning of the Battle of Nogales.

Captain Roy V. Morledge of Troop A was in Nogales when the shooting started. Recently he wrote me:

> I happened to be downtown near the depot when I heard some rifle shots, and then more. I saw them carrying a wounded soldier at the international street.
>
> Motor transportation was scarce in those days, but I had a good horse. I sped over the hills a couple of miles to camp. On the way I passed Lieutenant Colonel Herman in a car. He had already gotten some news and told me to go on, get my troop out and notify Troop C and Troop F.
>
> Colonel Herman soon arrived and led the troops for the town at the gallop. I was sent down Morely Avenue. The place was a double street along the railroad tracks. At the little park the troop was dismounted, and one trooper detailed to hold each group of eight horses. Those left behind pleaded with me to go along.
>
> Dismounted, I told the men to follow me. Not far along before we got a lot of fire. There was so much it was hard to tell where it was coming from. Also it seemed as though everybody in Nogales was shooting from the windows toward the border.
>
> Reaching the line in spite of the fire, we dashed into a big building on the Mexican side without resistance, but bullets from up on a hillside were hitting the place. We ran forward into another connecting building. It was the Concordia Club. In there were some frightened senoritas wearing kimonas. I got a laugh when one of them spoke to a trooper, saying: "Sergeant Jackson! Are we all glad to see you!" But we did not have time to tarry for the soldier to alibi his acquaintanceship.
>
> Colonel Herman ordered us to the top of the hill. Up we went in waves of a squad at a time, firing at Mexicans off to one side. We took a position near some old buildings and a barricade. Down below were the Mexican depot and buildings. From there they were firing toward the American town, and some probably just hiding. They also started replying to our action.
>
> I hope we only hit those who were shooting. But there were a lot

> of bodies lying around. All of a sudden some one saw a long pole with a sheet tied on being waved from the top of the Mexican customs house down below.
>
> I ordered the men to cease fire. It was then 7:45 P.M., and getting dark. Where the time passed I do not know. We had five men wounded, and the others wanted to clean out the town. However First Sergeant LaMar and I quickly controlled our skirmish line of troopers.
>
> Finally orders came to move back across the border and bivouac in the park near the depot. There I saw Captain Caron with a bandaged wrist. Also the news came that Captain Hungerford of Troop C and Lieutenant L. W. Loftus of Company G, Thirty-fifth Infantry had been killed as well as several soldiers.

Captain Henry C. Caron and Troop F upon arriving downtown crossed over to Terrace Avenue on the right of Troop A. Lieutenant Colonel Herman assigned the troop to move forward and occupy Titcomb Hill. Years afterwards Captain Caron wrote:

> We left our horses at a lumber yard in the vicinity of the Bowman Hotel, and proceeded on foot up Terrace Avenue to our positions as designated. The Mexicans were on the flat house tops and the hills giving us a heavy fire, and we returned it.
>
> I was behind a telephone pole with first Sergeant Thomas Jordan and got hit in the right arm below the elbow.[4] Sergeant Jordan picked me up and carried me back out of range of the fire. He then took command of the troop until I returned from the doctor's office. I had no lieutenants with me at the time.

First Sergeant Thomas Jordan was given a commendation by Lieutenant Colonel Herman for taking command of Troop F during the absence of his commander.

Captain Joseph D. Hungerford and Troop C were assigned the left sector and moved forward toward the Reservoir Hill for control of the heights overlooking the town. The troop advanced to the position, then crossed the border, clearing the Mexicans out of their entrenchments on the heights. During this forward dash Captain Hungerford was shot through the heart and instantly killed. First Sergeant James T. Penny then took command of Troop C. Subsequently he received a special commendation for his initiative and the handling of the troopers.

Meanwhile Major Herbert E. Marshburn, Thirty-fifth Infantry, arrived in town from Camp Little with contingents of Companies F, G, and H coming along in quartermaster trucks. Company H was held in reserve and moved to the railroad depot near the border.

Company G was assigned to support Troop F, Tenth Cavalry, moving on Titcomb Hill. Near the line the doughboys became heavily engaged. A bullet killed Lieutenant L. W. Loftus, and Corporal Barney Lots was also fatally shot. Along a street Corporal A. L. Whitworth was hit in the groin and dropped in front of a house. Mrs. Emma Budge and Mrs. Jones, braving the fire, ran out and assisted the wounded man to shelter.

Upon arrival of Company F, Thirty-fifth Infantry, it got action in the support of Troop C on the Reservoir Hill sector. A private was hit and fell across the street from the home of "Colonel" A. T. Bird. June Reed, a niece of the Birds, and Miss O'Daley ran out the back way and called to the man. He crawled across the street and was helped into the house. We young cavalry officers were very proud of June for the brave deed. She had favored our acquaintance and company over that of the infantry at the hops and Sunday horseback rides. After her display of courage she increased in favor as our special girl friend.

During the earlier part of the engagement another of our cavalry girls became involved. Pat Shannon, who lived in a hotel fronting Morley Avenue and near the line, had her share of excitement. Two armed citizens used the upstairs window of her room for a firing station. Pat stood close by them, handing out ammunition as the guns were emptied. She was the daughter of a Chicago physician and employed as pianist by the Nogales Theatre moving picture house. Some weeks after the affray Pat and Lieutenant "Dee" de Lorimier, Tenth Cavalry, were married.

In addition to the citizenry, who shared the gun fight, there were some unattached officers and soldiers engaged.

The sergeant of Ordnance Depot No. 2 near the cavalry camp told me that during the fight overtown and while loading a truck with ammunition a colored trooper came galloping up, dressed only in a hospital gown and riding bareback with a halter shank to guide his mount. The "sick" soldier begged for a rifle and shells so as to join his troop. Army Regulations to the contrary notwithstanding, the old sergeant picked out a rifle, had the trooper sign a receipt, and gave him a couple of bandoliers of ammunition. Off he went at an extended gallop, the loose hospital gown floating out like a sail, and his bare legs thumping the ribs of the horse in an urge for more speed.

The records show that Quartermaster Sergeant Victor Arana, with the Thirty-fifth Infantry, was wounded. It is probable that the sergeant abandoned his truck detail and chose to get on the firing line for the battle.

Lieutenant William Scott, Tenth Cavalry, was riding a motorcycle into town on business from Fort Huachuca. Nearing the cavalry camp he heard the firing. Speeding up he took a familiar back track for the high ground above the Sonora town. Arriving close to the place, the cycle was hidden, and he crept to the brow of the hill overlooking the scene of conflict. Besides his .45 pistol Scotty was armed with a new Winchester, which he had "souvenired" some months before at the Yaqui fight in Bear Valley. From his solitary station he spent the time picking off snipers from the rooftops below. Whenever there was a scarcity of targets, he kept in practice by potting chickens that were running in and out of the adobe shacks. Scotty was a former sergeant out of the Texas Big Bend border service. He had been on the Punitive Expedition into Mexico with the Sixth Cavalry.

Captain James T. Duke, Tenth Cavalry (now a retired brigadier general) was in Nogales on business and volunteered his services. After the death of Captain Hungerford, he was detailed to command Troop C. Major H. B. Cheadle, Infantry, on leave in town, also was assigned duties. Lieutenant James B. Potter, Tenth Cavalry, Adjutant of the Nogales subdistrict, served on the line. Lieutenant S. M. Lockwood of Troop A had duty as an aide for Lieutenant Colonel Herman during the affray. His liaison duties were doubled after the commander suffered a slight but hampering leg wound.

When the white flag was displayed, Colonel Herman had buglers sound "Cease Fire." A Messenger from the Mexican consul in his office on the American side gave the information that the Mexican commandante and officials wanted a conference in the American consulate building located on the Sonora side. Sniping continued from various locations, but disregarding the danger, the commanding officer with Lieutenant Robert S. Israel of the Intelligence section proceeded to the appointed place. A truce was quickly arranged. The next day Brigadier General DeRosey C. Cabell, the Arizona District commander, arrived from Douglas. After a meeting with the Mexican official party regarding the situation, the hostilities were resolved.[5]

That ended another Battle of Nogales.

L. Bjorklund

The Yaqui Indian Fight

Colonel H. B. Wharfield

Did you know that the United States Cavalry had the last Indian fight as recently as January 9, 1918?

On the afternoon of that day a band of some thirty Yaqui opened fire on Troop E of the Tenth Cavalry (Negro) under command of Captain Frederick H. L. Ryder in Atasco Canyon, a spur of Bear Valley, west of Nogales, Arizona. The well-armed Indians were but slightly outnumbered and gave a good account of their fighting prowess against the pursuing cavalry. Following the battle tactics of the Southwest Indians they took full advantage of the boulders and brush cover in the canyon, hiding, shooting, scattering, and avoiding a stand-up fight.

Not since the campaigns of the previous century against the Apache, Sioux, Kiowas, Comanche, Cheyenne, as well as other tribes, and also the Chippewa in Minnesota during 1898 had United States troops exchanged shots with hostile Indians.

This last Indian fight might have caught the interest and imagination of the American public had it occurred during peace times. But the desperate struggle of World War I was waging, and only the scant reports in the Arizona papers, perhaps a few others, and some military correspondence were given to the border incident. There was a

Reprinted (in excerpted form) from Colonel H. B. Wharfield, *Tenth Cavalry and Border Fights* (El Cajon, California: 1964), with permission.

single military report by the Headquarters Southern Department at Fort Sam Houston, Texas to the War Department regarding the skirmish.

Report No. 251, January 19, 1918:

Reported from Douglas, Arizona, January 10, 1918, that a detachment of American Cavalry sent into Bear Valley, 25 miles west of Nogales to observe trails, clashed with a band of Yaqui Indians, captured Ten, one of whom died in a hospital at Nogales of wounds, according to a telegram from the commander at Nogales.

For some months during the late fall of 1917 ranchers in the rough country south of Arivaca had seen evidences of the Yaqui's illegal crossings of the United States-Mexican border line. A few complaints to peace officers were made that remains of partially butchered cattle were found, showing that the meat was used by trespassers from across the border and not local cattle rustlers. The American cowmen along the line west of Nogales were all riding armed because of these outsiders; however there had been no violence on the United States side, and most of the slaughtered cattle were "downed" or recent "winter killed" animals weakened by the poor range and bad weather conditions.

Even though the cattlemen as well as the miners were not troubled by any overt acts, they did not feel entirely safe with the Yaqui traveling clandestinely across the region, coupled with the possibilities of violence in case of a meeting. A miner at Ruby, a mining community below Arivaca, had a scare one night while coasting in a Model T Ford down a long grade. Around a bend of the mountain road he almost ran over a band of Yaqui, who were armed and crossing southward toward Mexico. Thereafter he quit traveling at night.

John Maloney at Ruby told some cavalry officers that once he unexpectedly had come upon a group in daylight while riding horseback to a mining claim. He greeted them in native Spanish and turned off in the opposite direction. John gave the impression that the Yaqui would not bother whites. However his daughter, Aileen,[1] knowingly commented that she thought her father put the spurs to the horse the moment he was out of their sight. It had been common knowledge for a number of years that the Indians were sneaking across the border to get into the Tucson and Phoenix areas for work in citrus and cotton ranches and the mines. Many of them used their wages to purchase firearms and ammunition, which were smuggled back into Mexico for use of their tribesmen in conflicts with the Mexicans.

Diplomatic relations with Mexico were in somewhat of a delicate balance growing out of various conflicts of interest including the 1916 Punitive Expedition into Mexico in pursuit of Pancho Villa, the neutraility of Mexico during the then raging World War I involving suspicions that German spies were being harbored there, and various unresolved United States business and property interests in Mexico. That government through General Plutarco Elias Calles in the state of Sonora – subsequently he was President of Mexico from 1924 to 1928 – informally requested that the Yaqui be stopped from purchasing weapons in Arizona and gunrunning the contraband back into Mexico for rebellious purposes.

United States army forces for a number of years had been stationed along the entire border, and the cavalry used for patrolling to stop bandit raids on the line, smuggling, and cattle and horse stealing[2] by renegades of both sides. The War Department took cognizance of the increased seriousness of Yaqui arms smugglers. During 1917 the Nogales army subdistrict command of Colonel J. C. Frier of the Thirty-fifth Infantry increased the number of cavalry patrol camps along the border toward the mining communities of Ruby and Oro Blanco with a main camp at Arivaca, as well as eastward to Lochiel.

The Tenth Cavalry with headquarters at Fort Huachuca, had a squadron cavalry camp at Nogales located a half mile or so up a draw from the Thirty-fifth Infantry Camp Stephen D. Little.[3] The infantry commander let it be known that we were to encamp far enough away so the horse smell and flies would not contaminate his barracks. We young cavalry officers made the most of his proclamation by greeting his junior officers with such remarks as "get some horse aroma on your uniforms and smell like men," and other inconsiderate remarks.

The Second Squadron under command of Captain Otto Wagner maintained troop outposts to the east at Lochiel and Campini, and another troop to the west at a strategic natural crossing in the Bear Valley as well as detachments at Arivaca and toward Oro Blanco.

The Bear Valley camp in Atasco Canyon was located alongside the log corral of the early day Johnny Vogan[4] homestead. Military information obtained by the Nogales subdistrict indicated that this area was the frequented route used by the Yaqui for their Mexican trail. It was an uninhabited region and a reputed area for people to travel in pairs for safety sake. Various tales – all vague and unconfirmed – were current among the people of Ruby and Arivaca of mysterious disappearances in the border country.

After the New Year celebration in January 1918 Captain Blondy Ryder and his Troop E of the Tenth Cavalry drew the assignment to the general Bear Valley area for border patrol. The troop took the Oro Blanco trail along the border, sending the impedimenta around by Arivaca and thence southward past Ruby to the Johnny Vogan place. This location was about a mile from the border fence.

The terrain was well suited for the patrol work. A high ridge east from the camp gave a wide view of the region. Here a stationary sentinel look-out was established with visual signal communications in view of a camp sentry. In addition daily patrols rode the trails looking for signs, as well as any wanderers, in the border land.

One day Phil Clarke, a cattleman and Ruby storekeeper, stopped by for a visit. He reported that a neighbor had seen fresh Yaqui signs in the mountains to be north where a winter-killed cow had been partly skinned and sandals cut out of the hide.[5] The next morning on the ninth of January, 1918, Captain Ryder decided to strengthen the observer post by sending First Lieutenant William Scott along with the detail. They had orders to maintain a constant surveillance of the area with field glasses for any movement along the trails.

About the middle of the afternoon Lieutenant Scott signaled "attention." Upon acknowledgment from the camp sentry he gave the message "enemy in sight," and pointed toward a low ridge west of camp a quarter of a mile or more distant. The sentry hollered to First Sergeant Samuel H. Alexander, who was sitting under a nearby mesquite with several other noncommissioned officers. The shout brought everyone to their feet. On the skyline of the ridge could be seen a long column of Indians crossing to the other side. The horses had been under saddle with loose cinches all day tied up in the corral; so within a few minutes the troop was mounted.

When the soldiers left the corral the Yaqui were out of sight, but Lietuenant Scott kept pointing generally south in the direction of the border fence.

Galloping up to the crest the troop dropped over into a shallow brushy draw, dismounted, and tied the horses to each other in circles by squad. Leaving a guard, it formed a skirmish line and moved forward up the side of the canyon through the mesquite trees and brush. Nearing the top, nothing was seen of the Indians, so orders were given to return to the horses by a different route. Part way down the canyon the troopers came upon hastily abandoned packs. Sensing that the Yaqui were somewhere in that vicinity, the captain ordered an advance up the canyon in a southeasterly direction. Within only a short distance the hiding Indians were flushed and opened up a hot fire on the soldiers. Luckily the shooting was wild. The bullets could be heard whistling and cracking overhead. Captain Ryder shouted the command to commence firing and keep advancing under cover.

The fighting developed into an old kind of Indian engagement with both sides using all the natural cover of boulders and brush to full advantage. The Yaqui kept falling back, dodging from boulder to boulder and firing rapidly. They offered only a fleeting target, seemingly just a disappearing shadow. The officer saw one of them running for another cover, then stumble and thereby expose himself. A corporal alongside of the captain had a good chance for an open shot. At the report of the Springfield a flash of fire enveloped the Indian's body for an instant, but he kept on to the rock.

The cavalry line maintained its forward movement, checked at times by the hostile fire, but constantly keeping contact with the Indians. Within thirty minutes or so the return shooting lessened. Then the troop concentrated heavy fire on a confined area containing a small group, which had developed into a rear guard for the others. The fire effect soon stopped most of the enemy action. Suddenly a Yaqui stood up waving his arms in surrender. Captain Ryder immediately blew long blasts on his whistle for the order to "cease fire," and after some scattered shooting the fight was over.

Then upon command the troopers moved forward cautiously and surrounded them. This was a bunch of ten Yaqui, who had slowed the cavalry advance enough to enable most of their band to escape. It was a courageous stand by a brave group of Indians; and the cavalrymen treated them with the respect due to fighting men. Especially astonishing was the discovery that one of the Yaqui was an eleven year old boy. The youngster had fought bravely alongside his elders, firing a rifle that was almost as long as he was tall.

Many years after his Indian fight I asked Captain Ryder, now a retired army colonel, to give me his recollections of the engagement. In addition to the above factual material, he wrote:

> Just think, that Indian fight happened over forty-four years ago when you and I were with the Tenth Cavalry. Though time has perhaps dimmed some details, the fact that this was my first experience under fire – and it was a hot one even though they were poor marksmen – most of the action was indelibly imprinted on my mind.
>
> After the Yaqui were captured we lined them up with their hands above their heads and searched them. One kept his hands around his middle. Fearing he might have a knife to use on some trooper, I grabbed his hands and yanked them up. His stomach practically fell out. This was the man who had been hit by my corporal's shot. He was wearing two belts of ammunition around his waist and more over each shoulder. The bullet had hit one of the cartridges in his belt, causing it to be exploded; making the flash of fire I saw. Then the bullet entered one side and came out the other, laying his stomach open. He was the chief of the group. We patched him up with first-aid kits, mounted him on a horse, and took him to camp. He was a tough Indian, made hardly a groan and hung onto the saddle. If there were more hit we could not find them. Indians do not leave any wounded behind if they can possibly carry them along.
>
> One of my men spoke a mixture of Spanish, and secured the information from a prisoner that about twenty others got away. I immediately sent Lieutenant Scott, who had joined the fight, to take a strong detail and search the country for a few miles. However they did not find anything of the remainder of the band. It was dark when we returned to camp.
>
> I sent some soldiers to try and get automobile or any transportation at the mining camps for the wounded Yaqui, but none could be located until morning. He was sent to the army hospital at Nogales and died that day.[6]
>
> We collected all of the packs and arms of the Indians. There were a dozen or more rifles, some 30-30 Winchester carbines and German Mausers, lots of ammunition, powder and lead, and bullet moulds.
>
> The next day when you and Captain Pink Armstrong with Troop H came in from the squadron camp to relieve us, we pulled out for Nogales. The Yaqui were mounted on some extra animals, and not being horse-Indians were a sorry sight when we arrived in town. Some were actually stuck to the saddles from the bloody chafing and raw blisters they had stoically endured during the trip. Those Yaqui were just as good fighting men as any Apache of which race they have some ancient kinship, I understand.

Within a week or so we were ordered to Arivaca for station, and had to take our Indian prisoners along because the Thirty-fifth Infantry colonel, who was also the subdistrict commander, did not want to be bothered with guarding them.

They proved to be good workers and kept the campsite immaculately clean. At the corral nary any droppings were allowed to hit the ground. During the day the Indians would stand around watching the horses. Whenever a tail was lifted, out they rushed with their scoopshovels and caught it before the manure could contaminate the ground. It certainly helped in the decline of the fly population.

A few of the Yaqui spoke understandable Spanish, and some of the troopers talked a lot with them. We learned that the reason they fired upon us was they thought the Negro soldiers were Mexican troops that were on the American side of the border. Also, they were traveling in daylight because no United States troops were there three months before when they came into the country.

The Yaqui were so pleased with the routine soldier life, three square meals a day, a cot with a straw matress, and G.I. blankets at night that they all volunteered to enlist in the army. But the United States Department of Justice had other plans and took them to Tucson for legal action. That's the last I ever heard of them.

Some of the Arizona newspapers of 1918 had brief accounts of this Indian fight. From the research of these sources[7] I subsequently learned that the captured Yaqui were indicted by a United States grand jury and tried in the federal District Court at Tucson. On a trip to Arizona during August 1962 with Colonel Ryder, we looked up the court files in the case.

The grand jury had indicted the nine Yaqui on February 9, 1918 on the charges (that they) " . . . did wrongfully, unlawfully, and feloniously export to Mexico certain arms and ammunition, to-wit: 300 rifle cartridges and about 9 rifles without first procuring an export license issued by the War Trade Board of the United States."

On February 16, 1918 U. S. District Judge William H. Sawtelle entered an order for dismissal of the charges against Antonio Flores, the eleven year old boy, and accepted the plea of guilty from the others.

In the meantime the Mexican consul presented a request of General Calles, the military governor of Sonora, that the captured Yaqui be deported and turned over to his government. Calles was having serious trouble with the Indians, and had recently issued a proclamation urging the death and destruction upon all rebels. Only a few months before, a passenger train of the Sud Pacifico de Mexico Railroad had been held up by Yaqui south of Nogales in Sonora, and a number of the passengers wantonly killed.

Under the conditions in Sonora it appeared probable that the deportation of the Yaqui would result in their execution.

Federal Judge Sawtelle in passing sentence evidently took all circumstances of the Yaqui-Mexican government relations into consideration. He was a Westerner who believed in the right of everyone to have a chance to survive. On April 8, 1918 he sentenced the eight adult Yaqui to thirty days imprisonment in the Pima County, Arizona, jail; which precluded deportation.

Full dress uniform, 1880

Conclusion

In comparing their Negro soldiers with white troops in the early post-Civil War period, the officers of the colored regiments were convinced the Negro was more obedient and more loyal to his superiors than was the average white soldier. In the beginning, the newly freed Negro undoubtedly deserved this characterization. Suddenly elevated to the position of a soldier in arms, subordinate to the very men who had won him his freedom, still imbued with a heritage of inferiority, the Negro soldier gave freely of his loyalty and faithfulness.

Slowly this sense of servility gave way to individualism. The years of campaigning on the frontier, marked with success in battle, the development of traditions, and a growing pride in self and regiment, worked a subtle change on the Negro soldier's character. On the eve of the Spanish-American war he knew he was more than just a freedman. He had an awareness that he had performed well and that his record was as good as his white comrade's. There was a slow but steady change too in the kind of soldier and officer to be found in the colored regiments. Over the years recruits, who had no memory of slavery, were added to the rosters. Born and reared in freedom, some of them

Reprinted from Erwin N. Thompson, "The Negro Regiments of the U.S. Army, 1866-1900," unpublished M.A. thesis (University of California: 1966), with permission.

possessing a modicum of education, these young soldiers were not overwhelmed by the heritage of past bondage. The officers, particularly those assigned to the companies, were different too. The Civil War veterans were retiring or accepting promotions in the field grades, and lieutenants fresh out of West Point were coming into the regiments in increasing numbers. While these young officers upheld the traditions and conservativism of their predecessors, their elders had been the ones who had ended slavery, not they. The result was that relationships between the younger officers and the soldiers gradually became more like those found in the rest of the army. The sense of paternalism lesssened and a modicum of independence and initiative evolved.

The democratic social structure of the frontier also worked an effect on the Negro soldier. Although his social freedom was limited in the western communities, he did not come up against the total segregation that the South was instituting in the 1890s. When the Negro regiments arrived in the South in 1898, they were shocked and angry when southerners refused to sell them meals or drinks, when they found separate waiting rooms at the railway depots, and when they heard the hated epithet "nigger" at every turn.

For thirty years the Negro soldier had been able to live with segregation and had patiently accepted white leadership. The war with Spain and its aftermath were to reveal that both were now inadequate. In the bright light of nationwide publicity, the colored regiments fought bravely and well, unexcelled by any white unit. This brief moment of glory and recognition swiftly passed. The Negro troops, knowing they were equal to the best, felt resentment now because their color was a barrier to reward. the army continued to believe that the Negro was inferior and incapable of leadership. The generals held to their old concepts that if the Negro was led by white officers he would fight, but that was the limit of his capacity for soldiering.

General Miles, whose own service with Negro troops was thirty years behind him, recognized the quality of their performance in Cuba, then patronizingly concluded, "what may we expect of the (Negro) race when it shall have experienced as many generations of growth and development as the Anglo-Saxons who now dominate the thought, the inventive genius, the military prowess, and the commercial enterprise of the world."[1] Major General Merritt also continued in the old terms, "I have always found the colored race represented in the army obedient, intelligent and zealous in the discharge of duty, brave in battle, easily disciplined, and most efficient in the care of their horses, arms, and equipment." [2] This kind of priase was once important to the Negro, but he resented it after 1898. The Negro chaplain of the Twenty-fifth Infantry, T. G. Steward, expressed the new and growing discontent forcibly, "The colored American soldier, by his own prowess, has won an acknowledged place by the side of the best trained fighters with arms. In the fullness of his manhood he has no rejoicing in the patronizing paean, 'the colored troops fought nobly,' nor does he glow at all when told of his 'faithfulness' and 'devotion' to his white officers, qualities accentuated to the point where they might well fit an affectionate dog." [3] Steward's protests, and others like them, went unheard.

Another symptom of the dissatisfaction the Negro soldiers felt was the growing number of incidents arising primarily from racial strife between Negro troops and white communities. There had been violence on occasion before the Spanish-American war, such as at Sturgis City, Dakota Territory, and at San Angelo, Texas. Now such incidents increased in number and size. At Huntsville, Alabama, on their return from Cuba, troopers of the Tenth Cavalry engaged in a gun battle with a white provost guard at the railroad depot. In 1899, soldiers from the Twenty-fourth and Twenty-fifth Infantry, en route to the Philippine Islands, shot up and destroyed a bar in Winnemucca, Nevada, during a train stopover. The outraged citizens placed all the blame on the Negro soldiers, but the Negro's view has not been recorded. At El Paso, Texas, 1900, the city police arrested and jailed two members of the Twenty-fifth Infantry. The prisoners' comrades then marched on the jail and a sharp gun duel ensued between the soldiers and the police, with one fatality on each side.

The commanding officer of the Department of Texas at the time of the El Paso incident, Colonel James W. Hull, had a better understanding of the Negro soldier's problems in his relations with white citizens, especially southerners, than most officers. He recognized there was still "a very strong prejudice throughout all the old slave states against colored troops, and this is quite a separate feeling from the ordinary race prejudice. . . . A colored man in uniform represents authority, and this idea suggests superiority, which is bitterly resented."[4]

Despite Colonel Hull's warning, the army continued to station

Negro units in southern-oriented communities. The climax to this ill-founded policy occured at Brownsville, Texas, in 1906, when 10 or 20 soldiers of the recently-arrived Twenty-fifth Infantry shot up a part of town, killing one civilian and wounding the chief of police.[5] Brownsville had seen a Negro garrison as early as 1867, when two companies of the Ninth Cavalry were stationed there. However in recent years white troops had occupied old Fort Brown, and the change to a Negro garrison in 1906 disrupted that part of the town's economy that catered to the soldiers. With rigid segregation firmly entrenched, the saloon keepers and brothel managers could not accept the colored soldiers' trade and suffered financial setbacks. Their best customers had been the white troops and, resenting the change, they treated the Negro replacements with numerous indignities, forcing the soldiers to react finally in rebellious ways.[6]

The most significant result of the incident was not the immediate transfer of the Twenty-fifth Infantry to a western post, it was the intervention of President Theodore Roosevelt. When neither the soldiers involved nor their comrades would testify in the army's investigations of the affair, the president ordered the immediate dismissal from the army, without honor, of three companies of the Twenty-fifth composed of 160 enlisted men including six holders of the Medal of Honor. When this action came under strong attack in the United States Senate, Roosevelt insisted he had had no choice and would have done exactly the same had they been white troops. His solution was drastic, perhaps impulsive, but Roosevelt believed he had made the right decision.

The incident had remarkably little effect on Roosevelt's future with American Negroes. At a World War I meeting of the Circle of Negro War Relief in New York City, the candid ex-president announced that had he been allowed he would have formed and commanded a Negro division for duty in France. "It is perfectly possible, of course," he said, "that there is more than one colored man in the country fit for the difficult task of commanding one such colored regiment . . . But it happens that I only knew of one and that was Colonel Charles Young."[7]

Roosevelt's frank expression on the inadequacies of Negro leadership was representative of the First World War. The Negro soldiers in the training camps in the United States and in the army in France found themselves mistrusted and despised by their fellow Americans. Organized into two infantry divisions, the Ninety-second and the Ninety-third in the American Expeditionary Force, the colored troops were officered mostly by whites, many of whom hated their assignments and who treated their men with contempt and intolerable arrogance. The commanding general of the Second Army, in which the Ninety-second Division was assigned, General Robert Lee Bullard, wrote "Poor Negroes! They are hopelessly inferior." "Altogether" he said "my memories of the Ninety-second Negro Division are a nightmare." He concluded, "If you need combat soldiers, and especially if you need them in a hurry, don't put your time on Negroes."[8] Contending with the prejudice, even racial hatred, that existed among so many of their commanders, the Negro soldiers fought in France with a morale that was desperately low. Considered fit only to be laborers in the supply line, barely trusted to hold even small segments of the front line trenches, they suffered through the war, descending into what has been described as the lowest reputation the Negro soldier ever reached.[9]

None of the four regular army Negro regiments served as a unit in France during World War I. Although a large percentage of the soldiers from these regiments transferred to the Ninety-second and Ninety-third Division, and some received commissions in the lower grades, the units themselves remained at their stations, ranging from the Twenty-fifth Infantry's assignment in the Hawaiin Islands to patrols on the Mexican border, where the Tenth Cavalry had been a part of Pershing's expedition into Mexico against Pancho Villa in 1917. Whether in France or in Arizona, the Negro soldier felt the sting of prejudice at its bitterest since the emancipation of his race. The proofs of his abilities, won in the battles against the Indians and the Spanish, had come to naught. The stereotype of the loyal but undependable, the sober but superstitious Negro buried the proud record of the Tenth Cavalry at San Juan Hill.[10]

Twenty-five years later, in World War II, the Negro again underwent the agony of segregation and mistrust. A critic of this war has written, "By denying [Negroes] . . . the opportunity to become fully-developed citizens we have succeeded, really, in blunting not only the desires but the ability of most colored Americans to be good combat soldiers."[11] The battle record of Negroes, despite the torrent of wartime propaganda that tried to bolster their morale, was occasionally adequate but on the whole undistinguished. Out of the war, however, came the realization that the institution of segregation in the armed forces could not be continued much longer in the face of America's postwar problems at home and abroad.

Not until 1950 did the President of the United States, acting with courage and determination, order the end of segregation in the army. It was a bold but long-overdue act. Despite President Harry Truman's insistence that integration be expedited, the Twenty-fourth Infantry was thrown into the battle in Korea in July 1950, still an all-Negro regiment. The Twenty-fourth had been the first of the Negro regiments to meet the enemy, back in 1867. Now, as perhaps the last segregated unit to go into combat, it was to conclude its existence ingloriously. The pathetic record during July, August, and September, 1950, is the story of panic and one wild withdrawal after another, although a number of individuals in its ranks acted with supreme courage.[12] Caught in the tail end of the long-outmoded institution of segregation, the Twenty-fourth Infantry ended eighty years of service in disgrace when it was inactivated in 1951.[13] A Negro captain in Korea explained what had happened. A Negro in a colored regiment who "looks around him and sees nothing but Negroes . . . feels like somebody is using him as cannon fodder."[14] To repeat the crude slogan of the day, the Negro had decided that if he was to be treated as a second-class citizen then he would fight as a second-class soldier. Under Truman's insistence, integration proceeded swiftly throughout the army and with remarkable success – to the astonishment of the "old-army" officers. The Integrated Negro soldier fought through the rest of the Korean war in a superb manner. It was as simple as that.

In 1966, one hundred years after the first regular army Negro soldier enlisted, integration is complete in the armed forces of the United States. the problems today are not about segreation but involve numbers. While Negroes compose eleven percent of the population, they comprise five percent of the Navy, nine percent of the Marine Corps. ten percent of the Air Force, and eighteen percent of the army's airborne troops in Viet Nam. In the armed forces there is one Negro general officer. Among the army's officer corps. Negroes amount to only 3½ percent, and that is the highest percentage in the armed forces.[15] The Negro soldier is once again proving that he is the equal of any other. His conduct in today's combat reaffirms his predecessors' accomplishments in the Indian Wars and in Cuba.

One of the severest critics of the army's past approach to the problems of the Negro soldier, L. D. Reddick, has called the years between 1866 and 1900 the "Golden Day," the time during which Negroes received their greatest number of first-class military honors.[16] In some aspects, Reddick's descriptive term captures the quality of the first Negro regulars' service. In the earlier part of the period, when the victorious Union government was still concerned with the plight of the freed Negroes, the colored soldier proudly served in his separate units. For many, the army was an essential bridge that carried them out of slavery into the responsibilities of citizenship. As the century drew to a close, the Negro soldier had proven his abilities only to find that the small world of enlisted service in separate units circumscribed his potential and held him the prisioner of alleged inferiority.

The new century found the nation encouraging the development of Jim Crow laws at home, and assuming a share in the "white man's burden" abroad. Ironically, the Negro soldier was required to shoulder a part of this "burden" in subduing and controlling the new colonies and their colored populations. The "Golden Day" had long since ended, but it had passed on an inheritance of precedents that was to perpetuate the concept of Negro inferiority in the armed forces until the middle of the twentieth century.

Battle of Carrizo Canyon

NOTES

THE NEW WORLD

Pohe-yémo's Representative and the Pueblo Revolt of 1680

1. A general idea of these dissensions can be gathered throughout France V. Scholes, *Church and State in New Mexico, 1610-1650* (Albuquerque, 1937); also in *NMHR*, II, 1936, Nos. 1-4; 12, 1937, No. I and *Troublous Times in New Mexico, 1659-1670* (Albuquerque, 1942); also in *NMHR*, 12, 1937, Nos. 2, 4; 13, 1938, No. I; 15, 1940, Nos. 3-4; 16, 1941, Nos. 1-3).

2. The pueblo religio-civic government was and is in the hands of two main groups: 1) the *head representatives* (representing both the people and the "ancient ones" in their mythology) which consist of the chief representative (cacique), the two war chieftains and their assistants, and the heads of the kiva groups; 2) the *medicine men*, or heads of the various curing societies and their assistants. Bandelier divided them into three: warriors, medicine men, and the highest shamans. And what jealousy between the caciques and the shamans, and what rivalry between the *Yaya* (cacique) and the war captains! Adolph F. Bandelier, *Final Report of Investigations among the Indians of the Southwestern United States*, 2 parts (Cambridge, 1890, 1892), Part I, 148, 294. He refers in a note to Fray Alonso Benavides, who made two distinctions: *guerreros* and *hechiceros* (warriors and sorcerers, or medicinemen), who struggled against each other for dominion over the common people, and thus were the cause of internal and inter-tribal dissensions by which whole pueblos were laid desolate. *Ibid.*, part I, 148.

3. Charles W. Hackett and Charmion C. Shelby, *Revolt of the Pueblo Indians of New Mexico and Otermín's Attempted Reconquest, 1680-1682*, 2 Vols. (Albuquerque, 1942), I, 5. Italics mine.

4. *Ibid.*, 15-16. Italics mine. The introduction of a deified Montezuma, the Aztec Emperor, already points to a non-Pueblo Indian behind the message.

5. Father Vélez Escalante in his extracts of the Otermín journals: "That they as youths were totally ignorant of the motive, and only had heard it said that from very far away toward the north there had come an order from an Indian *teniente* of Pojéyemú for all of this kingdom to rise against the Spaniards . . . that the *teniente* of Pojéyemú was very tall, black, and with eyes big and yellow." Biblioteca Nacional, México (cited hereinafter as BNM), Leg. 3, No. I (20/428), Eleanor B. Adams transcript. He is the only source who aspirates the "h" and accents syllables. I am using the form and spelling "Pohé-yemo" as a compromise between old Spanish sources and the recordings of latter-day ethnologists.

6. The documents on the subject fill most of one volume: Archivo General de la Nación, Mexico (cited hereinafter as AGN), Tierras: Civil, tomo 426.

7. This I used, with other supporting documents, in an article, "Nuestra Señora de la Macana," *NMHR*, XXXIV (1959), 81-97. The idea was expanded into a "novel," both plot and characters taken entirely from the historical sources, entitled *The Lady from Toledo* (Fresno, 1960). Faulty deductions regarding the representative of Pohé-yemo are corrected in this present study.

8. The Negro Estevanico certainly played with Fray Marcos de Niza's high hopes and gullibility on the way to Cibola in 1539. The martyrdom of Fray Pablo de Acevedo in Sinaloa in 1561 was attributed to a mulatto interpreter who twisted his words. Even in this very year of 1680, a rebellion planned by the Indians south of Guadalupe del Paso was blamed on the insensate actions of a mulatto servant; Hackett and Shelby, I, 47. For the escapades of an African native before and after the Vargas Reconquest, see my article, "De Vargas' Negro Drummer," *El Palacio*, LVI (1949), 131-38.

9. This synthesis of pueblo beliefs is gleaned from outstanding ethnologists: Bandelier, *Final Report*, and *The Southwest Journals of Adolph F. Bandelier, 1880-1882*, Charles H. Lange and Carroll H. Riley (eds.) (Albuquerque and Santa Fe, 1966); Noel Dumarest, *Notes on Cochiti, New Mexico*, E.C. Parsons (ed.) (Lancaster, Pa., 1920); Elsie Clews Parsons, *The Pueblo of Jemez* (New Haven, 1925); Leslie A. White, *The Pueblo of San Felipe* (Menasha, Wis., 1932) and *The Pueblo of Santo Domingo* (Menasha, 1935); Charles H. Lange, *Cochiti* (Austin, 1959). My own observations and philosophical interpretation lead me to believe that there is no parallel here with the ancient deity religions of Asia Minor and Egypt, of Graeco-Roman mythology, or that of Aztec Mexico, much less with Judaeo-Christian religious concepts. Hence I studiously avoid any such confusing terminology as God, gods, spirit, worship, altar, priest, penitent, prayer, and the like. They have no relation to pure pueblo belief as such, even if the Indian himself, after early contact with Spanish Catholicity and now with the modern white man's parlance, has adopted such terms as Great Spirit, rain-gods, prayer sticks, etc.

10. Here I am using Keres terminology. The mythology is basically the same in all the pueblos, with local variations as to words and particular functions. The names vary according to language or dialect, even in their specific meaning, but there is always a general similarity in function and even nomenclature, for one linguistic group evidently borrowed from another, and vice versa. Since the tradition was entirely oral, it also suffered variation in neighboring pueblos of the same linguistic group. As ethnologists point out, the informants from each particular pueblo had confused ideas as to the exact nature and function of the "ancient ones."

11. Hackett and Shelby, I, 61.

12. *Ibid.*, 233-35.

13. *Ibid.*, 295. Note the Spanish interpretation of the "sun-father" Pohé-yemo, who made the sun shine when the people came out of Shipapu.

14. *Ibid.*, 345, 361.

15. *Ibid.,* 117, 120, 122, 177, 194. The Indians who did the most harm were those who had been most favored by the friars, and were the most intelligent, wrote Fray Antonio de Sierra, *ibid.,* 59.

16. *AGN,* Tierras: Civil, t. 426.

17. *Ibid.,* II B, Fol. 8.

18. George P. Hammond and Agapito Rey, *Don Juan de Oñate, Colonizer of New Mexico,* 1595-1628 (Albuquerque, 1953), Part I, 559, 562-63.

19. *Ibid.,* 155, 227, 233, 267, 299.

20. *Ibid.,* 146, 267. In the index the editors fail to distinguish fully between Alonso Naranjo, a native of Valladolid, 164, 292, who did not remain in New Mexico, and *Alonso Martines* or *Martín* or *Martín Naranjo,* a native of Estremadura. The latter's son was undoubtedly the Diego Martines Naranjo killed by the Jemez around 1640-1645, Hackett and Shelby, II, p. 266. Perhaps also a Bartolo Martín (?) Naranjo. See note 67, *infra.* It is quite possible that this Spanish or part-Spanish family passed down as *Martín Barba,* for there are no Spaniards named Naranjo for the remainder of the century. See my book, *Origins of New Mexico Familes in the Spanish Colonial Period* (cited hereinafter as *NMF)* (Santa Fe, 1954), 71, 221.

21. Hammond and Rey, part 2, 561.

22. *Ibid.,* 559, 563.

23. *AGN,* Tierras: Civil, t. 426, II A, Fol. 2.

24. *Ibid.,* II B, Fol. 8. There were no Spanish Naranjos at all in the Otermín refugee lists of 1680-1681, save possibly the Martín Barba family. The only man of this name was Pascual Naranjo, a mulatto of the Analco ward in Santa Fe, about whom more later.

25. Hackett and Shelby, II, pp. 211-12. Referring to the archives in 1766, Gov. Cachupín stated that "in the entry which Otermino made around the year eighty-three *[sic]*. . . he arrested in the pueblo . . . of La Isleta, an Indian called Naranjo." *AGN,* Tierras: Civil, t. 426, III, Fols. 74-75.

26. Hackett and Shelby, II, 245-49. Father Vélez Escalante simply mentions an Indian called Pedro Naranjo, a great idolator and sorcerer, who had come from the upper pueblos to Isleta, sent there by the rebel leaders, BNM, Leg. 3, No. I (20/428). In his written opinion, December 23, 1681, Fray Francisco de Ayeta said: "He is under arrest in this camp, is eighty years of age, and is a consummate sorcerer, and as such is noted and highly esteemed among them, as is proven by his having been found in La Isleta, teaching the diabolical manner and circumstances in which they must dance in their infamous and most obscene juntas (which they call cazinas) . . . . " Hackett and Shelby, II, 308-39. Father Ayeta goes on to relate all that Naranjo divulged to Otermín, but ends by attributing the Revolt to El Popé. But an Indian captive, Juan of Tesuque, declared that the rebel leaders had arranged for the destruction of the Isleta people, and that Naranjo had come down for this purpose. *Ibid.,* 329-30.

27. One Spaniard recalled how Gov. Argüello (1640, 1645) hanged 29 Jemez Indians for allying themselves with the Apache for a rebellion, and imprisoned others for killing a certain Diego Martines Naranjo. Another said he hanged more than forty. They claimed that Gov. Concha in 1650 discovered a plot by the Indians of Isleta, Alameda, San Felipe, Cochiti, and Jemez. They had agreed to turn loose all the Spaniards' horses, which were "the nerve of warfare," for the Apache to grab under pretense of a raid; then the Pueblos would pounce on the Spaniards while they were assembled in prayer on Holy Thursday. As a result nine leaders were hanged and others sold as slaves for ten years. Then, under Gov. Villanueva (1664), six

Piro of Senecú were hanged and others imprisoned for joining the Apache in an ambuscade that killed five Spaniards. Later, all the Piro Pueblos of Las Salinas under Don Estéban Clemente "whom all the kingdom obeyed," plotted a general uprising, likewise planning to surprise the Spaniards on Holy Thursday. But the plot was discovered and the leader was hanged. *Ibid.*, 266, 299-300. Note the title and full name of Don Estéban Clemente; they stamp him as non-Pueblo, another intelligent hybrid full of resentment against the Spaniard.

28. Communication by means of deerskin paintings is a Plains Indian feature. Perhaps the Taos acquired it from their close contact with them.

29. Francisco Xavier and Luis de Quintana, natives respectively of Sevilla and Balmaseda, and Diego López Sambrano, a native New Mexican of Santa Fe, were a trio whom the Indian ritual leaders hated the most. They were the officials who for the last five years under Governors Treviño and Otermín (1675-1680) had gone about destroying kivas and Indian shrines, and severely punishing the ritual leaders. Under Treviño they carried out a terrible witch hunt occasioned by the complaints of the voluble and superstitious Fray Andrés Durán of San Ildefonso. Forty-seven Tewas were arrested for witchcraft, and four of them were hanged for alleged witchcraft and murder. When the leaders were asked why they rebelled, both by Otermín in 1681 and by Vargas in 1692-1693, they referred time and again to this hated trio. For their lives, see *NMF*, 58, 89, 113.

30. In the previous year the Spanish clerk described the knotted cord as being made of thongs of animal hide. Perhaps the "timetable" sent to some other pueblos was on cords made of yucca fiber.

31. The representative of Pohé-yemo at Taos, and therefore himself and/or Domingo Naranjo. He certainly would not have himself identified and then be hanged like the Piro Estéban Clemente mentioned in note 27, *supra.*

32. *Degollados.* A purely Spanish form of execution. It was decapitation by first slitting the throat and then the entire neck.

33. The Pueblos were strictly monogamous. Even if considerable liberty was allowed to the young, until conception took place for a pair, after marriage there was only one wife, and adultery was severely punished. The polygamy offered here is African and Aztec.

34. Pedro Naranjo's entire declaration is in Hackett and Shelby, II, pp. 245-49.

35. Naranjo says that the three spirits went underground, but then adds that one of them *(El Caudi)* remained to give orders with El Popé, and thus *El Caudi* suggests one of the names of the high priest of Tlascala, *Achcautli.* See Fray Gerónimo de Mendieta, *Historia Eclesiástica Indiana* (Mexico, 1870), Lib. 2, Cap. 7. When combined with the other two spirits, we have resemblance to the gods *Omacatl* (two reed) and *Ixtlilton* (little black face) who was also called *Tlaltetecuini* (earth stamper). Or, more significantly, the names of the three spirits recall *Fire* worshipped as a god under the names: *Ixcocauqui, Cuecaltzin, Ueueteotl.* See Arthur J. O. Anderson and Charles E. Dibble, *Florentine Codex*, edition of Fray Bernardino de Sahagún (Santa Fe, 1950), Book I, *The Gods*, Part 2, 14-15, 39, 42. During the Fire Festivals honoring this god, the lords and consuls were elected, and "after these feasts, they forthwith proclaimed war against their foes." *Ibid.* It would be most natural for Naranjo to have an imperfect grasp of names in Aztec-Tlascaltec myth, as received from parents who themselves probably had a garbled memory of them.

36. Bandelier thought that "Copala" was a copyist's error for *Ci-bo-bé*, the Tewa word for *Shipapu. Final Report*, Part 2, 29-30. However, the original texts have *Copala*, and the context calls for it. Vélez Escalante places an accent on the last syllable, *Copalá.* The genesis of the Copala legend can be outlined as follows:

Sixteenth-century writers related legends of the Toltecs, Aztecs, and Chichimecas, as how they had come down from the north in slow stages from a place called *Aztlan* or *Huehuetlalpallan* or *Tlalpallan.* One group on the way down lingered at a place called "Seven Caves." Different friars and colonists heard the story from different natives, and so the legend and the terminology varied, and more so with repetition.

Tlalpala became identified, if incorrectly, with the place of the Seven Caves, and these with the "Seven Cities" of a Portuguese romance which the Spaniards of those times took for history. This is what led Fray Marcos de Niza to look for them in 1539 in the far north whence the Mexican nations had come. But he and Coronado in 1540 were sadly disappointed with the Seven Cities of Cibola, for the mud Zuñi villages had neither glamour nor gold. Yet the Spanish imagination would not give up. There had to be, somewhere in the *north,* that fabulous and rich place of the original inhabitants of Mexico, the birthplace of *"Montezuma,"* as the imperial name had become confused with those of the original leaders and gods of the Mexicans. Its fabled treasures made it *another* Mexico, a *new* Mexico, in the minds of adventurers.

There was a town of *Copala* on the flanks of the Colima range, an area where rich mining operations were going on in the 1530's, and this could have helped confuse it with *Tlalpala.* At any rate, the fortune hunters by the middle of the century were referring to the northern home of the Mexicans as Copala, which Coronado must have missed when he came upon Cibola. This prompted several forays into what is now northern Mexico, the chief of which was Ibarra's "quest of Copala." In 1563 he came upon a populous fertile valley, and reported that he had found the legendary Copala; the place was a disappointment, but the name stuck. In 1582 three friars and some soldiers reached the Rio Grande pueblos and said they had found "the *new* Mexico." Suddenly, the names of Copala and New Mexico became interchangeable. There was a lake into which the Rio Nazas emptied (near Ibarra's Copala), which was given the name "Lago de Nuevo Mexico," and this seems to be where Copala became a lake.

Soon after New Mexico was colonized in 1598, the Lake of Copala became a "fact." In 1605 Oñate had made his famous trip in search of the South Sea and here, wrote Father Zárate Salmerón, "was the first news they had of the lake of Copala, whence it is presumed the Mexicans came who settled New Spain." Oñate's men had asked the natives living near the mouth of the Colorado about this lake of Copala and they, like other natives before them and aferwards, pleased their visitors by describing such a fantastic lake and city toward the north. Thus it became the subject of fireside chats and dreams among the pioneer settlers of New Mexico – and among these were the first and second generations of the black Naranjos. Now a Naranjo was further confusing the legendary Copala with the Pueblo Indians' own mythical place of origin, the Hole of Shipapu. Bandelier and Cushing relate pueblo folktales in which the lake-idea of Copala and the hole-idea of Shipapu have become further confused, particularly among the Jémez and the Zuñi. Bandelier, *Final Report* Part 2, 29-30, 207, 587. But these are relatively modern accretions, not the original myth. Who knows but that they started around 1680?

37. *AGN,* Tierras: Civil, t. 426, II A, Fol. 3. Here I am using the old forms "Joseph" and "Josephe" as found in the manuscripts (in those times pronounced "Josép" and "Josépe," hence the diminutive "Pepe") to distinguish him more easily from the others named "José" in the same narratives.

38. *Ibid.,* II B, Fol. 47

39. *Ibid.,* Fol. 78.

40. Hackett and Shelby, II, 231. Juan of Tesuque, who blamed El Popé for the rebellion, had been an employed servant of Francisco Xavier, the nemesis of the ritual leaders and their kivas. Here it is mentioned that Xavier lost two mulatto slaves at Picuris. These were Francisco Blanco de la Vega, native of Puebla, and María Madrid or "La Mozonga," who was

taken captive with her children and was later rescued by the Vargas forces in 1692. See *NMF*, 307, and "Rendón" in *El Palacio*, LXIV, (May-June, 1957), 180-81.

41. Joseph's entire testimony, Hackett and Shelby, II, 238-42. Sebastián de Herrera Corrales had taken his family up to Taos on a visit, while he and Sargento Mayor Fernando de Chávez went further on to trade with the Ute. Both their families were wiped out by the Taos. On their return the two officers, and a Chávez youth who was with his father, saw what had happened and fled south past the besieged villa of Santa Fe, and caught up with the refugees of the Río Abajo. *NMF*, 21-22, 47. Hence young Joseph must have accompanied Herrera to the Ute country and thus escaped south with him and the two Chávez men.

42. Hackett and Shelby, II, pp. 243-45. Yet, this Lucas might have been what he said, and not Josephe's brother. But strangely enough, Lucas Naranjo was tied in with some Piro Indians in the uprising of 1696.

43. *Ibid.*, 231-32, 249-53.

44. *Ibid.*, I, 12. At the same time Otermín sent another trusted Indian, Juan el Tano, to see what his people were doing in Galisteo; but he returned as the leader of the Tano rebels. *Ibid.*, 12-14. I identify this Juan as the desecrator of the Macana image who was hanged by the Devil in the form of a black giant after having repented his sacrilege, for he fits in perfectly with the Macana leged. See notes 7, *supra*, and 78, *infra*.

45. On October 2, 1680, "Pascual Naranjo, mulatto, pitifully poor, passed muster on foot and without any arms, with a family of wife and six children. He did not sign because of not knowing how." Hackett and Shelby, I, 158. Pascual's wife was María Romero, nicknamed "Cota, la Naranja." This family, and practically all the Analco people, remained at Guadalupe del Paso instead of returning to Santa Fe in 1693. Two of their children married at Guadalupe del Paso in 1692 and 1698, NMF, 80. Most likely another son was the José Naranjo who testified for another former resident of Analco at Guadalupe del Paso in 1692. See note 50, *infra*. Earlier in the century Don Pedro de Chávez had equipped Pascual Naranjo with a cutlass and two horses during a campaign against the wild Indians, Hackett and Shelby, II, 177. Chávez' father, Don Pedro I, had owned a mulatto servant by the name of Diego de Santiago, whom he kept employed at his Rancho del Tunque near San Felipe Pueblo in the 1630s. Diego's wife was Felipilla, most probably from the pueblo, AGN, Inquisición, t. 372, exp. 19, fols. 17-18v. My guess is that Diego de Santiago was a brother of Domingo and/or Pedro Naranjo, and that he and Felipilla were the parents of Pascual Naranjo of Analco and of the mulatto woman living at "the rancho near San Felipe," the mother of the slain Bartolomé Naranjo and his two half-brothers, the Lorenzo boys. Father Vélez Escalante is the only writer who refers to *Tlascaltecas* living in Analco before the Revolt. In 1680 there were eight Analco families designated as "Mexican Indians." Probably, like Pascual Naranjo, they also had Tlascaltec antecedents, in the other two daughters of Don Joseph de Tepeaca and other women in the Oñate lists. It is not impossible that the padre heard this from the descendants of Pascual Naranjo and other such folk, and so was prompted to make the statement.

46. Hackett and Shelby, II, 362-63.

47. *AGN*, Historia, t. 37, No. 6, Fols. 124 *et seq.*

48. In 1631 the young mestizo Gerónimo Pacheco (perhaps the father of this Francisco Pacheco) was a good friend of the young mulatto Diego de Santiago treated in note 45, *supra*. Father Vélez Escalante relates an interesting episode which seems to refer to this Francisco Pacheco. Treating of this submission of the Taos to Gov. Vargas, he mentions Pacheco, but not Josephillo, then goes on to relate this incident which he took from an authentic testimonial of March 1681. It was given at Guadalupe del Paso by Alonso Shimitihua, cousin of the rebel

mestizo Alonso Catiti of Santo Domingo. Gov. Otermín had sent Shimitihua with some other trusted Indians to confer with the rebels and persuade them to make peace. Some of his companions defected to the rebels, and he was made prisoner and taken to Taos. There he witnessed the desecration of a statue of the Virgin Mary together with some Spanish cadavers. This image had been discovered in the house of an Indian "mestizo" married to a Taos woman and nicknamed "el Portugués." Shimitihua later escaped and returned to tell the Spaniards of his adventures, BNM, Leg. 3, No. I (20/428).

49. *AGN*, Historia, t. 37, No. 6. In the 1766 controversy, Gov. Cachupín stated, after consulting the archives, that Vargas in an early entrada found a mestizo (Pacheco) and one of those called Naranjo (Josephillo) at Taos. *AGN*, Tierras: Civil, t. 426, III, Fol. 74v. But then Cachupín confused Josephillo with the Naranjo (Lucas) who led the Tewas, Picuris, and Taos in the Revolt of 1696. *Ibid.* He also said that Vargas made Joseph Naranjo his pet – "Acarició a Joseph Naranjo." *Ibid.*, II B, Fol. 8.

50. On January 19, 1692, a Joseph Naranjo at Guadalupe del Paso had testified that he was 22 years old and had known young Juan de León Brito all his life, for they were reared together, Archives of the Archdiocese of Santa Fe, Diligencias Martrimoniales, 1692, No. 3. The León Britos were also "Mexican Indians" from Analco in Santa Fe, hence this Joseph Naranjo must be a son of Pascual Naranjo. See note 46, *supra.*

51. *AGN*, Historia, t. 38, Pt. I, Fol. 72; Vélez Escalante, BNM, Leg. 3, No. I (20/428). Gov. Cachupín mistakenly identified him as Joseph Naranjo. *Ibid.;* Tierras: Civil, t. 426, III, Fol. 74v.

52. Spanish Archives of New Mexico, State Records Center and Archives, Santa Fe (cited hereinafter as SANM), No. 60a; *Old Santa Fe*, III (October 1916), 368.

53. Lucas was clearly implicated by the declarations of several witnesses, SANM, No. 60a; *Old Santa Fe*, III, 359-65. "Su primer motor de este levantamiento nombrado Naranjo." AGN, Historia, t. 38, Fols. 50-52.

54. *AGN*, Tierras: Civil, t. 426, II A, Fol. 3; II B, Fols. 8-8v. The witness was wrong concerning the last accusation, for the Cuartelejo episode took place many years later when Joseph Naranjo was already a trusted and sincere ally of the Spaniards. But it is evident that Naranjo had left an enviable reputation as a linguist.

55. Letter of Father Garaycocchea, Zuñi, May 28, 1700. Here the padre refers to him as Joseph López Naranjo. BNM, Leg. 3, No. I (20/428).

56. This declaration and the certifications which follow are all written in the same clear hand, including all signatures with their rubrics. They are no doubt a copy of originals. Joseph's signature and rubric are obviously a deliberate sham by the copyist, for he could not sign his name in 1681, nor afterwards in his declarations of 1702, 1719, 1720. SANM, Nos. 84, 301.

57. AGN, Tierras: Civil, t. 426, Fols. 37-38. The year is thus written out for 1698, a mistake by the mid-eighteenth century copyist. Fray Agustín de Colina, in 1704, substantiates Naranjo's statement that he had indeed saved the lives of the padres when they went to the Hopi pueblos in 1700, BNM, Leg. 5, No. 5, Leg. 7, No. I, Fols. 42-43.

58. SANM, Nos. 301, 308.

59. Bancroft Library, University of California, Berkeley, New Mexico Originals (cited hereinafter as NMO), 1702. In 1766 Gov. Cachupín stated from the archives that Joseph Naranjo had been useful to Vargas, who commissioned him in these enterprises to the extent of sending him to Zuni and the Hopi pueblos, and naming him Major War-Captain of all the Indians "so that he might with greater authority be a part of the entire reduction." AGN, Tierras: Civil, t. 426, III, Fols. 75-75v.

60. SANM, No. 84.

61. Vélez Escalante, BNM, Leg. 3, No. I (20/428).

62. SANM, No. 99.

63. AGN, Provincias Internas, t. 36, Pt. 4, Fols. 359v-368.

64. Padrón de la Parroquia de Santa Cruz de los Espanoles, 1707, BNM, Leg. 6, No. I (25/487).

65. *NMF*, 241.

66. SANM, No. 154.

67. *Ibid.*, No. 199.

68. NMO, 1715.

69. The name is carved in large letters, JOSEPH NARANJO, without any date. It bears no relation to a much later carving beneath it, of 1774. Photo reproductions in John M. Slater, *El Morro, Inscription Rock* (Los Angeles, 1961), Plate 36, 93. It could have been carved for Naranjo by some literate companion when he traveled back and forth between Acoma and Zuñi as Alcalde Mayor of these two pueblos from 1700 to 1703; or else during the Ulibarrí campaigns of 1701 or 1709, when the latter left his inscriptions on the rock. Naranjo's name is about a hundred feet from them. There is another Naranjo signature next to an inscription of 1620: BARTOLOM NARANJO, with a rubric and a nick above the "M." *Ibid.*, Plate 83, 120. Slater and others have deciphered it as "Bartolome Naranjo." To me it looks rather like an abbreviated "Bartolo Martín Naranjo," hence possibly a literate individual of the early seventeenth century, perhaps another son of Alonso Martín Naranjo. Cf. note 20, *supra.*

70. SANM, Nos. 301, 308.

71. AGN, Tierras: Civil, t. 426, II B, Fols. 47, 49, 75v *et seq.*

72. *NMF*, p. 241.

73. AGN, Tierras: Civil, t. 426, II B, Fols. 70v-74, 79v.

74. *Ibid.*, Fols. 76, 78.

75. *Ibid.*, Fols. 82-84.

76. *NMF*, pp. 241-42.

77. See note 7, *supra.* Gov. Vargas must have heard the Macana tradition of 1680 from the refugee colonists at Guadalupe del Paso, for, to heighten the drama of his own reconquest of Santa Fe in 1693, he referred to it in his official report as actually happening at this time. Vélez Escalante, BNM, Leg. 3, No. I (20/428). This Macana tradition is entirely distinct from that of La Conquistadora. See my books on this particular Marian image, *Our Lady of the Conquest* (Santa Fe, 1948) and *La Conquistadora: The Autobiography of an Ancient Statue* (Paterson, N.J., 1954).

78. White, *Santo Domingo*, pp. 178-79. This seems to be the end of the original tale, in which God-Friar-Spaniard has been pitted against Pohé-yemo-Medicineman-Indian.

79. *Ibid.* This last paragraph is a confused reference to the Christian Last Judgment and Salvation, regarding which the Indian expresses his doubt by the last remark. But even this is a very old Spanish expression: "El día que pare la mula."

NOTES

DeVargas' Negro Drummer

1. Archdiocese of Santa Fe: *Informationes Matrimoniales* (1689), No. 1.

2. *Ibid.* (1692), No. 1.

3. *Ibid.* (1697), No. 7. She seems to have been the third and last wife of Captain Juan Madrid – *Ibid.* (1690), No. 2; (1703), No. 1; (1710), No. 13. She was also a member of the confraternity of La Conquistadora – Fray Angelico Chavez, *Our Lady of the Conquest* (Santa Fe: 1948), 67.

4. *Ibid.* (1697), No. 7.

5. *Ibid.* (1694), No. 32.

6. J.M. Espinosa, *First Expedition of Vargas into New Mexico, 1692* (Albuquerque, 1940), 50.

7. Museum of New Mexico: *Spanish Archives*, I, No. 730. Antonio Lucero's land was Bounded on the north by an arroyo coming down from the *sierra*, on the east by the path leading to Tesuque, on the west by the land of his father, Juan Lucero de Godoy, and on the south by the Santa Fe River bordering on the land of Alonso Maese – *Ibid.*, No. 423. Hence, Rodriguez's property was next to Lucero's but on the south side of the river. Alonso Maese was the stepfather of Rodriguez's wife, Juana de Apodaca or Maese.

8. *Inf. Matrim.* (1698), No. 6.

9. *Sp. Arch.*, II, No. 94a.

10. *Ibid.*, No. 99.

11. *Ibid.*, No. 1028.

12. Archdiocese of Santa Fe, unnclassified document.

13. New Mexico Archives, A.G.N., Mexico, Inquisición, 735.

14. *Sp. Arch.*, II, Nos. 250, 400, 538.

York

1. Bernard DeVoto (ed.), *The Journals of Lewis and Clark* (Boston, 1953).

2. Albert and Jane Salisbury, *Two Captains West* (Seattle, 1950).

3. John C. Ewers, "The Plains Indian Reactions to the Lewis and Clark Expedition," *Montana, The Magazine of Western History*, XVI (Winter, 1966), No. 1.

4. Albert Salisbury, *Ibid.*

5. DeVoto, *Ibid.*

6. *Ibid.*

7. *Ibid.*

8. *Ibid.*

9. Salisbury and Salisbury, *Ibid.*

10. Ella E. Clark, "Sesquicentennial Remembrances," *Montana, The Magazine of Western History*, V (Spring, 1955), No. 2.

THE FOUR BLACK UNITS

The Twenty-fifth Regiment of Infantry

1. The first regiment of this number and name was raised in Connecticut and organized under the act approved June 26, 1812; it was discontinued by the act approved March 3, 1815. The officers retained in service were transferred to other regiments May 17, and the rest discharged June 15, 1815, with three months' pay. From brevets conferred upon its officers it would appear that the regiment participated in the battles of Chrystler's Fields, Upper Canada, Nov. 11, 1813; Chippewa Falls, U.C., July 5, 1814, and Niagara Falls (Lundy's Lane) U.C., July 25, 1814.

Under the provisions of the act of July 28, 1866, the Second Battalion of the Sixteenth Infantry was constituted the Twenty-fifth Regiment, which was merged in the Eighteenth by the Act of March 3, 1869.

THE FORTS

Quitman: The Worst Post at Which I Ever Served

1. Zenas R. Bliss, *Memoirs,* 1854-1894 (unpub., The University of Texas typescript), 220.

2. Albert D. Richardson, *Beyond the Mississippi* (New York, 1867), 236.

3. Report of Jos. K. F. Mansfield, colonel and inspector general, United States Army, regarding his inspection of the department of New Mexico during the summer and fall of the year 1853, as quoted in Richard K. McMaster, "The Mansfield Report," *Password,* IV, July, 1959, No. 3, 110.

4. Eagle Springs is located 5 miles west southwest of Hot Wells, which is 23 miles southeast of Sierra Blanca on the Southern Pacific RR. It is also 3½ miles south southwest of Torbert, 19 miles from Sierra Blanca on the SP RR. Remains of rock walls there may be those of the stage station or later construction connected with mining activities.

5. Brigadier General Garland, Hqs. Dept. of NM to Adjutant General of Army, 5 June 1854, Letters Sent (LS), Letter Book (LB) Dept. of NM. All references to Letters Sent and Letters Received are from originals in National Archives, Old Army Branch (OAB). Also Report of Secretary of War, 1854, Executive Document, 33rd Congress, Second Session.

6. General David Twiggs, Hqs. Dept of Texas to War Dept., 24 August 1858. Report of Secretary of War, House Executive Document No. 2, Thirty-fifth Congress, Second Session, 6 Dec. 1858, 261. Twiggs to Adjutant General (AG), 9 August 1858.

7. Orders 18, Hqs. Dept of Texas, 23 July 1858. Order Book, Dept. of Texas, OAB.

8. Returns, Eighth Infantry Regt., September 1858. All references to designations of units moving to or from Ft. Quitman, strengths of units or names of commanders are from respective company, regimental, or post returns on file in National Archives, for the month and year indicated and will not be further footnoted.

9. Orders 19, Hq. Dept. of Texas, 8 September 1858. Letter Captain A.T. Lee, Eighth Inf. to AG, Dept. of Texas, 1 April 1859.

10. Special Orders (SO) 108, Hq. Dept. of Texas, 22 November 1858.

11. Letter Twiggs to AG, 5 February 1859 and 16 February 1859.

12. Letter Second Lt. J.G. Taylor, to AG Dept. of Texas, 30 June 1859. Letter Major Bomford, Annual Report to Hq. Dept. of Texas, 1 July 1859.

13. George G. Smith, "Parson's Progress to California," *The Quarterly* (Historical Society of Southern California), XXI (June-September, 1939), No. 2, 59-60.

14. Roscoe P. and Margaret B. Conkling, *The Butterfield Overland Mail,* 2 vols. (Glendale, California, 1947), II, 41-42.

15. Returns, Co. F, Ninth Cavalry, December 1867.

16. Regt. returns, Ninth Cavalry, January 1868.

17. SO 36, Hqs. District of Texas, 25 February 1868; SO 44, 10 March 1868.

18. Lydia Spencer Lane, *I Married a Soldier* (Philadelphia, 1893), 186.

19. Co. and Post Returns.

20. Letter Commanding Officer Ft. Quitman to Hqs. Dept. of Texas, July 1870.

21. Letter Major Morrow to Inspector General, Dept. of Texas, 6 July 1870.

22. Organization and post returns.

23. Letter Commanding Officer Ft. Quitman to Commanding General Dept. of Texas, 14 February 1872.

24. Letter Bentzoni to Hqs. Dept. of Texas, Report of Inspection, December 1872.

25. Circular 8, 221.

26. Letter Bentzoni to Assistant Adjutant General, Dept. of Texas, 27 November 1875.

27. SO 224, Hq. Dept. of Texas, 12 December 1876.

28. GO 11, Hqs. Ft. Quitman, 5 January 1877.

29. Third Endorsement by Hqs. Military Division of Missouri, 23 October 1877 to Letter First Lt. L. H. Rucker, Ninth Cav. to Adjutant General, New Mexico District, 4 October 1877.

30. Letter Commanding General Division of Missouri to Adjutant General's Office, 5 December 1877.

31. Report of Commanding Officer, District of New Mexico to Secretary of War, 6 September 1879, as published in *Annual Report of Secretary of War,* 19 Nov., 1879.

32. Orders 25, Hqs. Fort Davis, 14 February 1880.

33. Regimental returns, 10th Cav.

34. Mrs. O.L. Shipman, "Fort Quitman was Key Station in Colorful Frontier Days," *El Paso Times,* October 17, 1947.

35. GO 5, Hqs. Dept. of Texas, 1 February 1881.

36. Orders 7, Hqs. Fort Davis, 11 January 1881.

37. SO 74, Hqs. Fort Davis, 7 April 1881.

38. SO 202, Hqs. Fort Davis, 26 September 1881.

39. Letter Adj. Ft. Davis to Nordstrom, 12 April 1882.

40. Regimental returns, Tenth Cav.

41. Fort Quitman was no longer needed with the establishment of Camp Rice, whose subsequent location became Fort Hancock. For the story of Fort Hancock see George Ruhlen, "Fort Hancock: Last of the Frontier Posts," *Password*, IV (January, 1959), No. 1, 19-30.

THE CAVALRY

The Tenth Cavalry in the Early Days

1. The term Company was changed to Troop on January 1, 1881.

2. During the Geronimo campaign of 1885-86 Lt. Colonel (Brevet Brigadier General) George A. Forsyth, Fourth Cavalry, had command of the field troops of the Arizona Southwest District with headquarters at Fort Huachuca.

3. A resume of Major Carr's military career, including the Cibicu Fight of August 30, 1881, appears in the article by Thomas Peterson, Jr., "Eugene Asa Carr: War Eagle" *Arizoniana*, II (Fall, 1961), No. 3.

4. A letter of more recent times from the files of Presidio of San Francisco also illustrates the paper battles, frequently ludicrous, when personalities clash. In this matter Capatin M.S. Crissy, Coast Artillery Corps, at Fort Winfield Scott in the Presidio area submitted a fifteen-dollar charge to the post surgeon for services of a battery bull to a hospital cow. The formal reply to the claim is of interest.

Post Hospital
May 10, 1912

Sir:

I have the honor to acknowledge receipt of the enclosed bill and to say that the services of a bull for the hospital cow were neither requested nor desired by me or anyone connected with the Hospital.

. . . If a kind and virtuous cow cannot be left at large on a military reservation without the liability of being the victim of the unsought attention of a licentious bull, it is thought that the owners of the cow ought to be awarded not only consequential damages for the injuries inflicted, but exemplary damages as well.

Very Respectfully,

E.B. Frick
Lieut. Col. Med. Corps, U.S.A.
Surgeon

5. The camp was a third and permanent location established in 1859 by Captain Earl Van Dorn, Second Cavalry (subsequently a major general C.S.A. in the Civil War) and named for Lieutenant Charles Radziminski of the Second who had recently died of consumption.

For the protection of the horse herd when out grazing the animals were taught to gallop into camp at the slightest alarm, thus avoiding a possible stampede and loss to marauding Indians.

Troops from this camp engaged in a defeat of the Comanche. Among the wounded by the savages' arrows was Lieutenant Fitzhugh Lee, who a few years later became a Confederate general. The arrowhead was never removed from the officer's chest.

In 1941 while attending an artillery firing school at Fort Sill, I, together with my wife Myrtle and two daughters Katie and Jeanne, visited the site of the old camp. We found bone buttons, hand-made nails, parts of an iron kettle, and pieces of champagne bottles. The latter articles evidenced that soldiering was not all drudgery and hardship in the early days. Also the well was located.

6. Grierson Hill, Davidson Hill, and Pratt Hill are land features on the Fort Sill Military Reservation named for Tenth Cavalry officers.

7. Major George W. Schofield was active at Fort Sill both in the field and as frequent post commander during the Tenth Cavalry station there. He was a younger brother of Major General John Schofield, who for a period in 1868-1869 was secretary of war and in the early 1890s the commanding general of the army.

Major Schofield was interested in the field howitzer, and had patented a revolver known as the Schofield-Smith & Wesson.

While with the Sixth Cavalry at Fort Apache, Arizona, he committed suicide with one of his revolvers on December 12, 1882. The facts brought out at the board of inquiry showed that he had become a subject of deep melancholy since the death of his wife a few years before. He was buried in the post cemetery. The records state that his remains were disinterred on November 30, 1884 and removed to some other locality, but not a military cemetery. In 1918 there was a gravestone propped up in a corner of the Fort Apache cemetery. It had the name of a lieutenant colonel, but I have no further recollection

8. Henry O. Flipper was graduated in 1877 from the Military Academy and assigned to the Tenth Cavalry. After a brief service in the Indian wars, he was courts-martialed for carelessness in handling a commissary and dismissed from the army.

Upon leaving the service he spent thirty-seven years as a civil and mining engineer in the southwest and Mexico. "Colonel" Bill Greene of Arizona mining and cattle prominence hired him in the early 1900s. Albert B. Fall (involved in the Teapot Dome oil scandal while Secretary of Interior) employed him in 1908, where he remained at El Paso until 1919. That year he went to Washington and served in Fall's subcommittee. In 1921 when Fall became Secretary of Interior, Flipper was appointed as assistant to the secretary, serving until 1923. Thereafter he worked for petroleum companies in Central and South America until 1931. He died at Atlanta, Georgia in 1940; aged 84 years. "Negro Frontierman," Texas Western College Press, 1963, contains a sketch of his career together with Flipper's memoirs for the period 1877-1916.

ACTION ON THE FRONTIER

Colonel B. H. Grierson's Victorio Campaign

1. *New York Times,* October 29, 1880, 4:4, 5.

2. General John Pope was anxious to have the Tenth Cavalry join forces with the already fatigued and demoralized troops in New Mexico. Cf. *Army and Navy Journal,* XVII, No. 43, whole No. 875 (May 29, 1880), 884.

3. R.K. Grierson, "Journal kept on the Victorio Campaign in 1880." Copy of manuscript made available to the writer, by Mr. Barry Scobee of Fort Davis, Texas.

4. Grierson to wife, letter of August 2, 1880, in Grierson's Collected Papers, Newberry Library, Chicago.

5. J. Bigelow, Jr., "Historical Sketch of the Regiment from its organization to April 5th, 1890, the date of General Grierson's promotion to Brigadier General, U.S. Army." Microfilm copy from U.S. National Archives.

6. G.W. Baylor, commenting on an article in an El Paso newspaper, in W.K. Baylor, "The Old Frontier," *Frontier Times,* II, No. 11 (August, 1925), 12.

7. Letter reproduced in A.E. Sweet and J.A. Knox, *On a Mexican Mustang Through Texas* (London, 1884) 525-26.

8. L.L. Byrne to Grierson, letter of October 24, 1880, in Grierson's Collected Papers, Illinois State Historical Library, Springfield.

9. Grierson to J.N. Tyner, U.S. Acting Postmaster General, letter of September 18, 1878, in Grierson's Collected Papers, Newberry Library, Chicago.

10. R.G. Smither to T.N. Vincent, letter of August 22, 1880, in Grierson's Collected Papers, Newberry Library, Chicago.

11. R.G.Smither to editor of *Indianapolis News,* letter of August 30, 1880, in Grierson's Collected Papers, Newberry Library, Chicago.

12. U.S. Secretary of War, "Report," Forty-sixth Cong., Third session, House Exec. Doc. 1, Pt. 2 (Washington, 1881), 162.

13. *Ibid.*

14. *Army and Navy Journal,* XV, No. 41, whole No. 769 (May 18, 1878), 666.

15. *Army and Navy Journal,* XVII, No. 34, whole No. 866 (March 27, 1880), 683.

16. *Galveston Daily News,* October 5, 1880, 1:5.

17. J. Pope, "Report," 46 Cong., 2 sess., House Exec. Doc. 1, Pt. 2 (Washington, 1880), 85.

18. *Galveston Daily News,* October 20, 1880, 1:5.

The Battle at Rattlesnake Springs

1. From the diary of Robert Grierson on the day following the fight: "I wish Papa had gone with the troops yesterday after the Indians – the movements could've been decidedly better made – a lot of Indians ought to've been captured. Papa wishes he'd gone, but he supposed the movements would be made according to his directions."

The Thornburgh Battle with the Utes on Milk Creek

1. Report of Secretary of War, in *Messages and Documents, War Dept.,* 1879-1880, I, 9.

2. *Ibid.*

3. Capt. J.S. Payne, "The Campaign Against the Utes," in *United Service,* (Jan., 1880).

4. *Ibid.*

5. Report of Secretary of Interior, in *Messages and Documents, Interior Dept.,* 1879-1880, I, 93.

6. Report of Secretary of War, *op cit.*

7. Testimony of Henry James, in relation to the Ute Indian Outbreak, in *House Misc. Doc. 38,* 46 Cong., 2 Sess., 204.

8. Report of Secretary of War, *op cit.*

9. Testimony of Capt. J.S. Payne, in relation to the Ute Indian Outbreak in *Misc. Doc.* 38, *op cit.,* 172.

10. Testimony of Lieut. S.A. Cherry, in relation to the Ute Indian Outbreak, in *Misc. Doc.* 38, 67.

11. Testimony of Henry James, *op cit.,* 204.

12. J.S. Payne, "The Campaign Against the Utes," *op cit.*

13. Testimony of Lieut. Cherry, *op cit.,* 64.

14. Testimony of Capt. Payne, *op cit.,* 172.

15. This canyon, known as Coal Creek Canyon, through which the road to Meeker ran, followed Coal Creek, a tributary of White River.

16. Testimony of Capt. Payne, *op cit.,* 172.

17. Testimony of Lieut. Cherry, *op cit.,* 64.

18. Report of Secretary of War, *op cit.*

19. *Ibid.*

20. M.W. Rankin, *Reminiscences of Frontier Days,* 67. Mr. Rankin, who is a relative of Joe Rankin, the scout, reached the scene several days after the battle.

21. *Ibid.*

22. Testimony of Lieut. Cherry, *op cit.,* 70.

23. Testimony of Capt. Payne, *op cit.,* 177.

24. Capt. J.S. Payne. "The Campaign Against the Utes," *op cit.*

25. Testimony of Capt. Payne, *op cit.,* 173.

26. Testimony of Lieut. Cherry, *op cit.,* 64.

27. Testimony of Capt. Payne, *op cit.,* 173.

28. Testimony of Lieut. Cherry, *op cit.*, 64.

29. *Ibid.,* 69.

30. Special Telegram, *Denver Daily News,* October 2, 1879. *History of Denver* (Baskin, 1880), 141. M.W. Rankin, *op cit.,* 68.

31. J.S. Payne, "Campaign Against the Utes," *op cit.*

32. Testimony of Capt Payne, *op cit.,* 173.

33. Testimony of Lieut. Cherry, *op. cit.,* 65.

34. *Ibid.*

35. M.W. Rankin, *op. cit.*, 68; Thos. F. Dawson, *History of the Ute War*, 22.

36. Testimony of Lieut. Cherry, *op. cit.*, 65; N. Robinson, "The Ute Massacre," *Frank Leslie's Popular Monthly* (Feb. 1880), 150.

37. A.M. Startzell, "Thornburgh Massacre at Meeker," mss. in Colorado State Historical Society Files.

38. Testimony of Lieut. Cherry, *op. cit.*, 65.

39. *Ibid.*, 69.

40. J.S. Payne, "Campaign Against the Utes," *op. cit.*

41. Testimony of Capt. Payne, *op. cit.*, 174.

42. Testimony of Lieut. Cherry, *op. cit.*, 65.

43. *Senate Ex. Doc. 83* 46 Cong., 2d Sess.

44. Testimony of Chief Jack in relation to the Ute Indian Outbreak, in *Misc. Doc.* 38, 193.

45. *Senate Ex. Doc. 31*, 46 Cong., 2d Sess., 14.

46. Testimony of Capt. Payne, *op. cit.*, 174.

47. *Ibid.*

48. M.W. Rankin, *op. cit.*, 69.

49. J.S. Payne, "Campaign Against the Utes, *op. cit.*

50. Testimony of Lieut. Cherry, *op. cit.*, 66.

51. Theo. F. Rodenbough, *Uncle Sam's Medal of Honor*, 359. This brave feat has been ascribed to a Mr. Donovan, but careful search of the official records fails to substantiate the statement.

52. J.S. Payne, "Campaign Against the Utes, *op. cit.*

53. Sidney Jocknick, *Early Days on the Western Slope of Colorado*, 186.

54. Theo. F. Rodenbough, *op. cit.*, 355.

55. *Ibid.*, 356.

56. Testimony of Capt. Payne, *op. cit.* 179.

57. M.W. Rankin, *op. cit.*, 69.

58. Testimony of Capt. Payne, *op. cit.*, 175.

59. J.S. Payne, "Campaign Against the Utes," *op. cit.*

60. Testimony of Capt. Payne, *op. cit.*, 175; Theo F. Rodenbough, *op. cit.*, 362.

61. M.W. Rankin, *op. cit.*, 70.

62. J.S. Payne, "Campaign Against the Utes," *op. cit.* Theo F. Rodenbough, *op. cit.*, 362.

63. J.S. Payne, "Campaign Against the Utes," *op. cit.*

64. John Keith, in a letter written by him to Albert W. Johnson. Ms. in the Colorado Historical Society files.

65. J.S. Payne, "Campaign Against the Utes." *op. cit.*

66. John Keith, *op. cit.*

67. M.W. Rankin, *op. cit.,* 70.

68. Testimony of Lieut. Cherry, *op. cit.,* 66.

69. *Ibid.*

70. Testimony of Capt. Payne, *op. cit.,* 176.

71. M.W. Rankin, *op. cit.,* 71.

72. *Ibid.;* J.S. Payne, "Campaign Against the Utes," *op. cit.;* Theo F. Rodenbough, *op. cit.,* 366.

73. John Keith, *op. cit.*

74. M.W. Rankin, *op. cit.,* 71.

75. *Senate Ex. Doc. 31, op. cit.,* 106-108.

76. *Ibid.*

77. M.W. Rankin, *op. cit.,* 72.

78. *Senate Ex. Doc. 31, Op. cit.,* 108.

79. J.S. Payne, "Campaign Against the Utes," *op. cit.*

80. M.W. Rankin, *op. cit.,* 73; Sidney Jocknick, *op. cit.,* 186.

81. E.V. Sumner, "Beseiged by the Utes," *Century Magazine* (Oct. 1891), 837.

82. J.S. Payne, "Campaign Against the Utes," *op. cit.*

83. Gen. Wesley Merritt, "Three Indian Campaigns," in *Harper's New Monthly Magazine* (April, 1890), 736.

84. *Ibid.*

85. J.S. Payne, "Campaign Against the Utes," *op. cit.*

THE OFFICERS AND THE ENLISTED MEN

The Negro Soldier and His Officers

1. Brainerd Dyer, "The Treatment of Colored Union Troops by the Confederates, 1861-1865," *The Journal of Negro History*, XX (July 1935), 285-86.

2. U.S., *Congressional Globe,* 39th Cong., 1st Sess., 1866, 36:1, 265-66; and 36:2, 1379.

3. Recommendation from George W. Howard, AAG, 18 February 1866, Box 1, Folder 1, Shafter Papers, Stanford University Library.

4. John Nankivell, *History of the Twenty-Fifth Cavalry*, 7.

5. S. E. Whitman, *The Troopers, An Informal History of the Plains Cavalry, 1865-1890,* (New York, 1962), 34.

6. Bigelow, *Santiago Campaign,* 23-24.

7. Glass, *History of the Tenth Cavalry,* 17-18; Hutcheson, "The Ninth Regiment of Cavalry," *Army of the United States . . . ,* 282-83.

8. Haley, *Fort Concho,* 263-64, quoting from the "Medical History, Fort Concho," CCCI, 124, 147, 177.

9. Frances M. A. Roe, *Army Letters From an Officer's Wife, 1871-1888* (New York, 1909), 55, 103.

10. Letter from E. O. C. Ord to Shafter, April 1, 1876, Box 5, Folder 44, Shafter Papers, Stanford University Library.

11. Haley, *Fort Concho,* 270, quoting General Ord but giving no citation.

12. Report from Col. George L. Andrews to the AAG, Dept. of Texas, November 21, 1872, copy on file Fort Davis NHS.

13. *Ibid.*

14. Armes, *Ups and Downs,* 307.

15. Wheeler, *Buffalo Days,* 250-52.

16. Armes, *Ups and Downs,* 484.

17. Letter from E. O. C. Ord to Shafter, October 3, 1877, Box 1, Folder 3, Shafter Papers, Stanford University Library.

18. Sheffy, "Letters . . . of . . . Baldwin . . ." *Panhandle-Plains,* XI, 24.

19. Mills, *My Story,* 46.

20. Glass, *History of the Tenth Cavalry,* 140-41.

21. Henry O. Flipper, *The Colored Cadet at West Point, Autobiography* (New York, 1878), 2-13, 30.

22. *Ibid.,* 35, 288; George L. Andrews, "West Point and the Colored Cadets," *The International Review,* IX (November 1880), 479.

23. Flipper, *Colored Cadet,* 135.

24. Henry O. Flipper, *Negro Frontiersman: The Western Memoirs of Henry O. Flipper,* ed. Theodore D. Harris (El Paso, 1963), 8.

25. *Ibid.,* 2-3.

26. *Ibid.,* 8.

27. *Ibid.,* 20.

28. Heitman, *Historical Register and Dictionary,* I, 156.

29. Flipper, *Negro Frontiersman,* 39.

30. Heitman, *Historical Register and Dictionary,* I, 1066, Riddick; "Negro Policy of the United States Army," *Journal of Negro History,* XXXIV (January 1949), 19-20.

31. Steward, *The Colored Regulars,* 88-89; Cashin, *Under Fire With The Tenth Cavalry,* 289.

32. Scobee, *Fort Davis Texas,* 105-106.

33. David G. Mandelbaum, *Soldier Groups and Negro Soldiers* (Berkeley, 1952), 92. The same thought is expressed in Reddick, "Negro Policy of the Army," *Journal of Negro History*, XXXIV, 18-19.

34. Nankivell, *History of the Twenty-Fifth Infantry*, 6.

35. U.S., *Congressional Globe*, 39th Cong., 1st Sess., 1866, 36:2, 1385.

36. *Ibid.*, 1380.

37. Sheffy, "Letters. . . . of . . . . Baldwin . . . ." *Panhandle-Plains*, XI, 13.

38. Pratt, *Battlefield and Classroom*, 7.

39. Don Rickey, Jr., *Forty Miles a Day on Beans and Hay, The Enlisted Soldier Fighting the Indian Wars*, (Norman, 1963), 19.

40. Rickey, "The Negro Regiments," 4.

41. *Ibid.*

42. National Park Service, "Private Bentley's Buzzard," ms, 2.

43. Rickey, *Forty Miles a Day . . .*, 17-32.

44. Hutcheson, "The Ninth Cavalry of Infantry," *Army of the United States . . .* 281-82.

45. Nankivell, *History of the Twenty-Fifth Infantry*, 18, quoting from an inspection report by the AIG, Dept. of Texas, 1870.

46. Erna Risch, *Quartermaster Support of the Army, A History of the Corps, 1775-1939* (Washington, 1962), 489-90.

47. Report of the Post Surgeon, Fort Davis, March, 1869, copy on file at Fort Davis NHS.

48. *Ibid.*, May 1873, June 1875.

49. Rayford W. Logan, *The Betrayal of the Negro, from Rutherford B. Hayes to Woodrow Wilson* (New York, 1965), 325. In 1870 only 18.6 percent of American Negroes were literate; in 1890, 55.5 percent were.

50. Illustrations of this are to be found in Glass, *History of the Tenth Cavalry*, 17-18, and in any of the photographs of the companies of these regiments.

51. Report of the Post Surgeon, Fort Davis, April, 1877, copy on file at Fort Davis NHS.

52. John Bigelow, Jr., *On the Boody Trail of Geronimo* (Los Angeles, 1958), 197-98.

53. Drawings in Box 6, Folder 55, Shafter Papers, Stanford University Library.

54. Report of the Post Surgeon, Fort Davis, June, 1876, copy on file at Fort Davis NHS.

55. Risch, *Quartermaster Support*, 487-89.

56. Robert G. Athearn, *William Tecumseh Sherman and the Opening of the West* (Norman, 1956), 63.

57. Ray Brandes, *Frontier Military Posts of Arizona* (Globe, 1960), 35.

58. Report of Post Surgeon, Fort Davis, January, 1869, copy on file at Fort Davis NHS.

59. *Ibid.*, September, 1873.

60. Roe, *Army Letters,* 65.

61. Scobee, *Fort Davis Texas,* 110, quoting Col. Daniel B. Cullinane.

62. *Ibid.,* 111.

63. Jocelyn, *Mostly Alkali,* 320.

64. Armes, *Ups and Downs,* 460, 508.

65. Report of Post Surgeon, Fort Davis, July 1873, copy on file at Fort Davis NHS.

66. *Ibid.,* March 1870, March 1874, and July 1876.

67. *Report of the Secretary of War, 1868,* 974; *1869,* 422-23; *1870,* 273; *1871,* 328-39; *1872,* 300-301; *1873,* 212-13.

68. *Ibid.,* 1874, 232.

69. Rickey, *Forty Miles a Day,* 159.

70. This summary of diseases is based mostly on the Reports of Post Surgeon, Fort Davis, 1868-78, copies on file Fort Davis NHS.

71. Brandes, *Military Posts of Arizona,* 35-39.

72. U.S., Congress, Senate, *Discharge of Enlisted Men of the Twenty-Fifth United States Infantry, Brownsville Affray, August 13 and 14, 1906,* 59th Cong., 2d Sess., 1907, Senate Doc. 155, 329.

73. *Report of the Secretary of War, 1875,* 5; Whitman, *The Troopers,* 145; Haley, *Fort Concho,* 270.

74. Martha Summerhayes, *Vanished Arizona, Recollections of My Army Life* (Philadelphia, 1963), 230; Bigelow, *On the Bloody Trail,* 62.

75. Report of Post Surgeon, Fort Davis, August, 1879, copy on file Fort Davis NHS.

76. Report by Col. George Andrews to the AAG, Dept. of Texas, November 21, 1872, copy on file Fort Davis NHS.

77. *Report of the Secretary of War, 1867,* 6, 416; and *1868,* 726, 768-69.

78. *Report of the Secretary of War, 1867,* 164-65; *1870,* 41; and *1871,* 7.

79. Whitman, *The Troopers,* 172; Rickey, *Forty Miles a Day,* 143-44.

80. Report of Post Surgeon, Fort Davis, December, 1873, copy on file Fort Davis NHS.

81. *Ibid.,* June 1878 and September 1878.

82. Rickey, *Forty Miles a Day*, 173; Report of Post Surgeon, Fort Davis, January 1869, copy on file Fort Davis NHS.

83. Wheeler, *Buffalo Days,* 250-52.

84. Miles, *My Story,* 109-11.

85. Summerhayes, *Vanished Arizona,* 231-32.

86. Report of Post Surgeon, Fort Davis, May, 1873, copy on file at Fort Davis NHS.

87. *Report of the Secretary of War, 1873,* 6.

88. Roe, *Army Letters,* 65.

89. Rickey, *Forty Miles a Day,* 57, 187.

90. Charles King, *Campaigning With Crook and Stories of Army Life* (New York, 1890), 8.

91. Haley, *Fort Concho*, 262.

92. *Ibid.*, 274-75.

93. *Ibid.*, 277, 284.

94. U.S. Congress, Senate, *Discharge of Enlisted Men of the Twenty-Fifth Infantry*, 409.

95. *Ibid.*

96. Report of Post Surgeon, July, 1876, copy on file at Fort Davis NHS.

97. Utley, *Fort Davis*, 22.

98. U.S., Congress, *Medal of Honor Recipients*, 626, 653.

99. *Ibid.*, 653, 701, 712, 717, 718; Glass, *History of the Tenth Cavalry*, 35-36.

100. *Ibid.*, 676.

Captain Nolan's Lost Troop on the Staked Plains

1. T.B. Gibson, "Texas Rangers Scout After Apache Indians," *Frontier Times* (February, 1934).

SOME HEROIC INDIVIDUALS

The Seminole-Negro Indian Scouts, 1870-1881

1. Melville J. Herskovits has pointed out that Negroes have "mingled with the American Indians on a scale hitherto unrealized." Approximately one-third of the general Negro population in the United States, according to samplings, are of partial Indian ancestry. *The American Negro* (New York, 1928), 3, 9, 16.

2. Dindie Factor (ca. 1874), personal interview, Nacimiento, Coahulla, 1913. Factor is the son of Pompey Factor and the grandson of Scout Hardy Factor; His grandmother was a Biloxi.

3. For discussion of relations between Seminole Indians and Negroes in Florida, see William Hayne Simmons, *Notices of East Florida* (Charleston, 1822), 44-45, 50, 76; George A. McCall, Letters from the Frontiers (Philadelphia, 1868), 160; Jedidiah Morse, *A Report to the Secretary of War on Indian Affairs* (New Haven, 1822), 149-50, 309-11; John Lee Williams, *The Territory of Florida* (New York, 1837), 214; William Kennedy, *Texas, Its Rise, Progress and Prospects*, 2 vols. (London, 1841), I, 350; *American State Papers: Documents, Legislative and Executive, of the Congress of the United States, from the First Session of the Fourteenth to the Second Session of the Nineteenth Congress, Inclusive, Commencing December 4, 1815, and Ending March 3, 1827; Class II, Indian Affairs, Volume II* (Washington, 1834), 412; *American State Papers: Documents, Legislative and Executive, of the Congress of the United States, From the First and Second Sessions of the Twenty-fourth Congress, Commencing January 12, 1836,*

and Ending February 25, 1837; Military Affairs, Volume VI (Washington, 1861), 465, 533-34.

4. John T. Sprague, *The Origin, Progress, and Conclusion of the Florida War* (New York, 1848), 81, 100, 166, 309; *Army and Navy Chronicle,* IV, 12, 80, quoting from New Orleans *Bulletin,* January 7, 1837; Lieutenant Colonel W.S. Harney, Fort Mellon, East Florida, to Major General T. S. Jessup, dated May 4, 1837 (photostat in possession of Florida Historical Society, St. Augustine); journal of Captain J. Rhett Motte (ms. in possession of Florida Historical Society), 255.

5. See appropriate sections in Grant Foreman, *Indian Removal* (Norman, 1933) and The Five Civilized Tribes (Norman, 1934).

6. Documentary material on the kidnapping of Seminole Negroes is to be found in the Seminole Files, Indian Office, Department of the Interior, National Archives, Washington, D.C., and in the Quartermaster General's Office, War Department National Archives. See also Grant Foreman, *Pioneer Days in the Early Southwest* (Cleveland, 1926), 174, and Grant Foreman, *Advancing the Frontier* (Norman, 1933), 69.

7. The history of the Seminole Indians and Negroes in Mexico is treated in the author's "The Seminole in Mexico, 1850-1861," *Hispanic-American Historical Review*, XXXI, 1-36. The chief printed sources on the flight of the Seminole from the United States and their Indian-fighting activities in Mexico are: "Indians – Creek and Seminole," *House Executive Documents,* 33d Cong., 2d Sess., No. 15; *Reports of the Committee of Investigation Sent in 1873 by the Mexican Government to the Frontier of Texas* (New York, 1875), 188-94, 303-304, 327, 331, 407-12.

8. *Annual Report of the Commissioner of Indian Affairs to the Secretary of the Interior for the Year 1870* (Washington, 1870), 328-29; Ninth United States Census (1870), Population Schedule, Texas, Uvalde County (microfilm, Archives Collection, University of Texas Library); Rosa Fay (ca 1860-), widow of Scout Adam Fay and sister of Scout Joe Dixey (Dixon), personal interview, Brackettville, Texas, 1942; John Jefferson (1879-), former scout and also former sergeant in the Tenth Cavalry, son of Scout Joe Coon and grandson of Chief John Horse, personal interview, Del Rio, Texas, 1941; Bill Daniels (ca 1868-1950), son of Sergeant Elijah Daniel, Creek Negro band chieftain, and brother of Scout John Daniels, personal interview, 1942.

9. Numerous similarly-named government documents of this general period, as well as of the pre-Civil War period, deal with Indian depredations on the Texas frontier. One of the most informative is "Texas Frontier Troubles," *House Report*, 45th Cong., 2d Sess., III, No. 701, especially pp. 31-35. Others are: "Depredations on the Frontiers of Texas," *House Executive Documents,* 42d Cong., 3d Sess., VII, No. 39; *ibid.,* 43d Cong., 1st Sess., XVII, No. 257. Still others will be cited in connection with activites of the Seminole scouts in thwarting or punishing these raids. J. Frank Dobie, *Tongues of the Monte* (New York, 1935), 243-46, graphically epitomizes the Comanche raids.

10. Deposition No. 545. John Kibbets, in "Depredations on the Frontiers of Texas," *House Executive Documents,* 43d Cong., 1st Sess., XVII, No. 257, 22; "Texas Frontier Troubles," *House Report,* 45th Cong., 2d Sess., III, No. 701, 224; Captain J. D. De Gress, Fort Duncan, to Brevet Brigadier General H. Clay Wood, assistant adjutant general, dated March 17, 1870 (MS., Adjutant General's Office, 488M, War Department, National Archives, Washington, D.C.); F. H. French, second lieutenant, 19th Infantry, Fort Clark, to Adjutant General, Department of Texas, San Antonio, dated May 23, 1883 (MS., Seminole File 1882-11398, Indian Office, Department of the Interior, National Archives); Lieutenant Colonel Z. R. Bliss, Fort Clark, to Adjutant General, Department of Texas, dated August 26, 1884 (MS., Seminole File 1884-18287, Indian Office, Department of the Interior, National Archives); *Report of*

Commissioner of Indian Affairs, 1870, 328-29; *Report of Committee of Investigation,* 415; Notes by the late General John L. Bullis, U.S. Army, Commanded the Scouts from '72 to '81 (MS., General Service Files 123, 14308-1914, Indian Affairs, National Archives); J. H. Bliss, assistant secretary Committee on Indian Affairs, Public Lands, to the Commissioner of Indian Affairs, dated August 18, 1932 (MS., Indian Affairs Office, Department of the Interior, National Archives); Laurence Foster, *Negro-Indian Relationships in the Southeast* (Philadelphia, 1930), 46; Julia Payne (ca 1862-1946), step-granddaughter of Sergeant John Kibbitts and widow of Scout Issac Payne, personal interview, Nacimiento, Coahuila, 1944; Curley Jefferson (1881-), former scout, personal interview, Del Rio, Texas, 1941; John Jefferson, personal interview, 1941.

11. Dolly July (1870-), daughter of Sergeant John Ward (Warrior) and widow of Scout Billy July, personal interview, Brackettville, Texas, 1941; John Jefferson to K.W.P., 1948 (letter in possession of author).

12. Useful sources of information on the Seminole scouts are the Monthly Reports, 1870-1881, and the Enlistment Records, Seminole Negro-Indian Scouts (MS., Adjutant General's Office, War Department, National Archives). See also Ninth United States Census (1870), Population Schedule, Texas, Maverick, and Uvalde counties (microfilm); Tenth United States Census (1880), Population Schedule, Texas, Kinney County (National Archives).

13. *Report of Commissioner of Indian Affairs,* 328-29; Notes by General Bullis (MS.).

14. Major Henry C. Merriam, Fort Duncan, to the Commanding Officer, Fort Clark, dated July 8, 1872, and August 5, 1872; Special Orders No. 96, Second Lieutenant H. F. Leggett, 24th Infantry, post adjutant, Fort Duncan, dated August 3, 1872, in memoranda relative to Seminole Negro Indians, Military Division of Missouri, dated August 5, 1872 (MS., War Department, National Archives). Rebecca Wilson, daughter of Sergeant Sampson July, niece of Chief John Horse, and wife of Scout Bill Wilson, Brackettville, Texas, 1941.

15. Major Henry C. Merriam, Fort Duncan, to Assistant Adjutant General, Department of Texas, dated August 5, 1872, in memoranda relative to Seminole Negro Indians (MS.).

16. Ninth United States Census (1870), Population Schedule, Texas, Maverick, and Uvalde counties (microfilm).

17. Frank D. Reeve (ed.), "Frederick E. Phelps: A Soldier's Memoirs," *New Mexico Historical Review,* XXV, 113; W. C. Parker, first lieutenant and adjutant, 4th Cavalry, Fort Clark, to Lieutenant J. L. Bullis, dated July 10, 1873 (MS., in possession of General Bullis' daughter, Mrs. W. S. Halcomb of San Antonio, Texas).

18. Bill Daniels, personal interview, Brackettville, Texas, 1943; Adam McClain (?-1950), former scout, personal interview, Brackettville, 1943.

19. Henry W. Strong, *My Frontier Days and Indian Fights on the Plains of Texas* (n. p., n. d.), 51-53; Curley Jefferson, personal interview, 1941; Penny Factor (1874-), daughter of Scout Ben Wilson, Sr., personal interview, Brackettville, Texas, 1943.

20. Zenas R. Bliss, Reminiscences (typescript, University of Texas Library), V, 106-109.

21. *Ibid.,* 126-27; Mrs. Orsemus Bronson Boyd, *Cavalry Life in Tent and Field* (New York, 1894), 336-37.

22. This statment concerning the scouts' linguistic ability is contradicted, so far as English is concerned, from two quarters. A former Negro cavalryman, Jacob Wilks ("A Negro Trooper of the Ninth Cavalry," *Frontier Times,* IV, 9-11) says of Bullis' scouts: "They all spoke Spanish; only a few of them, the Texas ex-slaves, spoke any English." Lieutenant Frederick E. Phelps (Reeve (ed.), "Phelps: A Soldier's Memoirs," *New Mexico Historical Review,* XXV, 216)

says that "Mexican . . . was the langauge the Seminoles used" and tells a story based on the fact that a particular Seminole "could talk very little English and perhaps understand less." These, however, are the only suggestions encountered that the Seminole Negroes could not speak English, and both the Negro cavalryman and the lieutenant make statements about their origins which indicate that, although they undoubtedly served with the scouts, their knowledge of them was not particularly intimate. Some of the young scouts, in their twenties or less, who had been born and reared in Mexico may have been deficient in English, but it seems unlikely that those in their thirties or older who had been brought up entirely in the United States and whose prestige with both Indians and whites had depended to a large extent on thier ability as interpreters would have completely forgotten the English language. All the writer's conversations with widows and children of scouts, themselves contemporary with the Indian-fighting days, indicate that the Seminole at that time were basically an English-speaking people. Those in Brackettville, Texas, today are entirely bilingual, and although the Seminole in Nacimiento have now been living in Mexico for sixty or seventy years, all but the young children speak both English and Spanish fluently.

23. Martin L. Crimmins, "The Border Command: Camp Bullis," *The Army and Navy Courier*, II, 20-21; *Who was Who in America, 1897-1942* (Chicago, 1943), 164; Francis B. Heitman, *Historical Register and Dictionary of the United States Army*, 2 vols. (Washington, 1903), I, 261.

24. Reeve (ed.), "Phelps: A Soldier's Memoirs," *New Mexico Historical Review*, XXV, 203.

25. "Record of Engagements with Hostile Indians in Texas, 1868 to 1882," *West Texas Historical Association Year Book*, IX, 101-18, abstracted from *Record of Engagements with Hostile Indians within the Military Division of the Missouri from 1868 to 1882, Lieutenant-General P. H. Sheridan, Commanding* (Washington, 1882); Heitman, *Historical Register of the Army*, II, 439-46; "Mexican Border Troubles," *House Executive Documents*, 45th Cong., 1st Sess., No. 13, especially pp. 187-96; "Texas Border Troubles," *House Miscellaneous Documents*, 45th Cong., 2d Sess., VI, No. 64.

26. Carl Coke Rister, *The Southwestern Frontier* (Cleveland, 1928), 153-54; Robert G. Carter, "Raid Into Mexico," *Outing*, XII, 2ff; Martin L. Crimmins, "General Mackenzie and Fort Concho," *West Texas Historical Association Year Book*, X, 16-31; Frost Woodhull, "The Seminole Indian Scouts on the Border," *Frontier Times*, XV, 120-21; Crimmins, "Border Command," *Army and Navy Courier*, II , 20-21; San Antonio *Daily Express*, May 29, 1873, p. 3, col. 1.

27. Deacon Warren (Juan) Perryman, son of Scout James Perryman and Teresita, personal interview, Brackettville, 1941; Penny Factor, personal interview, 1943; John Jefferson, Del Rio, to K. W. P., letters dated November 4, 1948, and December 18, 1948 (in possession of writer).

28. Robert G. Carter, *The Old Sergeant's Story* (New York, 1926), 102-11; W. S. Nye, *Carbine and Lance* (Norman, 1937), 284-89; J. Evetts Haley, *Charles Goodnight: Cowman and Plainsman* (Boston, 1936), 196-97; J. Marvin Hunter (ed.), "The Battle of Palo Duro Canyon," from Captain George E. Albee's account in the New York *Herald* of October 16, 1874, *Frontier Times*, XXI, 177-81; Strong, *Frontier Days and Indian Fights*, 51-53; One Who Was There, "Scouting on the Staked Plains' (Llano Estacado) with Mackenzie in 1874," *United Service*, XIII, 400-12, 532-43; Woodhull, "Seminole Indian Scouts on Border," *Frontier Times*, XV, 124-25.

29. Lieutenant John L. Bullis, 24th Infantry, Fort Clark, to Lieutenant G. W. Smith, 9th Cavalry, post adjutant, April 27, 1875, in General Orders No. 10, Headquarters Department

of Texas, San Antonio, Texas, dated May 12, 1875 (photostat of orders in possession of Colonel Martin L. Crimmins of San Antonio, Texas); Mrs. O. L. Shipman, *Taming the Big Bend* (n. p., 1926), 58-63; Woodhull, "Seminole Indian Scouts on Border," *Frontier Times,* XV, 121-22; Crimmins, "Border Command," *Army and Navy Courier,* II, 20-21. The Medal of Honor awarded to Pompey Factor was in the possession of his son, Dindie Factor, in 1943.

30. Colonel Commanding, Fort Clark, to Assistant Adjutant General, Department of Texas, dated July 10, 1873, in memoranda relative to Seminole Negro Indians (Ms.).

31. Petition of Eligah [sic] Daniel, Fort Clark, dated June 28, 1873; order for termination of issuance of rations to other than enlisted men, dated December 22, 1873; Bullis to Assistant Adjutant General, Department of Texas, dated May 28, 1875; and Sergeant John Kibbets, Fort Duncan, to Assistant Adjutant General, Department of Texas, dated February 8, 1874, endorsed by Lieutenant Bullis on February 9, 1874, in memoranda relative to Seminole Negro Indians (MSS.); Bullis to Lieutenant George W. Smith, post adjutant, dated May 1, 1875 (MS., Seminole File 1875-B791, Indian Office, Department of the Interior, NAtional Archives).

32. Transcript of talk, John Horse, San Antonio; to Brigadier General C. C. Augur, on December 10, 1873; transcript of talk, John Kiveth [sic], San Antonio, to Brigadier General Augur, on December 10, 1873; Augur to Adjutant General of the Army, dated February 21, 1874, in memoranda relative to Seminole Negro Indians (MSS.).

33. Record of Engagements with Hostile Indians," *West Texas Historical Association Year Book,* IX, 101-18.

34. H. M. Atkinson, Special Indian Commissioner, Fort Duncan, to Edward P. Smith, commissioner of Indian affairs, Washington, November 16, 1874 (MS., Seminole File 1874-A1085, Indian Office, Department of the Interior, National Archives, Washington, D.C.); *Annual Report of the Commissioner of Indian Affairs to the Secretary of the Interior for the Year 1875* (Washington, 1875).

35. Bullis to Assistant Adjutant General, Department of Texas, dated May 28, 1875; Hatch to Assistant Adjutant General, Department of Texas, dated August 9, 1875; "Elizey Danuel," Fort Clark, to "Genuel," dated March 7, 1876, endorsed by Colonel R. S. Mackenzie, Fort Sill, I. T., on April 20, 1876, and Lieutenant General P. H. Sheridan, Headquarters, Military Division of the Missouri, Chicago, on April 29, 1876, in memoranda relative to Seminole Negro Indians (MSS.).

36. John Jefferson, personal interview, 1941.

37. Rebecca Wilson, personal interview, 1943.

38. John Jefferson, personal interview, 1941; Elsa Payne (ca 1860-1949), daughter of Scout Caesar Payne and widow of Scouts Sandy Fay and Bill Williams, personal interview, Nacimiento, Mexico, 1943.

39. Martin L. Crimmins, "Shafter's Explorations in Western Texas, 1875," *West Texas Historical Association Year Book,* IX, 82-96.

40. Reeve (ed.), "Phelps: A Soldier's Memoirs," *New Mexico Historical Review,* XXV, 203, 214; Frederic Remington, "On the Indian Reservations," *Century Magazine,* XXVIII, 395-96; testimony of Scout Joe Phillips in Foster, *Negro-Indian Relationships,* 47-48, and Woodhull, "Seminole Indian Scouts on Border," *Frontier Times,* XV, 120; Crimmins, "Border Command," *Army and Navy Courier,* II, 20-21.

41. Retired Sergeant John Jefferson states that, according to his mother, he was visited shortly after his birth by Lieutenant Bullis.

42. Woodhull, "Seminole Indian Scouts on Border," *Frontier Times,* XV, 122; Theodore F. Rodenbough and William L. Haskins (eds.), *The Army of the United States* (New York, 1896), 295.

43. Colonel Mackenzie, Fort Sill, I. T., to the Secretary of War, dated April 20, 1876, in memoranda relative to Seminole Negro Indians (MS.); Statement by P. H. Sheridan (MS., Seminole File 1883-20047, Indian Office, Department of the Interior, National Archives); Reeves (ed.), "Phelps: A Soldiers's Memoirs," *New Mexico Historical Review,* XXV, 203.

44. Dora Neill Raymond, *Captain Lee Hall of Texas* (Norman, 1940), 54-56; Mrs. Albert Maverick, "Ranch Life in Bandera County in 1878," *Frontier Times,* XVIII, 141-46; Frank H. Bushick, *Glamorous Days* (San Antonio, 1934), 174-81; Herman Lehman (1888-), sheriff, Maverick County, personal interview, Eagle Pass, Texas, August 22, 1950; Julia Payne, personal interview, 1942. See also murder indictments against John King Fisher, Maverick County courthouse, Eagle Pass, Texas.

45. W. A. Bonnet, "King Fisher," *Frontier Times,* III, 36-37; Adolfo Sierra (1864-), former sheriff of Maverick County, personal interview, Eagle Pass, Texas, August 22, 1950; Julia Payne, personal interview, 1944; John Jefferson to K. W. P., dated May 27, 1949 (letter in author's possession). Scout Dan Johnson may also have been wounded in the fight, as he was noted as suffering from a wound at the same time as George Washington.

46. "Journal of William H. C. Whiting," *Exploring Southwestern Trails, 1846-1854,* "Southwest Historical Series," VII (Glendale, 1938), 347-48; Maria Brace Kimball, *A Soldier-Doctor of Our Army* (Boston, 1917), 119-21; John C. Reid, "Reid's Tramp," *Frontier Times,* XX, 198-99, Julia Payne, personal interview, 1942.

47. Petition of thirty-five citizens of Kinney County, Fort Clark, dated April 24, 1876, for removal of Seminole Negroes; and Colonel Gregg, Fort Clark, to Assistant Adjutant General, Department of Texas, dated May 23 and 25, 1876, endorsed by General E. O. C. Ord, in memoranda relative to Seminole Negro Indians (MSS.); Rebecca Wilson, personal interview, 1941; Curly Jefferson, personal interview, 1941; John Jefferson, personal interview, 1941; Julia Payne, personal interview, 1942; Rosa Fay, personal interview, 1942.

48. Curley Jefferson, personal interview, 1941; John Jefferson, personal interview, 1941; Penny Factor, personal interview, 1943; Julia Payne, personal interview, 1942.

49. Bliss, Reminiscences (MS.), VI, 160; Charles Judson Crane, *The Experiences of a Colonel of Infantry* (New York, 1923), 74.

50. Of the hundred or som men whose names at one time or another appeared on the roster of the Seminole scouts during the Indian fighting period of 1870-1881, about one-third were discharged Negro soldiers, Texas Negroes, Mexicans, and Indians, some of whom intermarried with the Seminole. The backbone of the organization, however, both in numbers and in length and quality of service, was the Indian Negro element from Mexico which made up two-thirds of the total personnel.

The surnames, which, according to the best information obtainable, were borne by Indian Negro scouts from Mexico, in the order of their numbers, were Wilson, 9; Payne, 8; Bruner, 6; Factor, 5; Bowlegs, July, and Thompson, 4; Daniel, Perryman, Phillips, and Warrior (Ward), 3; Fay, Gordon, Johns[t]on, Kibbitt[s], and Washington, 2; Coon, Dixie or Dixey (Dixon), Grayson, Kennard, McCallip, Williams, Wood, 1. Most Indian Negroes derived their surnames from the Indian chiefs who were their ancestors' masters or patrons—Payne, Bowlegs, Factor, Perryman, Thompson, etc. Others adopted parental personal names as surnames – July, Fay (Felipe), perhaps Daniel. Hohn Horse's nephews assumed the surname of Washington, and his son Joe's surname of Coon was originally a nickname.

The Wilsons, Warriors, and Daniels, as also Grayson, Kennard, and McCallip, were Creek;

the Thompsons were Cherokee. The Gordons are traditionally said to have become "Seminole" – runaways or secessionists – by running away to Mexico from slavery in Georgia. Those named Payne, Bruner, Factor, Bowlegs, July, Perryman, Phillips, Fay, Kibbits, Johns[t]on, Washington, Coon, Dixie, Wood, and Williams (?) were of Florida Seminole origin. Since Seminole Indians were essentially Creeks who had moved to Florida, the line between Creek names and Seminole ones is rather uncertain.

51. Haley, *Charles Goodnight,* 196-97; Crane, *Experiences of a Colonel,* 106.

52. John Jefferson, personal interview, 1941; "Texas Border Troubles," *House Miscellaneous Documents,* 45th Cong., 2d Sess., VI, No. 64, 267-68. The Bullis Papers (MSS. in possession of General Bullis' daughter, Mrs. W. S. Halcomb of San Antonio, Texas) contain mention of one Julian, in all probability Longorio, who evidently operated as a spy in Mexico and as such was frequently sought by Mexican police.

53. Carlysle Graham Raht, *The Romance of Davis Mountains and Big Bend Country* (El Paso, 1919), 205; "Mexican Border Troubles," *House Executive Documents,* 45th Cong., 1st Sess., No. 13, 171-89.

54. *Ibid.,* 240; Rodenbough and Haskin (eds.), *Army of the United States,* 275.

55. Reeve (ed.), "Phelps: A Soldier's Memoirs," *New Mexico Historical Review,* XXV, 206ff; Rister, *Southwestern Frontier,* 187-89.

56. James Parker, *The Old Army: Memories, 1872-1918* (Philadelphia, 1929), 99.

57. Alexander E. Sweet and J. J. Amory Knox, *On a Mexican Mustang Through Texas* (St. Louis, 1884), 520-21; Rister, *Southwestern Frontier,* 189-90; Woodhull, "Seminole Indian Scouts on Border," *Frontier Times,* XV, 124-25; Grace Lowe Butler, "General Bullis: Friend of the Frontier," *Frontier Times,* XII, 358-62.

58. On October 20, 1881, Sergeant Bobby Kibbitts and nine men recovered thirteen horses from seven Indians near the Rio Grande, but this encounter is not listed in Heitman's *Historical Register* as an engagement.

59. Julia Payne, personal interviews, 1942, 1944.

60. Woodhull, "Seminole Indian Scouts on Border," *Frontier Times,* XV, 122-23; Rister, *Southwestern Frontier,* 267-68; A. J. Sowell, "Last Indian Raid in Frio Canyon," *Frontier Times,* XXIV; Crimmins, "Border Command," *Army and Navy Courier,* II, 20-21.

61. Rister, *Southwestern Frontier,* 268-69.

62. For additional comments of contemporaries on the Seminole scouts' trailing and fighting skill, see Parker, *Old Army,* 99; Vinton Lee James, *Frontier and Pioneer* (San Antonio, 1938), 26; Florence Fenley, *Oldtimers* (Uvalde, 1939), 185-87, quoting David W. Barnhill.

63. The swords are on exhibition in the Witte Museum, San Antonio.

64. *Who Was Who in America,* 164; Crimmins, "Border Command," *Army and Navy Courier,* II, 20-21.

65. Raht, *Romance of Davis Mountains,* 198.

66. The older generation of Seminole Negroes at Brackettville are fimly convinced that if General Bullis had lived, this disbandment would not have taken place. John Jefferson tells the story that Bullis was ill in his home in San Antonio when news of the intended disbandment reached him. He immediately called for his clothes and began to dress. "General, what are you doing out of bed? Don't you realize that you are a sick man?" the nurse protested. "Colonel ---- says he's going to disband my old scouts." the general replied. "I'm going to Fort Clark

and stop him" According to the story, the general then collapsed and died. As a matter of fact, the general died of a heart attack at a boxing match on May 26, 1911, and the final order for the disbanding of the scouts was not issued until July 10, 1914. The story, however, is indicative of the feeling between Bullis and the scouts even though the details do not jibe with the actualities.

67. Memoranda relative to Seminole Negro Indians (MSS.); Woodhull, "Seminole Indian Scouts on Border," *Frontier Times,* XV, 126-27.

BLACK-WHITE RELATIONS ON THE FRONTIER

The United States Army in the Aftermath of the Johnson County Invasion

1. The story of Wyoming's buffalo hunters has never been brought together in one place, but is mentioned and dated in John Barsom's fine article "Freund & Bro., Gunmakers on the Frontier," in the 1957 *Gun Digest,* John T. Amber, editor, Gun Digest Publishing Co., Chicago.

2. Walter von Richtofen, *Cattle Raising on the Plains of North America* (Norman, Oklahoma, reprint, 1964.)

3. Paul C. Henlein, *The Cattle Kingdom in the Ohio Valley,* 1783-1860 (Lexington, 1958).

4. Edward E. Dale, *The Range Cattle Industry* (Norman, Oklahoma, 1930).

5. The classic exposition of the so-called "Johnson County War," is of course Asa S. Mercer's *Banditti of the Plains,* most readily available in the University of Oklahoma Press reprint of 1954. Other useful collections of fact and opinion are: Daisy F. Baber, *The Longest Rope,* (Caldwell, Idaho, 1959). Frank M. Canton, *Frontier Trails,* (N.Y. 1930). Robert B. David, *Malcolm Campbell, Sheriff,* (Casper, Wyo., 1932). Bohlen and Tisdale, *An Era of Violence,* (Cheyenne, 1963).

6. Robert M. Utley, *Last Days of the Sioux Nation,* (New Haven, 1964).

7. Letter, Major H. C. Egbert, 17th Infantry to Adjutant General, Department of the Platte, April 23, 1892.

8. Fort McKinney, Wyoming, Post Return for April, 1892.

9. Report of Examiner F. B. Crossthwaite, Department of Justice, to the Attorney General of the United States, November 2, 1892.

10. Telegram, Colonel J. J. Van Horn to Adjutant General, Department of the Platte, April 11, 1892.

11. Telegram, Colonel J. J. Van Horn to Adjutant General, Department of the Platte, April 12, 1892.

12. Telegram, Brigadier General John R. Brooke to Major General Schofield, Commanding the Army, Washington D. C., April 12, 1892, quoting a telegram he had just received from Acting Governor Barber of Wyoming.

13. Telegram, Acting Governor Barber, Cheyenne, to the President of the United States, Washington, D.C. April 12, 1892.

14. Telegram, Acting Governor Barber to Secretary of War Elkins, April 12, 1892.

15. The arms of this company of the Wyoming National Guard had been routinely turned in for replacement during the winter, and were not yet replaced. There is abundant correspondence in the Fort McKinney letters received file on this point.

16. Telegram, General Schofield to General Brooke, April 12, 1892. Two telegrams, Brooke to Schofield April 12, 1892.

17. See Mercer, pp. 50-51, and others on this point.

18. Letter, Col. Van Horn to Adjutant General, Department of the Platte, April 13, 1892.

19. Three successive telegrams, General Brooke to General Schofield, April 13, 1892.

20. Telegram, General Brooke to General Schofield, April 14, 1892.

21. Telegram, Secretary of War Elkins to Senator Francis E. Warren, April 14, 1892 and duplicate of same date to Senator J. M. Carey.

22. Endorsement by Van Horn on writ presented by Johnson County, April 14, 1892, also letter Colonel Van Horn to Adjutant General, Department of the Platte, April 15, 1892.

23. Telegram, Sheriff W. G. Angus to President Benjamin Harrison, April 15, 1892.

24. Letter, Colonel Van Horn to Adjutant General, Department of the Platte, April 15, 1892.

25. Telegram, Secretary of War Elkins to General Brooke, April 15, 1892.

26. Telegram, Secretary of War Elkins to Governor Barber, April 15, 1892.

27. Telegram, General Brooke to Secretary of War Elkins, April 15, 1892.

28. Telegram, General Brooke to Secretary of War Elkins, April 16, 1892.

29. Telegram, Secretary of War Elkins to General Brooke, April 16, 1892.

30. Telegram, General Brooke to Elkins, 9 P.M., April 16, 1892.

Note on military sources: All the military correspondence cited above will be found in one of the following:
"A. G. Document File 29763, PRD 1892" Records of the Adjutant General's Office, RG 94. Post Records Fort McKinney, Wyoming; Post Records Fort D. A. Russell, Wyoming; Records of the Department of the Platte; all RG98 "Records of U. S. Army Commands" National Archives, Washington, D. C. (microfilm copies have been placed on file with the State Archives and Historical Dept.)

Racial Troubles on the Conchos

1. The newspapers of the time vividly point up the widespread violence, while the army's oppressive measures sometimes checked and again accentuated it. See especially the *San Antonio Express* for the years 1867 and 1869, and for the above mentioned mutiny the issue of May 8, 1867.

2. *Medical History*, as cited, CCCI, 124, 147, 177.

3. *Medical History*, Fort McKavett, 1870, 169.

4. The saga of Humpy Jackson is told in N. H. Pierce's *The Free State of Menard* (Menard, Texas, 1946), 99 ff., 135 ff. The account of the frontier chronicler, John W. Hunter, is reproduced. It is elaborated here from these sources, from an original use of the War Records, at Washington, and hitherto unpublished recollections set down by the author.

5. Pierce, as cited, 99, 134-36; Special Order 67, Fort McKavett, June 9, 1869, *Army Commands.*

6. Summary of information from War Records in letter of E. G. Campbell to O. C. Fisher, August 26, 1926; Pierce, as cited.

7. Mrs. A. W. Noguess to J. E. H., September 23, 1946; Pierce, as cited, 100.

8. Pierce, as cited, 102-104; "Special Orders, no. 67," R. S. Mackenzie to Brvt. Colonel H. Clay Wood, February 3, 1870, and same, February 15, 1870, *Army Commands,* Fort McKavett; *Medical History,* Fort McKavett, p. 157; *Medical History,* Fort Concho, CCCI, 157.

9. Captain Henry Carroll Report, April 20, 1870; John L. Bullis to Henry Carroll, April 19, 1870; *Army Commands,* Fort McKavett; Pierce, as cited, 105.

10. *Record of Deeds,* Vol A, 19, Menard County; Pierce, as cited, 107.

11. General E. O. Ord to Assist. Adj. Gen., May 20, 1875, *Letters Sent,* Department of Texas, 886.

12. W. F. Buchanan to Post Adjut., *Letters Received,* July 13, 1875.

13. William Bulger to Company Commander, May 10, 1875, *Letters Received,* Fort Concho.

14. See Miss Kubela's thesis, "History of Fort Concho, Texas," 65, University of Texas Archives.

15. *Medical History*, CCCI, 157.

16. *Ibid.,* 185.

17. *Ibid.,* 214.

18. For further comment on the nature of Saint Angela, see Captain R. G. Porter, *On The Border With Mackenzie,* 53-54.

19. Noah Armstrong to J. E. H., April 25, 1945 and July 10, 1946.

20. A detailed account of this trouble may be found in the *Galveston Daily News,* March 1, 1878, quoted from the *San Saba News.*

21. Kubela, "History of Fort Concho," as cited, 86-88.

22. *Galveston News,* February 17, 1881.

23. John A. Loomis to J. E. H., January 31, 1946.

24. *Dallas Herald,* February 6, 1881; *Galveston News,* as cited.

25. Sancho Mazique to J. E. H., October 10, 1946; Loomis, as cited.

26. *Galveston News,* January 21, 1881.

27. *Galveston News,* February 3, 1881.

28. Reprinted in *Dallas Herald,* February 5, 1881.

29. B. H. Grierson to Adjt. Gen., February 8, 1881, *Army Commands,* Fort Concho.

30. "Monthly Return," February 18, 1881, Frontier Battalion, State Archives, Austin; *Austin Statesman,* February 8, 1881; Kubela, as cited, 95.

31. J. Evetts Haley, *Jeff Milton, A Good Man With A Gun* (Norman, 1948), 36.

32. Martin to Co. O., Fort Concho, February 8, 1881, *Army Commands.*

33. Marsh to Jones, as cited, *Adjutant General's Papers,* State Library.

34. C. O. to Colonel B. H. Grierson, February 14, 1881.

35. *San Angelo Standard,* May 3, 1924; Dallas Herald, February 26 and November 13, 1881.

THE TWENTIETH CENTURY

The Fight at Carrizal

1. The unit was commanded by Captain Lewis S. Morey.

2. Houston doubltess refers to the Colt. 45 caliber semiautomatic pistols with which the Tenth Cavalry had been supplied before leaving the United States. These were not revolvers.

3. This is probably General Felix U. Gomez mentioned by Karl Young in his recent article *(The American West* magazine, Spring, 1966: "A Fight That Could Have Meant War"). Young, however, says the message was carried by an American, Lemuel H. Spilsbury.

Border Fight at Nogales

1. Colonel Emilio Kosterlisky, the picturesque native Russian commander of the federal Mexican Rurales, was among the forces seeking refuge on the American side. In accordance with the European military custom he surrendered his sabre to Captain Cornelius C. Smith, Troop G, Fifth Cavalry. This historic Damascus blade is now in the possession of Dr. Cornelius C. Smith, Jr., a son of the officer. During 1918-19 Colonel Smith was the commanding officer of the Tenth Cavalry.

2. Almost two years before (June 21, 1916) in front of Carrizal, Mexico, Troop C, had made a gallant, though futile fight against overwhelming Mexican forces. Battling until out of ammunition and its officers and a number of non-coms killed, the small group of troopers inflicted large casualties on Carranzistas before the end. A number of the men in the Nogales fight were veterans of the Carrizal conflict.

3. Captain Henry C. Caron resigned his commission in 1920. For the next eighteen years he was a newspaper man on the New York City News and wire editor for the New York Journal American. Returning to Arizona in 1938 he engaged in newspaper work and also served with the State employment bureau. He died at Phoenix on December 2, 1957.

4. Who of our days with the Tenth will ever forget that incident on the Nogales streets during the fight. It was something of a whimsy of fate, and gave us many a chuckle. The captain, slight of built and of medium stature, was standing well protected behind a telephone pole together with huge, bulging First Sergeant Jordan. During a hot exchange of rifle fire and while pointing out a sniper, he was hit and the mostly exposed trooper went unscratched.

5. The town of Nogales, Sonora has erected the "Twenty-Eighth of August Monument" at a location on Calle (street) Obregon, with an inscription recording the names of Mexican citizens killed in the battle. The date used was that of the settlement of the affray.

The Yaqui Indian Fight

1. Aileen Maloney (Mrs. Jess W. Taylor, Tucson) was one of our cavalry belles at Nogales. Her father was a miner both in spirit and fact, preferring the hills to city life. After grade school – the family lived in Nogales – the mother took her and the others to Los Angeles for schooling in order to "civilize Aileen." However she spent vacations and other periods with her father in the Ruby diggings.

After the publication of the Yaqui fight article in 1963 Myrtle and I made one of our visits to her. Besides the cavalry, the life in the Ruby country was a main topic of conversation. Some quotes of her statements well reflect the lure of the life and the boisterous days along the border.

"Even in my time with Dad at his mine there were robberies, people shot, and it was a wild place; but we didn't think so then.

"I was with my father at the mine when the battle with the Yaqui took place. I got the first account of it at a dance held a few days later at Clarke's general store. We were not at all upset about the Yaqui going through the country, but felt very sorry for them as the Mexicans treated them so badly.

"I suppose those were rugged days. In 1920 Clarke sold his store to the Frasier brothers from New York. They were murdered and the store robbed by two Mexicans, one was a miner who worked for Dad. The men fled into Mexico. A year later a family named Pearson took over the store. They put iron bars on the windows and went around armed. A few months later they were also robbed and killed. I guess those were wild times after all. But it was a wonderful place, though. We all go back about once a year to refresh our souls. The old hills never change."

2. Years ago in the Big Sandy country out from Kingman Arizona I saw a beautiful bay stallion that had been "rustled" from a Mexican ranch. A stock buyer, while loading a car of cattle at a siding on the American side, made a deal with a vacquero to bring the animal across the Rio Grande River. Upon delivery the Mexican was given sixty dollars gold.

3. This camp had been used by border troops since 1910. In 1915 it received the formal name of Camp Stephen D. Little by the Southern Department. The site was named for Private Stephen D. Littles, (The order missipelled the name.) of Company L, 12th Infantry, who was killed in 1915 by a shot from Mexican soldiers along the Nogales border. The camp was abandoned in 1931.

4. The Johnny Vogan place was located about 1876 near a seepage in the canyon. There Johnny built an adobe house and mesquite log corral. In 1918 only the corral remained but the waterhole had been dug out by the cattlemen in the region.

Just across a low divide, a mile or so distant, and near the head of Sycamore Canyon, was Yank Springs. This place was an early day ranch of a colorful character named Yank Bartlett. He had settled there after his job as packmaster for the United States Boundary re-survey party. Lieutenant John Bigelow, Jr. tells about Indian depredations in 1886 near the ranch house.

Yank had previously served as a packer with General George Crook. Captain John G. Bourke, "On the Border with Crook", wrote: "The names of Hank 'n Yank (Hewitt and Bartlett) and many other scouts, guides, and packers of that onerous, dangerous and crushing campaign (1872-73) should be inscribed on the brightest page in the annals of Arizona."

5. The Yaqui sandal was made by placing a foot on the hair side, then cutting the shape with tabs on each side of the ankle. A piece of rawhide was drawn through a slit between the large toe and the next, being tied to the side tabs. This made good footwear for walking in the mountains as long as it remained pliable.

6. On May 3, 1964 we learned a sequel about the wounded Yaqui from Val Cason, now living in his cabin near the Pena Blanca Wash some fifteen miles west of Nogales on Highway 289.

A party of us were searching out old sites of the border region: Colonel Blondy Ryder, Mrs. Jess(ie) Rider Fickas who was one of the Douglas girls frequently visiting army families at Fort Huachuca during our Tenth Cavalry days, Lieutenant Colonel John H. and Ila Healy also of the old Tenth, and my wife, Myrtle, and I.

Early in the day we stopped at Arivaca and looked over the area of a cavalry border camp, locating the still-standing iron flag pole and an adobe buiding where the officers were quartered. Journeying southeasterly we saw the ghost town of Ruby – now locked up by the owners – and continued searching for the border camp in Atasco Canyon.

Just beyond Sycamore Canyon, near Yank Springs, was the roadside sign of the Claude Henson Bear Valley ranch. We drove down to the house. Above the home was an old mesquite log corral with some additional fencing. Blondy and I went there, and found that it was the old camp site; even the lone big mesquite was still standing.

We trod on "hallowed" ground that Sunday. There to the front was the outpost hill. South was the ridge where the Yaqui were sighted, the area fought over was mostly within view. The skyline of hills compared the same with a photo Blondy had. Everything was similar, not much changed; excepting that Scotty, Pink, the colored troopers, pup tents, horses in the corral, and we of our youthful days were all of the past.

Talking with Claude Henson we learned that Val still lived in the country.

Journeying on to the Pena Blanca Wash we located him, hale and hearty in his eighties, mentally keen and alert, but a little slowed by a slight stroke of the year before. What a talkfest we had about the old border days and incidents of his many years in the region. He told us of his acquaintance with John Slaughter – the Cochise County sheriff of 1887 to 1891 – fighting with Mexican bandits, killings in the early lawless days, cattle rustling, and the incident of bringing out the wounded Yaqui in the Model T Ford over the rough road.

The eleven year old Yaqui boy was the grandson. He sat in the back seat holding the wounded man's head. They got out as far as the Wash. Going up a hill, the boy suddenly exclained, "Papa grandes muerto!"; and then the little fellow began to cry. Val drove on to the Nogales army camp. The boy held his dead grandfather's head in his lap all the way to the town.

7. Mrs. Marguerite B. Cooley, Director, Department of Library and Archives, State of Arizona, researched the Arizona newspapers on the subject. Her assistance on this and other historical projects has been invaluable to me.

Conclusion

1. Steward, *Colored Regulars,* 7-8, from a foreword by Gen. Nelson A. Miles.

2. *Ibid.,* 88n.

3. *Ibid.,* 326-27.

4. U. S. Congress, Senate, *Discharge of Enlisted Men . . . Brownsville Affray,* 59th Cong., 2d Sess., 353.

5. Ganoe, *History of the U. S. Army,* 434.

6. U. S. Congress, Senate, *The Brownsville Affray*, 60th Cong., 1st Sess., 1908, Senate Doc. 389, 28-29, 33-34, 37, and 42.

7. Emmett J. Scott, *Scott's Official History of the American Negro in the World War* (no publisher, 1919), 18.

8. Robert Lee Bullard, *Personalities and Reminiscences of the War*, (New York, 1925), 291-98.

9. Reddick, "Negro Policy of the U. S. Army," *Journal of Negro History*, XXXIV, (January, 1949), 20.

10. Schoenfeld, *The Negro in the Armed Forces*, 24.

11. Warman Welliver, "Report on the Negro Soldier," *Harper's Magazine*, CXCII (April, 1946), 337.

12. Roy E. Appleman, *United States Army in the Korean War, South to the Naktong, North to the Yalu (June-November, 1950)*, (Washington, 1961), 193-94, 270, 285, 373, 440 and 479-86.

13. *Ibid.*, 486n.

14. Mandelbaum, *Soldier Groups*, 123.

15. Walter Cronkite, "Integration in the Military," a special news feature, Columbia Broadcasting System, presented July 3, 1966.

16. Reddick, "Negro Policy of the U. S. Army," *Journal of Negro History*, XXXIV (January, 1949), 18-19.

BIBLIOGRAPHY

BOOKS

Armes, Colonel George A. *Ups and Downs of an Army Officer.* Washington, D.C.: 1900.

Athearn, Robert C. *William Tecumseh Sherman and the Settlement of the West.* Norman: University of Oklahoma Press, 1956.

Bennet, Jr., Lerone. *Before the Mayflower: A History of the Negro in America, 1619-1962.* Chicago: Johnson Publishing Company, 1962.

Beyer, Walter F. and Keydel, Oscar (eds.). *Deeds of Valor.* Vols. I & II, Detroit: Perrien-Keydel Company, 1903.

Blaustein, Albert P. and Zangrando, Robert L. (eds.). *Civil Rights and the American Negro.* New York: Washington Square Press, 1968.

Bontemps, Arna. *100 Years of Negro Freedom.* New York: Dodd, Mead & Company, 1961.

Bourke, John G. *An Apache Campaign In The Sierra Madre.* New York: Charles Scribner's Sons, 1886.

________. *On The Border With Crook.* New York: Charles Scribner's Sons, 1896.

Brady, Cyrus T. *Indian Fights and Fighters.* New York: McClure, Phillips and Company, 1904.

Brimlow, George F. *Cavalryman Out of the West: Life of General William Carey Brown.* Caldwell, Idaho: The Caxton Printers Ltd., 1944.

Buchanan, James S. and Dale, Edward E. *A History of Oklahoma.* New York: Row, Peterson and Company, 1924.

Carter, Robert G. *On The Border With Mackenzie.* Washington, D.C.: Eynon Printing Company, 1935.

Casey, Robert J. *The Texas Border and Some Borderliners.* New York: The Bobbs-Merrill Company, Inc., 1950.

Cashin, Herschel V., *et al.* (eds.). *Under Fire With The Tenth United States Cavalry.* New York: F. Tennyson Neely, 1899.

Clark, Dan E. *The West in American History.* New York: Thomas Y. Crowell, 1937.

Cook, John R. *The Border and the Buffalo.* Topeka: Crane & Co., 1907.

Cruse, Thomas. *Apache Days and After.* ed. Eugene Cunningham. Caldwell, Idaho: The Caxton Printers, Ltd., 1941.

Custer, Elizabeth B. *Following the Guidon.* New York: Harper & Bros., 1890.

________. *Tenting On the Plains.* New York: C.L. Webster and Company, 1887.

DeVoto, Bernard (ed.). *The Journals of Lewis & Clark.* Boston: Houghton-Mifflin Company, 1953.

Dick, Everett. *The Sod-House Frontier, 1854-1890.* Lincoln, Nebraska: Johnsen Publishing Company, 1954.

Dixon, Joseph K. *The Vanishing Race.* Garden City, New York: Doubleday, Page and Company, 1913.

Downey, Fairfax. *Indian Fighting Army.* New York: Charles Scribner's Sons, 1941.

DuPuy, Captain William A. and Jenkins, John Wilbur (eds.). *The World War and Historic Deeds of Valor.* 6 Vols. Chicago: National Historic Publishing Association, 1919.

Flipper, Henry O. *The Colored Cadet at West Point.* New York: Homer & Lee, 1878.

________. *Negro Frontiersman.* ed. Theodore D. Harris. El Paso: Texas Western College Press, 1963.

Frazer, Robert W. *Forts of the West.* Norman: University of Oklahoma Press, 1965.

Glass, Edward L.N. *The History of the Tenth Cavalry: 1866-1921.* Tuscon, Arizona: Acme Printing Company, 1921.

Graham, Colonel W.A. *The Custer Myth.* Harrisburg, Pa.: The Stackpole Company, 1953.

Guzman, Martin. *Memoirs of Panco Villa.* Translated by Virginia H. Taylor. Austin, Texas: University of Texas Press, 1965.

Haley, J. Evetts. *Fort Concho and the Texas Frontier: 50 Years of Western History In Its Most Dramatic Era.* San Angelo, Texas: San Angelo Standard-Times, 1952.

Herr, John K. and Wallace, Edward S. *The Story of the U.S. Cavalry.* Boston: Little, Brown & Company, 1953.

Horan, James D. and Sann, Paul. *Pictorial History of the Wild West.* New York: Crown Publishers, Inc. 1954.

Kain, Robert C. *In The Valley of the Little Big Horn.* np, Newfane, Vt.: 1969.

Katz, William L. *Eyewitness: The Negro In American History.* New York, Pitman Publishing Corporation, 1967.

Keim, De Benneville R. *Sheridan's Troopers on the Border: A Winter Campaign on the Plains.* Philadelphia: David McKay Co., Inc., 1885.

King, Captain Charles. *Campaigns With Crook and Stories of Army Life.* New York: Harper & Brothers, 1905.

Leckie, William H. *The Buffalo Soldiers: A Narrative of the Negro Cavalry In The West.* Norman: University of Oklahoma Press, 1967.

Lee, Irvin H. *Negro Medal of Honor Men.* New York: Dodd, Mead & Company, 1967.

Luce, Edward S. *Keogh, Comanche and Custer.* np, 1939.

Marquis, Thomas B. *A Warrior Who Fought Custer.* Minneapolis: The Midwest Company, 1931.

Marshall, Otto M. *The Wham Paymaster Robbery, Boldest In Arizona History, May 11, 1889.* Pima, Arizona: np, 1967.

Miles, General Nelson A. *Personal Recollections of General Nelson A. Miles.* Chicago: Werner Company, 1896.

Muller, William G. *The Twenty-fourth Infantry, Past and Present, 1869-1922.* np, 1923.

Nankivell, Captain John H. *History of the Twenty-fifth Regiment United States Infantry, 1869-1926.* Denver: Smith-Brooks Printing Co., 1927.

Ploski, Harry A. and Brown, Roscoe C., Jr. (eds.). *The Negro Almanac.* New York: Bellweather Publishing Company, Inc., 1967.

Pratt, Richard Henry. *Battlefield And Classroom, Four Decades With The American Indian.* ed. Robert Utley. New Haven: Yale University Press, 1964.

Rickey, Don, Jr. *Forty Miles A Day On Beans and Hay.* Norman: University of Oklahoma Press, 1963.

Rister, Carl C. *Land Hunger: David L. Payne and the Oklahoma Boomers.* Norman: University of Oklahoma Press, 1942.

Rodenbough, Theodore F. and Haskin, William L. (eds.). *The Army of the United States.* New York: Maynard, Merrill & Company, 1896.

Rodney, George B. *As A Cavalryman Remembers.* Caldwell, Idaho: The Caxton Printers, Ltd., 1944.

Salisbury, Albert & Jane. *Two Captains West.* Seattle: Superior Publishing Company, 1950.

Scobee, Barry. *Old Fort Davis.* San Antonio: Naylor Company, 1947.

Stewart, Edgar I. *Custer's Luck.* Norman: University of Oklahoma Press, 1955.

Terrell, John Upton. *Estevanico the Black.* Los Angeles: Westernlore Press, Publishers, 1968.

Thompkins, Frank. *Chasing Villa.* Harrisburg, Pa.: The Military Service Publishing Company, 1934.

Toulouse, Joseph H. & James R. *Pioneer Posts of Texas.* San Antonio: Naylor Company, 1936.

Vestal, Stanley. *Sitting Bull, Champion of the Sioux.* Norman: University of Oklahoma Press, 1957.

Wagner, Glendolin Damon. *Old Neutriment.* Boston: Ruth Hill, Publisher, 1934.

Wellman, Paul I. *The Indian Wars of the West.* New York: Doubleday and Company, 1947.

Wharfield, Colonel H.B. *Tenth Cavalry & Border Fights.* El Cajon, California: np, 1964.

Whitman, S.E. *The Troopers.* New York: Hastings House, Publishers, Inc., 1962.

PERIODICALS

Baird, Major George W. "General Miles' Indian Campaigns," *Century Magazine* (July, 1891).

Bigelow, Lieutenant John. "After Geronimo," *Outing Magazine* (February, 1886-January, 1887).

Buchanan, William J. "Legend of the Black Conquistador," *Mankind Magazine,* I, 5 (February, 1968).

Clark, Ella E. "Sesquicentennial Remembrances," *Montana, the Magazine of Western History*, V, 2 (Spring, 1955).

Dorst, Captain Joseph. "Ranald Slidell Mackenzie," *Cavalry Journal*, X (December 1897).

Ege, Robert J. "Braves of All Colors," *Montana, The Magazine of Western History*, XVI, 1 (Winter, 1966).

Ewers, John C. "The Plains Indians Reactions to the Lewis and Clark Expedition," *Montana, The Magazine of Western History*, XVI, 1 (Winter, 1966).

Forsyth, George A. "A Frontier Fight," *Harper's Monthly Magazine*, XCI (June, 1895).

Godfrey, Brig. General E.S. "Some Reminiscences, Including The Washita Battle, November 29, 1868," *Cavalry Journal*, XXXVII, 153.

Hunter, John Warren. "A Trooper of the Ninth Cavalry," *Frontier Times*, IV, 7 (April, 1927).

Merritt, Wesley. "Three Indian Campaigns," *Harper's New Monthly Magazine* (April, 1890).

Morey, Captain Lewis S. "The Cavalry Fight at Carrizal," *Journal of U.S. Cavalryman* (January, 1917).

Pratt, Richard, H. "Some Indian Experiences," *Cavalry Journal*, XVI (December, 1906).

Remington, Frederic. "A Scout With the Buffalo Soldiers," *The Century Magazine* (April, 1889).

________. "Vagabonding With the Tenth Horse," *The Cosmopolitan Magazine*, XXII, 4 (February, 1897).

Thompson, Erwin N. "The Negro Soldiers On The Frontier: A Fort Davis Case Study," *Journal of the West*, VII, 2 (April, 1968).

Thompson, Major W.A. "Scouting With Mackenzie," *Cavalry Journal*, X (December, 1897).

Troxel, Captain O.C. "The Tenth Cavalry in Mexico," *U.S. Cavalry Journal* (October, 1916).

Wharfield, Colonel H.B. "The Affair At Carrizal," *Montana, The Magazine of Western History*, XVIII, 4 (Autumn, 1968).

Woodhull, Frost. "The Seminole Indian Scouts on the Border," *Frontier Times*, XV, 3 (December, 1937).

Young, Karl. "A Fight That Could Have Meant War," *The American West*, III, 2 (Spring, 1966).

Author Unknown. "Practice Maneuvers in Arizona," *Harper's Weekly* (December 22, 1888).

Author Unknown. "Our Soldiers In The Southwest," *Harper's Weekly* (August 21, 1886).

Author Unknown. "Oklahoma," *Harper's Weekly* (March 28, 1885).

Author Unknown. "List of Actions, etc., With Indians and Other Marauders, Participated In By The Tenth U.S. Cavalry, Chronologically Arranged – 1867-1897," *Journal of the U.S. Cavalry* (December, 1897).

LEARNED SOCIETIES

Baldwin, Percy M. "Fray Marcos de Niza and His Discovery of the Seven Cities of Cibola." *New Mexico Historical Review*, I (April, 1926).

Basbett, James N. "A Study of the Route of Cabeza de Vaca," *Texas Historical Association Quarterly*, X (January-April, 1907).

BIBLIOGRAPHY

Bloom, Lansing B. "Was Fray Marcos A Liar?" *New Mexico Historical* Review, XVI (April, 1941).

________. "Who Discovered New Mexico?" *New Mexico Historical Review*, XV (April, 1940).

Braddy, Haldeen. "Panco Villa at Columbus, The Raid of 1916," *Southwestern Studies*, Texas Western University, III, 1 (1965).

Burkey, Elmer R. "The Thornburgh Battle With The Utes On Milk River," *The Colorado Magazine*, XIII, 3 (1936).

Carroll, H. Bailey. "Nolan's Lost Nigger Expedition of 1877," *Southwest Historical Quarterly*, XLIV (July, 1940).

Chapman, Berlin B. "Freedmen and the Oklahoma Lands," *Southwestern Social Science Quarterly*, XXIX (September, 1948).

Chavez, Fray Angelico. "De Vargas' Negro Drummer," *El Palacio* (May, 1949).

________. "Pohé-yemo's Representative and the Pueblo Revolt of 1860," *New Mexico Historical Review*, XLII, 2 (April, 1967).

Crimmins, Colonel M.L. "Shafter's Explorations In West Texas," *West Texas Historical Association Yearbook*, IX (October, 1933).

________. "Captain Nolan's Lost Troop On The Staked Plains," *West Texas Historical Association Yearbook*, X (October, 1934).

Howe, Jerome W. "Campaigning In Mexico, 1916," *Arizona Pioneers Historical Society* (1968).

Krogman, Wilton M. "The Racial Composition of the Seminole Indians of Florida and Oklahoma," *Journal of Negro History*, XIX (1934).

Libby, O.B. (ed.). "The Arikara Narrative of the Campaign Against the Hostile Dakotas, June, 1876," *North Dakota Historical Collection*, VI (1920).

McConnell, Ronald C. "Isaiah Dorman and the Custer Expedition," *Journal of Negro History*, XXXIII (July, 1948).

Miles, Susan. "Fort Concho, In 1877," "*West Texas Historical Association Yearbook*, XXXV (October, 1959).

Murray, Robert A. "The United States Army in the Aftermath of the Johnson County Invasion: April through November 1892," *Annals of Wyoming*, XXXVIII, 1 (April, 1966).

Nunn, Curtis, W. "Eighty-Six Hours Without Water On The Texas Plains," *Southwestern Historical Quarterly*, XLIII (January, 1940).

Perry, Lieutenant Alex W. "The Ninth United States Cavalry In The Sioux Campaign of 1890," *Journal of U.S. Cavalry Association*, IV (1891).

Porter, Kenneth W. "The Seminole-Negro Indian Scouts, 1870-1881," *Southwestern Historical Quarterly*, LV (January, 1952).

Porter, Kenneth W. "Negroes And Indians On The Texas Frontier," *Southwestern Historical Quarterly*, LIII (October, 1949).

________. "The Seminole In Mexico 1850-1861," *The Hispanic American Review*, XXXI (1951).

Reddick, L.D. "The Negro Policy of the U.S. Army 1775-1945," *Journal of Negro History*, XXXIV (January, 1949).

Ruhlen, George. "Quitman: The Worst Post at Which I Ever Served." *The El Paso County Historical Society*, VI, 3 (Fall, 1966).

Savage, W. Sherman. "The Negro In The Westward Movement," *Journal of Negro History*, XXV (1940).

________. "The Role od Negro Soldiers In Protecting The Indian Frontier from Intruders," *The Journal of Negro History*, XXXVI, 1 (January, 1951).

Sutton, Mary. "Glimpses of Fort Concho Through Military Telegraph," *West Texas Historical Association Yearbook*, XXXII (October, 1956).

Temple, Frank M. "Colonel B.H. Grierson's Victorio Campaign," *West Texas Historical Association Yearbook*, XXXV (October, 1959).

Waller, Reuben. "History of A Slave Written by Himself at the Age of 89 Years," *The Beecher Island Battle Memorial Association Annual* (1961).

GOVERNMENT PUBLICATIONS

Mooney, James, "The Ghost-dance Religion," *Fourteenth Annual Report of the Bureau of American Ethnology 1892-1893.*" Washington, D.C.: Government Printing Office, 1896.

No Author. "Rattlesnake Springs." unpublished manuscript, Fort Davis National Historic Site, Texas, March, 1964.

No Author. "Tinaja de las Palmas." unpublished manuscript, Fort Davis National Historic Site, Texas, February, 1964.

U.S. Inspector General's Office. "The Brownsville Affray," 60th Cong., 1st Sess., Sen. Doc. 389, Washington, D.C.: Government Printing Office, 1908.

Utley, Robert M. "Fort Davis National Historic Site," Historical Handbook 38, U.S. Department of Interior, National Park Service, Washington, D.C.: 1965.

SPECIAL SOURCES

Bagley, Asa Wallace. "The Negro of Oklahoma," unpublished Master's thesis, University of Oklahoma, 1926.

Benteen, Captain F.W. Letter exchanged between him and Theo Goldin of the 7th Cavalry, October 20, 1891, Gilcrease Institute of Western Art and History, Tulsa, Oklahoma.

Carroll, John M. "Bullets, Black Men and Bravery," unpublished manuscript, 1968.

________. "Lieutenant Henry Ossian Flipper," unpublished manuscript, 1968.

________. "York," unpublished manuscript, 1968.

Cole, George D. "Brush Fire War, 1916 Style," unpublished Master's thesis, Louisana State University, 1962.

Davidson, Major General Michael S. Address to 101st Anniversary Convention of the 9th & 10th Cavalry Regimental Association, 28 July, 1967.

Duncan, Otis D. "The Fusion of White, Negro and Indian Cultures at the Converging of the South and the West," Paper read before a meeting of the American Sociological Society, Philadelphia, December, 1933.

Fain, Samuel S. "The Pershing Punitive Expedition and Its Diplomatic Battlegrounds," unpublished Master's thesis, University of Arizona, 1951.

BIBLIOGRAPHY

Kubela, Marguerite E. "History of Fort Concho, Texas," unpublished Master's thesis, University of Texas, 1936.

Lewis, Eva P. "Social Life in the Territory of Oklahoma," unpublished Master's thesis, University of Oklahoma, 1954.

Rickey, Don, Jr. "The Negro Regulars: A Combat Record, 1866-1891," unpublished paper delivered at the Western History Association meeting at Helena, Montana, October, 1965.

Shadley, Frank W. "The American Punitive Expedition Into Mexico, 1916-1917," unpublished Master's thesis, College of the Pacific, 1952.

Thompson, Erwin N. "The Negro Regiments of the U.S. Army 1866-1900," unpublished Master's thesis, University of California, 1966.

———. "Private Bentley's Buzzard," unpublished manuscript, Fort Davis National Historic Site, Texas, April 2, 1965.

Tolson, Arthur. "The Negro In Oklahoma Territory, 1889-1907: A Study In Racial Discrimination," unpublished Ph.D. dissertation, University of Oklahoma, 1966.

Troxel, O.C. *et al.* (eds.). "Narrative of Service of the Tenth U.S. Cavalry in the Punitive Expedition," a pamphlet published by the Acme Printing Company, Tucson, Arizona, 1921.

Battle of Las Animas Canyon

INDEX